A Special Issue of
Neuropsychological Rehabilitation

Biopsychosocial Approaches in Neurorehabilitation:
Assessment and Management of Neuropsychiatric, Mood
and Behavioural Disorders

Edited by

W. Huw Williams

Washington Singer Laboratories,
University of Exeter, UK

and

Jonathan J. Evans

Oliver Zangwill Centre for Neuropsychological
Rehabilitation, Ely, Cambridgeshire, UK

 Psychology Press
Taylor & Francis Group

HOVE AND NEW YORK

Published in 2003 by Psychology Press Ltd
27 Church Road, Hove, East Sussex, BN3 2FA
www.psypress.co.uk

Simultaneously published in the USA and Canada
by Taylor & Francis Inc
29 West 35th Street, New York, NY 10001, USA

Psychology Press is part of the Taylor & Francis Group

© 2003 by Psychology Press Ltd

British Library Cataloguing in Publication Data
A catalogue record for this book is available from the British Library

ISBN 1-84169-945-4 (hbk)
ISSN 0960-2011

Cover design by Hybert Design
Typeset in the UK by Quorum Technical Services, Cheltenham, Gloucestershire
Printed in the UK by Henry Ling Ltd, Dorchester
Bound in the UK by TJ International, Padstow, Cornwall

Contents*

*This book is also a special issue of the journal *Neuropsychological Rehabilitation*, and forms issues 1 & 2 of Volume 13 (2003). The page numbers are taken from the journal and begin with p. 1.

Brain injury and emotion:
An overview to a special issue on biopsychosocial approaches in neurorehabilitation

W. Huw Williams

School of Psychology, University of Exeter, UK

Jonathan J. Evans

Oliver Zangwill Centre, Ely, Cambridgeshire, UK

Survivors of acquired brain injury (ABI) are at risk of a range of neuropsychiatric and behavioural disorders. Emotional disturbance, with reactive elements of mood disorder, such as depression and anxiety, appear particularly common. Specific anxiety disorders, such as post-traumatic stress disorder (PTSD) have also been identified. Pain syndromes are also common—particularly in those who have suffered Traumatic Brain Injuries (TBI). Survivors of ABI are often at risk of substance misuse and of irritability states. Their relationships may suffer from the stresses triggered by the aftermath of injury. Intimate, in particular, sexual relationships may be particularly affected. These effects are not, necessarily, only consequent of severe injuries, as mild TBI can also have, for some, significant neuropsychiatric effects. Assessment and management of such conditions are compromised by survivors of injury often having a limited insight into the sequelae of their injuries. Interventions for such disorders and forms of distress are increasingly available. This paper introduces the special issue of *Neuropsychological Rehabilitation* on biopsychosocial approaches in neurorehabilitation. A range of papers provide overviews for assessing and managing such neuropsychiatric, mood and behavioural (health and habit) disorders.

Correspondence should be addressed to Dr W. Huw Williams, Lecturer in Clinical Psychology, School of Psychology, University of Exeter, Exeter, EX4 4QG, UK. Phone: +44 1392 264661, Fax: +44 1392 264623, Email: w.h.williams@exeter.ac.uk

Much of what happens in neurorehabilitation involves work with, and through, the emotional crises of brain injury survivors and their families. Indeed, referrals to outpatient and outreach programmes are not often on the basis of a neurological issue or goal, but due to lack of insight, development of mood problems, chemical dependency, or family disintegration (see Harris, 1997). The importance of addressing the emotional needs of brain injured groups was highlighted by a recent large-scale population-based study by Teasdale and Engberg (2001). They found that people who suffer brain injuries are at particular risk of suicide. Calls have, subsequentlty, been made for more effective identification and treatment of mental health issues in brain injured groups (Lewis, 2001).

Neurorehabilitation has been seen as an activity concerned with the psychological adjustment of its recipients. For example, Wilson (1989, p. 117) noted that, in cognitive rehabilitation, the aim is to "enable clients or patients and their families to live with, manage, bypass, or reduce, or *come to terms with* cognitive deficits precipitated by injury to the brain" (emphasis ours). To do all, or indeed any, of these things requires creative solutions to complex problems. A literature that can inform clinicians charged with finding such solutions to emotional and mental health problems associated with neurological trauma is emerging. This special issue was conceived as providing a focus for the development of clinical practice and research for such conditions. Many people who suffer neurological injuries will not necessarily develop mental health disorders—but there is an elevated risk that they might. Indeed, such conditions may be subclinical, but in the context of other additional stressors (or lack of protective factors) become expressed. Indeed, research has shown that survivors typically experience greater emotional problems as time goes on. This special issue is not solely developed to address the extant mental health disorders of survivors. It also provides evidence upon which to base practice for such disorders, and emphasises the role that neuropsychological rehabilitation has in reducing the likelihood of such mental health conditions developing. The umbrella term "bio-psycho-social approaches" is used to highlight the necessity, when working with people with acquired brain injuries (ABI), of understanding the complex interaction of biological, psychological and social influences on affect and behaviour.

Many leading experts in neurorehabilitation were willing to contribute to the special issue. The papers presented provide a framework for understanding, assessing, and managing the various forms of mental health, psychological, and behavioural problems that routinely occur for survivors of brain injury. There are review, position, case and empirical papers that examine specific disorders and methods for their management. It is noted by many authors that various forms of distress, such as pain or anxiety, do not present in a "typical" manner in the context of the neurological and neuropsychological sequelae of brain injury. However, complexity does not preclude solutions.

The issue is in five sections: (1) Assessment, (2) mood and anxiety disorders, (3) behavioural, health, and habit disorders, (4) relationship issues, and (5) community services. These sections are not mutually exclusive—but papers do provide an overview of critical issues in each domain.

SECTION 1: ASSESSMENT

There are many issues relevant to the assessment of mental health issues in brain injury. Each paper provides guidance for specific areas of interest. However, in general, any assessment needs to take account of insight, level of injury, and pre-injury status. Therefore, we have a section dedicated to such issues.

Insight

Impairments of insight and awareness are common following brain injury and represent major challenges for rehabilitation services. Such problems have been clearly linked to poor functional and vocational outcomes. The specific relationship between insight problems, mood and behaviour is less well documented, although clinical experience would suggest that a failure to appreciate problems can protect against mood disorder associated with sense of loss, but create mood and behaviour problems associated with frustration at being unable to return to pre-injury roles. In this special issue, Prigatano and Johnson highlight the lack of a comprehensive theoretical model of such issues, which limits the design of assessment tools and interventions. Building on the work of Zeman (2001), they construct a model of the "three vectors of consciousness", and examine the implications of this model for assessment and treatment interventions.

Mild traumatic brain injury (MTBI)

Of growing concern to professionals in the area of assessment is the growing evidence that milder forms of TBI can be associated with subtle to severe neurobehavioural sequelae. Historically such "post-concussional" injuries have been considered to be potentially attributable—in good part—to pre-morbid psychiatric histories (see Lishman, 1998). However, there has been evidence that, for example, stress factors at the time of injury are not necessarily linked to symptoms (Watson et al., 1995), and there have been magnetic resonance imaging (MRI) and neuropsychological findings to support the view that structural impairments may occur even in very mildly brain injured survivors (see Voller et al., 1999). In a thorough review of the area Zasler and Martelli (this issue) note that MTBI accounts for approximately 80% of the estimated 373,000 traumatic brain injuries that occur each year in the United States. The effects of MTBI are likely to be underestimated, and are still poorly understood. They note that the consequences of MTBI can impede physical, emotional, social, marital, and vocational functioning. The identification of the consequences of MTBI is crucial, particularly in the medico-legal context. Zasler and Martelli provide criteria for identifying MTBI and its potential sequelae. However, they note how evaluation of impairment and disability presents a significant diagnostic challenge fraught with potential obstacles and confounding issues, especially when considering the potential for functional disability, and note that it is by "no means a simple undertaking".

Pre-injury factors

One of the most contentious areas of assessment of neuropsychiatric and mood disorders in TBI is that of pre-injury status. Indeed, there is an aphorism that holds that, "It is not only the kind of injury that matters, but the kind of head" (Symonds, 1937, p. 1092). Research on pre-injury characteristics has been focused on two main areas: The presence of positive personality traits that might enhance psychosocial outcome and the absence of such positive elements, which may be reflected in difficult premorbid psychosocial histories. While acknowledging that there may be some likelihood of such effects, Lishman (1998) noted that, "it has proved difficult to specify what special aspects of [premorbid] personality are important" (p. 174). Some studies have, though, shown that pre-injury misusage of substances may influence outcome (see Williams, 2003). It has been suggested that there may be particular patterns of pre-injury personality types that could exert an influence on how individuals react to their injuries and their aftermath. In an empirical paper that adds much to the debate, Tate (this issue) provides further evidence for the view that such factors as personality (as measured by the Eysenck Personality Questionnaire—Revised) may not be reliable indicators of outcome. She found that personality measures can be used to identify subgroups of survivors with elevated dispositional traits, but that such traits are not necessarily associated with psychosocial outcome. Tate found that post-traumatic amnesia (PTA) length was the best predictor of poorer outcome. As Tate (1998) previously noted, one of the key issues in understanding persistent variable in outcome in TBI is that young men are those most at risk of TBI and they "frequently tend to be nonconformist, risk takers, immature, have difficulty with authority and so forth simply by virtue of their life stage" (p. 8).

SECTION 2: DEPRESSION AND ANXIETY: "REACTIVE" DISORDERS

The most commonly diagnosed mood disorders after brain injury are depression and specific anxiety disorders, with a significant proportion of individuals having two or more diagnoses (Hibbard et al., 1998). Issues of prevalence, assessment and management of depression and anxiety disorders after brain injury are examined in several papers in this volume.

Depression

Fleminger, Oliver, Williams, and Evans (this issue) provide a neuropsychiatric overview of the assessment of depression in brain injury. They note how there may well be factors associated with the specific lesions involved that may lead to forms of depression. They discuss the difficulty in assessing and diagnosing depression following brain injury when depressive symptoms—such as irritability, frustration, fatigue, poor concentration and apathy—may occur as a direct result of brain damage rather than be symptomatic of depression. However, there do appear to be patterns of depression in brain injury. For example, as survivors become more aware of their losses and the implications of the injuries for their life goals and social roles they may suffer more emotional distress. There may well be a need to consider a range of treatment options for depression in brain injury, including pharmacological approaches and cognitive behaviour therapy (CBT). In a related paper, Khan-Bourne and Brown (this issue) provide an overview of how CBT may be modified for use for people with cognitive disabilities and discuss evidence for use of CBT for depression in brain injured groups. One particular trigger for depressive symptoms may be cognitive skills being compromised. Code and Herrman (this issue) provide an overview of the effects of stroke on language and subsequent presentation of depression. They discuss the relationships between recovery and emotional state and the clinical and psychosocial implications of these relationships. They also examine methods for assessment of psychosocial evaluation with this group and provide guidance for rehabilitation, including a section on pharmacological treatment for depression in aphasic people.

Anxiety

As a group, anxiety disorders are the most commonly diagnosed mental health disorder in general mental health settings. They are suspected to be common after brain injury, however, they may be under-diagnosed due to difficulties in identifying symptoms in the context of other issues (see Scheutzow & Wiercisiewski, 1999). For many, anxiety may be associated with the adjustment process to the brain injury and may, for example, be focused on feeling out of control and insecure over the future and social roles. Williams, Evans, and Fleminger (this issue) provide an overview of anxiety disorders in TBI with a focus on understanding mental health distress as a phenomenon that occurs along a "normative" continuum. They emphasise the importance of not only diagnosing anxiety disorders, but also the need to understand the mechanisms by which particular individuals have developed such disorders, so that intervention can be informed by accurate clinical formulation. A case illustration is provided for obsessive–compulsive disorder (OCD) following TBI in which CBT was integrated with cognitive rehabilitation. In a related paper, McMillan, Williams, and Bryant (this issue) provide an overview of recent developments in the literature on PTSD and brain injury and how such conditions are now more generally accepted as being possible in the context of brain injury. Indeed, recent evidence suggests that it is a relatively common disorder and, if left untreated, may severely limit a person's ability to function, and may often lead to adoption of unhelpful coping mechanisms, such as alcohol misuse.

SECTION 3: BEHAVIOURAL DISORDERS AND HEALTH STATUS

Reactions to acquired brain injury are often complicated by the presence of additional stresses, such as pain, comorbid behavioural disorders, such as habitual alcohol misuse, or acquired behavioural disorders, such as aggressive outbursts.

Alcohol and substance misuse

As noted above, misuse of drugs and alcohol is often cited as predictive of outcome. It is not surprising that drug and alcohol problems may well develop even in premorbid non-users, as such behaviours are common coping mechanisms in many societies. Such issues have often precluded survivors from rehabilitation—although it is becoming increasingly acknowledged that services should be developed to treat those with a brain injury who misuse drugs or alcohol. Alcohol and drug misuse put people at risk of having a brain injury. As Taylor, Kreutzer, Demm, and Meade (this issue) note, many accidents are alcohol or drug related, and a vast majority of victims test positive for alcohol or illicit drugs at the time of hospital admission. They provide a thorough review of substance misuse patterns, risk factors, and dangers of post-injury use. They provide an overview of critical features of treatment, prevention, and education which will be particularly helpful for clinicians who have to address these issues on daily basis.

Pain

Pain is one of the most commonly "missed" issues with which people with TBI present. Survivors tend to be poor in reporting (or monitoring and evaluating) such "physical" sense data, and rehabilitation staff may not be aware of how to assess and treat such conditions. It is crucial that the pain syndromes of persons with TBI are addressed as they are—evidently—distressing for the person, but also may well be associated with depression, anxiety and alcohol or drug misuse. Tyrer and Lievesley (this issue) describe the main pain syndromes in TBI and review management approaches. In a thorough overview, they discuss assessment in both acute and post-acute phases of rehabilitation.

Early assessment may require particular attention to non-verbal signs of pain. They note how persistent pain may arise from a combination of physical and psychological factors and is best managed in a multidisciplinary pain clinic. Treatments described include analgesic drugs, graded exercise, cognitive–behavioural therapy and transcutaneous electrical nerve stimulation. They highlight the importance of integrated pain management and neuropsychological rehabilitation for those with combined cognitive and pain problems arising in the context of brain injury.

Irritability and anger

It is well established that severe brain injury frequently leads to problems with anger and irritability (Brooks et al., 1987). Outcome studies have also identified irritability problems to be common after a mild and moderate head injury (Haboubi, Long, Koshy, & Ward, 2001; Deb, Lyons, & Koutzoukis, 1999). Alderman (this issue) notes how irritability is not a unitary clinical phenomenon and that it may have more than one underlying cause: the product of organic damage, abnormal electrical discharge, or an emotional response to residual disabilities and/or a learnt behavioural pattern for expressing needs. He recommends that the treatment of irritability requires careful, detailed assessment and that there is a growing range of therapy options available for treatment of pervasive irritability—ranging from psychotherapy and behaviour therapy to pharmacological intervention. Indeed, he notes that there is cause for optimism that such issues may be managed more effectively than they have been in the past, although he acknowledges that the "clinical reality" of the lack of availability of services tempers such hope (see Oddy & McMillan, 2001). Eames and Wood (this issue) discuss one subgroup of individuals who experience anger problems that are said to be primarily neurologically based. They discuss the evidence for what has come to be termed "episodic dyscontrol syndrome". They note that there is relatively little in the clinical literature on organic aggressive, or organic affective syndromes, that are episodic in nature. They suggest that such disorders require a specific diagnosis, a different classification, and a different approach to treatment, than has been possible to date. They provide guidance on how such disorders may be assessed, understood, and treated, emphasising the need for pharmacological input prior to insight oriented psychological therapies.

SECTION 4: PERSONAL RELATIONSHIPS

Family

Lezak (1986, 1988) reminded clinicians that "brain injury is a family affair" and that spouses frequently find themselves in "social limbo". The family often takes the fundamental role in supporting a survivor of brain injury. Also, improved family functioning is often a goal for rehabilitative efforts—be they spousal relationships, or, for example, in parenting style. Oddy and Herbert (this issue) note how there are frequent exhortations in the rehabilitation literature to include families in the rehabilitation process and not to neglect their needs. The promotion of the well-being of family members is, they argue, a worthwhile end in itself and it is not unreasonable to hypothesise that there will be positive benefits for the injured family member. However, they report that there are remarkably few studies evaluating the effectiveness of different types of family intervention. They provide a review that describes the current evidence base for family intervention following brain injury. When formal rehabilitation is available—and this may be rare—the family is, usually, involved in that process. Oddy and Herbert discuss models for understanding change in families (loss, coping, systems) and integrate these models with suggested practice. They note that, although there is no direct evidence concerning the efficacy of such interventions, there is a body of evidence concerning the impact of brain injury on the family which provides the evidence base for planning such interventions.

Sexuality

Oddy and Herbert introduce issues of sexuality in their paper. Ponsford (this issue) provides an empirical paper that is novel and needed in this area. In the first study of both men and women who have suffered brain injury, Ponsford highlights the impact on quality and frequency of sexual experiences. She reports the results of a study of sexuality with 208 participants with TBI and 150 controls. A significant number of TBI participants reported problems with sexual functioning including the reduction of opportunities and frequency of engaging in sexual activities, decline in giving partners satisfaction, decreased enjoyment of sexual activity, changes in ability to stay aroused and to climax, and loss of drive. The frequencies of such negative changes were significantly higher than those reported by controls. She also found that TBI participants reported decreased self-confidence, sex appeal, higher levels of depression, and decreased relationship quality with their sexual partner. Given that sexuality is a key aspect of human functioning and fulfilment, such a picture clearly demonstrates the need to develop ways and means of improving the sexual outcome of survivors and their spouses or partners. Indeed, many aspects of such issues might be addressed through psychosexual counselling—if it were available.

SECTION 5: COMMUNITY SERVICES

Efforts to develop inpatient and outpatient services are, rightly, valued. However, the effects of rehabilitation for individuals, in the long term, rests on adequate development of community-based resources. Often work undertaken in rehabilitative units may not generalise unless there are community supports. Rehabilitation, then, is not something that "stops" at the end of the hospital corridor. It is something that happens in the community—at least in some areas (see Wood & McMillan, 2001). In the concluding section there are papers that present how such community elements of rehabilitation may be organised in developed and developing world contexts.

Community enablement

Yates (this issue) notes how, since the adoption of the WHO ICF model of enablement (World Health Organisation, 2001), the challenge for rehabilitation professionals is to apply the substantial knowledge on psychological aspects of impairment and functioning following acquired brain injury to the environment in which the individual chooses to live and participate. It is noted that in working at this level, the potential net gains may include reduction in mood disorders, increased social support networks, improved social relationships, and meaningful vocational choices.

Developing world

Brain injuries are, of course, a global phenomenon. It is believed that road traffic accidents are a growing threat to life and health in the developing world. Indeed, 90% of disability caused by road traffic accidents is in developing countries (Nantulya & Reich, 2002). In such contexts it may well be difficult for services to be staffed and trained for the rehabilitation of brain injured groups. There may well be other pressing concerns. In an informative account, Judd (this issue) provides guidance as to how services in such societies may be developed to promote rehabilitative efforts. Examples are given from Judd's first-hand experience of working across cultures and in community settings in developing countries. Judd acknowledges that although experienced neurorehabilitation experts are "typically in awe of the number, complexity, and combinations of specific problems that can arise from brain disorders . . . [and there] may not always be solutions to all problems all of the time, a small number of simple concepts can be applied within a basic framework to alleviate considerable distress and disability". Moreover, the "potential [for well-being] can only be realised . . . in collaboration with the individuals, families, and communities affected by brain disorders".

CONCLUSIONS

This special issue was conceived with the aim of developing an evidence base for those who work with brain injured survivors and their families as to how emotional, behavioural, and neuropsychiatric conditions should be understood, assessed and treated. In doing so, it touches on areas of individual, spousal, family, social, community, and cultural concern. It is hoped that some answers may be found to some of the questions about what to do, and why, when confronted with such shattering forms of distress consequent upon neurological injuries. As well as developing increasingly sophisticated approaches to managing cognitive impairments, rehabilitation services should also be trying to enable survivors to manage pain, handle sadness, cope with anxiety, drink less alcohol, be less irritable, take care of their children, relate to their partners, and even have a better sex life. It is evident from this special issue that there is a body of evidence slowly emerging that should give hope for better, more complete, outcomes for survivors of brain injury and their families.

REFERENCES

Brooks, D. N., McKinlay, W., Symington, C., Beattie, A., and Campsie, L. (1987). The effects of severe head injury upon patient and relative within seven years of injury. *Journal of Head Trauma Rehabilitation, 2,* 1–13.

Deb, S., Lyons, I., & Koutzoukis, C. (1999). Neurobehavioural symptoms one year after a head injury. *British Journal of Psychiatry, 174,* 360–365.

Haboubi, N. H. J., Long, J., Koshy, M., & Ward, A. B. (2001). Short-term sequelae of minor head injury (6 years experience of minor head injury clinic). *Disability and Rehabilitation, 23,* 635–638.

Harris, D. P. (1997). Outcome measures and a program evaluation model for postacute brain injury rehabilitation. *Journal of Outcomes Measurement, 1,* 23–30.

Hibbard, M. R., Uysal, S., Keple, K., Bogdany, J., & Silver, J. (1998). Axis I psychopathology in individuals with traumatic brain injury. *Journal of Head Trauma Rehabilitation, 13,* 24–39.

Lewis, G. (2001). Mental health after head injury. *Journal of Neurology, Neurosurgery & Psychiatry, 71,* 431.

Lezak, M. D. (1986). Psychological implications of traumatic brain injury for the patients' family. *Rehabilitation Psychology, 31,* 241–250.

Lezak, M. D. (1988). Brain damage is a family affair. *Journal of Clinical and Experimental Psychology, 10,* 11–23.

Lishman, W. (1998). *Organic Psychiatry* (3rd edition). Oxford: Blackwell.

Nantulya, V. M., & Reich, M. R. (2002). The neglected epidemic: Road traffic injuries in developing countries. *British Medical Journal, 324,* 1139–1141.

Oddy, M., & McMillan, T. M. (2001). Future directions: Brain injury services in 2010. In R. Ll. Wood & T. M. McMillan (Eds.), *Neurobehavioural disability and social handicap following traumatic brain injury.* Hove, UK: Psychology Press.

Scheutzow, M. H., & Wiercisiewski, D. R. (1999). Panic disorder in a patient with traumatic brain injury: A case report and discussion. *Brain Injury, 13,* 705–714.

Symonds, C. P. (1937). Mental disorder following head injury. *Proceedings of the Royal Society of Medicine, 30,* 1081–1094.

Tate, R. L. (1998). "It is not only the kind of injury that matters, but the kind of head": The contribution of premorbid psychosocial factors to rehabilitation outcomes after severe traumatic brain injury. *Neuropsychological Rehabilitation, 8,* 1–18.

Teasdale, T. W., & Engberg, A. W. (2001). Suicide after traumatic brain injury: a population study. *Journal of Neurology, Neurosurgery, and Psychiatry, 71,* 436–440.

Voller, B., Benke, T., Benedettos, K., Schnider, P., Auff, E., & Aicher, F. (1999) Neuropsychological, MRI and EEG findings after mild traumatic brain injury. *Brain Injury, 123,* 821–827.

Watson, M. R., Fenton, G. W., McClelland, R. J., Lumsden, J., Headley, M., & Rutherford, W. H. (1995) The Post-concussional state: Neurophysiological aspects. *British Journal of Psychiatry, 167*, 514–521.

Williams, W. H. (2003). Neuro-rehabilitation and cognitive behaviour therapy for emotional disorders in acquired brain injury. In B. A. Wilson (Ed.), *Neuropsychological rehabilitation; Theory and practice* [In series *Studies in neuropsychology: Development and cognition*]. New York: Swets.

Wilson, B. A. (1989). Models of cognitive rehabilitation. In P. Eames & R. Wood (Eds.), *Models of brain rehabilitation* (pp. 117–141). London: Chapman & Hall.

Wood, R. Ll., & McMillan, T. M. (Eds.). (2001). *Neurobehavioural disability and social handicap following traumatic brain injury.* Hove, UK: Psychology Press.

World Health Organisation (2001). *International classification of functioning, disability and health—ICF.* Geneva, Switzerland: World Health Organisation.

Zeman, A. (2001). Invited review. Consciousness. *Brain, 124*, 1263–1289.

The three vectors of consciousness and their disturbances after brain injury

George P. Prigatano and Sterling C. Johnson

Barrow Neurological Institute, St. Joseph's Hospital and Medical Center, Phoenix, Arizona, USA

Based on the recent review of Zeman (2001) three "vectors" of consciousness are described. A model for understanding how they are related is outlined. Recent behavioural and neuroimaging studies are reviewed pertinent to this conceptualisation. Initial ideas for working with these disturbances in consciousness during neuropsychological rehabilitation are presented.

INTRODUCTION

The experience of attempting to rehabilitate post-acute traumatic brain injury (TBI) patients brought into focus the potential importance of disturbances in self-awareness for rehabilitation outcome (Prigatano et al., 1984). Since that time, studies have appeared which document that impaired awareness is related to employment outcome in TBI patients (Sherer et al., 1998a) and functional outcome after acute cerebrovascular accident (Pedersen et al., 1996). One interesting study documents the presence of impaired awareness early after stroke, which was related to worse functional outcome at 1 year follow-up (Jehkonen et al., 2000). The implication is that even when frank anosognosia disappears, there may be residual disturbances in self-awareness that continue and influence functional (including psychosocial) outcome. This is important from a theoretical perspective since it has recently been argued that disturbances in self-awareness change over time and that different syndromes may be

———————————

Correspondence should be addressed to George P. Prigatano, PhD, Clinical Neuropsychology, Barrow Neurological Institute, St. Joseph's Hospital and Medical Center, 350 West Thomas Rd., Phoenix, AZ 85013, USA. Phone: 602-406-3671; Fax: 602-406-6115, Email: gprigat@chw.edu identified that relate to neuropsychological rehabilitation outcome (Prigatano, 1999).

The persistent problem in studying such disturbances, however, has been the lack of a comprehensive theoretical model that accounts for the complexity of the disturbances observed and leads to better methods of measurement. Choosing the appropriate methods of measurement not only can aid the clinician, but also can provide construct validation when evaluating the usefulness of a given model.

A recent review paper by Zeman (2001) provided some interesting observations regarding human consciousness and addressed important questions from a biological and philosophical perspective. Based in part on the Zeman (2001) review paper, we suggest that three "vectors" of consciousness can be identified. These "directional" forces may be differentially disturbed after brain injury, as observed in many brain injury rehabilitation settings. We briefly describe those disturbances and outline methods for their measurement. We furthermore propose a simple correlational matrix, which helps predict a proposed relationship between these three vectors. We summarise recent neuroimaging findings relevant to this conceptual model. Finally, we briefly suggest ideas for addressing these related disturbances in consciousness during rehabilitation.

THE THREE MEANINGS OF CONSCIOUSNESS: ZEMAN'S 2001 ANALYSIS AND CLINICAL OBSERVATION

In an exceptionally useful review, Zeman (2001) distinguishes three principal meanings of the term "consciousness". Consciousness can refer to the waking state. In this sense, it is a matter of degree ranging from alertness to drowsiness through sleep and possibly into coma (in some instances). The second meaning is "consciousness as experience". It is the content of personal experience from moment to moment. It is the subjective sense of being aware of the self. The third meaning is "consciousness as mind". In this sense it is "any mental state with a propositional content . . ." He gives examples of how the term "consciousness" can be used. They are (p. 1266):

1. "After a lucid interval, the injured soldier lapsed into unconsciousness."
2. "I am conscious of a feeling of dread and an overpowering smell of burning rubber."
3. "I am conscious that I am straining your patience."

Brain damage can affect each "type" of consciousness. In the first sense of the term, it affects the arousal/alertness level that makes up the continuum of the sleep–wake cycle. When this type of disturbance occurs, patients are hypo-aroused, confused, and unable to respond meaningfully to the environment.

The Glasgow Coma Scale (GCS; Teasdale & Jennet, 1974) is a behavioural measure to assess this type of disruption of "consciousness", particularly following the acute stages after TBI. After acute cerebral vascular accident (CVA), patients may also be hypoaroused as witnessed by their sitting in wheelchairs with their heads slumped over. They also show reduced Galvanic skin responses when presented emotional and nonemotional material (Morrow, Vrtunski, Kim, & Boller, 1981). This may well be a physiological marker of this type of disturbance of consciousness.

Brain damage can also affect patients' personal experience of themselves. It is in this sense that Prigatano (1999) has described disorders of self-awareness. It is the second dimension of consciousness that becomes affected in frank anosognosia. This dimension is often measured indirectly by comparing the patient's self-reports to judgements of the observing clinician or relatives' ratings. Different methods for assessing such disturbances in self-awareness are listed in Table 1.

TABLE 1
Methods presently used to measure disturbances in self-awareness
(Vector 2 of consciousness)

Method 1	Clinician rates patient's level of awareness or anosognosia on a simple rating scale	Example: Anosognostic Questionnaire (Starkstein et al., 1992)
Method 2	Patients self-report via ratings on a questionnaire their level of competency on various behavioural dimensions. Ratings are obtained from someone who knows the patient well to obtain a discrepancy score as an indirect measure of impaired awareness	Examples: PCRS-P form versus PCRS-R form (Prigatano et al., 1986); also Awareness Questionnaire (Sherer et al., 1998b)
Method 3	Clinician records and rates different spontaneous responses to questions when giving feedback to brain dysfunctional patients	Example: Clinician's rating scale of impaired self-awareness and denial of disability (Prigatano & Klonoff, 1997).
Method 4	Correlation of what patients say they are capable of doing versus their actual performance on neuropsychological tests	Example: PCRS-P ratings are compared with total scores on the BNIS (Prigatano, Ogano, & Amukusa, 1997).
Method 5	Specific rules are outlined to determine if a complete vs. partial syndrome of impaired self-awareness is present and if a partial syndrome is present, whether the individual is using defensive versus nondefensive methods of coping	Example: Clinical decisions recently described by Prigatano (in press)

PCRS-P = Patient Competency Rating Scale—Patient; PCRS-R = Patient Competency Rating Scale—Relative; BNIS = BNI Screen for Higher Cerebral Functioning.

Because such disturbances affect people's own self-report of their subjective state, they are frequently difficult to separate from the psychological phenomenon of "denial" as a psychological method of coping versus a state of brain disorder. Some clinical guidelines have been offered to help with this separation (Prigatano & Klonoff, 1997).

Brain damage can also affect the patient's "insight" and "judgement" of other people's mental states as well as their own. This is the third dimension of consciousness that Zeman (2001) identifies. It touches on what is now being discussed as the "theory of mind". Zeman (2001) notes that Humphrey (1978) considers that the evolutionary value of this type of consciousness is that it allows an individual to judge what others are thinking and feeling before they act. This can have obvious advantages for survival and therefore it serves a clear role in "biological success" (p. 1281). The measurements of this type of disturbance of consciousness are just beginning to be identified as we will describe below.

THE THREE VECTORS OF CONSCIOUSNESS

It appears to us that these three "dimensions" of consciousness must: (1) interact; (2) be subserved by overlapping neurocircuits in the brain and brainstem; and (3) evolve to meet different needs of the organism that aid the never-ending processes geared towards survival. Moreover, (4) there is a "magnitude" and a "directional" component to these dimensions of consciousness that must be recognised and measured. Consciousness is a "force" (i.e., a push or pull that causes an object to accelerate; Huetinck & Adams, 2001). As a force, it acts on objects with some "directional pull" and displaces (shifts) mental energy. Thus, it has a "purpose".

In physics, the term "vector" is applied to a quantity completely specified by a magnitude and a direction (Bueche & Hecht, 2000). We believe consciousness exists in some "quantity" for a given individual and again has a directional component. Consequently, we propose the term "vectors" of consciousness. An added utility of the concept is that vectors more closely associated with one another share common space (vector space). Vectors can be added or subtracted. Vectors far removed from one another are less clearly related and therefore the magnitude of their relationship can be specified. This phenomenon allows for some modest predictions concerning relationships between measures of consciousness and their disturbances.

Given the known and suspected brain structures (and their functions) involved in these emergent forms of brain activity (i.e., different dimensions or vectors of consciousness), we propose a simple model for guiding measurements in these areas.

Vector 1—the wakefulness dimension of consciousness—clearly involves the upper brainstem, the posterior hypothalamus, and the thalamus (see Zeman,

2001). These are the key gatekeepers of the sleep–wakefulness continuum. Citing research by Macquet et al. (1996), Zeman (2001) notes that, "in REM sleep, regional blood flow increases in the rostral brainstem, thalamus, and limbic regions, . . . but declines in prefrontal and posterior cingulate cortex, and in some regions of the parietal cortex" (p. 1269). Macquet et al. (1997) also report that during human slow wave sleep, there is a decreased regional cerebral blood flow in the brainstem, thalami, basal ganglia, basal forebrain/ hypothalamus, orbital frontal cortex, anterior cingulate and precuneus. Mesial aspects of the right temporal lobe also seem to show decreased cerebral blood flow. Thus, brainstem and limbic structures which are more activated during dreaming (i.e., REM sleep) are less activated during nondreaming sleep.

We often feel "tired" after a vigorous night of dreaming, especially if the dreams have been disturbing to us. Also during the dreaming state, we "lose" conscious awareness of what is real. Many people report considerable relief when waking up from a "bad dream" and recognising that things they experienced in the dream were only "imagined". We follow Jouvet's (1999) notion that sleep may have many functions, including conservation and replacement of "energy" reserves via alteration of brain metabolism during the sleeping stages of life, as well as rehearsing certain emotional themes during dreaming in order to biologically maintain our individuality.

Thus, the first vector of consciousness allows for the biological foundation for knowing what is "real" and directly forms the basis of the second vector of consciousness, which involves other brain regions and subserves the experiential sense of "me" or "I" in the real world, now.

Prigatano (1991; 1999) has proposed that the heteromodal regions of the cerebral hemispheres are responsible for the emergence of this type of consciousness. Depending on how well developed these heteromodal regions are, different levels of sophistication concerning knowing who one is or one's sense of self may emerge. For example, a person with mild mental retardation can identify themselves versus another, but their level of self-awareness (consciousness as personal experience) seems to be diminished compared to other individuals with normal intelligence. Conversely, when different heteromodal regions are damaged, one may observe different disturbances in an altered sense of self. These are reflected in the classic anosognostic syndromes. Also, in normal development, heteromodal regions are least developed during early childhood and become more developed (particularly frontal and parietal areas) as the child develops. One can readily attest to a more enriched and sophisticated view of one's self throughout the ageing process (see Erik Erickson's theoretical formulations in Hall & Lindzey, 1978). Again, the development of the heteromodal cortex seems to be responsible for this developing phenomenological sense of self.

The "function" of a phenomenological sense of self appears to be related to making adaptive choices that subserve survival for the individual in the most rudimentary sense. For example, the statement that "this is my money, you can't have it" reflects a basic understanding of what I am and what I need. The statement, "I need water, I am thirsty" is another such example. While this vector of consciousness is crucial for meeting basic survival needs (the needs that are seen out in the wild, during child development, etc.), it further develops into another level of consciousness. This further developed level allows for "insight" into the workings of our own mind as well as the minds of others. It is the third vector of consciousness (i.e., consciousness as mind).

This third vector clearly is involved with "reading the minds" and preparing for potential actions of others. It appears to be a further development of consciousness where we can begin to empathise with others' thoughts and feelings, be prepared for things that they may or may not do, and develop "insight" into patterns of relationships that allow us to anticipate what another may do in relationship to us. This clearly has survival quality and appears also to be heavily dependent on enhanced heteromodal cortex. We would suggest that this third vector of consciousness is dependent on wakefulness (Vector 1), but like Vector 2, is distributed in their heteromodal cortex, but at another level of organisation. Vector 3 is a natural refinement of Vector 2. Therefore, while Vector 3 will rely on Vector 1, it is mostly closely associated with the emergence of Vector 2. The phrase, "it takes one to know one" is compatible with the view that self-knowledge is necessary in order to have knowledge of the other. People with frontal lobe brain injury have difficulty on "theory of mind" tasks that require the patient to make inferences about another person's intentions (Stuss, Gallup, & Alexander, 2001). Individuals with autism and schizophrenia also have difficulty on "theory of mind" tasks (Frith & Frith, 1999). The neural explanation of these deficits at this point is incomplete, but the frontal heteromodal cortex is strongly implicated as a crucial part of this system.

We have attempted to illustrate a potential hierarchical model of these vectors of consciousness in Table 2. The model attempts to relate brain structures which are important for each of the vectors and also to identify key brain structures in which the vectors blend into one another or share a common vector space.

As can be seen from this model, the upper brainstem, particularly the reticular activating system, is extremely important for consciousness as a wakeful state. Inputs between upper brainstem and the thalamus may be the point of shift between Vectors 1 and 2 where consciousness of the self may be experienced at a most rudimentary level. Vector 2 clearly emerges when there is interconnection between thalamus and limbic structures involved in the anterior and posterior cingulate. At this point, heteromodal cortex is involved in the emergence of Vector 2. The emergence of Vector 3 appears to reflect a "higher" level of organisation of heteromodal cortex and limbic structures.

This rudimentary model leads to predictions as to how different measures of these three vectors might relate to one another.

TABLE 2
Hierarchical model of three vectors of consciousness
and associated "key" brain structures*

Heteromodal cortex	Blending of Vectors 2 and 3 ↑	Vector 3	Consciousness as a mental state. Theory of own and others "mind"
Anterior and posterior cingulate (limbic structures)		Vector 2	Consciousness as a phenomenological state of the "me" and in the "here and now" (i.e., consciousness as experience)
Thalamus	Blending of Vectors 1 and 2 ↑		
Upper brainstem (reticular activating system)		Vector 1	Consciousness as wakefulness

* Note that each "vector" blends at key neurocircuits so that overlapping circuitry is responsible for different types of consciousness. Not depicted in this simple hierarchical model are the feedback loops, which must exist, so these vectors can influence one another.

Proposed methods of measurement and their level of relationship

Given the construct of three "vectors" of consciousness, we would propose that Vector 1 is more closely associated with Vector 2 (i.e., sharing more vector space). In contrast, Vector 3 is more closely associated with Vector 2 (theoretically they both evolve from the heteromodal cortex and therefore share a more common vector space), but is obviously reliant on Vector 1 (sharing, however, less vector space). Given this assertion, we suggest that the correlation of Vector 1 disturbances with Vector 2 disturbances would be in the neighborhood of .50 (shared vector space; using a pure linear model, which is a gross over-simplification). In contrast, Vector 1 disturbances would be less correlated with measures of disturbances than Vector 3 (further removed vector space). Again, using a linear model of shared vector space, we would estimate the relationship to be about .25. A predicted correlational matrix is provided in Table 3.

What is the empirical evidence and how do predicted correlations match up with observed relationships?

Sherer et al. (1998c) have reported a correlation between admitting GCS score (an early measure of impaired consciousness—Vector 1) with clinicians' ratings of patients' residual awareness after severe TBI (a later measure of impaired consciousness—Vector 2). They report a correlation of +.39. Studying a Spanish sample of TBI patients, Prigatano et al. (1998) correlated admitting GCS scores with measures of impaired awareness using the Patient Competency Rating Scales (patients' self-reports compared to relatives'). Again, an identical magnitude of correlation was found ($r = -.39$).

TABLE 3
Predicted correlational matrix of how measures of the three vectors would relate
to one another using a purely linear model (which is clearly an oversimplification)

	Consciousness as wakefulness (Vector 1)	Consciousness as personal experience (Vector 2)	Consciousness as awareness of "mind" (Vector 3)
Consciousness as wakefulness (Vector 1)	1.00	.50	.25
Consciousness as personal experience (Vector 2)	.50	1.00	.50
Consciousness as awareness of "mind" (Vector 3)	.25	.50	1.00

We would predict that a correlation between measures such as admitting GCS score (Vector 1 measurements) and later post-acute ratings of awareness of others' mental activities (theory of mind measurement; Vector 3 measurements) would be in the neighborhood of +.25. The predicted relationship between measures of impaired self-awareness (Vector 2) and awareness of insight into other's mental states would be in the range of .50. At this date, no such data are available. Further studies will be needed to test this hypothesis.

Impaired self-awareness and denial phenomenon: Past and recent observations

A historical review of anosognosia, impaired self-awareness, and denial phenomenon after brain injury can be found in Weinstein and Kahn (1955), Prigatano and Schachter (1991), and Prigatano (1999). A recent summary of the literature on anosognosia can also be found in Prigatano (in press).

Weinstein and Kahn (1955) noted that many patients who appear to be anosognostic actually have some "knowledge" of their impairments and disabilities, and therefore thought that they were "denying" their illness. Ramachandran (1994) has reawakened this perspective. Using caloric stimulation with a patient who showed anosognosia for hemiplegia, he argues that the patient actually remembers saying that her arm was not paralysed while the caloric effect was present. When the caloric effect wore off, she stated that her arm was not paralysed, but again, had the memory of saying that it was paralysed when she had caloric stimulation. He argues that "at some deeper level, she does indeed have knowledge about the paralysis" (p. 324).

One way to approach this is to argue that different brain mechanisms may be involved in "denial" when it exists as a defence mechanism versus impaired awareness, when it is secondary to brain dysfunction affecting particularly the heteromodal cortex. House and Hodges (1988) reported on an interesting case of "persistent denial" of a hemiplegic lady following a right basal ganglia lesion. At the time, it was difficult to explain why a basal ganglia lesion would cause persistent denial. However, recently Vuilleumier et al. (2001) provided suggestive evidence that patients who show hysterical paralysis (with the assumed mechanism of denial being active) showed a decrease of metabolic activity in the thalamus and in the caudate and putamen. Is it possible that the mechanism, as a defence, involves brain-stem and limbic structures? It should be noted that years ago Charcot (see Ellenberger, 1970, p. 91) suggested that hysterical patients lived "in a state of somnambulism". He felt that such patients could be induced to demonstrate a hysterical hemiparesis due to hypnosis, or conversely through suggestions imposed during the hypnotic state, could be relieved of their symptoms. In both cases, however, their being in a hypoaroused state was thought to relate to their hysterical symptomatology. It is fascinating that newer evidence may support, in part, such a theory.

We may assume, therefore, that denial phenomena actually may have more to do with Vector 1 type of consciousness than Vectors 2 or 3. As noted earlier, Prigatano (1991, 1999) has suggested that impaired self-awareness versus denial of disability in patients with severe TBI is most likely associated with disturbances of heteromodal cortex. Prigatano and Altman (1990) serendipitously observed that patients with severe TBI, who showed impaired awareness, tapped slowly on the Halstead Finger Tapping Test (Reitan & Wolfson, 1993). Some recent functional magnetic resonance imaging (fMRI) studies have emerged that shed light on the potential importance of this observation. In normal individuals, performance of the Halstead Speed of Finger Tapping Test activates the contralateral sensory motor strip, the ipsilateral cerebellar hemisphere, and at times the supplementary motor cortex as well as the ipsilateral sensory motor strip (Johnson & Prigatano, 2000). When normals are asked to sustain the speed of finger movement, some show bilateral activation of heteromodal regions (Johnson & Prigatano, 2000). We have recently reported on two TBI cases; one who shows impaired self-awareness; the other who shows primarily denial phenomena (Prigatano, 2002). The first individual's finger tapping was correlated with normal activation of the sensory motor strip and the ipsilateral cerebellum when simply carrying out the tapping task. When his performance was compared across trials (i.e., speed of finger tapping had to be sustained) he failed to show a normal pattern of heteromodal cortical activation. This was the first suggested evidence that impaired self- awareness (Vector 2) may indeed involve the heteromodal regions.

In contrast, the second patient, who had an orbital frontal injury and who appeared to be showing, at least in part, denial phenomena as a method of coping with partial awareness activated heteromodal regions when sustaining finger tapping over time. These two cases provide suggestive evidence that impaired self-awareness (Vector 2) involves primarily heteromodal regions and may not necessarily involve large activations of thalamus, basal ganglia, or brainstem structures. Because of the intimate connections between all of these regions, however, lesions at any level of the neural axis may directly affect the different vectors of consciousness, although differentially. We suggest, however, when denial is present, it may be precisely the deep brain structures that are less functional.

The fact that early measures of impaired consciousness actually relate to rehabilitation outcome up to one year post injury, provides again further evidence that there is a neurological basis of impaired awareness that has relevance to making appropriate choices later in life. In the introduction it was noted that this was observed in patients with TBI. A recent study by Sherer et al. (in press) extends these observations and shows that early measures of impaired awareness relate to employability at rehabilitation discharge. Thus, there is a growing body of literature that suggests that early disturbances of consciousness indeed carry with them residual effects and those effects can be seen some time past the acute stages.

FUNCTIONAL NEUROIMAGING STUDIES
AND THE THREE VECTORS OF CONSCIOUSNESS

Imaging studies of individuals in an altered state of consciousness versus regained consciousness can provide some insight into the first aspect of consciousness described by Zeman (2001). Coma, general anaesthesia, and stages of sleep have been examined with FDG positron emission tomography (PET).

In a resting but wakeful state, the posterior cingulate and retrosplenial regions exhibits the highest baseline state of energy metabolism (Gusnard & Raichle, 2001). The dorsal medial prefrontal cortex, anterior cingulate, and insula also exhibit prominent resting state metabolic (PET) and electrical (EEG) activity (Ingvar, 1979; Raichle et al., 2001).

Fiset and colleagues (1999) studied people in differing levels of uncon-sciousness induced by propofol anaesthesia. In that study, the medial thalamus, cuneus, precuneus, posterior cingulate, and orbitofrontal regions exhibited relatively greater reduction in energy metabolism. The findings led Fiset and colleagues to conclude that reduction of consciousness through anaesthesia is achieved by affecting these specific brain structures and pathways in the brain.

Imaging studies of sleep and wakefulness also provide a unique opportunity to examine brain activity with regard to consciousness. As noted above, during rapid eye movement sleep, the limbic system, including the anterior cingulate, is relatively more metabolically active compared to other regions. In contrast, during slow wave sleep, the medial prefrontal cortex and anterior and posterior cingulate exhibit decreased metabolic activity based on FDG PET (Braun et al., 1997; Finelli et al., 2000; Maquet, 1999).

Functional activation imaging of patients in coma may be of prognostic value and may help in making life-support decisions. These studies also inform us regarding brain reactivity in the absence of consciousness. Moritz et al. (2001) recently reported a case study of a patient who sustained multifocal cerebral injuries from a motor vehicle accident. The initial GCS was 11, but the patient deteriorated over the next 72 hours with increased cerebral pressure and herniation with associated ischaemia in the posterior circulation. A decompression craniotomy was performed to address the elevated intracranial pressure and swelling. Electrophysiological examination indicated absence of detectable thalamocortical response following median nerve stimulation and a poor prognosis for recovery. However fMRI examination of tactile, visual and auditory sensory cortex demonstrated unequivocal cerebral responses to all three stimulus inputs. The patient eventually improved. In the context of this discussion, the results of Moritz et al. (2001) would suggest that the brain can respond to sensory information despite a dramatically reduced level of consciousness/awareness.

There are several functional imaging reports in the literature that help us understand the second vector of consciousness and how it may relate to the third vector. In these studies, subjects have been asked to monitor their own mental states in the "here and now" (Blakemore, Wolpert, & Frith, 2000; Gusnard, Akbudak, Shulman, & Raichle, 2001; Lane, Fink, Chau, & Dolan, 1997; McGuire, Paulesu, Frackowiak, & Frith, 1996). Activations in these studies were within the anterior cingulate and paracingulate region, Brodmann Area 32 (Frith & Frith, 1999). For example, Lane et al. (1997) used PET and ^{15}O-water, and presented healthy subjects with pleasant, unpleasant and neutral pictures from the International Affective Picture System. In half the scans subjects selectively attended to their subjective emotional experience to the picture (an internal focus of attention). As each picture appeared, they indicated on a keypad whether the picture induced a pleasant, unpleasant or neutral feeling. In the other half of the scans they viewed matched pictures and attended to the spatial location of the scene (an external focus of attention). Results revealed robust activation in rostral anterior cingulate cortex when subjects attended to what they were feeling. Replication studies of this paradigm have found highly similar results (Gusnard et al., 2001; Lane et al., submitted).

Regarding the interface of Vectors 2 and 3 of consciousness, Johnson et al. (2002) studied normal volunteers with fMRI and asked the subjects to reflect on their own traits, beliefs, and abilities. During the experimental condition, subjects evaluated yes/no statements such as "I get along with others", I'm hopeful about the future", "I cry easily", or "I forget important things". In the comparison condition, subjects evaluated yes/no statements regarding general knowledge (e.g., "You need water to live", "10 seconds is more than a minute"). During the experimental condition in which subjects were required to access their own beliefs about themselves, each and every subject activated the anterior medial prefrontal cortex as well as the posterior cingulate region. Very similar results have been reported by Zysset, Huber, Ferstl, and von Cramon (2002).

Two previous PET studies examining "theory of mind" tasks also reported anterior medial prefrontal and posterior cingulate activity (Fletcher et al., 1995; Goel, Grafman, Sadato, & Hallett, 1995). The tasks used in these studies required the participant to "mentalise" about the beliefs and desires of others so as to predict their behaviour. Together, the results of the self-evaluative studies and the theory-of-mind studies suggest that overlapping neural systems are required for both types of task. This is very consistent with Zeman's (2001) idea of the third type of consciousness reflecting "anything that we believe, hope, fear, intend, expect, desire", whether or not those beliefs and expectations are about the self or about others.

The neuroimaging studies just reviewed indicate a network underlying consciousness involving the midbrain, thalamus, and some limbic and cortical structures including the anterior cingulate, anterior mesial prefrontal cortex, and retrosplenial cortex. The anterior mesial prefrontal cortex and retrosplenial region are of particular note as these appear to be involved in all three vectors of consciousness. These regions are differentially hypometabolic under conditions of unawareness (coma, anaesthesia, slow-wave sleep), and are activated during cognitive probes of the second and third vectors of consciousness.

Disturbances of consciousness and rehabilitation

Given the above theoretical model and empirical findings, we would suggest that there are three classes of disturbances of consciousness that need to be addressed in brain injury rehabilitation in general and neuropsychological rehabilitation in particular. The first set of disturbances has to do with the sleep–wake cycle that affects arousal/alertness. What is important about this dimension is that it is highly related to the energy level of the individual. It has been known for many years that brain injuries of various types affect energy level and patients frequently report fatigue when doing mental or physical tasks (Brodal, 1973). It is crucial that neurorehabilitationists consider methods for increasing the energy level of brain dysfunctional patients who show a disturbance of this type. We would anticipate that anything that helps the patient get a better night's sleep would be very helpful in improving this type of disturbance in consciousness. Also, medications that can increase levels of arousal during the waking stages might help "reactivate" Vector 1 or type 1 consciousness.

In the course of attempting to rehabilitate post-acute TBI patients, it was noted that those patients who worked at cognitive rehabilitation tasks for several hours a day reported sleeping better at night. Many of these patients' family members spontaneously noted that these patients appeared to be less irritable after a good night's sleep and extensive cognitive retraining (Prigatano et al., 1986). Perhaps the mere act of carrying out repetitive thinking tasks can increase the tolerance for such activity in some patients. While memory is "not a muscle", and exercise does not strengthen it, this may not be true for our mental energy. The more we work at carrying out certain kinds of cognitive exercises, perhaps we increase the potential of energy reserve. This is an area that needs to be further evaluated.

The second disorder of consciousness described here (Vector 2) has received more empirical attention. Individuals who have poor self-awareness are prone to make poor social choices, and this does relate to rehabilitation outcome (Prigatano, 1999; Prigatano et al., 1984; Sherer et al., 1998a; Sherer et al., in press). Methods have developed to assess this type of disturbance as listed in Table 1. While there are no systematic ways of improving this type of self-awareness, a combination of individual and group exercises seems to be helpful (see Prigatano, 1999). Much depends on the overall integrity of the heteromodal cortex as to whether or not this type of impaired awareness can improve.

As noted by Prigatano (1999), many patients with impaired awareness go from a complete syndrome to a partial syndrome. With partial knowledge, they may use both defensive versus nondefensive methods of coping. When nondefensive methods of coping are the primary methods of dealing with partial knowledge, the holistic programmes described by Ben-Yishay et al. and Prigatano et al. (see Prigatano, 1999) are perhaps most helpful. When patients use denial as a method of coping with partial knowledge, psychotherapeutic interventions may become crucial (see Prigatano 1999).

We are impressed that early work with impaired awareness may also have some practical consequences, in addition to working with this problem at the post-acute stage. Prigatano and Wong (1999) noted that the patient's capacity to predict accurately how many words they could recall during the first 30 days of rehabilitation was correlated to whether or not they actually obtained their rehabilitation goals. In fact, this measure of disturbed awareness was a strong predictor of achieving rehabilitation goals as was any other deficit (cognitive or affective). Vilkki (1992) also noted that after TBI, patients often had difficulty accurately predicting how they will perform on a task, even when given feedback after their performance. We suggest that during the acute stages of rehabilitation, patients be encouraged to make simple predictions of what they are able to do, based on feedback from all forms of therapy (speech therapy, physical therapy, etc.). Improving the accuracy of one's predictions may actually improve self-awareness and this may well have practical conse-quences, even following acute rehabilitation. Finally, in this regard, Borgaro and Prigatano (2002) recently reported that impaired awareness was equally affected after severe TBI as was memory and affective disturbances. Collectively, these studies suggest that impaired self-awareness should be worked with from a rehabilitation point of view during the acute stages, as well as the post-acute stages.

The third vector of consciousness, that is a developed sense of self and the capacity to "read" the minds of others, is also important. As suggested in this paper, it depends on Vectors 1 and 2 but may be at a different level of organisation to Vector 2. The development of delusions in various psychotic states may be specifically related to disturbances in Vector 3. It has been noted, for example, that individuals with schizophrenia often have very poor self-awareness and have difficulties interpreting the actions of others (Flashman et al., 2001). When this occurs, they are described as delusional. Prigatano (1988) noted that unresolved problems with anosognosia may well result in delusional behavior. A recent clinical example of this was reported in Prigatano (1999).

The implications for rehabilitation are obvious. During acute, intermediate and post-acute phases, brain dysfunctional patients should be asked to judge the intentions of others on a variety of cognitive remediation tasks. They should systematically go through what cues they use (visual, auditory, etc.) to make their judgements. Attempts to correct inaccuracies in their perception of others' "states of mind" may actually reduce their cognitive confusion early in rehabilitation and avoid later problems of suspiciousness, if not paranoid ideation several years post-brain injury. This is a new area of inquiry, but one that should be actively embraced within the context of neuropsychological rehabilitation.

SUMMARY

In this brief theoretical paper, we have attempted to summarise selected literature dealing with disturbances of consciousness and to build upon a model suggested by Zeman (2001). We believe that three basic disturbances of consciousness can be described. All forms of consciousness interact, but at different levels of organisation in the brain. Conceptualising disturbances of consciousness along these lines leads to predictions about how these disturbances may be related and tested through construct validation methods. The model also suggests initial ideas for working with these disturbances during different stages of brain injury rehabilitation.

REFERENCES

Blakemore, S. J., Wolpert, D., & Frith, C. (2000). Why can't you tickle yourself? *Neuroreport*, *11*(11), 11–16.

Borgaro, S., & Prigatano, G. P. (2002). Early cognitive and affective sequelae of traumatic brain injury: A study using the BNI Screen for higher cerebral functions. *Journal of Head Trauma Rehabilitation*, *17*(6), 526–534.

Braun, A. R., Balkin, T. J., Wesenten, N. J., Carson, R. E., Varga, M., Baldwin, P., Selbie, S., Belenky, G., & Herscovitch, P. (1997). Regional cerebral blood flow throughout the sleep–wake cycle. An H2(15)O PET study. *Brain, 120,* 1173–1197.

Brodal, A. (1973). Self-observations and neuro-anatomical considerations after a stroke. *Brain, 96,* 675–694.

Bueche, F., & Hecht, E. (2000). *College physics.* New York: McGraw-Hill.

Ellenberger, H. (1970). *The discovery of the unconscious. The history and evolution of dynamic psychiatry.* New York: Basic Books.

Finelli, L. A., Landolt, H. P., Buck, A., Roth, C., Berthold, T., Borbely, A. A., & Achermann, P. (2000). Functional neuroanatomy of human sleep states after zolpidem and placebo: A H2(15)O-PET study. *Journal of Sleep Research, 9*(2), 161–173.

Fiset, P., Paus, T., Daloze, T., Plourde, G., Meuret, P., Bonhomme, V., Hajj-Ali, N., Backman, S.B., & Evans, A.C. (1999). Brain mechanisms of propofol-induced loss of consciousness in humans: A positron emission tomographic study. *Journal of Neurosciences, 19*(13), 5506–5513.

Flashman, L. A., McAllister, T. W., Johnson, S. C., Rick, J. H., Green, R. L., & Saykin, A. J. (2001). Specific frontal lobe subregions correlated with unawareness of illness in schizophrenia: A preliminary study. *Journal of Neuropsychiatry and Clinical Neurosciences, 13*(2), 255–257.

Fletcher, P. C., Happe, F., Frith, U., Baker, S. C., Dolan, R. J., Frackowiak, R. S., & Frith, C. D. (1995). Other minds in the brain: A functional imaging study of "theory of mind" in story comprehension. *Cognition, 57*(2), 109–128.

Frith, C. D., & Frith, U. (1999). Interacting minds: A biological basis. *Science, 286*(5445), 1692–1695.

Goel, V., Grafman, J., Sadato, N., & Hallett, M. (1995). Modeling other minds. *Neuroreport, 6*(13), 1741–1746.

Gusnard, D. A., Akbudak, E., Shulman, G. L., & Raichle, M. E. (2001). Medial prefrontal cortex and self-referential mental activity: Relation to a default mode of brain function. *Proceedings of the National Academy of Science USA, 20,* 20.

Gusnard, D. A., & Raichle, M. E. (2001). Searching for a baseline: Functional imaging and the resting human brain. *Nature Review Neuroscience, 2*(10), 685–694.

Hall, C. S., & Lindzey, G. (1978). *Theories of personality* (3rd ed). New York: John Wiley & Sons.

House, A., & Hodges, J. (1988). Persistent denial of handicap after infarction of the right basal ganglia: A case study. *Journal of Neurology, Neurosurgery, and Psychiatry, 51,* 112–115.

Huetnick, L., & Adams, S. (2001). *Physics.* New York: Hungry Minds.

Humphrey, N. (1978). Nature's psychologists. *New Scientist, 29,* 900–903.

Ingvar, D. H. (1979). "Hyperfrontal" distribution of the cerebral grey matter flow in resting wakefulness; on the functional anatomy of the conscious state. *Acta Neurologica Scandinavia, 60*(1), 12–25.

Jehkonen, M., Ahonen, J.-P., Dastidar, P., Laippala, P., & Vilkki, J. (2000). Unawareness of deficits after right hemisphere stroke: Double-dissociations of anosognosias. *Acta Neurologica Scandinavia, 102,* 378–384.

Johnson, S. C., Baxter, L. C., Susskind-Wilder, L. S., Pipe, J. G., Heiserman, J. E., & Prigatano, G. P. (2002). Neural correlates of self-reflection. *Brain, 125,* 1808–1814.

Johnson, S., Baxter, L., Susskind-Wilder, L., & Prigatano, G. (2001). The neural substrates of self-reflective thought: Preliminary results. *Neuroimage, 13,* S422.

Johnson, S. C., & Prigatano, G. P. (2000). Functional MR imaging during finger tapping. *BNI Quarterly, 16*(3), 37–41.

Jouvet, M. J. (1999). *The paradox of sleep: The story of dreaming.* Cambridge, MA: MIT Press.

Lane, R. D., Fink, G. R., Chau, P. M., & Dolan, R. J. (1997). Neural activation during selective attention to subjective emotional responses. *Neuroreport, 8*(18), 3969–3972.

Lane, R., Fort, C., Johnson, S., Ryan, L., & Trouard, T. (submitted). Dissociable representations of emotional state in dorsal and ventral medial prefrontal cortices.

Macquet, P. (1999). Brain mechanisms of sleep: Contribution of neuroimaging techniques. *Journal of Psychopharmacology*, *13*(4 Suppl 1), S25–28.

Macquet, P., Degueldre, C., Delfiore, G., Aerts, J., Peters, J. M., Luxen, A., et al. (1997). Functional neuroanatomy of human slow wave sleep. *Journal of Neuroscience*, *17*, 2807–2812.

Macquet, P., Peters, J. M., Aerts, J., Delfiore, G., Degueldre, C., Luxen A., et al. (1996). Functional neuroanatomy of human rapid-eye-movement sleep and dreaming. *Nature*, *383*, 163–166.

McGuire, P. K., Paulesu, E., Frackowiak, R. S., & Frith, C. D. (1996). Brain activity during stimulus independent thought. *Neuroreport*, *7*(13), 2095–2099.

Moritz, C. H., Rowley, H. A., Haughton, V. M., Swartz, K. R., Jones, J., & Badie, B. (2001). Functional MR imaging assessment of a non-responsive brain injured patient. *Magnetic Resonance Imaging*, *19*(8), 1129–1132.

Morrow, L., Vrtunski, K., Kim, Y., & Boller, F. (1981). Arousal responses to emotional stimuli and laterality of lesion. *Neuropsychologia*, *19*, 65–71.

Pedersen, P. M., Jorgensen, H. S., Nakayama, H., Raaschou, H. O., & Olsen, T. S. (1996). Frequency, determinants, and consequences of anosognosia in acute stroke. *Journal of Neurological Rehabilitation*, *10*, 243–250.

Prigatano, G. (1988). Anosognosia, delusions, and altered self-awareness after brain injury: A historical perspective. *BNI Quarterly*, *4*(3), 40–48.

Prigatano, G. P. (1991). Disturbances of self-awareness of deficit after traumatic brain injury. In G. P. Prigatano & D. L. Schacter (Eds.), *Awareness of deficit after brain injury: Theoretical and clinical issues* (pp. 111–126). New York: Oxford University Press.

Prigatano, G. P. (1999). *Principles of neuropsychological rehabilitation*. New York: Oxford University Press.

Prigatano, G. P. (2002). *Awareness of deficit and psychological interventions after brain injury*. Proceedings of the Third World Congress of Neurological Rehabilitation, Venice, Italy (pp. 395–398).

Prigatano, G. P. (in press). The assessment and rehabilitation of anosognosia and syndromes of impaired awareness. In P. Halligan, U. Kischka, & G. Beaumont (Eds.), *Oxford handbook of clinical neuropsychology*. New York: Oxford University Press.

Prigatano, G. P., & Altman, I. M. (1990). Impaired awareness of behavioral limitations after traumatic brain injury. *Archives of Physical Medicine and Rehabilitation*, *71*, 1058–1064.

Prigatano, G. P., Bruna, O., Mataro, M., Munoz, J. M., Fernandez, S., & Junque, C. (1998). Initial disturbances of consciousness and resultant impaired awareness in Spanish patients with traumatic brain injury. *Journal of Head Trauma Rehabilitation*, *13*(5), 29–38.

Prigatano, G. P., Fordyce, D. J., Zeiner, H. K., Roueche, J. R., Pepping, M., & Wood, B. C. (1984). Neuropsychological rehabilitation after closed head injury in young adults. *Journal of Neurology, Neurosurgery, and Psychiatry*, *47*, 505–513.

Prigatano, G. P., Fordyce, D. J., Zeiner, H. K., Roueche, J. R., Pepping, M., & Woods, B. C. (1986). *Neuropsychological rehabilitation after brain injury*. Baltimore, MD: Johns Hopkins University Press.

Prigatano, G. P., & Klonoff, P. S. (1997). A clinician's rating scale for evaluating impaired self-awareness and denial of disability after brain injury. *The Clinical Neuropsychologist*, *11*(1), 1–12.

Prigatano, G. P., Ogano, M., & Amukusa, B. (1997). A cross-cultural study on impaired self-awareness in Japanese patients with brain dysfunction. *Neuropsychiatry, Neuropsychology, and Behavioral Neurology*, *10*(2), 135–143.

Prigatano, G. P., & Schacter, D. L. (1991). *Awareness of deficit after brain injury: Theoretical and clinical issues*. New York: Oxford University Press.

Prigatano, G. P., & Wong, J. L. (1999). Cognitive and affective improvement in brain dysfunctional patients who achieve inpatient rehabilitation goals. *Archives of Physical Medicine and Rehabilitation, 80*, 77–84

Raichle, M. E., MacLeod, A. M., Snyder, A. Z., Powers, W. J., Gusnard, D. A., & Shulman, G. L. (2001). A default mode of brain function. *Proceedings of the National Academy of Science USA, 98*(2), 676–682.

Ramachandran, V. S. (1994). Phantom limbs, neglect syndromes, repressed memories, and Freudian psychology. *International Review of Neurobiology, 37*, 291–372.

Reitan, R. M., & Wolfson, D. (1993). *The Halstead-Reitan Neuropsychological Test Battery: Theory and clinical interpretation* (2nd edition). Tucson, AZ: Neuropsychology Press.

Sherer, M., Bergloff, P., Boake, C., High, W., Jr, & Levin, E. (1998b). The Awareness Questionnaire: Factor structure and internal consistency. *Brain Injury, 12*(1), 63–68.

Sherer, M., Bergloff, P., Levin, E., High, W. M., Jr, Oden, K. E., & Nick, T. G. (1998a). Impaired awareness and employment outcome after traumatic brain injury. *Journal of Head Trauma Rehabilitation, 13*(5): 52–61.

Sherer, M., Boake, C., Levin, E., Silver, B. V., Ringholz, G., & High, W. M., Jr. (1998c). Characteristics of impaired awareness after traumatic brain injury. *Journal of International Neuropsychological Society, 4*, 380–387.

Sherer, M., Hart, T., Nick, T., Whyte, J., Thompson, R. N., & Yablon, S. (in press). Early impaired self-awareness after traumatic brain injury.

Starkstein, S. E., Fedoroff, J. P., Price, T. R., Leiguarda, R., & Robinson, R. G. (1992). Anosognosia in patients with cerebrovascular lesions. A study of causative factors. *Stroke, 23*(10), 1446–1453.

Stuss, D. T., Gallup, G. G., & Alexander, M. P. (2001). The frontal lobes are necessary for "theory of mind". *Brain, 124*, 279–286.

Teasdale, G. M., & Jennet, B. (1974). Assessment of coma and impaired consciousness: A practical scale. *The Lancet, 2*, 81–84.

Vilkki, J. (1992). Cognitive flexibility and mental programming after closed head injuries and anterior or posterior cerebral excisions. *Neuropsychologia, 30*(9), 807–814.

Vuilleumier, P., Chicherio, C., Assal, F., Schwartz, S., Slosman, D., & Landis, T. (2001). Functional neuroanatomical correlates of hysterical sensorimotor loss. *Brain, 124*, 1077–1090.

Weinstein, E. A. & Kahn, R. L. (1955). *Denial of illness. Symbolic and physiological aspects.* Springfield, IL: Charles C Thomas.

Zeman, A. (2001). Invited review. Consciousness. *Brain, 124*, 1263–1289.

Zysset, S., Huber, O., Ferstl, E., & von Cramon, D. Y. (2002). The anterior frontomedian cortex and evaluative judgment: An fMRI study. *Neuroimage, 15*(4), 983–991.

Mild traumatic brain injury:
Impairment and disability assessment caveats

Nathan D. Zasler

Concussion Care Centre of Virginia, Glen Allen, USA

Michael F. Martelli

Concussion Care Centre of Virginia,
and Virginia Commonwealth University Health System, Glen Allen, USA

Mild traumatic brain injury (MTBI) accounts for approximately 80% of all brain injuries, and persistent sequelae can impede physical, emotional, social, marital, vocational, and avocational functioning. Evaluation of impairment and disability following MTBI typically can involve such contexts as social security disability application, personal injury litigation, worker's compensation claims, disability insurance policy application, other health care insurance policy coverage issues, and the determination of vocational and occupational competencies and limitations. MTBI is still poorly understood and impairment and disability assessment in MTBI can present a significant diagnostic challenge. There are currently no ideal systems for rating impairment and disability for MTBI residua. As a result, medicolegal examiners and clinicians must necessarily familiarise themselves with the variety of disability and impairment evaluation protocols and understand their limitations. The current paper reviews recommended procedures and potential obstacles and confounding issues.

INTRODUCTION

Mild traumatic brain injury (MTBI), although quite prevalent, is still poorly understood. MTBI incidence, which is likely underestimated, accounts for approximately 80% of the estimated 373,000 traumatic brain injuries that occur each year in the US. The most frequent cause of MTBI is motor vehicle

Correspondence should be addressed to Nathan D. Zasler, CEO and Medical Director, Concussion Care Centre and Tree of Life, 10120 West Broad Street, Suites G, Glen Allen, Virginia 23060, Phone: 804-346-1803, Fax: 804-346-1956, Email: nzasler@cccv-ltd.cl

© 2003 Psychology Press Ltd
http://www.tandf.co.uk/journals/pp/09602011.html   DOI:10.1080/09602010

accidents and its victims are typically young males 15–24 years of age. Post-concussional sequelae may impede physical, emotional, social, marital, vocational, and avocational functioning. Awareness of community resources is a prerequisite to providing neuromedical, as well as non-medical services to this special patient population. The Brain Injury Association (BIA) is an excellent resource for information on brain injury for professionals, "survivors", and families (Kraus & McArthur, 1995).

Traditionally, severity of initial neurological injury is defined by the initial Glasgow Coma Scale score, presence and duration of amnesia (retrograde and anterograde), and alteration or loss of consciousness (and its duration) (Williams, Levin, & Eisenberg, 1990; Zasler, 1997). Mild traumatic brain injury has been defined as a traumatically induced physiological disruption of cerebral function, as manifested by at least one of the following: (1) loss of consciousness of no longer than 20 min; (2) any loss of memory, either retrograde or anterograde; (3) any alteration in mental status at the time of the accident, even in the absence of loss of consciousness or amnesia; (4) physical symptoms that are potentially brain-related (e.g., nausea, headache, dizziness, tinnitus, visual aberrations, olfactory deficits, or extended periods of fatigue); and (5) development of post-traumatic cognitive deficits that cannot be completely accounted for by emotional factors. By definition, severity must not exceed the following in order to qualify as "mild": (1) Glasgow Coma Scale score of 13 to 15 without worsening; (2) post-traumatic amnesia of ≤24 hours; and (3) loss of consciousness ≤30 minutes (Report of the TBI Special Interest Group, ACRM, 1993). Notably, individuals with intracranial lesions and those with lower GCS scores (e.g., 13 or 14) generally have poorer outcomes (Williams et al., 1990, p. 27; Culotta, Sementilli, Gerold, & Watts, 1996).

IMPAIRMENT AND DISABILITY ASSESSMENT IN MTBI

The clinician should include a thorough history, results of clinical evaluations, assessment of current clinical status, plans for future treatment, including rehabilitation and re-evaluation, diagnosis, and clinical impressions, and an estimate of time for full or partial recovery. The impact of the medical condition(s) on life activities, nature of the medical condition, or chance of sudden or subtle incapacitation should be assessed. The risk of injury, harm, or further impairment activity needed to meet life demands must also be addressed. Any restrictions or accommodations should be stipulated.

When a patient presents with multi-system trauma, there may be impairments involving several parts of the body including the nervous system. Individual impairments should be separately calculated and their whole-person values combined using the "combined values chart" in the AMA Guides for Evaluation of Permanent Impairment (American Medical Association, 1993).

In general, only the medical condition causing the greatest impairment should be evaluated. This presents a problem in a patient with post-concussive deficits concurrent with more significant bodily impairments such as loss of a limb.

NEUROPSYCHOLOGICAL ASSESSMENT IN NEUROLOGICAL CONTEXT

Neuropsychological assessment is a much more sensitive measure than bedside examination and currently represents the gold standard for assessment of cognitive dysfunction in MTBI. Given the importance of neuropsychological testing in the assessment of cognitive impairment in this patient population, evaluating clinicians should develop a relatively sophisticated appreciation of the sensitivity, specificity, validity, and reliability of the measures used. The following are 10 caveats to assess when reviewing the quality of neuropsychological testing.

1. Has pre-injury intellectual function been adequately estimated from educational and/or military standardised scores and/or age, education, and demographically adjusted statistical estimation procedures?

2. Was objective collateral information obtained regarding pre- and/or post-injury status?

3. Was pre-morbid medical (especially previous TBI) and psychological history adequately reviewed and considered?

4. Were other factors potentially impacting on test performance adequately considered for potential contribution (e.g., pain, emotional issues, vestibular symptoms, motivation)?

5. Were diagnostic inferences based on appropriately referenced normative group comparisons and actuarially based cut-off scores and comparisons with base rates or likelihood of symptom occurrence in peers without MTBI?

6. Were measures of validity, simulation and/or dissimulation included in the evaluation?

7. Was adequate consideration given for the initial degree of neurological insult relative to GCS score, duration of PTA, altered level of consciousness, etc., and was this correlated with symptom severity and onset relative to consistency with degree and temporal correlation of impairment?

8. Was the pattern of change across time analysed for consistency with anticipated recovery curves?

9. Was the impact of medication on test performance noted in the report?

10. Was the pattern of symptoms reported and temporal onset of symptoms correlated with anticipated complaints after equal magnitude injuries *and* with neuropsychological test results? (Zasler & Martelli, 1998.)

Nonetheless, neuropsychological assessment suffers several shortcomings: questionable ecological (real-world) validity for the less severely impaired, variable ability to detect malingering, and over-reliance on technicians for administering tests. Due to the nature of assessing cognitive functions in analogue situations, it too often falls short of predicting real work performance. Clinicians must remain aware of these shortcomings when performing impairment ratings (Dodrill, 1977; Report of the Therapeutic and Technology Assessment Subcomittee, AAN, 1996). Empirically validated "rating systems" for most of the deficits associated with these disorders are lacking. Evaluations are too often performed despite limited training in disability issues, application of complex differential diagnostic issues and the various potential ethical conflicts relevant to medicolegal evaluations. Even if problems relating to environmental incentives and other influences that contribute to bias in the examinee (and examiner) in medicolegal contexts were not present, disentangling the multiple contributors to impairment and disability would still represent a diagnostic challenge that requires careful scrutiny (Dodrill, 1997; Martelli, Zasler, & Bush, in press; Report of the Therapeutic and Technology Assessment Subcommittee, AAN, 1996; Zasler & Martelli, 1998).

FACTORS INFLUENCING PERFORMANCE AND PRESENTATION

In addition, we cannot ignore the effects of response bias as a critical element in the conduct of medicolegal evaluations. Response bias refers to a class of behaviours that reflect less than fully truthful, accurate or valid symptom report and presentation, whether deliberate or unconscious.

Given the frequent highly desirable incentives to distort performance, examinee motivation to provide truthful report and full effort is an extremely important prerequisite to valid assessment. Valid assessment is required for provision of: (1) Accurate diagnosis; (2) appropriate and timely treatment to promote optimal recovery; (3) prevention of iatrogenic impairment and disability reinforcement, and promulgation of unnecessary health care costs; and (4) appropriate legal compensation decisions based on causality and level of damages suffered. In the context of impairment and disability evaluations, or insurance-related evaluations, reports demonstrating high prevalence rates of response bias in examinees are proliferating (Binder & Rohling, 1996; Larrabee, 2000; Rohling, 2000; Rohling & Binder, 1995; Youngjohn, Burrows, & Erdal, 1995). Although most studies focus on exaggeration of impairments, incentives also exist for minimising deficits. Another too often neglected area of response bias is examiner response bias (Johnson, Krafka, & Cecil, 2000).

Although the incidence of response bias in various medical or psychological problems can only be estimated, it is increasingly evident that compensation is an important issue affecting presentation. The numerous reports demonstrating high prevalence rates of response bias show a significant impact on symptom report and test performance in medicolegal evaluations. In one study, poor effort was found to have a stronger effect on neuropsychological test scores than did severity of brain injury or neurological disease (Green, Rohling, Lees-Haley, & Allen, 2001). Financial incentives play a much stronger role in mild versus moderate and severe TBI. These findings imply that failure to control for effort level leads to false conclusions, not only for individual clinical diagnoses, but also for group data from which we derive clinical diagnostic information.

Although response bias is most commonly conceptualised as deliberate exaggeration of difficulty (e.g., symptom magnification, malingering), a continuum exists that extends from (1) denial or unawareness of impairments through (2) symptom minimisation, (3) normal or average symptom presentation, (4) sensitisation to subtle or benign symptoms or problems, (5) exaggeration or symptom magnification, and up to (6) frank malingering. This unidimensional conceptualisation likely represents an oversimplification that obscures the subtleties of a wide range of response biases that may be demonstrated, but nonetheless serves as a useful framework.

Unawareness and *denial* refer to neurological or psychological phenomena wherein impairments are under-appreciated due to dysfunction of cognitive operations subserving awareness, or personal shortcomings are psychologically repressed to guard against distressful realisations. *Symptom minimisation* is a more deliberate phenomenon, usually motivated by intention to limit impact of undesirable functional restrictions or distress, and engage in desired activities. Failure to detect such biases can result in overestimation of abilities that could potentially endanger the welfare of the examinee.

Medicolegal assessments should be concerned with people exaggerating normality or exaggerating deficits, and the legal system should be just as concerned with people being under-compensated as over-compensated. Sometimes subtle impairments are missed given a relative absence of self-reported problems and adequate neuropsychological test performance. Attention should be paid to corroboratory report of greater problems than described by the examinee, declining performance in work and other functional life areas as assessed by others that contradict examinee denial, and externalisation of blame (Sbordone, Seyranian, & Ruff, 2000). Notably, objective assessment procedures administered in a quiet, structured, and distraction-free testing environment are not always sensitive to difficulties with self-directed activity in the real world.

Undue *sensitisation* to distress from mild, negligible, or benign symptoms can lead to a spectrum of abnormal illness behaviours and response bias in reporting problems. Anxiety can augment symptom perception and health concerns. Sensitisation may be especially relevant for post-concussive symptoms that often appear with similar frequency in the general population (Lees-Haley & Brown, 1993; Lees-Haley et al., 1997). *Symptom magnification* refers to conscious or unconscious exaggeration of impairment and can reflect multiple factors, including financial reward and psychological needs, including: garnering attention that would otherwise not be forthcoming; resolving pre-existing life conflicts; retaliating against employer or spouse; finding more socially acceptable attribution for psychological disorders; reducing anxiety; and exerting a "plea for help" or soliciting acknowledgment of perceived difficulties. Excessive preoccupation with symptoms is involved in a number of DSM-IV somatoform disorders (American Psychiatric Association, 1994). Depression, post-traumatic stress disorder, and other anxiety conditions in which there can be sensitisation or magnification of symptoms can represent important imitators of bonafide physical and neurological impairment.

Malingering is the extreme form of response bias and reflects deliberate symptom production or gross exaggeration for purposes of secondary gain. In the medicolegal evaluation, it is often reflected by responses biased in the direction of false symptom reports or managed effort to produce poor performance on tests. Measures of this type of response bias should always be administered in cases of medicolegal presentation and where there is suspicion of any disincentive to exert full effort, or suspicion of sociopathic personality disorder (Martelli, Zasler, MacMillan, & Mancini, 1999b).

Response bias represents an especially important threat to validity of medicolegal assessments. Because assessments include and usually begin with an interview about self-reported symptoms and rely heavily on measures of performance on standardised tests, the validity of the results requires the veracity, co-operation, and motivation of the patient. However, patients seen for presumptive brain injury-related impairments often over-report pre-injury functional status in regard to post-concussive symptoms that often appear with similar frequency in the general population. Further, the ability of neuro-psychologists to accurately detect malingering in routine test protocols has been less than impressive (e.g., Loring, 1995). The same is unfortunately true for physicians as a group.

Medicolegal examiners and clinicians alike should also remember that such injuries often occur in conjunction with both cranial adnexal and musculo-ligamentous injuries, such as occurring following cervical acceleration/deceleration (whiplash) injury, requiring rating of these sequela and combined whole person impairments (Zasler, 1996a).

Notably, functional implications of each impairment should be discussed based on patient and corroboratory witness reports and anticipated norms. Examining clinicians should remember that the best way to assess a particular functional capability is to have the examinee do that activity, not some simulation of the activity that only approximates the behaviour in question. Symptom descriptors used as "diagnoses", such as "post-traumatic headache" and "post-traumatic dizziness", are not only incomplete but provide no patho-aetiological information which can translate to appropriate diagnostic and treatment strategies. Each condition/impairment should be listed with a presumptive patho-aetiology, such that "post-traumatic headache" might be "post-traumatic headache secondary to right greater occipital neuralgia, right-sided referred cervical myofascial pain and migraine without aura". Subjective symptoms should be differentiated from objective ones (Zasler, 1996b).

Importantly, the diagnosis of mild traumatic brain injury should be based on: patient and chart history; temporal relationship of symptoms to injury in question; nature of post-concussive complaints and "fit" with expected symptomatology; corroboration by others including "non-invested" individuals; and degree to which symptom improvement matches expected natural history of neurological recovery. Adequate consideration must be given to alternative explanations for each impairment. The examiner must assess each subjective impairment with appropriate bedside procedures and as necessary further diagnostic testing or recommendation for such. Assessment should also include testing to determine validity of symptom complaint (e.g., response bias testing) (Zasler, 1996b).

Employment determinations should be made based on the ability of the claimant to work, with or without accommodation, with impairment(s) and meet job demands and other conditions of employment, including travel to and from work (Zasler, 1996a). Importantly, impairment ratings may not adequately reflect functional disability in people following MTBI, where variability in impairment and functional disability following similar injuries is not uncommon. A growing body of literature describes the factors that impact on variability in long-term outcome following brain injury. The following variables have all been found to contribute to poorer outcome and higher levels of functional impairment and disability: (1) Injury context variables including collateral non-cerebral traumatic injuries, especially cervical injuries, multiple injuries, greater motor impairment, presence of chronic pain. (2) Pre-morbid biological variables such as previous brain injury and age greater than 40. (3) Pre- and post-injury psychosocial variables including lower intelligence, history of alcohol or substance abuse, psychiatric history, poor school achievement, not being married, deficient social support systems, and poor family support. (4) Personality and coping variables such as perceptions of victimisation, over-achievement, dependency, grandiosity, and borderline personality traits, along with childhood sexual abuse, post-traumatic stress, and post-traumatic depression. (5) Environmental variables including litigation-related financial incentives (Zasler, 1996b). Clearly, consideration of these variables is required in order to better understand the relationship between injury, severity of impairment, and degree of functional disability for any given individual.

RECOMMENDATIONS FOR PROMOTING
OBJECTIVE PRACTICE

The following recommendations are based on previous work and are offered in order specifically to promote objectivity and validity in assessments conducted in medicolegal contexts (Blau, 1984; Martelli, Zasler, & Grayson, 1999a, 2000; Martelli, Zasler & Johnston-Green, 2001). However, objectivity is equally important in clinical contexts. Because physician–patient relationships and absence of careful scrutiny too often foster uncritical acceptance of impairment, these recommendations have utility for clinical assessments more generally.

- Always assess response bias (including malingering) and make efforts to guard against motivational deficiencies as a threat to validity.
- Emphasise the importance of accurate report on all interview questions and full effort on tests to produce valid profiles that permit comparison with known symptom patterns.
- Rely on standardised, validated, and well-normed procedures and tests and use only appropriate normative data for comparisons.
- Take into account symptom base rates (i.e., how frequently the symptoms occur in the general population and in the absence of the injury for which they are being evaluated), other explanatory factors for symptoms (e.g., medications, sleep disturbance, depression, PTSD), symptoms typical for the medical condition (e.g., inherent somatic complaints of disorders like multiple sclerosis, Parkinson's disease, and chronic pain), relevant situational variables (e.g., attention fluctuation due to chronic pain conditions, fatigue, insomnia/sleep deprivation, chronic stress), sociocultural factors (e.g., rural impoverished backgrounds), and other contextual factors and considerations.
- Avoid joining the legal–client "team", respect role boundaries (e.g., the patient's doctor, expert, trial consultant) and emphasise objectivity. Arrive at opinions only after review of all available evidence. Monitor excessive favourability to the side of the retaining party. Objective opinions should vary in the same manner that truth varies. Balanced opinions are characterised by elements that are favourable to each side in the medicolegal context, both in terms of findings in any one case and for the sample of cases represented. Notably, Martelli et al. (2001) and Brodsky (1991) have attempted to offer very preliminary guidelines regarding the expected rates of disagreement in diagnostic conclusions (e.g., 25%).
- Dispute the opinion of other experts only in the context of a complete and accurate representation of their findings, inferential reasoning, and conclusions.

- Spend sufficient time evaluating and treating the patient population that you offer testimony about. Attempt to devise and employ a system that allows for monitoring the validity of diagnostic and prognostic statements against external criteria (i.e., actual social and occupational functioning).
- Develop a mechanism that facilitates feedback from peers on quality and objectivity.
- Recognise the limitations of medical and neuropsychological opinions, as few findings and symptoms are black or white or attributable to a single event (e.g., Ockham's Razor).
- Promote increased awareness of relevant issues relating to ethics and scientific objectivity, and utilisation of objective data, such as Brodsky's objectivity ratio (Brodsky, 1991) or the suggestions provided by Martelli et al. (1999a, 2001).

Especially in medicolegal evaluations, assessment of response bias is critical to ensuring accurate determination of symptom source or diagnosis and thereby appropriate decisions on treatment and compensation, and the prevention of iatrogenic complications. As much as possible, assessment of motivational issues should integrate information from a variety of sources rather than rely on individual indicators. Although there are many techniques to assess response bias, the methodology is still developing. At present, determination of response bias largely relies on clinical skill and judgement, without recourse to any simple tests and/or decision making algorithms. The more challenging problems include ferreting out mixtures of exaggeration and true symptomatology, understanding what aspects of response bias are consciously versus unconsciously determined, and appreciating what may be modified by psychosocial or biomedical manipulations. Further work is needed to disentangle and measure the impact of the variety of types of response biases. Finally, evidence suggests that the nature of the adversarial medicolegal system may be as important an impediment to post-injury recovery as any patient variable, and addressing its impact on response bias would seem to be an efficacious approach to enhancing neuropsychological and neuromedical assessment.

CONCLUSION

Evaluation of impairment and disability following physical, neurological or other injuries/diseases, as well as psychiatric disorders, typically involves such contexts as social security disability application, personal injury litigation, worker's compensation claims, disability insurance policy application, other health care insurance policy coverage issues, and the determination of competence to work, handle finances or fulfil other important life functions (e.g., parenting or driving). However, evaluation of impairment and disability presents a significant diagnostic challenge fraught with potential obstacles and confounding issues, especially in cases of functional disability following less conspicuously severe or catastrophic injury such as psychological, subtle neurological or soft tissue damage (Zasler, 1996b; Zasler & Martelli, 1998; Martelli, Zasler, & Grayson, 1999a, 2000; Martelli et al., 2001; Zasler & Martelli, 2002).

Impairment and disability evaluation is by no means a simple undertaking. Medicolegal examiners and clinicians must necessarily familiarise themselves with the variety of protocols for evaluation of disability and impairment and understand their limitations relative to MTBI. Presently, there is no ideal system for rating impairment and disability for MTBI residua (Zasler & Martelli, 1998). A thorough understanding of the underlying disease process and associated injuries is paramount for optimal evaluation, treatment, and prognostication.

REFERENCES

American Academy of Neurology, Report of the Therapeutics and Technology Assessment Subcommittee (1996). Assessment: Neuropsychological testing of adults. *Neurology, 47,* 592–599.

American Congress of Rehabilitation Medicine, Report of the Traumatic Brain Injury Committee of the Head Injury Interdisciplinary Special Interest Group (1993). Definition of mild traumatic brain injury. *Journal of Head Trauma Rehabilitation, 8*(3), 86–87.

American Medical Association (1993). *Guides to the Evaluation of Permanent Impairment* (4th ed.). Chicago, IL: AMA.

American Psychiatric Association (1994). *Diagnostic and Statistical Manual of Mental Disorders* (4th ed.). Washington, DC: American Psychiatric Association.

Binder, L. M., & Rohling, M. L. (1996). Money matters: A meta-analytic review of the effects of financial incentives on recovery after closed-head injury. *American Journal of Psychiatry, 153,* 1–7.

Blau, T. (1984). *The psychologist as expert witness.* New York: John Wiley & Sons.

Brodsky, S. L. (1991). *Testifying in court: Guidelines and maxims for the expert witness.* Washington, DC: American Psychological Association.

Culotta, V. P., Sementilli, M. E., Gerold, K., & Watts, C. C. (1996). Clinicopathological heterogeneity in the classification of mild head injury. *Neurosurgery, 38*(2), 245–250.

Dodrill, C. B. (1997). Myths of neuropsychology. *Clinical Neuropsychologist, 11,* 1–17.

Green, P., Rohling, M. L., Lees-Haley, P. R., & Allen, L. (2001). Effort has a greater effect on test scores than severe brain injury in compensation claimants. *Brain Injury, 15*(12), 1045–1060

Johnson, M. T., Krafka, C., & Cecil, J. S. (2000). *Expert testimony in federal civil trials: A preliminary analysis.* Washington, DC: Federal Judicial Center.

Kraus, J. F., & McArthur, D. L. (1995). *Epidemiology of brain injury.* Los Angeles, CA: University of California Los Angeles, Department of Epidemiology. Southern California Injury Prevention Research Center.

Larrabee, G. J. (2000). Neuropsychology in personal injury litigation. *Journal of Clinical and Experimental Neuropsychology, 22,* 702–707.

Lees-Haley, P., & Brown, R. S. (1993). Neuropsychological complaint base rates of 170 personal injury claimants. *Archives of Clinical Neuropsychology, 8,* 203.

Lees-Haley, P. R., Williams, C. W., Zasler, N. D., Margulies, S., English, L. T., & Steven K. B. (1997). Response bias in plaintiff's histories. *Brain Injury*, *11*(11), 791–799.

Loring, D. W. (1995). *Psychometric detection of malingering*. Presentation at the Annual Meeting of the American Academy of Neurology, Seattle.

Martelli, M. F., Zasler, N. D., & Bush, S. (in press). Assessment of response bias in impairment and disability evaluations following brain injury. In J. Leon Carrion & G. Zitnay (Eds.), *Practices in brain injury*. Philadelphia: CRC Press.

Martelli, M. F., Zasler, N. D, & Grayson, R. (1999a). Ethical considerations in medicolegal evaluation of neurologic injury and impairment. *NeuroRehabilitation: An interdisciplinary Journal*, *13*, 45–61.

Martelli, M. F., Zasler, N. D., & Grayson, R. (2000). Ethics and medicolegal evaluation of impairment after brain injury. In M. Schiffman (Ed.), *Attorney's guide to ethics in forensic science and medicine*. Springfield, IL: Charles C. Thomas.

Martelli, M. F., Zasler, N. D. & Johnson-Green, D. (2001). Promoting ethical and objective practice in the medicolegal arena of disability evaluation. *Physical Medicine and Rehabilitation Clinics of North America*, *12*(3), 571–584.

Martelli, M. F., Zasler, N. D., & MacMillan, R. (1998). Mediating the relationship between injury, impairment and disability: A vulnerability, stress and coping model of adaptation following brain injury. *NeuroRehabilitation: An interdisciplinary Journal*, *1*(1), 51–66.

Martelli, M. F., Zasler, N. D., Mancini, A. M., & MacMillan, P. (1999b). Psychological assessment and applications in impairment and disability evaluations. In R. V. May & M. F. Martelli (Eds.), *Guide to functional capacity evaluation with impairment rating applications*. Richmond: NADEP Publications.

Rohling, M. (2000). Effect sizes of impairment associated with symptom exaggeration versus definite traumatic brain injury. *Archives of Clinical Neuropsychology*, *15*(8), 843.

Rohling, M. L., & Binder, L. M. (1995). Money matters: A meta-analytic review of the association between financial compensation and the experience and treatment of chronic pain. *Health Psychology*, *14*(6), 537.

Sbordone, R. J., Seyranian, G. D., & Ruff, R. M. (2000). The use of significant others to enhance the detection of malingerers from traumatically brain injured patients. *Archives of Clinical Neuropsychology*, *15*(6), 465–477.

Williams, D. H., Levin, H. S., & Eisenberg, H. M. (1990). Mild head injury classification. *Neurosurgery*, *27*, 422–428.

Youngjohn, J. R., Burrows, L., & Erdal, K. (1995). Brain damage or compensation neurosis? The controversial post-concussion syndrome. *Clinical Neuropsychologist*, *9(2)*, 112.

Zasler, N. D. (1996a). Impairment and disability evaluation in post-concussive disorders. In M. Rizzo & D. Tranel (Eds.), *Head injury and post-concussive syndrome*. New York: Churchill Livingstone.

Zasler, N. D. (1996b). Neuromedical diagnosis and management of post-concussive disorders. In L. J. Horn, & N. D. Zasler (Eds.), *Medical rehabilitation of traumatic brain injury*. Philadelphia: Hanley and Belfus.

Zasler, N. D. (1997). Prognostic indicators in medical rehabilitation of traumatic brain injury: A commentary and review. *Archives of Physical Medicine and Rehabilitation*, *78*, (Suppl 4), 12–16.

Zasler, N. D., & Martelli, M. F. (1998). Assessing mild traumatic brain injury. *AMA Guides Newsletter, November/December*, 1–5.

Zasler, N. D., & Martelli, M. F. (2002). Functional disorders in rehabilitation medicine. *State of the art reviews in physical medicine and rehabilitation*, *16*(1). Philadelphia: Hanley and Belfus, Inc.

Zasler, N. D., & Martelli, M. F. (submitted). Impairment and disability evaluation. In M. Rizzo & P. Eislinger (Eds.), *Principles and practice of behavioral neurology and neuropsychology*.

NEUROPSYCHOLOGICAL REHABILITATION, 2003, *13* (1/2), 43–64

Impact of pre-injury factors on outcome after severe traumatic brain injury: Does post-traumatic personality change represent an exacerbation of premorbid traits?

Robyn L. Tate

*University of Sydney
and Royal Rehabilitation Centre Sydney, Australia*

Although personality change is a frequent and disabling consequence of severe degrees of traumatic brain injury (TBI), little information is available beyond descriptive statements. The present paper presents a brief overview of the literature on the effects of pre-injury variables on post-trauma psychosocial functioning, and makes specific examination of the effect of premorbid personality structure on the post-trauma personality in people with TBI. A close relative of 28 people undergoing rehabilitation after TBI completed the Eysenck Personality Questionnaire—Revised (EPQ-R) and Current Behaviour Scale (CBS) regarding the injured person's personality and character. Data were collected on three occasions: Ratings about premorbid status were taken as soon as feasible after admission, and follow-up ratings regarding current status were made at 6 and 12 months post-trauma. As a group, premorbid ratings indicated an unremarkable profile on the EPQ-R. Significant changes had occurred by 6 months post-trauma, which were sustained at 12 months post-trauma for both the EPQ-R and CBS. Yet none of the specific hypotheses regarding premorbid personality structure on the EPQ-R and post-trauma characterological deficits on the two CBS factors, Loss of Emotional Control (LEC) and Loss of Motivation (LM), was supported: There were no significant differences between subgroups with high or low premorbid levels of Extraversion, Neuroticism, Psychoticism, Addiction and Criminality and post-trauma CBS factors, LEC, and LM. These findings suggest that although personality changes occur as a result of traumatic brain injury, they are largely independent of the premorbid personality structure.

Correspondence should be addressed to Robyn Tate, Associate Professor, Rehabilitation Studies Unit, Department of Medicine, University of Sydney, Royal Rehabilitation Centre Sydney, PO Box 6, Ryde, NSW 1680, Australia. Phone: 61 2 9808 9236, Fax: 61 2 9809 9037, Email: rtate@med.usyd.edu.au

This study was funded by the Australian Research Council. Thanks are due to Silvia Maggiotto for assistance with data collection.

http://www.tandf.co.uk/journals/pp/09602011.html   DOI:10.1080/09602010244000372

In their seminal paper, Kendall and Terry (1996) propose a model, modified from the theoretical framework of Lazarus and Folkman (1984), to account for individual differences in outcome and adjustment after traumatic brain injury (TBI). The model consists of three main components: antecedent variables, mediating factors, and outcomes. The focus of the present paper is on the first component, antecedent variables, particularly those that are precursors to the injury. Kendall and Terry identify a range of antecedent variables: cognitive impairments, neurological factors (pertaining to variables such as injury severity and lesion locus), personal resources (including self-esteem, locus of control), environmental resources (such as social support, family style, financial stressors), and situational factors. Heading the list, however, is pre-injury psychosocial functioning, which they describe as an "imperative" consideration in understanding post-trauma outcome and psychosocial adjustment after TBI. Kendall and Terry (1996) are not the first to draw attention to the potential significance of pre-injury factors. Thirty years ago, Lishman (1973) identified factors he described as "indirectly related to the injury", such as environmental factors, emotional repercussions of the injury, and in particular, premorbid personality and mental constitution. These factors, he believed, contributed significantly to the postmorbid clinical picture. They are also important considerations in the neuropsychological assessment process to formulate and guide rehabilitation strategies (Alberts & Binder, 1991; Kay, 1992; Prigatano, 1999).

Yet, perusal of those multivariate studies addressing the influence of pre-injury factors in the TBI group reveals that many focus upon a fairly limited set of variables, frequently of the demographic type. The most commonly examined variables are age at injury, sex and years of education, and less commonly, premorbid occupational status (often used as a surrogate for socio-economic status) and marital status. In terms of age, a number of studies have found that it significantly contributes to post-injury psychosocial functioning (e.g., Bowman, 1996; Fleming, Tooth, Hassell, & Chan, 1999; Heinemann & Whitneck, 1995; Ip, Dornan, & Schentag, 1995; Ponsford, Olver, Curran, & Ng, 1995). Other studies, however, report negative results (e.g., Ezrachi, et al., 1991; Tate & Broe, 1999; Vogenthaler, Smith, & Goldfader, 1989). Very few studies have found sex to predict specific aspects of psychosocial adjustment, exceptions being Bowman (1996) and Heinemann and Whiteneck (1995). Findings regarding the significance of years of education are also equivocal, with Heinemann and Whiteneck (1995) reporting in the positive, compared with negative findings reported by Fleming et al. (1999), Tate and Broe (1999) and Vogenthaler et al. (1989). By contrast, there is little evidence to suggest that either premorbid marital status (Ip et al., 1995; Vogenthaler et al., 1989) or premorbid occupational status (e.g., Bowman, 1996; Ip et al., 1995; Ponsford et al., 1995; Vogenthaler et al., 1989; Tate & Broe, 1999) significantly contribute to psychosocial outcomes post-injury, although the occasional study reports significant results (e.g., Fleming et al., 1999; Greenspan et al., 1996). Although Prigatano's (1999) recent writings indicate demographic variables such as age, education, and possibly level of intelligence, exert powerful influences on post-trauma functioning, he is writing in the context of their effect upon neuro-psychological test performance rather than psychosocial outcome.

Thus, with the possible exception of age, there is little evidence that common demographic variables, in isolation, impact upon post-injury psychosocial functioning. An important next step will be to consider the combination of such variables, in particular, whether some demographic variables may mediate the effects of others, as the work of Novack, Bush, Meythaler, and Canupp (2001) suggests. Additionally, a broader range of variables should be considered, including contextual variables such as environmental and family supports (Kendall & Terry, 1996; Webb, Wrigley, Yoels, & Fine, 1995), even though these are more difficult to measure than the simple, well-known demographics characterising the TBI group: age (peak incidence in the 15–24 year age group), sex (males outnumber females in the ratio at least 2:1), and road traffic accidents as the most common cause of injury (Kraus et al., 1984; Tate, McDonald, & Lulham, 1998).

Moreover, there is evidence that the TBI group has a specific premorbid psychosocial profile. A large proportion of those injured in road traffic accidents have a high blood alcohol level at the time of the injury, with it being in excess of 100 mg/dl in 31–58% of cases (Corrigan, 1995). Lower socio-economic groups are over-represented in the TBI population (Field, 1976; Kraus et al., 1986; Selecki, Hoy, & Ness, 1967). Furthermore, Tsuang, Boor, and Fleming (1985) have indicated that those involved in road traffic accidents have particular personality characteristics (e.g., being risk-takers, having diffi-culty with authority figures, less maturity and conformity, less control of hostility and anger). The epidemiological study of Jamieson and Tait (1966) commented upon the "undue proportion of social deviates", but critical analysis of their operational definitions suggests that they had overstated the case (see Tate, 1998). More reasoned figures available from specific samples estimate bet-ween 15–20% of the TBI group have histories of criminal convictions (Brooks, 1988; Kreutzer, Harris Marwitz, & Witol, 1995). Recent prospective studies on pre-morbid substance dependency suggest high figures, with Corrigan (1995) estimating it to be between 50% and 66%. Even so, Tate (1998) noted that in the absence of a community reference group matched for the age, sex, and socio-economic biases of the TBI population, it is difficult to interpret whether such figures represent higher, lower or comparable rates to people without TBI. This is important because, as Tsuang and colleagues have pointed out, the psycho-social characteristics of the TBI group are also a feature of their life stage.

Taken together, these studies suggest that the TBI group is characterised by adolescent and young adult males, from lower socioeconomic strata, whose psychosocial characteristics suggest antisocial tendencies, and who sustain their injuries in road traffic accidents, frequently when intoxicated. Two related implications can be drawn from this epidemiological snapshot. First, the suggestion that such pre-existing psychosocial characteristics adversely affect outcome and psychosocial adjustment, and second, that post-trauma (neuro-psychological) functioning is simply a reflection of the premorbid clinical picture (cf. "he was always like that"). These propositions have explicit expression in the literature. Brooks (1984, p. 139) expanded upon comments made earlier by London (1967), that "in most cases after severe head injury, the personality and behavioural changes that occurred 'tend either to be an exaggeration of previous traits or to occur in patients that might have been expected to develop mental disorder without having had their brains damaged.'" What is the evidence for these opinions?

In terms of the first proposition that pre-existing antisocial characteristics (including substance usage, psychiatric histories, and legal infringements) adversely affect outcome, a number of investigators have specifically addressed this issue in severely injured samples. Although the reading of some overviews (e.g., Martelli, Zasler, & MacMillan, 1998; Zasler, 1997), suggest the case is clear-cut with poor premorbid functioning exerting an adverse effect upon outcome, in reality the findings have been mixed: Bogner, et al. (2001) and MacMillan, Hart, Martelli, and Zasler (2002) reported that premorbid psychosocial problems predicted post-trauma productivity, but this was not found by Ezrachi et al. (1991) nor Vogenthaler et al. (1989), and in studies reporting significant findings no control was made for possible pre-trauma differences in occupational functioning. For example, in the sample of Bogner and colleagues, 36% of those with a history of substance abuse were "not productive" premorbidly, compared with 9% of those without history of substance abuse. Similarly, premorbid substance dependency was found to be predictive of post-trauma independent living by MacMillan et al., but not by Bogner et al., or Vogenthaler and colleagues. Neither Hall, Wallbom, and Englander (1998) nor Tate and Broe (1999) found that pre-injury psychosocial problems predicted overall outcome or psychosocial adjustment, respectively, and Tate (1998) found no differences between groups with good versus problematic premorbid functioning.

A number of investigators have suggested that the influence of premorbid factors may be more relevant in mildly rather than severely injured groups (Kendall & Terry, 1996), and others have formulated their arguments specifi-cally for the mild TBI group (Kay, 1992). Even so, the results of a number of studies using samples of mildly injured patients have been negative. Ponsford et al. (2000), did not find evidence of either an increased incidence of premorbid psychosocial problems compared with a non-injured group, nor did the subset of patients with continuing psychosocial symptomatology at 3 months post-trauma have higher premorbid psychopathology than the subset without such symptomatology. Similarly, Robertson et al. (1994) reported no differences in premorbid psychopathology between mild TBI and non-injured groups. Their TBI group, however, had significantly larger numbers with heavy premorbid alcohol, but not illicit drug, use.

The second proposition, that post-trauma (neuropsychological) functioning is simply a reflection of the premorbid clinical picture, is the focus of the remainder of this report. A number of studies have addressed the issue of the effect of premorbid substance usage on post-trauma neuropsychological functioning (e.g., Barker et al., 1999; Dikmen et al., 1993; Tate et al., 1995), but these are not germane to the specific issue of this paper, which is the influence of pre-morbid personality on post-trauma personality.

Personality is defined as: "Patterns of emotional and motivational responses that develop over the lifetime of the organism, are highly sensitive to biological and environmental contingencies, are formed in large part during early child-hood experiences, and are resistant to change but are, nevertheless, modifiable through continued learning and experience." (Prigatano, 1987a, p. 217). Changes in personality and emotional disturbance after severe degrees of TBI have been described as serious, persistent and having a major functional impact (Brooks, 1988). They are also frequent, with 74% of relatives of people with TBI reporting personality or characterological changes persisting in the longer-term (Brooks et al., 1986). This frequency is comparable to those reported by other investigators (e.g., Thomsen, 1984; Tyerman & Humphrey, 1984; Weddell, Oddy, & Jenkins, 1980). The types of personality changes identified after TBI span a broad range. Using relative's reports, Brooks and McKinlay (1983), for example, found that at 12 months post-trauma, significant changes occurred in 14 of 18 traits examined. These included a range of changes, such as being more quick-tempered, reliant upon others, disliking of company, unhappy, lifeless, childish, and changeable. Other investigators have described similar domains of change after TBI (Tyerman & Humphrey, 1984; Prigatano, 1992). These characterological changes are similar to (although usually more attenuated than) the classical case descriptions, such as those of Phineas Gage (MacMillan, 1996) and Brickner's Patient A (Damasio & Anderson, 1993), who suffered dramatic alterations in personality, consequent upon acquired brain injury, specifically involving the frontal lobes.

Prigatano (1987b; 1999) suggests that the sum total of personality change may arise from any of three levels: (1) neuropsychologically based personality disorders due to the neurological disturbances of brain structures that mediate emotional and motivational responses; (2) reactionary disturbances comprising those emotional and motivational responses that reflect failures in coping with environmental demands; and (3) the premorbid personality, in terms of pre-existing patterns of emotional and motivational responses that will emerge and be modified in the light of the two above-mentioned areas of disturbance. A number of investigators (e.g., Goldstein & Levin, 1989; Prigatano, 1987a) have observed that very little progress has been made in developing a working model of personality change after TBI, although the seminal work of Luria (1969; 1973) provides the foundation for organically determined characterological changes. He drew a distinction between two main variants: (1) euphoria, impulsiveness and inadequate actions, which may be superimposed on a background of disinhibition, and (2) generalised emotional indifference, superimposed on a background of general inhibition and torpidity. Rosenthal and Bond (1990) recommend this framework for the TBI group, and for the purposes of the present paper, these characterological impairments of organic aetiology are labelled Disorder of Control and Disorder of Drive, respectively.

The clinical descriptions drawn by Bond (1984) serve to highlight the variability and complexity characterising this area. He described a case where personality change appeared to be an exacerbation of premorbid traits, another where personality change seemed to have ameliorated previous objectionable behaviour, and cases where positive premorbid qualities clearly contributed to adjustment to disability, as well as others "without strong premorbid traits" (p. 174) showing manifestation of symptomatology commonly described in post-traumatic personality change. Although investigators in the late 1980s called for more attention to be focused on clarifying issues on the role of premorbid personality (e.g., Goldstein & Levin, 1989; Prigatano, 1987b), little progress has been made to date, and there is only anecdotal evidence regarding the suggestion that post-trauma personality changes are an exacerbation of premorbid traits.

The aim of the present study is to examine the general influence of premorbid personality on the manifestation of personality change in a group of patients followed over a 12-month period after TBI. Scales such as the Eysenck Personality Questionnaire—Revised (EPQ-R; Eysenck & Eysenck, 1991) and Current Behaviour Scale (CBS; Elsass & Kinsella, 1989; Kinsella, Packer, & Olver, 1991) are ideally suited to explore all these issues. The EPQ-R is a widely used, standardised test of personality. It comprises three primary scales: Extraversion, Neuroticism (also described as stability or emotionality), and Psychoticism (also described as toughmindedness, reflecting an underlying dispositional trait of psychoticism). Two subsidiary scales are Addiction and Criminality. The CBS was specifically designed to measure characterological deficits after TBI. Two factors, Loss of Emotional Control (LEC) and Loss of Motivation (LM), reflect Disorder of Control and Disorder of Drive, respectively.

Specific predictions were made:

1. It was hypothesised that the premorbid personality structure of the TBI group will be similar to that of age- and sex-matched people in the general population.
2. The occurrence of the TBI will cause a change in the personality structure of the individual.

3. Recovery of such personality change will be observed over time, in particular, between 6 and 12 months post-trauma, as occurs for the pattern of cognitive recovery.
4. For the proposition that post-trauma personality is an exaggeration of premorbid traits, it was hypothesised that patients with higher premorbid levels of Extraversion will have significantly higher scores on the CBS factor (LEC) examining Disorder of Control than patients with lower premorbid levels of Extraversion.
5. Conversely, patients with lower premorbid levels of Extraversion will have significantly higher scores on the CBS factor (LM) examining Disorder of Drive than patients with higher premorbid levels of Extraversion.
6. Patients with higher premorbid levels of Psychoticism, Addiction or Criminality will have significantly higher scores on the CBS factor (LEC) examining Disorder of Control than patients with lower premorbid levels of Psychoticism, Addiction, or Criminality.

METHOD

Participants

Study participants were recruited from patients consecutively admitted to the Lidcombe/Liverpool Hospitals Brain Injury Rehabilitation Unit. This service has a specific catchment area for southern and south-western Sydney, with a population of approximately 1.1 million residents. Selection criteria for the study comprised age (15 to 50 years at the time of injury), a recent severe TBI, and duration of PTA in excess of one week. Patients were excluded if there was a premorbid history of neurological events or major psychiatric illness.

There are inevitable methodological limitations in a study of personality change after TBI, a number of which have been addressed by other investigators (Gainotti, 1993; Gass & Ansley, 1995; Kurtz, Putnam, & Stone, 1998; McKinlay & Brooks, 1984). Of central importance are practical issues about how information should be collected and from whom. Patient self-report is problematic particularly in the very early post-trauma stages when the severity of cognitive impairments frequently precludes reliable insights into changes that have occurred from the premorbid state. Moreover, reports from relatives may be subject to unreliability, particularly given the emotional distress and other stressors incurred by the injury. Clinical staff personnel are at a distinct disadvantage given that they did not know the patient before the injury and thus are not able to independently assess whether observed behaviours are a change from the premorbid state. On balance, reports provided by a close relative or other person who knew the patient well before injury are probably the most appropriate source of information, and have been widely used by other investigators, although it is recognised that caveats apply to such data. The present study used a close relative as informant and so an additional selection criterion was the relative's proficiency in English in order that questionnaires could be completed.

Materials

The Eysenck Personality Questionnaire—Revised (EPQ-R) was used to measure the personality traits of the patients. It is a 106-item forced-choice questionnaire, in which six scales are described. Three relate to the major dimensions of personality: Extraversion (E scale); Neuroticism (N scale); and Psychoticism (P scale). Two subsidiary scales are A (Addiction) and C (Criminality). The final scale is a validity scale, labelled L (Lie), reflecting the tendency to give socially desirable responses or dissimulate. All scales have acceptable psychometric properties, including internal consistency (alpha coefficients ranging from .76 to .90) and stability over a one-month period (range .76–.89). Raw scores were converted to z-scores (Mean = 0, SD = 1), using the age and gender norms provided in the manual, and statistical analyses used z-scores for each of the scales. For the L scale, the normative data corresponding to the age and gender of the informant, not the TBI referent person, were used. No normative data are provided for females for the C scale, and so analyses using this scale were conducted with a reduced data set of the male participants.

The Current Behaviour Scale (CBS) was selected to measure characterological changes occurring as a result of the injury. It consists of 25 items in which bipolar adjectives are rated on a 7-point scale, with higher scores indicative of greater disturbance. The CBS has good psychometric properties. It is a reliable scale, with high internal consistency (Cronbach's alpha coefficient .80), and shows good stability with test–retest correlations over a 1-week period of $r = .83$ for "close others" of TBI patients. A principal components analysis identified two factors, Loss of Emotional Control (LEC) and Loss of Motivation (LM), together accounting for 43% of the variance (Kinsella et al., 1991). The LEC factor received loadings from items such as impulsivity, aggression and restlessness, consistent with Disorder of Control, whereas the LM factor had loadings from items such as lacking energy, disinterested and lacking initiative, consistent with Disorder of Drive. Analyses in this report used both total scores (range 7–175) and mean scores from the two factors (range 1–7).

Procedure

Approval to conduct the study was given by the Ethics Committee of the South Western Sydney Area Health Service. As soon as feasible after admission to the Rehabilitation Unit, a close relative was approached and invited to participate in the study. Those who agreed provided written consent and were interviewed about the patient's psychosocial and medical history, on average at 8.2 weeks post-trauma. They then completed the EPQ-R and CBS regarding the patient's *premorbid* personality and character (referred to as the Premorbid rating). This method of rating premorbid personality after brain injury has previously been used by other investigators (Dodwell, 1988; Kurtz et al., 1998). The relatives were reinterviewed with the EPQ-R and CBS at 6 months post-trauma (first follow-up rating) and again at 12 months post-trauma (second follow-up rating). On these occasions they completed the questionnaires according to the patient's *current* personality and character (referred to as the Post-trauma ratings).

RESULTS

Sample characteristics

Of 165 patient admissions to the rehabilitation unit over a 3-year period, the relatives of 45 TBI patients were eligible for and agreed to participate in the study. It was possible to follow up 30 of the 45 relatives at 6 months post-trauma and 28 relatives at 12 months post-trauma. The reasons that relatives were not followed up were as follows: Medical deterioration of the patient or he or she remained in the persistent vegetative state at first follow-up ($n = 5$), time of follow-up occurred after study completion ($n = 6$ and a further two for the 12-month follow-up), geographical relocation ($n = 3$), and declined further participation ($n = 1$). Most participants from this series have been described in reports on other aspects of the study (Tate, 1998, 1999). The 28 relatives followed up on both occasions comprised parent ($n = 19$), spouse or partner ($n = 4$), sibling ($n = 3$), adult daughter ($n = 1$), and grandmother ($n = 1$) with whom the patient had been living prior to the TBI.

The demographic characteristics of the brain-injured participants were consistent with the epidemiological features of this clinical population, documented in both Australia and other countries (Jennett, 1996; Kraus et al., 1984; Tate et al., 1998). The participants were mostly males ($n = 24$, 85.7%), aged an average of 26.82 years (SD = 8.79), with limited formal education (Mean = 10.29 years, SD = 1.38). Road traffic accident was the most common cause of the injury, occurring in 21 cases (75%), followed by assault ($n = 5$), fall ($n = 1$), and the final participant sustained his injury in an indoor soccer match. The individuals were severely brain-injured: The average duration of PTA was 64.46 days (SD = 50.53, range 14–224 days), with 70% having a duration of PTA in excess of one month. With one exception, all patients had abnormal computerised tomography (CT) scans, with 17 individuals classified as having structural lesions in the frontal lobes, mainly contusions, haematoma, and haemorrhage. Table 1 summarises the CT scan results for the individuals.

TABLE 1
CT scan results in participants with TBI

Subject no.	Patient ID	Type and location of pathology
1	1	L F extracranial haematoma, L thalamic haemorrhage, shear haemorrhages in L caudate nucleus and L cerebral peduncle
2	2	B F haematomas, L T haematoma, L T contusions, burst R T, R T lobectomy
3	3	B F and T contusions
4	4	Large R subdural haematoma, partial R T lobectomy and drainage of haematoma. Follow-up scan: generalised ventricular enlargement
5	5	R subdural haematoma with midline shift
6	6	Small amount of blood in posterior horn of R lateral ventricle with some asymmetry of Sylvian fissure, more poorly defined on R
7	7	Haemorrhage in inferior part of R F
8	8	L F and mid P extradural haemorrhage, contusion of L T
9	9	L subdural haematoma and L T lobectomy
10	10	Diffuse B F and L T contusions. Follow-up scan: extensive low density changes in B F and L T lobes consistent with post-traumatic infarction related to previous contusions
11	11	B F chronic subdural haematoma
12	12	Acute subdural haematoma with mass effect and R T haematoma
13	13	L F contusion and fracture to base of skull
14	14	R F-T extradural haematoma with contrecoup L F-T contusion
15	15	Fracture L T bone, L P-T subdural haematoma and intracerebral blood in L T. Midline shift to R
16	16	Multiple haemorrhagic contusions, diffuse R cerebral contusions
17	17	Contusion of R T with surrounding oedema, L extradural haematoma
18	18	Multiple B F and P contusions and small area of haematoma in brain stem
19	19	Small R F-P subdural haematoma, small L T contusion
20	20	Hypolucency in B T-P, L F, L basal ganglia, R thalamus
21	21	Squamus T bone fractures, R F and P extradural haematoma
22	22	R F subdural haematoma, L F-P haematoma
23	23	Vertical fracture through O bone, moderate subdural haematoma along falx and interhemispheric region, subdural blood over L F lobe and within basal cisterns and in IV ventricle
24	24	Hyperdensity in B F-P areas consistent with contusions
25	25	Fracture to face and R F vault, low density in L F region consistent with contusions
26	26	L O contusion
27	28	Fracture R P bone, posterior R P extracranial haematoma, small sheer haemorrhages in grey matter of posterior R P, L F-P subdural haematoma
28	31	Multiple shearing haemorrhages and white matter contusions throughout both hemispheres

R = right, L = left, B = bilateral, F = frontal lobe, T = temporal lobe, P = parietal lobe, O = occipital lobe, NAD = no abnormality detected.

27/28 patients (ID 1–26 and 28) were described in a previous report (Tate, 1999).

52

Data screening

Initial screening of the data from the EPQ-R and CBS revealed that although virtually all variables at each test occasion were normally distributed, the EPQ-R P and A scales showed significant skewness and kurtosis. All data were thus analysed with nonparametric statistics, using Mann-Whitney U tests for group comparisons and Wilcoxon Signed Ranks tests for repeated measures analyses of changes over time. Table 2 provides descriptive statistics for the dependent variables. In statistical analyses, Bonferroni adjustments were made to the alpha level to control for an inflated Type 1 error rate due to multiple comparisons. Accordingly, for the EPQ-R variables the critical alpha level was set at $p < .01$ (.05/5) for each set of comparisons (Premorbid versus first follow-up, and first versus second follow-ups). For the CBS variables, the critical alpha level was set at $p < .025$ (.05/2) for each set of comparisons.

As a validity check on the data, attention is drawn to the high EPQ-R: L score (comparable to the 89th percentile). In discussing high L scores, the manual suggests that in addition to dissimulation, L measures some stable personality characteristic, such as social naivety or conformity. The authors argue that where dissimulation is the primary reason for the high L scores, then intercorrelation between L and N scores is high. Conversely, intercorrelation is low or absent "when conditions are such as to provide little motivation for dissimulation" (Eysenck & Eysenck, 1991, p. 14). In the present sample, the correlation between N and L was not statistically significant ($rs = -.29$,

TABLE 2
Means and standard deviations of the EPQ-R scales
and CBS factors at premorbid, first follow-up (6 months post-trauma)
and second follow-up (12 months post-trauma)

	Premorbid		First follow-up		Second follow-up	
	Mean	SD	Mean	SD	Mean	SD
EPQ-R						
E	0.35	0.81	−0.08	0.97	−0.36	0.98
N	−0.64	0.82	0.12	0.80	0.39	0.91
P	−0.31	1.23	−0.19	1.20	0.09	1.63
L	1.23	1.19	1.21	1.32	1.04	1.46
C	0.17	1.07	0.85	1.02	1.03	1.30
A	−0.93	0.96	−0.32	1.19	0.08	1.22
CBS						
LEC	3.01	1.01	3.74	1.05	3.84	1.15
LM	2.76	0.62	3.38	0.89	3.49	0.86

Note: EPQ-R = Eysenck Personality Questionnaire—Revised; CBS = Current Behaviour Scale; EPQ-R: E = Extraversion; N = Neuroticism; P = Psychoticism; L = Lie; C = Criminality; A = Addiction; CBS: LEC = Loss of Emotional Control; LM = Loss of Motivation

$p > .05$). As a further check on the data, the manual suggests that subgroups scoring high and low on L be formed, using a median split on the data, and compared on the N score. If no significant group differences are observed, it is acceptable to use a single data set of the combined subgroups. In the present sample the Mann-Whitney U test was non-significant ($z = -1.49$, $p > .05$). Additionally, as in the standardisation sample, the three primary scales were independent, as indicated by the lack of significant correlation among them. Spearman rank order correlation coefficients for the premorbid data were as follows: E versus N = 0.15; E versus P = 0.24; N versus P = 0.36.

Premorbid personality profile

Graphical representation of the EPQ-R scales is provided in Figure 1. The premorbid ratings indicate that, as a group, the patients had an unremarkable profile. With reference to the three major dimensions of personality, E, N, and P, they were somewhat more extraverted than their normative group (E comparable to 64th percentile), had lower levels of psychopathology (P at 38th percentile) and were less emotional or unstable (N at 26th percentile). Similarly, they were within normal limits on the two subsidiary scales,

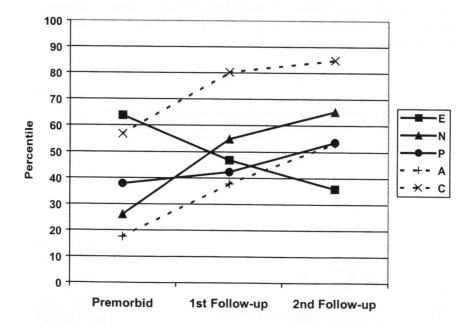

Figure 1. Percentile scores for EPQ-R scales for premorbid, first follow-up (6 months post-trauma) and second follow-up (12 months post-trauma) ratings. E = Extraversion, N = Neuroticism, P = Psychoticism, A = Addiction, C = Criminality.

Addiction (18th percentile) and Criminality (57th percentile). Inspection of the raw data indicated that, at an individual level, only the occasional participant scored above two standard deviations on any scale. This pattern of results was essentially the same in the larger group of 45 who were interviewed for the premorbid rating: E = 67th percentile, P = 34th percentile, N = 23rd percentile, A = 16th percentile, and C = 47th percentile.

Effect of the injury

Figure 1 also shows changes between the premorbid and post-trauma ratings on the three primary EPQ-R scales. The data were analysed using Wilcoxon Signed Ranks tests and descriptive statistics are provided in Table 2. Three of the five EPQ-R scales showed significant changes between the premorbid and first follow-up ratings: The direction of the mean scores indicated that participants showed increases in N ($z = -3.49$, $p < .001$), A ($z = -2.62$, $p < .01$) and C ($z = -2.62$, $p < .01$). No significant change occurred for P ($z = -0.56$, $p > .01$) or E ($z = -2.46$, $p > .01$), although the latter was significant at the traditional $p < .05$ level. There were no significant differences on any scale between the ratings at the two follow-up occasions, at 6 and 12 months post-trauma, suggesting that the elevated N, A, and C scales did not revert to premorbid levels. The mean scores of the E scale showed further decrease between first and second follow-ups, although again it did not meet the critical alpha level ($z = -2.36$, $p = .018$).

On the CBS, the scores of the participants were compared to the data reported in Elsass (1991), although she reports on the total scores, not the two factors. The total score for the present sample at first follow-up ($M = 92.61$, SD = 16.26) was similar to the "close other" ratings of her TBI group at 6 months post-trauma ($M = 86.34$, SD = 17.60). Similarly, premorbid ratings were comparable between the present sample and that of Elsass ($M = 77.84$, SD = 13.34 and $M = 72.74$, SD = 15.01, respectively). Results of Wilcoxon tests for the two CBS factors showed significant differences between the premorbid and post-trauma ratings, both for LEC ($z = -3.20$, $p = .001$) and LM ($z = -3.41$, $p = .001$). The direction of the mean scores indicated an increase in disturbance at the post-trauma rating. There were, however, no significant differences between first and second follow-ups for the CBS factors, suggesting that the scores at second follow-up remained elevated in comparison with premorbid levels.

Effect of premorbid personality

Median splits on the data of the premorbid EPQ-R scales were performed and the two groups (High versus Low) were compared on the two CBS factors at first and second follow-ups. Descriptive statistics are presented in Table 3.

TABLE 3
Means and standard deviations of the CBS factors at first and second follow-up for each of the EPQ-R scales classified as High or Low on the premorbid scales

CBS	First follow-up				Second follow-up			
	Loss of Emotional Control		Loss of Motivation		Loss of Emotional Control		Loss of Motivation	
	Mean	SD	Mean	SD	Mean	SD	Mean	SD
Premorbid EPQ-R								
E: High	3.91	0.76	3.28	0.93	3.99	1.04	3.19	0.73
Low	3.57	1.29	3.47	0.87	3.69	1.26	3.79	0.89
N: High	4.04	1.00	3.26	0.78	3.90	1.19	3.28	1.05
Low	3.45	1.05	3.49	1.01	3.78	1.14	3.71	0.58
P: High	4.02	1.13	3.50	0.91	4.02	1.25	3.61	0.97
Low	3.46	0.92	3.25	0.89	3.66	1.05	3.37	0.74
A: High	4.04	0.96	3.51	0.80	4.16	1.07	3.51	1.05
Low	3.45	1.08	3.24	0.99	3.52	1.17	3.47	0.65
C: High	4.08	0.98	3.51	0.89	4.01	1.21	3.35	1.10
Low	3.29	0.92	3.16	0.89	3.48	1.10	3.44	0.58

See Table 2 for description of abbreviations.

Contrary to Hypotheses 4 to 6, there were no statistically significant differences between the groups scoring High and Low on any of the EPQ-R scales and either CBS factor, LEC or LM. More specifically, with reference to Hypothesis 4, at the first follow-up it was found that individuals showing higher premorbid levels of Extraversion did not demonstrate a significantly higher score on CBS LEC than individuals with lower premorbid levels of Extraversion ($z = -1.31$, $p > .01$). Nor, conversely, (Hypothesis 5), did individuals with lower premorbid levels of Extraversion have a significantly higher score on CBS LM than individuals with higher scores on Extraversion ($z = -0.58$, $p > .01$). Hypothesis 6 examined premorbid social maladjustment, but individuals with higher premorbid scores on the EPQ-R psychopathology scales of Psychoticism, Addiction, and Criminality did not show significantly higher scores on CBS LEC ($z = -1.15$, -1.70, -1.85, respectively, all $ps > .01$). Essentially the same pattern of results was found for the second follow-up data set.

It is reasonable to expect that the present sample was heterogenous with respect to characterological changes, consisting of those who did or did not show evidence of significant post-traumatic personality changes. As a further extension of the hypotheses, it was expected that those showing characterological changes would have a different premorbid personality profile on the

EPQ-R than those without such change. Characterological changes were determined by calculating the minimum difference on the total CBS score that was necessary to establish a reliable change in scores that was not due to measurement error of the test. The formula provided by Ley (1972)[1] was used for this purpose. The minimum difference was 8.65, with 15 of the 28 participants showing a reliable change on CBS scores between the premorbid and first follow-up ratings.

The group showing characterological changes had somewhat lower total scores for the premorbid CBS rating than the group without change ($M = 73.07$, SD = 10.71 and $M = 83.35$, SD = 14.67, respectively), but the difference was not statistically significant. As expected, that group also had substantially higher scores for the post-trauma CBS rating ($M = 100.40$, SD = 13.61 and $M = 83.62$, SD = 14.67 respectively; $z = -2.49, p < .02$). There were, however, no group differences on any of the premorbid EPQ-R variables, with none of the results even approaching significance.

Because of the close relationship between characterological changes and frontal systems dysfunction, it was anticipated that individuals with evidence of frontal lesions on CT scan would have greater degree of characterological changes than those without such changes. Although 9 of the 15 individuals with frontal lesions demonstrated significant characterological changes, a chi-square test, comparing subgroups with and without significant characterological changes on the CBS by lesion site (frontal versus nonfrontal), was not significant.

DISCUSSION

In summary, the present study found that the premorbid personality structure of this TBI sample was unremarkable when compared to age- and sex-appropriate norms. Changes in personality occurred as a consequence of the injury on major dimensions of personality, with increases in Neuroticism, Addiction, and Criminality, with a trend to decrease in Extraversion. These changes were also corroborated on a scale specifically designed to measure characterological changes after TBI. No amelioration of these changes occurred between test

---

[1]The minimum difference (MD) required for the change in score between the premorbid and post-trauma ratings to be reliable was calculated using the following formula: $MD = z_{MD} \sqrt{2 \times \sigma^2 (1-r_{xx})}$, where z_{MD} is the z-score associated with a change in test score of magnitude MD between premorbid and post-trauma; σ is the standard deviation of the premorbid rating of the normal control group (SD = 11.8) reported in Elsass and Kinsella (1989); r_{xx} is the test–retest correlation coefficient of that group ($r = .93$). Given that scores could either increase or decrease over time, a two-tailed test of significance was used and thus $z_{MD} = 1.96$.

occasions at 6 and 12 months post-trauma on either of the scales. There was no evidence to suggest that the post-trauma changes in personality were an exacerbation of premorbid characteristics, even in the subset of patients who demonstrated significant characterological changes. Nor were there differences in the premorbid personality between subgroups comprising those with and without significant characterological changes.

Few empirical studies of the role of premorbid personality on the development of characterological deficits and personality changes after TBI have been reported. In the present sample, the premorbid personality profile was unremarkable, well within the normal range on all scales of the EPQ-R, including the psychopathology scales. These findings are in general agreement with those of Kurtz and colleagues (1998), using a different personality inventory (and they too found elevated premorbid scores on Extraversion). As noted, although the review of Tsuang et al. (1985) suggested that people involved in road traffic accidents have a particular personality profile, they observed that these types of traits also characterise the life stage of the highest incidence group (viz. young adult males). The fact that the EPQ-R scales are age- and sex-corrected removes any bias. Thus, in comparison with their peers, the TBI group was similarly extraverted, stable and showed comparable levels of psychopathology.

The present study also found a significant increase in disturbance on the CBS between the premorbid and post-trauma ratings, suggestive of characterological deficits indicative of both Disorder of Control and Disorder of Drive. Similarly, statistically significant changes were observed on three of the five EPQ-R scales (N, A, and C, with a trend to significance on the E scale). Although it was expected that some recovery of function would occur between the 6- and 12-month post-trauma test occasions, no change was documented on either the CBS or EPQ-R. Further longitudinal studies are needed to document the natural recovery of characterological changes. Although there have been many reports of post-traumatic personality change in the TBI literature, until recently few group studies have used standardised instruments. Additionally some recent reports are difficult to interpret because ratings of both premorbid and post-trauma status are taken at a single point in time (Lannoo et al., 1997) or a cross-sectional design is used, comparing different groups at various times post-trauma (Malia, Powell, & Torode, 1995). Neither of these designs is appropriate to the study of characterological changes. The former is problematic because of confounds well-described by Brooks and colleagues (1986) including attribution, sensitisation to problems over time, and thresholds of tolerance, whereby the risk is that the premorbid state is idealised; and the latter because only a longitudinal design can validly comment upon changes over time.

The current findings regarding personality changes between premorbid and post-trauma ratings are contrary to the conclusions drawn by Kurtz et al. (1998)

from a broadly similar study, but using the NEO Personality Inventory (NEO-PI-R). Two of the NEO-PI-R factors, Extraversion and Neuroticism, have comparable parallels in the EPQ-R (the remaining three NEO-PI-R factors being Openness, Agreeableness, and Conscientiousness). They reported few differences between ratings made for the premorbid period and those of current functioning at six months post-trauma. They did find, however, a statistically significant decrease in Extraversion, a trend that was observed in the present sample. Differences between the conclusions reached may, therefore, be partly a function of emphasis of interpretations. Whereas Kurtz and colleagues interpret their findings as evidence of only "modest personality change" (p. 11), and hence argued for the "stability of normal personality traits" after TBI, changes observed on the EPQ-R in the present study raise the issue of the effect of the injury on personality structure.

Is the patient's personality so radically altered that it could be said he is "no longer Gage"? (Stuss, Gow, & Heatherington, 1992). Using single-case methodology, a proportion of the present sample ($n = 15$) was identified as demonstrating significant characterological change on the CBS. However they did not show a different pre-trauma personality profile on the EPQ-R than the group without significant change. This is not to deny that specific individuals with pathognomonic changes will not have particular premorbid traits, but it would appear that the effect size from group studies is not a large one. There was also no association between lesion location (frontal versus nonfrontal) and characterological changes. It is acknowledged that the TBI group is not a suitable population in which to study clinico-pathological correlations, due to the multifocal pathology that characterises this clinical group. Moreover, it is entirely possible that structural lesions external to the frontal lobes may nonetheless disrupt frontal function by disconnecting vital pathways.

A literal interpretation of the results of the EPQ-R, namely, that the present sample is more unstable and tough-minded, with greater degrees of addiction and criminality, is misleading. Criticism has been made about the simplistic application and interpretation of labels from scales of personality and psychopathology to the neurological population (Gainotti, 1993; Prigatano, 1987a). The problem is that many of the items are likely to be endorsed if the person is brain injured. Woessner and Caplan (1995) for instance, found that 50% of the items from the Obsessive–Compulsive dimension of the Symptom Checklist-90—Revised were classified as "brain injury symptoms" by expert judges. Alfano, Finlayson, Stearns, and Neilson (1990) have also demonstrated such problems with the Minnesota Multiphasic Personality Inventory, wherein clinical neuroscience specialists rated between 1.7% (for Mf scale) and 39.4% (for Hs scale) of items from the clinical scales as having neurological content.

The EPQ-R is subject to similar limitations with a brain-injured population. Taking the C scale, for instance, a number of items from this construct are commonly experienced as a direct result of TBI: "Do you stop to think things over before doing anything?", "Are you an irritable person?", "Does it worry you if you know there are mistakes in your work?", "Do you like to arrive at appointments in plenty of time?" These items tap into the characterological changes so frequently described in this clinical group: impulsivity, irritability, carelessness, and poor planning, respectively, rather than "criminality" per se. This is not to deny, of course, that in certain individuals there may be onset or exacerbation of criminal behaviour after the injury. Other EPQ-R scales have similar limitations in item content. "Decreases" in E will be found when individuals respond in the negative to items such as "Are you a talkative person?" or "Do you have many friends?" "Increases" in N will be found when items such as "Do you feel your life is very dull?" or "When your temper rises, do you find it difficult to control?" These types of items tap into organic impairments which individuals may or may not experience as a direct result of a TBI. In one sense, this is to be an expected result, because the theory of personality developed by Eysenck (1981) derives from a biological basis.

There are a number of possibilities to account for the failure of the present study to produce significant results with respect to the specific hypotheses under examination. Although both the EPQ-R and CBS provided evidence of post-traumatic changes in personality, there was no association with particular premorbid traits. The small sample size may not have had sufficient power to detect significant results. Another related possibility is that the patients in this series may not have had sufficient aberration in their premorbid personality to enable an adequate test of the hypotheses. In other words, it may be the case that only people whose premorbid personality traits were either extreme and/or somewhat disturbed show an exacerbation of premorbid traits following the injury. As the results from this study showed, when compared with normative data, the premorbid personality functioning of the present sample was unremarkable.

Alternatively, perhaps it is the case that post-traumatic personality change does not represent an exacerbation of premorbid traits. Indeed, in Lishman's (1998, p.188) opinion, "frontal lobe personality change bears a definitive stamp which in large measure cuts across differences in premorbid personality". Yet, at the clinical level, it is frequently the case that the vivid impact caused by the exceptional patient who disobeys the rule will outweigh the many more whose profiles conform to the rule. Patient RW is a case in point. Prior to his injury he was a member of a biker gang, and post-trauma, he had a superimposed disorder of control, screaming and bellowing, throwing food and (full) urinal bottles, terrorising staff and patients alike (Tate, 1987). In this context, Prigatano's (1987b, p. 17) observation is particularly apt: There is "little evidence for a close correlation between pre-trauma personality characteristics and post-trauma behavior. Nevertheless, in the clinical setting one is often convinced that such a correlation exists".

REFERENCES

Alberts, M. S., & Binder, L. M. (1991). Premorbid psychosocial factors that influence cognitive rehabilitation following traumatic brain injury. In J. S. Kreutzer & P. H. Wehman (Eds.), *Cognitive rehabilitation for persons with traumatic brain injury. A functional approach* (pp. 95–103). Baltimore: Paul H Brooks.

Alfano, D. P., Finlayson, M. A. J., Stearns, G. M., & Neilson, P. M. (1990). The MMPI and neurologic dysfunction: Profile configuration and analysis. *Clinical Neuropsychologist, 4,* 69–79.

Barker, L. H., Bigler, E. D., Johnson, S. C., Anderson, C. V., Russo, A. A., Boineau, B., & Blatter, D. D. (1999). Polysubstance abuse and traumatic brain injury: Quantitative magnetic resonance imaging and neuropsychological outcome in older adolescents and young adults. *Journal of the International Neuropsychological Society, 5,* 593–608.

Bogner, J. A., Corrigan, J. D., Mysiew, W. J., Clinchot, D., & Fugate, L. (2001). A comparison of substance abuse and violence in the prediction of long-term rehabilitation outcomes after traumatic brain injury. *Archives of Physical Medicine and Rehabilitation, 82,* 571–577.

Bond, M. (1984). The psychiatry of closed head injury. In N. Brooks (Ed.), *Closed head injury. Psychological, social and family consequences* (pp. 148–178). Oxford: Oxford University Press.

Bowman, M. L. (1996). Ecological validity of neuropsychological and other predictors following head injury. *Clinical Neuropsychologist, 10(4),* 382–396.

Brooks, N. (1984). Head injury and the family. In N. Brooks (Ed.), *Closed head injury. Psychological, social and family consequences* (pp. 123–147). Oxford: Oxford University Press.

Brooks, N. (1988). Personality change after severe head injury. *Acta Neurochirurigica (Supplementary), 44,* 59–64.

Brooks, N., Campsie, L., Symington, C., Beattie, A., & McKinlay, W. (1986). The five year outcome of severe blunt head injury: A relative's view. *Journal of Neurology, Neurosurgery and Psychiatry, 49,* 746–770.

Brooks, D. N., & McKinlay, W. (1983). Personality and behavioural change after severe blunt head injury—a relative's view. *Journal of Neurology, Neurosurgery and Psychiatry, 46,* 336–344.

Corrigan, J. D. (1995). Substance abuse as a mediating factor in outcome from traumatic brain injury. *Archives of Physical Medicine and Rehabilitation, 76,* 302–309.

Damasio, A. R., & Anderson, S. W. (1993). The frontal lobes. In K. M. Heilman & E. Valenstein (Eds.), *Clinical neuropsychology* (pp. 409–460, 3rd edition). New York: Oxford University Press.

Dikmen, S. S., Donovan, D. M., Loberg, T., Machamer, J. E., & Temkin, N. R. (1993). Alcohol use and its effects on neuropsychological outcome in head injury. *Neuropsychology, 7,* 296–305.

Dodwell, D. (1988). Comparison of self-ratings with informant-ratings of premorbid personality on two personality rating scales. *Psychological Medicine, 18,* 495–501.

Elsass, L. (1991). Behaviour following traumatic head injury—a prospective study. Unpublished PhD thesis, La Trobe University, Australia.

Elsass, L., & Kinsella, G. (1989). Development of a scale for measuring behaviour change following closed head injury. In V. Anderson & M. Bailey (Eds.), *Proceedings of the Fourteenth Annual Brain Impairment Conference* (pp. 124–131). Melbourne: Australian Society for the Study of Brain Impairment.

Eysenck, H. J. (Ed.). (1981). *A model for personality.* New York: Springer-Verlag.

Eysenck, H. J., & Eysenck, S. B. G. (1991). *Manual of the Eysenck Personality Scales (EPS Adult).* London: Stoughton & Houghton.

Ezrachi, O., Ben-Yishay, Y., Kay, T., Diller, L., & Rattock, J. (1991). Predicting employment in traumatic brain injury following neuropsychological rehabilitation. *Journal of Head Trauma Rehabilitation, 6*(3), 71–84.

Field, J. H. (1976). *Epidemiology of head injuries in England and Wales.* Leicester, UK: HMSO.

Fleming, J., Tooth, L., Hassell, M., & Chan, W. (1999). Prediction of community integration and vocational outcome 2–5 years after traumatic brain injury rehabilitation in Australia. *Brain Injury, 13(6)*, 417–431.

Gainotti, G. (1993). Emotional and psychosocial problems after brain injury. *Neuropsychological Rehabilitation, 3*, 259–277.

Gass, C. S., & Ansley, J. (1995). Personality assessment of neurologically impaired patients. In J. N. Butcher (Ed.), *Clinical personality assessment: Practical approaches* (pp. 192–207). New York: Oxford University Press.

Goldstein, F. C., & Levin, H. S. (1989). Manifestations of personality change after closed head injury. In E. Perecman (Ed.), *Integrating theory and practice in clinical neuropsychology* (pp. 217–243). Hillsdale, NJ: Lawrence Erlbaum Associates, Inc.

Greenspan, A. I., Wrigley, J. M., Kresnow, M., Branche-Dorsey, C. M., & Fine, P. R. (1996). Factors influencing failure to return to work due to traumatic brain injury. *Brain Injury, 10*, 207–218.

Hall, K. M., Wallbom, A. S., & Englander, J. (1998). Premorbid history and traumatic brain injury. *NeuroRehabilitation, 10*, 3–12.

Heinemann, A. W., & Whiteneck, G. G. (1995). Relationships among impairment, disability, handicap, and life satisfaction in persons with traumatic brain injury. *Journal of Head Trauma Rehabilitation, 10*(4), 54–63.

Ip., R. Y., Dornan, J., & Schentag, C. (1995). Traumatic brain injury: Factors predicting return to work or school. *Brain Injury, 9*(5), 517–532.

Jamieson, K. G., & Tait, I. A. (1966). *Traffic injury in Brisbane. Report of a general survey* (Special Report No. 13). Canberra: National Health and Medical Research Council.

Jennett B. (1996). Epidemiology of head injury. *Journal of Neurology, Neurosurgery, and Psychiatry, 60*, 362–369.

Kay, T. (1992). Neuropsychological diagnosis: Disentangling the multiple determinants of functional disability after mild traumatic brain injury. In L. J. Horn & N. D. Zasler (Eds.), *Rehabilitation of post-concussive disorders* (pp. 109–127). Philadelphia: Hanley & Belfus.

Kendall, E., & Terry, D. J. (1996). Psychosocial adjustment following closed head injury: A model for understanding individual differences and predicting outcome. *Neuropsychological Rehabilitation, 6*, 101–132.

Kinsella, G., Packer, S., & Olver, J. (1991). Maternal reporting of behaviour following very severe blunt head injury. *Journal of Neurology, Neurosurgery and Psychiatry, 54*, 422–426.

Kraus, J. F., Black, M. A., Hessol, N., Ley, P., Rokaw, W., Sullivan, C., Bowers, S., Knowlton, S., & Marshall, L. (1984). The incidence of acute brain injury and serious impairment in a defined population. *American Journal of Epidemiology, 119*, 186–201.

Kraus, J. F., Fife, D., Ramstein, K., Conroy, C., & Cox, P. (1986). The relationship of family income to the incidence, external causes, and outcomes of serious brain injury, San Diego County, California. *American Journal of Public Health, 76*, 1345–1347.

Kreutzer, J. S., Harris Marwitz, J., & Witol, A. D. (1995). Interrelationships between crime, substance abuse and aggressive behaviour among persons with traumatic brain injury. *Brain Injury, 9*, 757–768.

Kurtz, J. E., Putnam, S. H., & Stone, C. (1998). Stability of normal personality traits after traumatic brain injury. *Journal of Head Trauma Rehabilitation, 13*(3), 1–14.

Lannoo, E., De Deyne, C. D., Colardyn, F., De Soete, G., & Jannes, C. (1997). Personality change following head injury: Assessment with the NEO Five-Factor Inventory. *Journal of Psychosomatic Research, 43*, 505–511.

Ley, P. (1972). *Quantitative aspects of psychological assessment. An introduction.* London: Duckworth.

Lazarus, R. S., & Folkman, S. (1984). *Stress, appraisal, and coping.* New York: Springer.

Lishman, W. A. (1973). The psychiatric sequelae of head injury: A review. *Psychological Medicine, 3,* 304–318.

Lishman, W. A. (1998). *Organic psychiatry. The psychological consequences of cerebral disorder* (3rd edition). Oxford: Blackwell Scientific Publications.

London, P. S. (1967). Some observations on the course of events after severe injury of the head. *Annals of the Royal College of Surgeons of England, 41,* 607–614.

Luria, A. R. (1969). Frontal lobe syndromes. In P. J. Vinken & G. W. Bruyn (Eds.), *Handbook of Clinical Neurology* (Vol. 2, pp. 725–757). Amsterdam: North-Holland.

Luria, A. R. (1973). *The Working Brain.* London: Penguin.

Macmillan, M. (1996). Phineas Gage: A case for all reasons. In C. Code, C.-W. Wallesch, Y. Joanette, & A. R. LeCours (Eds.), *Classic cases in neuropsychology* (pp. 243–262). Hove, UK: Psychology Press.

MacMillan, P. J., Hart, R. P., Martelli, M. F., & Zasler, N. D. (2002). Pre-injury status and adaptation following traumatic brain injury. *Brain Injury, 16,* 41–49.

Malia, K., Powell, G., & Torode, S. (1995). Personality and psychosocial function after brain injury. *Brain Injury, 9,* 607–618.

Martelli, M. F., Zasler, N. D., & MacMillan, P. (1998). Mediating the relationship between injury, impairment and disability: A vulnerability, stress and coping model of adaptation following brain injury. *NeuroRehabilitation: An interdisciplinary journal, 11,* 51–66.

McKinlay, W., & Brooks, D. N. (1984). Methodological problems in assessing psychosocial recovery following severe head injury. *Journal of Clinical Neuropsychology, 6,* 87–99.

Novack, T. A., Bush, B. A., Meythaler, J. M., & Canupp, K. (2001). Outcome after traumatic brain injury: Pathway analysis of contributions from premorbid, injury severity, and recovery variables. *Archives of Physical Medicine and Rehabilitation, 82,* 300–305.

Ponsford, J. L., Olver, J. H., Curran, C., & Ng, K. (1995). Prediction of employment status 2 years after traumatic brain injury. *Brain Injury, 9(1),* 11–20.

Ponsford, J., Willmott, C., Rothwell, A., Cameron, P., Kelly, A.-M., Nelms, R., Curran, C., & Ng, K. (2000). Factors influencing outcome following mild traumatic brain injury in adults. *Journal of the International Neuropsychological Society, 6,* 568–579.

Prigatano, G. P. (1987a). Psychiatric aspects of head injury: Problem areas and suggested guidelines for research. In H. S. Levin, J. Grafman, and H. M. Eisenberg (Eds.), *Neurobehavioral recovery from head injury* (pp. 215–231). New York: Oxford University Press.

Prigatano, G. P. (1987b). Neuropsychological deficits, personality variables, and outcome. In M. Ylvisaker & E. M. R. Gobble, (Eds.), *Community re-entry for head injured adults* (pp. 1–23). Boston: Little, Brown & Co.

Prigatano, G. P. (1992). Personality disturbances associated with traumatic brain injury. *Journal of Consulting and Clinical Psychology, 60,* 360–368.

Prigatano, G. P. (1999). *Principles of neuropsychological rehabilitation.* New York: Oxford University Press.

Robertson, E., Rath, B., Fournet, G., Zelhart, P., & Estes, R. (1994). Assessment of mild brain trauma: A preliminary study of the influence of premorbid factors. *Brain Injury, 8,* 69–74.

Rosenthal, M., & Bond, M. R. (1990). Behavioral and psychiatric sequelae. In M. Rosenthal, E. R. Griffith, M. R. Bond, & J. D. Miller (Eds.), *Rehabilitation of the adult and child with traumatic brain injury* (pp. 179–192). Philadelphia: FA Davis Co.

Selecki, B. R., Hoy, R. J., & Ness, P. (1967). A retrospective survey of neuro-traumatic admissions to a teaching hospital: Part 1. General aspects. *Medical Journal of Australia, July 15,* 113–117.

Stuss, D. T., Gow, C. A., & Heatherington, C. T. (1992). "No longer Gage": Frontal lobe dysfunction and emotional changes. *Journal of Consulting and Clinical Psychology, 60,* 349–359.

Tate, P. S., Freed, D. M., Bombardier, C. H., Lewis Harter, S., & Brinkman, S. (1999). Traumatic brain injury: Influence of blood alcohol level on post-acute cognitive function. *Brain Injury*, *13*, 767–784.

Tate, R. L. (1987). Behaviour management techniques for organic psychosocial deficit incurred by severe head injury. *Scandinavian Journal of Rehabilitation Medicine*, *19*, 19–24.

Tate, R. L. (1998). "It is not only the kind of injury that matters, but the kind of head": The contribution of premorbid psychosocial factors to rehabilitation outcomes after severe traumatic brain injury. *Neuropsychological Rehabilitation*, *8*(1), 1–18.

Tate, R. L. (1999). Executive dysfunction and characterological changes after traumatic brain injury: Two sides of the same coin? *Cortex*, *35*, 39–55.

Tate, R. L., & Broe, G. A. (1999). Psychosocial adjustment after traumatic brain injury: What are the important variables? *Psychological Medicine*, *29*, 713–725.

Tate, R. L., McDonald, S., & Lulham, J. M. (1998). Incidence of hospital-treated traumatic brain injury in an Australian community. *Australian and New Zealand Journal of Public Health*, *22*, 419–423.

Thomsen, I. V. (1984). Late outcome of very severe blunt head trauma: A 10–15 year second follow-up. *Journal of Neurology, Neurosurgery, and Psychiatry*, *47*, 260–268.

Tsuang, M. T, Boor, M., & Fleming, J. A. (1985). Psychiatric aspects of traffic accidents. *American Journal of Psychiatry*, *142*, 538–546.

Tyerman, A., & Humphrey, M. (1984). Changes in self-concept following severe head injury. *International Journal of Rehabilitation Research*, *7*(1), 11–23.

Vogenthaler, D. R., Smith, K. R., & Goldfader, P. (1989). Head injury, a multivariate study: Predicting long-term productivity and independent living outcome. *Brain Injury*, *3*(4), 369–385.

Webb, C. R., Wrigley, M., Yoels, W., & Fine, P. R. (1995). Explaining quality of life for persons with traumatic brain injuries 2 years after injury. *Archives of Physical Medicine and Rehabilitation*, *76*, 1113–1119.

Weddell, R., Oddy, M., & Jenkins, D. (1980). Social adjustment after rehabilitation: A two year follow-up of patients with severe head injury. *Psychological Medicine*, *10*, 257–263.

Woessner, R., & Caplan, B. (1995). Affective disorders following mild to moderate brain injury: Interpretative hazards of the SCL-90-R. *Journal of Head Trauma Rehabilitation*, *10*(2), 78–89.

Zasler, N. D. (1997). Prognostic indicators in medical rehabilitation of traumatic brain injury: A commentary and review. *Archives of Physical Medicine and Rehabilitation*, *78 (Supp. 4)*, S12–S16.

NEUROPSYCHOLOGICAL REHABILITATION, 2003, *13* (1/2), 65–87

The neuropsychiatry of depression after brain injury

Simon Fleminger, Donna L. Oliver

Lishman Brain Injury Unit, Maudsley Hospital, London, UK

W. Huw Williams

School of Psychology, University of Exeter, Exeter, UK

Jonathan Evans

Oliver Zangwill Centre for Neuropsychological Rehabilitation, Ely, UK

Biological aspects of depression after brain injury, in particular traumatic brain injury (TBI) and stroke, are reviewed. Symptoms of depression after brain injury are found to be rather non-specific with no good evidence of a clear pattern distinguishing it from depression in those without brain injury. Nevertheless symptoms of disturbances of interest and concentration are particularly prevalent, and guilt is less evident. Variabilitiy of mood is characteristic. The prevalence of depression is similar after both stroke and TBI with the order of 20–40% affected at any point in time in the first year, and about 50% of people experience depression at some stage. There is no good evidence for areas of specific vulnerability in terms of lesion location, and early suggestions of a specific association with injury to the left hemisphere have not been confirmed.

Insight appears to be related to depressed mood with studies of TBI indicating that greater insight over time post-injury may be associated with greater depression. We consider that this relationship may be due to depression appearing as people gain more awareness of their disability, but also suggest that changes in mood may result in altered awareness.

The risk of suicide after TBI is reviewed. There appears to be about a three to fourfold increased risk of suicide after TBI, although much of this increased risk may be due to pre-injury factors in terms of the characteristics of people who

Correspondence should be addressed to Dr Simon Fleminger, Consultant Neuropsychiatrist, Lishman Brain Injury Unit, Maudsley Hospital, Denmark Hill, London SE5 8AZ, UK. Phone: +44 20 7919 2092, Fax: +44 20 7919 2087, Email: s.fleminger@iop.kcl.ac.uk

© 2003 Psychology Press Ltd
http://www.tandf.co.uk/journals/pp/09602011.html   DOI:10.1080/09602010244000354

suffer TBI. About 1% of people who have suffered TBI will commit suicide over a 15-year follow-up.

Drug management of depression is reviewed. There is little specific evidence to guide the choice of antidepressant medication and most psychiatrists would start with a selective serotonin reuptake inhibitor (SSRI). It is important that the drug management of depression after brain injury is part of a full package of care that can address biological as well as psychosocial factors in management.

INTRODUCTION

In this paper we review several aspects of depression after brain injury that are of particular relevance to the biological origins of depressive symptoms, their impact on risk management and their drug treatment. Much of the research on mood disorders in ABI has been conducted on traumatic brain injury (TBI) and stroke. Other forms of acquired brain injury have received relatively little attention. This has inevitably meant that this review will focus primarily on studies in TBI and stroke.

If depressive symptoms after brain injury are highly determined by the fact that the brain has been injured, rather that due to a psychological reaction to the injury and disability, then one might expect to see a pattern of symptoms that was distinct from that seen in depression in the absence of brain injury, and a strong relation to lesion location. The specificity and prevalence of depressive symptoms after brain injury, and their relation to lesion location, will therefore be reviewed.

Management of the brain injured person is not infrequently complicated by poor insight. The poor insight may be so severe that issues related to risk management become evident, for example, if the patient with a severe dysexecutive syndrome demands to be allowed to leave hospital and return to work. In our experience recovery of insight is related to depression, and we explore this relationship in this paper. However, depression brings with it the risk of suicide and the relationship between suicide and brain injury is also reviewed. We then review the value of biological treatments for depression after brain injury. Finally we consider how biological approaches fit with other treatment options, in particular, neurological rehabilitation and cognitive behaviour therapy, to provide multi-modal treatment strategies.

PRESENTATION OF DEPRESSION

A question that is often posed is whether depression following brain injury resembles depression experienced by those without neurological damage. Symptoms such as irritability, frustration, fatigue, and poor concentration commonly occur after brain injury independently of depression, i.e., they occur as a direct result of the brain damage rather than a manifestation of depression. Accordingly, it is not uncommon for brain injured patients to report a high rate of depressive symptoms even though, clinically, they are not depressed. For example, Kreutzer, Seel, and Gourley (2001) in a sample of TBI patients found that the most frequently endorsed symptoms of depression were: feeling tired (46%), being frustrated (41%), and having poor concentration (38%).

Few studies have attempted to make a direct comparison of the symptom profiles of depressed brain injured patients, non-depressed brain injured patients and depressed patients without brain injury. For example, Jorge, Robinson, and Arndt (1993a) compared the frequency of psychological (e.g., worrying, loss of interest, lack of confidence, guilt) and vegetative (e.g., insomnia, loss of libido, weight loss) symptoms in depressed and non-depressed TBI patients. Those with depression reported a significantly higher occurrence of psychological and vegetative symptoms compared to those who were not depressed. Also, the only symptoms that distinguished those who were depressed from those who were not, throughout the 12-month follow-up period, were the psychological symptoms relating to changes in self-attitude (i.e., lack of confidence, feelings of hopelessness, self-depreciation) and the vegetative symptom of lack of energy. In contrast to Jorge et al. (1993a), Aloia, Lang, and Allen (1995) using a statistical method, indirectly compared the symptom profiles of depression in head injured patients and non-head injured patients. The findings suggested that the picture of depression in head injury was similar to that in non-head injury.

Given the paucity of studies making a direct comparison of the rates of symptom endorsement between the differing clinical groups, it is difficult to confirm the symptoms that specifically characterise depression following brain injury. However, Kreutzer et al. (2001), by reviewing the literature, identified the symptoms irritability, lack of interest, moving slowly, fatigue, and forget-fulness as being more common after brain injury regardless of depression.

Apathy, or loss of motivation, is frequently observed among brain injured patients and is often associated with depression. In a consecutive series of 83 TBI patients, Kant, Duffy, and Pivovarnik (1998) found 60% were rated as both depressed and apathetic on the Beck Depression Inventory (BDI) and Apathy Evaluation Scale (AES-Self-rated). Of the sample, 10% were rated as apathetic but not depressed and an equal number depressed but not apathetic. Starkstein et al. (1993), in a consecutive series of 96 stroke patients, found 23% had symptoms of apathy of whom 11% were also suffering from depression. A further 23% were rated as depressed but not apathetic. In this study the Present State Exam was used to reach a diagnosis of depression and apathy was assessed using the Apathy Scale. Marin (1990, 1991) draws a distinction between apathy as a symptom of depression and "true" apathy, arguing that the latter "describes only those patients whose lack of motivation is not attributable to a diminished level of consciousness, an intellectual deficit or emotional distress" (p. 22). Hence, on the basis of this distinction a diagnosis of apathy must first rule out depression.

The reader is referred to the review by Aben et al. (2001) for a discussion on the presentation of post-stroke depression where the story regarding specificity of symptoms is rather similar (see also Code and Herrmann, this volume).

PREVALENCE OF DEPRESSION

A wealth of studies have examined the prevalence of depression after brain injury, whether the brain injury results from traumatic brain injury (TBI) or stroke. In particular, such studies have sought to illuminate a number of issues, namely, the commonality of depression, its duration, and when it is likely to occur after the brain injury has been sustained. Undoubtedly, these studies are useful when attempting to draw definitive conclusions as to the true prevalence of depression and its natural course following brain injury. But all to often, the findings lack consistency.

Traumatic brain injury

It is useful to distinguish those studies that have examined depression during the first year after TBI from those that have examined it, on average, 2 years and beyond.

Turning to the former, prevalence rates from a low of 18% (Satz et al., 1998) to a high of 39% (Bowen et al., 1999) are identified. One of the most informative of the early studies is Jorge et al.'s (1993b). This study examined 66 consecutively admitted TBI patients to a shock trauma centre who underwent psychiatric interview, within 1 month of injury, and were re-assessed at 3, 6, and 12 months. At 1 month, 26% were diagnosed with major depression, quantified using the Hamilton Rating Scale, and 3% with minor depression. At 3, 6, and 12 month follow-up, the prevalence of major depression remained relatively constant, being respectively, 22.2%, 23.2%, and 18.6%. Of those not diagnosed as depressed at 1 month, 10% developed depression at 3 months. New cases were further diagnosed at the rate of 15% at 6 months, and 12% at 12 months. Jorge et al. (1993b) found that by examining the course of depression in the 17 patients diagnosed with major depression at 1 month, depression persisted, on average, for 4.7 months with a minimum duration of 1.5 months to a maximum of 12 months. Within the sample, 79% completed the initial assessment and a minimum of two follow-up assessments.

Similar findings were also reported by Kersel, Marsh, Havill, and Sleigh (2001) and Bowen et al. (1999). At 6 months, Kersel et al.'s (2001) study found 24% to be classified as clinically depressed, based on scores on the short form of the Beck Depression Inventory. Further, 9% of this 24% scored in the mild depression range and 16% in the severe depression range. At 12 months, similar rates of depression were observed; 24% were considered to be clinically depressed, of whom 14% were rated as mildly depressed and 10% as severely depressed. It must be noted that those who fell within the "6 month" follow-up, may have been assessed at any time between 153 to 277 days (equating to a range of 5.1 to 9.2 months) and, those within the "12 month" follow-up, between 345 to 497 days (equating to 11.5 to 16.5 months). This aside, the 6 month prevalence reported by Kersel et al. (2001), and Jorge et al. (1993b), is in line with that reported by Satz et al. (1998) at 18%. Higher estimates of 35% at 6 months and 39% at 12 months have, however, been reported by Bowen et al. (1999), although these estimates are based on the presence of mood disorders in a sample of 99 TBI patients, rather than the presence of depression specifically.

An important conclusion that may be drawn from these studies is that depression is no more common in the acute phase than the later stages of recovery during the first year after TBI. The Kersel et al. (2001) and Bowen et al. (1999) findings reveal considerable individual variation in the occurrence and resolution of depression during the first year. For example, in Kersel et al.'s (2001) study, half of the depressed TBI patients at 6 months reported a lessening of their symptoms, or complete recovery by 12 months, and none reported an increase in severity between 6 and 12 months. At 12 months, only six (10%) new cases of depression were identified.

In contrast, higher prevalence has been reported in studies that recruited TBI patients at varying times post-injury. In the largest study to date, Kreutzer et al. (2001) examined 722 patients with mild-to-severe brain injuries, referred to a regional level I trauma centre for out-patient assessment, and who's average time post-injury was 2.5 years, ranging from 3 months to 9 years. Within this study, 42% met DSM-IV criteria for a major depressive episode, based on analysis of scores using the Neurobehavioural Functioning Inventory, a self-report questionnaire. The generalisability of this study's findings are, however, acknowledged as being weakened by the fact that all the patients were recruited from a single out-patient centre and it relied upon patients' self-reports (Kreutzer et al., 2001). These findings are in line with Hibbard et al. (1998) and Hoofien, Gilboa, Vakil, and Donovick (2001). Hibbard et al. (1998) diagnosed 48% with major depression post-TBI; of whom, 38% were suffering from major depression at the time of interview. The sample consisted of 100 TBI patients with injuries of varying levels of severity, averaging 7.6 years post-injury and assessed at three points in time relative to the injury: before TBI, post TBI, and at time of interview. When the sample included both patients who had previously been diagnosed with major depression, and patients with post-TBI depression, prevalence increased to 61%. Hibbard et al. (1998) acknowledged an inherent limitation in their study regarding interpretation of the pre-TBI and post-TBI depression, data. As the TBI patients were required to provide a retrospective account of their affective state, such data may be obscured by neurocognitive and awareness deficits. In contrast, Hoofien et al. (2001) found that 45% of its sample of 76 patients with severe TBI, and on average 14.1 years post-injury, were suffering from depression, as indicated by an elevated score on the Symptom Checklist 90—Revised. Slightly higher prevalence rates of 57% and 59% have, respectively, been reported by Douglas and Spellacy (2000), and Glenn et al. (2001). Douglas and Spellacy's (2000) study comprised 35 patients with severe TBI and who averaged 7 years post-injury (range = 3.5–10 years), and Glenn et al.'s (2001) study comprised 41 patients with TBI of mild-to-severe severity and averaged 3.4 years post-injury.

With the exception of Kreutzer et al. (2001) and Glenn et al. (2001), these studies have examined the prevalence of depression in TBI patients at least 3.5 years post-injury. They therefore lend support to the argument, given the high occurrance reported, that the prevalence of depression within TBI patients increases with time after the first year post-injury.

Stroke

As with TBI, prevalence estimates for post-stroke depression (PSD) vary enormously between 64% and 10% (Aben et al., 2001); the literature is plagued with inconsistent findings. However, in contrast to the post-TBI depression literature, few studies have examined the frequency of depression in stroke patients more than 2 years post-stroke (Dam, 2001). Rather, considerable attention has focused on the prevalence of PSD at a given time during the first year post-stroke.

Examining the acute phase post-stroke, Ramasubbu et al.'s (1998) study of 626 hospital-based stroke patients, found 13% scored in the severe depression category and 13% in the moderate depression category. The study assessed patients using the Centre for Epidemiological Studies Depression Scale (CES-D), 7–10 days post-stroke. Ramusubbu et al.'s (1998) prevalence estimate for major depression is lower than the 20% reported by Downhill and Robinson (1994) but considerably higher than the 5.6% reported by Berg et al. (2001). Downhill and Robinson's (1994) sample of 309 hospital-based stroke patients were, on average, 11.3 days post-stroke and assessed on the basis of DSM-III and the Hamilton Depression Rating Scale. Similarly, Berg et al. (2001) utilised the same diagnostic instruments and also recruited a hospital-based sample of 100 consecutive stroke patients who were 2 weeks post-stroke.

Of the studies examining PSD at the post-acute stage, Morris et al. (1992) diagnosed 18% of their sample with major depression and 20% with minor depression based on DSM criteria. Kauhanen et al. (1999) reported that, at 3 months post-injury, the prevalence of major depression was 9% and minor depression 44%. At 12 months post-stroke, 16% showed major depression and 26% minor depression. In contrast, House (1991) reported only 5% suffering from major depression at 12 months, based on DSM criteria. House's (1991) study used an unselected community sample of 128 patients. Kauhanen et al.'s (1999) sample composition, which was similar to Morris et al.'s (1992), was a series of consecutive hospital-based stroke patients ($n = 106$), who underwent psychiatric interview for the diagnosis of depression based on DSM-III-R criteria. Finally, looking at the longer-term occurrence of PSD, Dam (2001), in a 7-year follow-up study consisting of 99 hospital-based patients, found major or mild depression in 20% of their sample.

With regard to the course of depression, Kauhanen et al. (1999) suggest that the prevalence of major depression increases over the first year post-stroke. Similar findings have been reported by Gainotti, Antonucci, Marra, and Paolucci (1999) who found major depression based on DSM criteria, in 29% at 2 months, increasing to 32% at 2–4 months and to 60% at 4 months or more. However, other studies have failed to corroborate these findings (Herrmann et al., 1998; Kotila, Numminen, Waltimo, & Kaste, 1998). Robinson, Bolduc, and Price (1987) found the prevalence of the major depression did not change significantly between the 12 and 24 months follow-up, while House (1991) found that the prevalence of depression declined over the year. House's (1991) findings challenge the view that mood disorders after stroke are persistent (Robinson et al., 1987; Wade, Legh-Smith, & Hewer, 1987).

As in the TBI literature, individual variation in the course of PSD during the first year has been observed. The study by Herrmann et al. (1998) found that 30% of patients with significant depressive symptoms at 3 months had recovered by 1 year, while depression continued to persist in 45% of patients between the 3 and 12-month assessments. The cumulative prevalence of PSD, the chance that an individual will suffer depression during a given time interval, is a more informative measure of the frequency of PSD (Aben et al., 2001) and deserves greater attention. Of the few studies considering the cumulative prevalence of PSD, Andersen, Vestergaard, Riis, and Lauritzen (1994) distinguished patients who had previously had a stroke and those that were first-ever stroke patients. During the first year post-stroke, 41% of the former group and 33% of the latter developed depression. Of those who were not depressed at 3 months, 25% went on to develop depression. Similarly, of House's (1991) total sample ($n = 128$), 39% were identified as depressed based on the BDI (≥ 10) at some point during the first year post-stroke.

Conclusion

It is not possible to draw tidy conclusions with regard to the course and duration of depression following TBI and stroke, given the results reported in the above studies. Studies in both areas have produced inconsistent findings.

Review of study findings must be considered in the context of the differences in methodology and sample composition (Kreutzer et al., 2001). All of the studies have differed greatly in terms of sample size, assessment tools, the level or range of injury severity, type of injury, the time post-injury, and the inclusion/exclusion criteria. There is some evidence that hospital-based samples of stroke suffer higher rates of depression than community-based populations, presumably partly reflecting the fact that they are more severe strokes.

Issues that must also be considered include, for example, that the diagnosis of depression in both populations is extremely problematic (Aben et al., 2001; Evans & Levine, 2002). There is an overlap between somatic and cognitive symptoms of depression and the sequelae of TBI and stroke. Poor concentration, slowed motor and cognitive speed, fatigue and apathy, as well as problems with sleep, which are common manifestations of depression, are also frequently reported by non-depressed TBI patients. The symptoms of stroke also mimic depression, e.g., poor facial expression, motor or speech retardation, loss of initiative (see Code & Herrmann, this volume), and diagnosis is often confounded by the ward environment which may disrupt sleep and eating habits (Gall, 2001).

In a recent review of the PSD literature, which may also be applied to TBI, Aben et al. (2001) highlighted several methodological difficulties that complicate the interpretation of findings on PSD. For example, several studies have imposed inclusion criteria to restrict the sample to a particular homogeneous group, others have used broader criteria. As recognised by House (1991) most studies recruit stroke patients who have been admitted to hospital and, as noted by Gall (2001), have excluded patients with dysphasia or comprehensive deficits and patients with moderate to severe cognitive impairments. The use of such hospital-based samples may, accordingly, be biased in terms of age, severity (and type) of brain injury and thereby be unrepresentative. Therefore, the composition of the sample may limit the extent to which findings can be generalised.

Further, the diagnosis of depression in the TBI literature has often relied upon self-rating scales that have been designed for the psychiatric population (Kreutzer et al., 2001). There are few, if any, validated scales for use in the TBI population. Gordon et al. (1991) devised the Structured Assessment of Depression in Brain Damaged Individuals, but it has not been widely adopted (Aben et al., 2001). One must also take into consideration when using self-report scales that responses of TBI patients may be obscured by deficits in awareness (Kreutzer et al., 2001). For example, Satz et al. (1998) found a discrepancy in the prevalence of depression when measured using a self-report scale and an examiner-rated scale.

LESION SITE AND DEPRESSION

Considerable research has centred on the neuroanatomical correlates of depression in brain injured patients. Greater attention has been focused on the relationship between lesion location and depression in stroke than in TBI. This may be as a result of the difficulty localising the precise neuroanatomical regions damaged by TBI; typically lesions associated with TBI are more diffuse than lesions observed in stroke patients (Rosenthal, Christense, & Ross, 1998).

Robinson and others were the first to propose that depression following stroke may be related to the location of the lesion. Based on the findings of a series of studies, Robinson proposed that major depression is associated with lesions in the left-hemisphere, specifically the anterior region (Robinson & Szetela, 1981; Robinson et al. 1984). These assertions have caused many to attempt to replicate these findings, some producing supportive evidence (Vataja et al., 2001) others not (Gainotti, Azzoni, & Marra, 1999; Herrmann, Bartels, Schumacher, & Wallesch, 1995; House et al., 1990; Kim & Choi-kwon, 2000).

The most informative study is the systematic review undertaken by Carson et al. (2000). A comprehensive and systematic search of the literature identified 143 studies, of which 48 met pre-defined inclusion criteria. Of these 48 studies, 38 found no association between the risk of depression and lesion location, two studies reported that the risk of depression was increased with left-sided lesions, while seven reported an increased risk with right-sided lesions, and the remaining study reported a relationship between depression and lesions located in the right parietal region or the left frontal region. As 35 of the 48 studies had made a categorical diagnosis of post-stroke depression, these studies were included in the meta-analysis, which went on to find no evidence to support the hypothesis that depression is more commonly associated with left-hemisphere strokes than with right-hemisphere strokes (RR 0.95; 95% CI 0.83–1.10). Anterior stroke lesions were the most common and therefore carried the greatest absolute risk of depression, but there was no evidence for a selective relative risk for anterior lesions. Nor was there any support for the hypothesis that depression is more commonly associated with lesions of the left anterior brain than with other regions (RR 1.17; 95% CI 0.87–1.62). Further analysis, taking into consideration the time interval between stroke and diagnosis of depression, was not significant.

Two studies that have sought to extend their findings from stroke research to TBI are Fedoroff et al. (1992) and Jorge et al. (1993b). These studies lend some support for the assertions made by Robinson. Fedoroff et al.'s (1992) study of 66 patients with acute closed head injuries, admitted consecutively to a shock trauma centre, underwent semi-structured psychiatric interview within 1 month of injury. Patients were grouped according to depression status (i.e., depressed and non-depressed), on the basis of DSM. The nature and location of lesions were determined from CT scans taken within the first day after trauma and repeated 1–2 weeks later. A significant relationship between depression following TBI and site of lesion was observed. The likelihood of post-TBI depression was greater in those with left anterior lesions. In contrast, using a logistic regression model the likelihood of depression diminished with frontal lesions (i.e., right, left, or bilateral frontal including orbitofrontal) or purely cortical lesions. Jorge et al. (1993b) followed Fedoroff et al.'s (1992) sample over a 12-month period, during which they were reassessed at 3, 6, and 12 month intervals. Only in the acute phase were lesions located in the left anterior significantly associated with major depression. Jorge et al. (1993b) suggested that the findings were in line with the hypothesis that major depression may be triggered by disruption of the ascending nonadrenergic and serotonergic pathways that leads to a depletion of these neurotransmitters.

INSIGHT AND MOOD

There are indications in the literature that depression following brain injury may be related to insight or awareness of disability. Boake, Freeland, Ringholz, Nance, and Edwards (1995) have reported that up to 45% of individuals with moderate-to-severe TBI suffer diminished or complete lack of insight of the impairments they have sustained as a result of their brain injury. While cognitive impairment, personality change and behavioural dysfunction may be clearly evident to others, to the head-injured patient with limited insight such deficits may simply not be "seen", or dismissed as insignificant (Flashman, Amador, & McAllister, 1998). Further, the head-injured patient with limited insight may also fail to appreciate how such impairments affect various domains of everyday functioning and so may hold unrealistic expectations about resuming their pre-injury lifestyle.

Poor insight, which is often associated with behavioural problems, tends to occur early during recovery and usually resolves (Ponsford, Sloan, & Snow, 1995). Some of the depression and emotional distress that may follow brain injury may be understood as a psychological reaction to awareness of disability. The patient may be faced with the stark reality that they are unable to resume pre-injury vocational and recreational activities. Recognition of such losses may trigger a psychological response such as depression (Morton & Wehman, 1995), a hypothesis supported in the brain injury literature (e.g., Gainotti, 1993; Ownsworth & Oei, 1998). Insight deficits following TBI have also been regarded as a motivated form of denial (McGlynn & Schacter, 1989); a psychological defence mechanism to preserve self-esteem and fend off depression. However, this strategy may fail if the patient attempts to pursue pre-injury activities and is unsuccessful. The experience of failure may force the patients to confront their impairments and disabilities and thus trigger a catastrophic reaction such as severe depression (Ownsworth & Oei, 1998).

If depression is a reaction to awareness of disability then increasing depression and emotional distress would be expected to accompany improving insight. Godfrey, Partridge, Knight, and Bishara (1993) observed that the onset of emotional dysfunction (i.e., depression, anxiety, and poor self-esteem) coincided with improving insight of behavioural, cognitive and social impairments in a sample of closed head injury (CHI) patients. In addition to undertaking a social skills exercise, patients completed various self-report measures in order to assess their current levels of behavioural impairment, perceived cognitive deficits, and emotional adjustment. A close relative also undertook these measures, in order to provide an "objective" rating of the patient's level of impairment in the various domains. A group of orthopaedic patients acted as control group. At 6 months post-injury, the CHI patients displayed limited insight into the behavioural and neuropsychological problems that they were experiencing together with a tendency to overestimate the competency of their social abilities. This was evident from the finding of the self-ratings by the CHI patients in that they did not differ significantly from those of the control group. Further, the close relatives rated the CHI group as significantly more impaired in the various domains than the control group. At this 6 month stage, there was no evidence of increased levels of emotional dysfunction. However, at 1 year and 2–3 year follow-up, the CHI patients demonstrated greater insight into their behavioural impairments as indicated in the consistency between the patients' self-ratings of their behavioural problems and the reports of a close relative. At this stage, higher levels of depression anxiety, and lower levels of self-esteem were reported by the CHI patients. Wallace and Bogner (2000) have also reported a relationship between self-awareness and depression in TBI patients. Their sample consisted of 50 moderate-to-severe TBI patients who averaged 1.95 years post injury (SD = 2.09, range = 0.19–9.44 years). Awareness of deficits was measured by examining the discrepancy between the patients' scores on the Patient Competency Rating Scale and the rating of a close relative. TBI patients who lacked insight into their impairments were less likely to report symptoms of depression and anxiety while those who showed good insight were more likely to express significant emotional distress.

Similar findings have been reported in the Post-traumatic Stress Disorder (PTSD) literature in neurological conditions. For example, Williams, Evans, Wilson, and Needham (in press) reported that lowered insight was associated with lowered ratings of PTSD symptoms. However, they noted that although participants may lack insight, they may in fact have troubling symptoms, but are unable to report them. Interpretation of these results, in general, is, however, reliant upon close relatives providing an objective measure of the patient's social functioning. Relatives tend to experience increased levels of depression caring for a brain-injured individual (Marsh, Kersel, Havill, & Sleigh, 1998) and therefore their opinion may be biased by their own subjective well-being (Kersel et al., 2001).

Finally, a cluster analysis by Fleming, Strong, and Ashton (1998) revealed that TBI patients in the high self-awareness group demonstrated more emotional distress and motivation to change their behaviour than the low self-awareness group.

The above studies provide evidence to support the argument that depression after TBI may *result* from improving insight. However, is this relationship unique to TBI patients? One way to examine this is to look at the relationship between depression and insight in non-TBI populations. In a sample of 46 patients who met DSM-IV criteria for chronic schizophrenia or schizoaffective disorder, Smith, Hull, Israel, and Willson (2000) found an association between higher levels of depression and better insight indicated by lower symptom unawareness and misattribution. Similarly, Sanz et al. (1998), in a sample of 33 in-patients meeting DSM-IV for non-organic psychotic illness, reported that the more depressed patients scored highest on measures of insight. These findings have been corroborated (Dixon, King, & Steiger, 1998; Caroll et al., 1999; Moore, Cassidy, Carr, & O'Callaghan, 1999).

However, some of these studies also provide evidence for an alternative hypothesis: depression may *produce* better insight. Iqbal, Birchwood, Chadwick, and Trower (2000) examined the vulnerability of a sample of 105 schizophrenic patients to post-psychosis depression (PPD) over a 12-month period. Those patients who developed PPD did not differ from those who did not develop PPD on any measure of insight prior to the onset of the PPD. However, once depressed, the PPD group showed greater insight, including awareness of illness, relabelling of symptoms and the need for treatment, than the non-PPD group.

This hypothesis finds support from studies of manic-depressive illness where the change in mood can be regarded as the primary event. Peralta and Cuesta (1998) assessed insight in 54 patients fulfilling DSM-III-R criteria for manic or major depressive episodes on admission to a psychiatric unit, and on discharge. On admission, insight in manic patients was found to be more impaired than in patients with major depression. However, during the course of treatment, as the acute episode remitted, levels of insight in the manic patients improved. These findings are in line with Michalakeas et al. (1994) and Gheami, Stoll, and Pope (1995).

The explanation that depression may make one more insightful is consistent with cognitive models of depressive realism. Depressive realism suggests that depression is a realistic and rational response to a negative event (Moorey, 1996). This position challenges the view of Beck, and others, who maintain that depression results from a distorted style of thinking that is negatively biased (Beck, 1963). Experimental studies in the normal population have provided some limited evidence for the concept of depressive realism. For example, mood induction studies looking at the effects of mood on attributional biases have shown mood does influence attribution. In particular, errors in judgement are most likely when one is in a good mood while a depressed mood tends to produce more accurate judgements (Forgas, 1998). Alloy and Abramson (1979) have shown that depressed college students have a more accurate view of reality than non-depressed college students. However, these results have not been replicated in realistic or emotionally engaging situations (Pacini, Muir, & Epstein, 1998). It has also been reported that a good mood is associated with a tendency to attribute success to stable, internal causes and, in the face of failure, blame to unstable, external/situational causes. In contrast, a depressed mood produces the reverse effect: Success is attributed to situational factors outside the individual's control, while failure is attributed to internal causes (Forgas, Bower, & Moylan, 1990). On the basis of these findings, one may speculate that a depressed mood may enhance insight, i.e., depressed brain-injured individuals become much more aware of their disabilities and are more realistic in respect of their outlook.

To conclude, studies in the brain-injured and other populations support an association between depression and insight. This association may be bidirectional: On the one hand depression may result from improving insight, and on the other depression may produce better insight. However, it has not yet been established whether these relationships are causal. In fact, Prigatano (1997) suggests one should not assume that increased awareness after brain injury automatically leads to depression. Based on clinical experience, Prigatano (1997) suggests that rather than leading to depression, increased insight may "give patients a better appreciation of the problems they face, and with that knowledge, they may feel better prepared to cope with life's difficulties" (p. 309).

SUICIDE AFTER BRAIN INJURY

The best way to determine whether brain injury is a risk factor for suicide is to calculate the standardised mortality ratio (SMR) for suicide deaths in a large cohort of brain injury survivors. The SMR compares the rate of suicide in the index cohort with the expected rate of suicide in the population from which the cohort comes, taking into account the fact that the risk of suicide is highly dependent on the age, sex, and sociocultural background of the subjects. It is usually expressed as a percentage; an SMR of 100% indicating the risk of suicide is the same as the control population.

Harris and Barraclough (1997) undertook a large meta-analysis of suicide following various medical and psychiatric conditions. With regard to traumatic brain injury they identified the large study by Achte et al. (1970) of 6500 brain injured survivors from the Finnish–Russian war of 1940 followed up for about 25 years. Of those studied 107 committed suicide; only 32 would have been expected to do so. In addition they found five studies of civilian brain injury, largely from England, with a total 650 patients followed up for up to 40 years. There was a total of 5 suicides, with an expected rate of 1.4. For both civilian and war brain injuries the SMR was about 350, indicating that the risk of suicide after brain injury was raised over three-fold.

Since that study there have been two relevant studies. Tate, Simpson, Flanagan, and Coffey (1997) followed up 896 patients admitted to a brain injury rehabilitation unit, of whom 8 died from suicide, all of whom were male, over a follow-up period of up to 18 years. The time interval between injury and death was from 1 to 11 years. These patients had had severe brain injuries with post-traumatic amnesic periods on average of several weeks. Most of the patients had active psychiatric problems at the time of suicide, including five with mood disturbance and one with a psychotic disorder. In four there was a history of previous suicide attempts following the brain injury, and in one the brain injury was itself a result of attempted suicide. In several cases there had been repeated expressions of suicidal intent. Alcohol and drug abuse was not particularly evident. The authors did not attempt to calculate an SMR, noting that the index population was highly selected. If we assume an average follow-up period of 9 years the suicide rate was about 112 per 100,000 population per annum, i.e., at least four times greater than the figure they quote of 25 per 100,000 per annum for men aged 15–44 years in Australia.

Teasdale and Engberg (2001) identified all cases in Denmark admitted with a diagnosis of traumatic brain injury between 1979 and 1993 and these cases were then screened in the national register of deaths for the period up to and including 1993 to identify those cases that had gone on to commit suicide. Using ICD, (8th Edition) codes they identified 126,000 cases of concussion, 7560 cases of skull fracture, and 11,700 cases of intracerebral contusion or haemorrhage. These cases were followed up for up to 15 years. Suicide was identified in 750, 46, and 99 cases respectively, giving SMRs of 3.0 (concussion), 2.7 (skull fracture), and 4.1 (intracerebral contusion or haemorrhage). The increased risk of suicide was significantly greater in the intracerebral contusion/haemorrhage group, compared with the two other groups. They plotted survival curves and found no period of particular greater risk; the risk of suicide remained fairly constant over time. Suicide was associated with comorbid drug/alcohol abuse. Men were at slightly greater absolute risk, over and above their greater risk of sustaining a brain injury, but, because of their low absolute risk of suicide, the SMR for women was greater for all three groups.

There was a surprisingly high rate of suicide in the concussion group. Few of these patients would have sustained significant brain injury and the increased risk in these patients was interpreted as due to the particular vulnerability of patients who sustain head injuries. In other words a considerable proportion of the increased risk of suicide after brain injury is due to the personality and cultural factors of those who are at risk of sustaining brain injuries. Nevertheless, the greater risk in those with significant brain injury does indicate a specific contribution of brain injury and its disability.

In conclusion all three studies suggest that over a 15-year period following head injury the suicide rate is approximately 1%, which is at least three times the standard suicide rate. Some of the excess risk is due to pre-injury factors.

There has been little work on the risk of suicide attempts, without completed suicide, after brain injury. This is of interest given that brain injury may may be a risk factor for the development of borderline personality disorder (Hibbard et al., 2000; Streeter, Van Reekum, Schorr, & Bachman, 1995), which is itself associated with deliberate self-injury.

BIOLOGICAL TREATMENT OF DEPRESSION

The evidence for the efficacy of antidepressant medication after stroke has been thoroughly reviewed in a recent article by Turner-Stokes and Hassan (2002). Nortriptyline, a tricyclic, fluoxetine and citalopram, selective serotonin reuptake inhibitors (SSRIs), and trazodone, have been used in randomised controlled trials (RCT) of post-stroke depression. All have been found to be effective in treating depression, although their effects on improving functional outcomes have been less impressive. However, Gainotti et al. (2001) in an observational study of antidepressant use, suggest that these drugs are able to improve functional outcomes in patients who are depressed after brain injury. Given the vulnerability of patients with stroke to cardiovascular side-effects of medication, most psychiatrists would therefore recommend an SSRI as the first line treatment of depression after stroke. Preference should be given to those drugs with less potential for interactions with other drugs, through protein binding or enzyme induction. Citalopram or sertraline would seem sensible drugs to choose.

Lability of mood, or emotional incontinence, after stroke appears to respond to antidepressants and there is good evidence for fluoxetine (Brown, Sloan, & Pentland, 1998). Amitriptyline has successfully been used for emotional incontinence in multiple sclerosis (Schiffer, Herndon, & Rudick, 1985). Anecdotal evidence supports the use of SSRIs in brain injury (Sloan, Brown, & Pentland, 1992).

There have been no RCT evaluations of antidepressant efficacy for depression after traumatic brain injury. A controlled comparison by Dinan and Mobayed (1992) found that patients who were depressed following head injury appeared to respond less well to amitriptyline than depressed patients without a head injury. This is consistent with the clinical impression that depression following brain injury may be more difficult to treat. Most neuropsychiatrists would recommend starting with an SSRI, partly because these drugs probably have less effect on reducing seizure threshold particularly when compared with tricyclic antidepressants.

There have been no trials of the treatment of mania after head injury. In those patients with rapid-cycling mood disorders, or with bipolar affective disorders with periods of mania and depression, a mood stabiliser should be considered. Given lithium's potential for side-effects in the brain injured (Schiff et al.,

1982) valproate or carbamazepine is probably the drug of first choice, although there is no good evidence of efficacy.

Electro-convulsive therapy (ECT) is a highly controversial intervention within mental health fields. It appears that the use of ECT is declining in the UK (see Bhat & Sibisi, 2000). It has been argued that there is no clear exposition of a biological mechanism for supporting its use for purported mood disorder (Abrams, 1992). ECT's proponents have argued that it may be effective for severe depression and should remain as a possible treatment option in such cases (see Freeman, 1995). A study by Kant, Coffey, and Bogyi (1999) suggested that it might be used safely with patients after a head injury. However, this was based on a case series of 11 patients using measures of gross global functioning, which may not have been sensitive to cognitive changes (the Neurobehavioral Cognitive Status Examination, NCSE, and Mini-Mental State Examination, MMSE). An RCT study, by Yao et al. (2000), of the effects of ECT on the memory functioning of 77 people with schizophrenia revealed that memory function continuously decreased in the ECT group. There have been no RCT evaluations of ECT's effectiveness in brain injury. Current guidelines being developed in the UK by the National Institute for Clinical Excellence may provide a framework for its future use (see www.nice.org.uk/article.asp?a=25969).

BIOPSYCHOSOCIAL MANAGEMENT OF DEPRESSION

We have described, above, biological aspects of depression following brain injury. We noted that lesion site may influence the nature of depression, but does not fully explain the occurrence and severity of depression, and that depression appears to be more of a risk with time after the injury. We noted how insight may be a factor within this relationship. To further explain such findings it is important to explore how depression may be understood in terms of a psychological reaction to injury and its aftermath. The stress-coping models, which are in part evolved from grief models, and also cognitive behavioural theory are presented below, as biopsychosocial frameworks for understanding the complex interaction of pre-injury, injury, and post-injury factors on mood and behaviour.

Psychological reaction to injury

In general, reactions to loss may involve initial stages of shock and denial, followed by stages of anger and depression, leading through to adjustment and reintegration (see Jackson, 1988). Importantly, there is not necessarily a progression through all stages of grief, as it is possible to have different combinations of each form of emotion at the same time, with one possibly being more salient (see discussion in Code & Herrmann, this issue, and Yates, this issue). TBI leads to a particularly complicated form of grief, or psychological adjustment, because emotional denial may well follow anosognosia. Furthermore, the person may have lost the very skills and opportunities for reinvestment in life. Moreover, losses may also be cumulative and ongoing for survivors and a pervasive sense of grief may occur in the context of a disintegrated sense of self (see Williams, Williams, & Ghadiali, 1998). Stress-coping theories of adaptation have as their key theme the interaction of pre-injury coping styles and stress caused by the demands and conflicts of the aftermath of the injury (see Kendall & Terry, 1996). The person's adjustment is thus influenced by successive efforts to master the demands and conflicts triggered by their trauma, with, over time, adaptive or unhelpful coping styles being developed. Such conceptualisations are argued to be consistent with the general stress and coping literature (Folkman et al., 1986) and the literature on coping in physical illness (Moos & Schaefer, 1984).

Research by Moore and Stambrooke (1995) and Malia, Powell, and Torode (1995) revealed that ABI survivors were shown to be less likely to have good psychosocial outcomes if their coping styles were avoidant, emotion-focused or "wishful". More recently, Finset and Anderson (2000) investigated coping styles of 70 ABI survivors and a non-injured control group. They reported that the ABI group tended to have a less differentiated coping style than the controls. They also found a lack of active-approach coping responses was associated with apathy, and avoidant coping was associated with depression. Unfortunately, it was not possible to control for dysexecutive problems contributing to the coping responses described in these studies. Also, studies did not investigate the relative contributions of pre-morbid, event-related and post-injury factors on coping styles.

In general, additional factors that need to be addressed in their effect on a survivor's psychological reaction and adjustment include the following: The emotional trauma of the event, such as in PTSD (see McMillan, Williams, and Bryant, this issue); breakdown of partnership and/or changes in family roles (see Kendall & Terry, 1996; also see Oddy & Herbert, this issue); physical disabilities causing additional stress; problems with pain, particularly headache, and in TBI, pain due to orthopaedic injuries (see Tyrer, this issue); primary and/or secondary sleep disorders (Cohen, Oksenberg, Snir, & Stern, 1994); and misuse of alcohol and/or drugs (see Kreutzer, this issue, and see Taylor, Kreutzer, Demm, & Meade, this issue).

Biopsychosocial treatment of depression

It is beyond the scope of this review to address the full spectrum of treatment approaches for mood and mental health disorders in ABI groups. However, we do wish to emphasise that it is unlikely, as in general mental health fields, that one treatment option will provide for effective and efficient intervention, particularly in the case of preventing relapse. Usually a combination of approaches is needed. Developments, as represented in papers in this volume suggest that people with ABI may require components of neurorehabilitation, pharmacological intervention, cognitive behaviour therapy, and other treatment options, through other modalities (from post-acute, outreach to community interventions) depending on their mental health status, cognitive profile, insight, and personal goals (see Ownsworth & Oei, 1998 for a discussion of management of depression).

Cognitive behaviour therapy requires particular mention in the context of depression. We have explored above the possible mediating factors for mood disorders in brain injury, such as coping styles, and such issues may be addressed through CBT. Also, CBT provides systematic means for addressing such issues as: negative automatic thoughts; negative cognitive schemas; unhelpful behaviour profiles; social engagement and, importantly, hope. CBT has been shown to be particularly effective in the management of depression in general mental health groups (Roth & Fonagy, 1996). CBT is advocated as particularly suited for people with ABI as it contains systems for managing generalisability of "therapeutic work" from the treatment session (diaries and workbooks, etc.) and promotes social and emotional control skills learning (Ponsford et al., 1995; Williams & Jones, 1997). Cases to illustrate the use of CBT for TBI survivors for depression in the context of other conditions (such as PTSD) have been described in the literature (see Williams et al., in press).

A further area of particular note is the management of suicide risk. In general, the following issues may need to be addressed in managing suicide risk in ABI: Lack of planning and problem solving for "getting out" of depressed mood; poor memory that affects ability to cope with problematic situations; emotional lability and/or dis-inhibition and impulsiveness that might increase the risk of acting without considering the consequences of actions; poor emotional expression, leading to depressed state going unnoticed; and perseveration over negative material, leading to a spiral of negative thinking (see Klonoff & Lage, 1995; Tate et al., 1997 for risk factors, assessment, and recommendations for management of suicide). Staff training and support regarding suicide risk must also be addressed.

CONCLUSION

Depression after brain injury needs careful evaluation (Evans & Levine, 2002). It can probably jeopardise functional recovery, and is related to insight into disability as well as suicide risk. There is much scope for effective biopsychosocial management of depression after ABI. However, given the complex issues involving the myriad of factors inherent in neurological trauma, there is little hard evidence on which to base practice in this area. There is an urgent need to develop the literature on the management of mood disorders for survivors of ABI.

REFERENCES

Aben, I., Verhey, F., Honig, A., Lodder, J., Lousberg, R., & Maes, M. (2001). Research into the specificity of depression after stroke: A review on an unresolved issue. *Progress in Neuro-Psychopharmacology & Biological Psychiatry*, *25*(4), 671–689.

Abrams, D. (1992). *Elecetroconvulsive therapy*. (2nd edition), Oxford: Oxford University Press.

Achté, K. A., Lönnqvist, J., & Hillbom, E. (1970). Suicides of war brain injured veterans. *Psychiatrica Fennica*, *1*, 231–239.

Alloy, L. B., & Abramson, L. Y. (1979). Judgment of contingency in depressed and nondepressed students: Sadder but wiser? *Journal of Experimental Psychology*, *108*(4), 441–485.

Aloia, M. S., Long, C. J., & Allen, J. B. (1995). Depression among the head-injured and non-head-injured: A discriminant analysis. *Brain Injury*, *9*(6), 575–583.

Andersen, G., Vestergaard, K., Riis, J., & Lauritzen, L. (1994). Incidence of post-stroke depression during the first year in a large unselected stroke population determined using a valid standardized rating scale. *Acta Psychiatrica Scandinavica*, *90*(3), 190–195.

Beck, A. T. (1963). Thinking and depression: 1. Idiosyncratic content and cognitive distortions. *Archives of General Psychiatry*, *9*, 324–333.

Berg, A., Palomaki, H., Lehtihalmes, M., Lonnqvist, J., & Kaste, M. (2001). Poststroke depression in acute phase after stroke. *Cerebrovascular Diseases*, *12*(1), 14–20.

Bhat, M., & Sibisi, C. (2000). *Electroconvulsive therapy practice in an inner city London teaching hospital over the last 3 years*. Annual Meeting, Royal College of Psychiatry Conference, Edinburgh, 7th July 2000.

Boake, C., Freeland, J. C., Ringholz, G. M., Nance, M. L., & Edwards, K. E. (1995). Awareness of memory loss after severe closed-head injury. *Brain Injury*, *9*, 273–283.

Bowen, A., Chamberlain, M. A., Tennant, A., Neumann, V., & Conner, M. (1999). The persistence of mood disorders following traumatic brain injury: A 1 year follow-up. *Brain Injury*, *13*(7), 547–553.

Brown, K. L., Sloan, R. W., & Pentland, B. (1998). Fluoxetine as a treatment for post-stroke emotionalism. *Acta Psychiatrica Scandinavica*, *98*, 455–458.

Carroll, A., Fattah, S., Clyde, Z., Coffey, I., Owens, D. G., & Johnstone, E. C. (1999). Correlates of insight and insight change in schizophrenia. *Schizophrenia Research*, *35*(3), 247–253.

Carson, A. J., MacHale. S., Allen, K., Lawrie, S. M., Dennis, M., House, A., & Sharpe, M. (2000). Depression after stroke and lesion location: A systematic review. *Lancet*, *356*(9224), 122–126.

Cohen, M., Oksenberg, A., Snir, D., & Stern, M.J. (1994). Temporally related changes in sleep complaints in traumatic brain injured patients. *Journal of Neurology, Neurosurgery and Psychiatry*, *55*, 313–315.

Dam, H. (2001). Depression in stroke patients 7 years following stroke. *Acta Psychiatrica Scandinavica*, *103*(4), 287–293.

Dinan, T. G., & Mobayed, M. (1992). Treatment resistance of depression after head injury: A preliminary study of amitriptyline response. *Acta Psychiatrica Scandinavica*, *85*(4), 292–294.

Dixon, M., King, S., & Steiger, H. (1998). The contribution of depression and denial towards understanding the unawareness of symptoms in schizophrenic out-patients. *British Journal of Medical Psychology*, *71* (Pt 1), 85–97.

Douglas, J. M., & Spellacy, F. J. (2000). Correlates of depression in adults with severe traumatic brain injury and their carers. *Brain Injury*, *14*(1), 71–88.

Downhill, J. E. Jr, & Robinson, R. G. (1994). Longitudinal assessment of depression and cognitive impairment following stroke. *Journal of Nervous & Mental Disease*, *182*(8), 425–431.

Evans, J. J., & Levine, B. (2002). Mood disorders: Issues of prevalence, misdiagnosis, assessment, and treatment. *Neuropsychological Rehabilitation, 12*(2), 167–170.

Fedoroff, J. P., Starkstein, S. E., Forrester, A. W., Geisler, F. H., Jorge, R. E., Arndt, S. V., & Robinson, R. G. (1992). Depression in patients with acute traumatic brain injury. *American Journal of Psychiatry, 149*(7), 918–923.

Finset, A., & Andersson, S. (2000). Coping strategies in patients with acquired brain injury: Relationships between coping, apathy, depression and lesion location. *Brain Injury, 14*, 887–905.

Flashman, L. A., Amador, X., & McAllister, T. W. (1998). Lack of awareness of deficits in traumatic brain injury. *Seminars in Clinical Neuropsychiatry, 3*(3), 201–210.

Fleming, J. M., Strong, J., & Ashton, R. (1998). Cluster analysis of self-awareness levels in adults with traumatic brain injury and relationship to outcome. *Journal of Head Trauma Rehabilitation, 13*(5), 39–51.

Folkman, S., Lazarus, R. S., Dunkel-Schetter, C., DeLongis, A., & Gruen, R. J. (1986). The dynamics of stressful encounters: Cognitive appraisal, coping, and encounter outcomes. *Journal of Personality & Social Psychology, 50*, 992–1003.

Forgas, J. P. (1998). On being happy and mistaken: Mood effects on the fundamental attribution error. *Journal of Personality & Social Psychology, 75*(2), 318–331.

Forgas, J. P., Bower, G. H., & Moylan, S. J. (1990). Praise or blame? Affective influences on attributions for achievement. *Journal of Personality & Social Psychology, 59*(4), 809–819.

Freeland, J. (1996). Awareness of deficits: A complex interplay of neurological, personality, social and rehabilitation factors. i.e. *Magazine, 4*, 32–34.

Freeman, C. (1995) *The ECT handbook*. London: Royal College of Psychiatrists Publications.

Gainotti, G. (1993). Emotional and psychosocial problems after brain injury. *Neuropsychological Rehabilitation, 3*(3), 259–277.

Gainotti, G., Antonucci, G., Marra, C., & Paolucci S. (2001). Relation between depression after stroke, antidepressant medication and functional recovery. *Journal of Neurology, Neurosurgery, and Psychiatry, 71*, 258–261.

Gainotti, G., Azzoni, A., & Marra, C. (1999). Frequency, phenomenology and anatomical-clinical correlates of major post-stroke depression. *British Journal of Psychiatry, 175*, 163–167.

Gall, A. (2001). Post stroke depression. *Hospital Medicine (London), 62*(5), 268–273.

Ghaemi, S. N., Stoll, A. L., & Pope, H. G., Jr. (1995). Lack of insight in bipolar disorder. The acute manic episode. *Journal of Nervous & Mental Disease, 183*(7), 464–467.

Glenn, M. B., O'Neil-Pirozzi, T., Goldstein, R., Burke, D., & Jacob, L. (2001). Depression amongst outpatients with traumatic brain injury. *Brain Injury, 15*(9), 811–818.

Godfrey, H. P., Partridge, F. M., Knight, R. G., & Bishara, S. N. (1993). Course of insight disorder and emotional dysfunction following closed head injury: A controlled cross-sectional follow-up study. *Journal of Clinical and Experimental Neuropsychology, 15*(4), 503–515.

Gordon, W. A., Hibbard, M. R., Egelko, S., Riley, E., Simon, D., Diller, L., Ross, E. D., & Lieberman, A. (1991). Issues in the diagnosis of post-stroke depression. *Rehabilitation Psychology, 36*, 71–87.

Harris, E. C., & Barraclough, B. (1997). Suicide as an outcome for mental disorders: A meta-analyis. *British Journal of Psychiatry, 170*, 205–228.

Herrmann, M., Bartels, C., Schumacher, M., & Wallesch, C. W. (1995). Poststroke depression: Is there a pathoanatomic correlate for depression in the postacute stage of stroke? *Stroke, 26*(5), 850–856.

Herrmann, N., Black, S. E., Lawrence, J., Szekely, C., & Szalai, J. P. (1998). The Sunnybrook Stroke Study: A prospective study of depressive symptoms and functional outcome. *Stroke, 29*(3), 618–624.

Hibbard, M. R., Bogdany, J., Uysal, S., Kepler, K., & Silver, J. (2000). Axis II psychopathology in individuals with traumatic brain injury. *Brain Injury, 14*, 45–61.

Hibbard, M. R., Uysal, S., Kepler, K., Bogdany, J., & Silver, J. (1998). Axis I psychopathology in individuals with traumatic brain injury. *Journal of Head Trauma Rehabilitation*, *13*(4), 24–39.

Hoofien, D., Gilboa, A., Vakil, E., & Donovick, P. J. (2001). Traumatic brain injury (TBI) 10–20 years later: A comprehensive outcome study of psychiatric symptomatology, cognitive abilities and psychosocial functioning. *Brain Injury*, *15*(3), 189–209.

House, A. (1991). Mood disorders in the first year after stroke. *British Journal of Psychiatry*, *158*, 83–92.

House, A., Dennis, M., Warlow, C., Hawton, K., & Molyneux, A. (1990). Mood disorders after stroke and their relation to lesion location. A CT scan study. *Brain*, *113* (Pt 4), 1113–1129.

Iqbal, Z., Birchwood, M., Chadwick, P., & Trower, P. (2000). Cognitive approach to depression and suicidal thinking in psychosis. 2. Testing the validity of a social ranking model. *British Journal of Psychiatry*, *177*, 522–528.

Jackson, H. (1988). Brain, cognition and grief. *Aphasiology*, *2*, 89–92.

Jorge, R. E., Robinson, R. G., & Arndt, S. (1993a). Are there symptoms that are specific for depressed mood in patients with traumatic brain injury? *Journal of Nervous & Mental Disease*, *181*(2), 91–99.

Jorge, R. E., Robinson, R. G., Arndt, S. V., Starkstein, S. E., Forrester, A. W., & Geisler, F. (1993b). Depression following traumatic brain injury: A 1 year longitudinal study. *Journal of Affective Disorders*, *27*(4), 233–243.

Kant, R., Coffey, C. E., & Bogyi, A. M. (1999). Safety and efficacy of ECT in patients with head injury: A case series. *Journal of Neuropsychiatry and Clinical Neuroscience*, *11*, 32–37.

Kant, R., Duffy, J. D., & Pivovarnik, A. (1998). Prevalence of apathy following head injury. *Brain Injury*, *12*(1), 87–92.

Kauhanen, M., Korpelainen, J. T., Hiltunen, P., Brusin, E., Mononen, H., Maatta, R., Nieminen, P., Sotaniemi, K. A., & Myllyla, V. V. (1999). Poststroke depression correlates with cognitive impairment and neurological deficits. *Stroke*, *30*(9), 1875–1880.

Kendall, E., & Terry, D. J. (1996). Psychosocial adjustment following closed head injury: A model for understanding individual differences and predicting outcome. *Neuropsychological Rehabilitation*, *6*, 101–132.

Kersel, D. A., Marsh, N. V., Havill, J. H., & Sleigh, J. W. (2001). Psychosocial functioning during the year following severe traumatic brain injury. *Brain Injury*, *15*(8), 683–696.

Kim, J. S., & Choi-Kwon, S. (2000). Poststroke depression and emotional incontinence: Correlation with lesion location. *Neurology*, *54*(9), 1805–1810.

Klonoff, P. S., & Lage, G. A. (1995). Suicide in patients with traumatic brain injury: Risk and prevention. *Journal of Head Trauma Rehabilitation*, *10*, 16–24.

Kotila, M., Numminen, H., Waltimo, O., & Kaste, M. (1998). Depression after stroke: Results of the FINNSTROKE Study. *Stroke*, 29(2), 368–372.

Kreutzer, J. S., Seel, R. T., & Gourley, E. (2001). The prevalence and symptom rates of depression after traumatic brain injury: A comprehensive examination. *Brain Injury*, *15*(7), 563–576.

Malia, K., Powell, T., & Torode, M. (1995). Coping and psychosocial function after brain injury. *Brain Injury*, *9*, 607–618.

Marin, R. S. (1990). Differential diagnosis and classification of apathy. *American Journal of Psychiatry*, *147*(1), 22–30.

Marin, R. S. (1991). Apathy: A neuropsychiatric syndrome. *Journal of Neuropsychiatry & Clinical Neurosciences*, *3*(3), 243–254.

Marsh, N. V., Kersel, D. A., Havill, J. H., & Sleigh, J. W. (1998). Caregiver burden at 1 year following severe traumatic brain injury. *Brain Injury*, *12*(12), 1045–1059.

McGlynn, S. M., & Schacter, D. L. (1989). Unawareness of deficits in neuropsychological syndromes. *Journal of Clinical & Experimental Neuropsychology*, *11*(2), 143–205.

Michalakeas, A., Skoutas, C., Charalambous, A., Peristeris, A., Maronos, V., Keramari, E., & Theologou, A. (1994). Insight in schizophrenia and mood disorders and its relation to psychopathology. *Acta Psychiatrica Scandinavica*, *90*(1), 46–49.

Moore, O., Cassidy, E., Carr, A., & O'Callaghan, E. (1999). Unawareness of illness and its relationship with depression and self-deception in schizophrenia. *European Psychiatry: The Journal of the Association of European Psychiatrists, 14*(5), 264–269.

Moore, A. D., & Stambrook, M. (1995). Cognitive moderators of outcome following traumatic brain injury: A conceptual model and implications for rehabilitation. *Brain Injury, 9,* 109–130.

Moorey, P. (1996). When bad things happen to rational people: Cognitive therapy in adverse life circumstances. In P. M. Salkovskis (Ed.), *Frontiers of cognitive therapy.* London: Guilford Press.

Moos, R., & Schaefer, J. A. (1984). The crisis of physical illness: An overview and conceptual approach. In R. Moos (Ed.), *Coping with physical illness: New directions.* New York: Plenum Press.

Morris, P. L., Robinson, R. G., Raphael, B., Samuels, J., & Molloy, P. (1992). The relationship between risk factors for affective disorder and poststroke depression in hospitalised stroke patients. *Australian & New Zealand Journal of Psychiatry, 26*(2), 208–217.

Morton, M. V., & Wehman, P. (1995). Psychosocial and emotional sequelae of individuals with traumatic brain injury: A literature review and recommendations. *Brain Injury, 9*(1), 81–92.

Ownsworth, T. L., & Oei, T. P. (1998). Depression after traumatic brain injury: Conceptualization and treatment considerations. *Brain Injury, 12*(9), 735–51.

Pacini, R., Muir, F., & Epstein, S. (1998). Depressive realism from the perspective of cognitive-experiential self-theory. *Journal of Personality & Social Psychology, 74*(4), 1056–1068.

Peralta, V., & Cuesta, M. J. (1998). Lack of insight in mood disorders. *Journal of Affective Disorders, 49*(1), 55–58.

Ponsford, J. L., Sloan, S., & Snow, P. (1995). *Traumatic brain injury: Rehabilitation for everyday adaptive living.* Hove, UK: Psychology Press.

Prigatano, G. P. (1997). The problem of impaired self-awareness in neuropsychological rehabilitation. In J. Leon-Carrion (Ed.), *Neuropsychological rehabilitation: Fundamentals, innovations and directions.* Florida: GR/St. Lucie Press.

Ramasubbu, R., Robinson, R. G., Flint, A. J., Kosier, T., & Price, T. R. (1998). Functional impairment associated with acute poststroke depression: The Stroke Data Bank Study. *Journal of Neuropsychiatry & Clinical Neurosciences, 10*(1), 26–33.

Robinson, R. G., Bolduc, P. L., & Price, T. R. (1987). Two-year longitudinal study of poststroke mood disorders: Diagnosis and outcome at one and two years. *Stroke, 18*(5), 837–843.

Robinson, R. G., Kubos, K. L., Starr, L. B., Rao, K., & Price, T. R. (1984). Mood disorders in stroke patients. Importance of location of lesion. *Brain, 107,* 81–93.

Robinson, R. G., & Szetela, B. (1981). Mood change following left hemispheric brain injury. *Annals of Neurology, 9*(5), 447–453.

Rosenthal, M., Christensen, B. K., & Ross, T. P. (1998). Depression following traumatic brain injury. *Archives of Physical Medicine & Rehabilitation, 79*(1), 90–103.

Roth, A. D., & Fonagy, P. (1996). *What works for whom? A critical review of psychotherapy research.* New York: Guilford Press.

Sanz, M., Constable, G., Lopez-Ibor, I., Kemp, R., & David, A. S. (1998). A comparative study of insight scales and their relationship to psychopathological and clinical variables. *Psychological Medicine, 28*(2), 437–446.

Satz, P., Forney, D. L., Zaucha, K., Asarnow, R. R., Light, R., McCleary, C., Levin, H., Kelly, D., Bergsneider, M., Hovda, D., Martin, N., Namerow, N., & Becker, D. (1998). Depression, cognition, and functional correlates of recovery outcome after traumatic brain injury. *Brain Injury, 12*(7), 537–553.

Schiff, H. B., Sabin, T. D., Geller, A., Alexander, L., & Mark, V. (1982). Lithium in aggressive behavior. *American Journal of Psychiatry, 139*(10), 1346–1348.

Schiffer, R. B., Herndon, R. M., & Rudick, R. A. (1985). Treatment of pathologic laughing and weeping with amitriptyline. *New England Journal of Medicine, 312,* 1480–1482.

Sloan, R. W., Brown, K. W., & Pentland, B. (1992). Fluoxetine as a treatment of emotional lability after brain injury. *Brain Injury*, *6*, 315–319.

Smith, T. E., Hull, J. W., Israel, L. M., & Willson, D. F. (2000). Insight, symptoms, and neuro-cognition in schizophrenia and schizoaffective disorder. *Schizophrenia Bulletin*, *26*(1), 193–200.

Starkstein, S. E., Fedoroff, J. P., Price, T. R., Leiguarda, R., & Robinson, R. G. (1993). Apathy following cerebrovascular lesions. *Stroke*, *24*(11), 1625–1630.

Streeter, C. C., Van Reekum, R., Schorr, R. I., & Bachman, D. L. (1995). Prior head injury in male veterans with borderline personality disorder. *Journal of Nervous and Mental Disease*, *183*, 577–581.

Tate, R., Simpson, G., Flanagan, S., & Coffey, M. (1997). Completed suicide after traumatic brain injury. *Journal of Head Trauma Rehabilitation*, *12*, 16–28.

Teasdale, T. W., & Engberg, A. W. (2001). Suicide after traumatic brain injury: A population study. *Journal of Neurology, Neurosurgery, and Psychiatry*, *71*, 436–440.

Turner-Stokes, L., & Hassan, N. (2002). Depression after stroke: A review of the evidence base to inform the development of an integrated care pathway. Part 2: Treatment alternatives. *Clinical Rehabilitation*, *16*, 248–260.

Vataja, R., Pohjasvaara, T., Leppavuori, A., Mantyla, R., Aronen, H. J., Salonen, O., Kaste, M., & Rekinjuntti, T. (2001). Magnetic resonance imaging correlates of depression after ischemic stroke. *Archives of General Psychiatry*, *58*(10), 925–931.

Wade, D. T., Legh-Smith, J., & Hewer, R. A. (1987). Depressed mood after stroke. A community study of its frequency. *British Journal of Psychiatry*, *151*, 200–205.

Wallace, C. A., & Bogner, J. (2000). Awareness of deficits: Emotional implications for persons with brain injury and their significant others. *Brain Injury*, *14*(6), 549–562.

Williams, W. H. (in press). Rehabilitation of emotional disorders following acquired brain injury. In B. A. Wilson (Ed.), *Neuropsychological rehabilitation; Theory and practice*.

Williams, W. H., Evans, J. J., Wilson, B. A., & Needham, P. (in press). Neurological, cognitive and attributional predictors of posttraumatic stress symptoms after traumatic brain injury. *Journal of Traumatic Stress*.

Williams, W. H., & Jones, R. S. (1997). Teaching cognitive self-regulation of independence and emotion control skills. In B. S. Kroese, D. Dagnan, & K. Loumidis (Eds.), *Cognitive therapy for people with learning disabilities*. London: Routledge.

Williams, W. H., Williams, J. M. G., & Ghadiali, E. J. (1998). Autobiographical memory in traumatic brain injury: Neuropsychological and mood predictors of recall. *Neuropsychological Rehabilitation*, *8*, 43–60.

Yao, Shaomin; Zhang, Zhenlan; Luo, Suqin; Qi, Jianying; Li, Zhi; Liu, Xinmin; An, Airong; & Wu, Jianbin (2000). Memory deficiency of schizophrenics after electro-nonconvulsive or electro-convulsive therapy (ECT). *Chinese Mental Health Journal*, *14*(6), 388–390.

NEUROPSYCHOLOGICAL REHABILITATION, 2003, *13* (1/2), 89–107

Cognitive behaviour therapy for the treatment of depression in individuals with brain injury

N. Khan-Bourne[1,2] and R. G. Brown[2]

[1]*Lishman Brain Injury Unit, Maudsley Hospital, South London and Maudsley NHS Trust, London, UK*

[2]*Department of Psychology, Institute of Psychiatry, King's College London, London, UK*

This article focuses on depression and its psychological management following brain injury or stroke in the adult population. The presentation of depression in the context of brain injury is discussed and a summary of the psychosocial aetiological factors for the development of depression in this context is provided. The links between depression and neuropsychological functioning are explored and the significant impact of depression on neurorehabilitation outcome highlights the need for the development of effective interventions in this area. Cognitive behaviour therapy (CBT) is presented as a potentially suitable treatment: The model is described with ideas for the clinician on how to adapt the delivery of CBT for clients with neuropsychological impairment. To date, there have been a very small number of studies evaluating CBT for the treatment of depression in brain injury, however their results have been promising. It is concluded that further research is necessary.

Depression is a frequent complication following brain injury and with multiple biological, psychological and social factors involved in its onset and maintenance. Depression after a brain injury may in turn affect rehabilitation outcome, through its additional impact on cognition mood and motivation. However, despite recent advances in the psychological treatment of depression in the non brain-injured population, particularly using cognitive behaviour therapy (CBT), there has been very little work on the value of such techniques

---

Correspondence should be addressed to Dr R. G. Brown, Department of Psychology, PO77, Institute of Psychiatry, De Crespigny Park, London SE5 8AF.

This work was supported in part by the James S. McDonnell Foundation.

© 2003 Psychology Press Ltd
http://www.tandf.co.uk/journals/pp/09602011.html   DOI:10.1080/09602010244000318

in the brain injury population. This paper is directed at clinicians and clinical researchers working with brain injured individuals. It aims to summarise current knowledge about psychosocial factors implicated in the aetiology of depression, to show how depression may interact with cognitive functioning, and to consider the delivery of CBT in clinical practice in the context of neurorehabilitation.

Depressive disorders

Before discussing depression in patients with brain injury it is worth considering the disorder and its impact in non-injured individuals. The symptoms of depression fall into four categories: emotional (persistent sad mood), cognitive (feelings of worthlessness or inappropriate guilt), motivational (lack of interest), and physical (appetite or sleep disturbance). Clinical depression contrasts with the normal emotional experiences of sadness, in being extreme, persistent, and disabling. Depression is one of the most common psychiatric illnesses and can have a major impact on people's health and quality of life. The prevalence of depressive disorders (based on DSM-IV criteria) in a representative sample of 4,972 of the UK general population was around 5% with the rate slightly higher for women (5.9%) than men (4.2%) (Ohayon, Priest, Guilleminault, & Caulet, 1999). The literature suggests that the course of depression varies between individuals, as does the response to treatment. Depression also carries a high probability of relapse. For example, Coyne, Pepper, and Flynn (1999) found that 85% of currently depressed individuals in primary care and 78% in psychiatric settings had had prior episodes of depression, while Piccinelli and Wilkinson (1994) found that 75% of individuals followed up over 10 years had relapsed and 10% suffered a persistent depression.

Depression often coexists with other affective disorders. In a prospective study, Angst (1996) examined the risk of major depressive episodes and recurrent brief depression associated with other psychiatric disorders. Over a 10 year period the following disorders were shown to have increased risk (odds-ratio) of co-morbid depression: dysthymia (4.4), generalised anxiety disorder (4.4), panic disorder (2.7), hypomania (2.6), agoraphobia (2.6), and social phobia (2.4).

The cost of depression to society was estimated by Chisholm (2001) who included care costs, productivity costs, and psychosocial costs falling upon the individual, their families and friends, employers, and to society as a whole. The total estimated cost in the UK amounted to £3.4 billion, based on 1990 prices. It has been further estimated that depression accounts for around 10% of life years lost to disability for the working population and the cost to the healthcare system increases with the length of illness (Asvall, 2001).

Against this background it can be seen that depression is a major problem even in the non-brain injured population. A review of the literature in brain injury gives a wide variation in prevalence rates for depression ranging from 24% (Guth, 2000) to 70% (Kersel, Marsh, Havill, & Sleigh, 2001; Kreutzer, Seel, & Gourley, 2001), in traumatic brian injury (TBI) and from 20–63% after stroke (Leung, 1997; Sandin, Cifu, & Noll, 1994). This variability is likely to result from differences in assessment methods and diagnostic criteria, and heterogeneity in the brain injury population. Diagnosis is complicated by the fact that the expression of affective disorder in the brain-injured population is frequently atypical, and there is considerable overlap between the symptoms of brain injury and the symptoms of depression (Raskin & Stein, 2000). Depression may be overestimated if too much emphasis is given to the non-affective symptoms (e.g., motivational, physical) particularly when using cut-off scores on questionnaires, or underestimated if depressive symptoms are confused with other sequelae of the brain injury.

The timing of the assessment following injury may also affect estimates of the severity and prevalence of depression. Whilst Bowen et al. (1999) found that the frequency of mood disorder after TBI remains largely unchanged in individuals between 6 months and 12 months post-injury, several studies (e.g., Perino et al., 2001) have indicated that the onset of depression may be more likely to occur after the initial phase of recovery. Some investigators (e.g., Wallace, 2000) have suggested that this is due to the development of awareness of the full impact of the brain injury, which generally becomes apparent after the acute phase when the recovery curve has slowed. Conversely, others have suggested that depression is more likely where individuals have poor insight into their difficulties (Ownsworth & Oei, 1998). This issue is discussed in detail elsewhere in this special edition.

Despite the variability in estimated prevalence, it is clear that depression is common in the brain-injured population and may well be under-diagnosed (Jean-Bay, 2000), and may persist for many years post-injury (e.g., Hoofien, Gilboa, Vakil, & Donovick, 2001; Linn, Allen, & Willer, 1994). As in non-brain injury populations, co-morbidity is high, with 44% of individuals presenting with two or more DSM axis-1 disorders (Fleming, Strong, & Ashton, 1998).

Cognitive impairment and depression

Depression interacts with both cognitive and motivational processes as evidenced by experimental analogue research in healthy individuals and in depressed individuals, with and without brain injury.

Individuals with depression show deficits on a range of cognitive tests (Brown, Scott, & Bench, 1994) with the pattern of dysfunction having many of the characteristics associated with fronto-subcortical impairment. Reischies and Neu (2000) found that depressed non-brain injured individuals displayed mild cognitive impairments in comparison with matched controls, particularly in the areas of "averbal" memory, psychomotor speed and verbal fluency. In non-brain injured individuals there appears to be considerable variation in recovery of cognitive function with remission of the depressive episode. In individuals with brain injury, there is some evidence that treatment of the depression may have a more positive impact on cognition. Fann, Uomoto, and Katon (2001) found a considerable improvement in individuals with mild TBI (MTBI) following eight weeks of treatment with antidepressants, although the study was uncontrolled and did not assess the impact of practice or spontaneous improvement.

Some symptoms associated with depression may also interfere with cognition. Rumination, common in individuals with affective disorder, is associated with poor performance on tests of executive function such as the Wisconsin Card Sorting Task (Davis, Armstrong, Donovan, & Temkin, 1984). A recent study by Watkins and Brown (2002) suggested that rumination has a direct causal role in disrupting ongoing, demanding cognitive tasks. Depressed individuals also show a loss of enjoyment and decreased interest in previous activities, which can result in a reduction in purposeful or "goal-directed" behaviour. Motivational deficits will interact with cognitive function. Bernstein and de Ruiter (2000) compared non-brain injured and MTBI groups on a range of cognitive tasks. They manipulated motivation by telling the students that performance would be a good indicator of their overall degree result. This manipulation resulted in improved performance of healthy controls while for the individuals with MTBI (an average of 6.4 years after injury) performance was unaffected.

The implication then, is that depression causes its own problems, which may be superimposed on the primary cognitive deficits resulting from the brain injury. Left untreated, studies indicate that depression will increase patient handicap, interfere with participation in rehabilitation, and impact on the recovery of cognitive and psychosocial function (Parikh et al., 1990; Pohjasvaara et al., 2001). For example, the latter authors examined the influence of depression on the long-term outcome of stroke a large-scale study of ischaemic stroke patients aged 55–85 years. Patients were assessed on a variety of factors, using various methodologies (e.g., Beck's Depression Inventory, BDI; handicap, Rankin scale; assessment of activities of daily living, Barthel Index; medical, neurological, and radiological stroke evaluation and a comprehensive psychiatric evaluation) 3 months after stroke and then at follow-up, 15 months later. The diagnosis of depressive disorders was made using DSM-III-R criteria. It was found that patients with a BDI score of 10 or more at 3 months was correlated with poorer functional outcome as measured by the Barthel Index and the Rankin Scale. Poorer functional outcome at 3 months also correlated with depression at 15 months. Thus, it is clear that it is necessary to address the depression as part of the neurorehabilitative process.

Risk factors for depression following brain injury

Several factors have been implicated in the development of depression following brain injury (Lishman, 1987), although a comprehensive model has yet to be proposed or tested. Poorer initial recovery status (as measured by the Glasgow Outcome Scale), is associated with a greater likelihood of depression (Satz et al., 1998), while the location of the brain injury and the level of insight into functional deficits may also play a role. In addition to such organic risk factors Ownsworth and Oei (1998) considered the possible role of pre-morbid factors, and the psychosocial consequences of the brain injury to the patient's life.

Pre-morbid psychiatric disturbance may be an important predictor of post-injury depression. In some cases the TBI itself may well be an indirect result of pre-morbid psychiatric problems, for example where the TBI is a consequence of high-risk behaviour or a suicide attempt. Pre-morbid personality factors, cognitive assets, and family support are also associated with post-brain injury depression. In particular, it is suggested that individuals who coped well with stress before their brain injury are likely to have skills that protect them from developing depression or enhance recovery from it (Ownsworth & Oei, 1998). Although post-injury coping may not always reflect pre-morbid styles, Malia, Powell, and Torode (1995) found that brain injured individuals use in the main four strategies for coping: problem-focused, emotion-focused, avoidance, and wishful thinking. Emotion-focused coping, avoidance, and wishful thinking were more likely to be associated with poorer psychosocial functioning.

Curran, Ponsford, and Crowe (2000) failed to find any specific pattern of coping in individuals with TBI and severely injured orthopaedic individuals, but confirmed the general association between depression and anxiety with a coping style characterised by wishful thinking and self-blame. Finally, Finset and Andersson (2000) found that avoidant coping was associated with depression for individuals with severe TBI, stroke, or hypoxic brain injury and that these individuals tended to display less differentiated coping styles. Together, such data suggest that the coping style should be assessed as a potential determinant of patient functioning likely to influence long-term adjustment to brain injury, and is a valid target for psychological intervention.

Family functioning can have an important impact on the individual's susceptibility to depression after brain injury. Families that were "dysfunctional" pre-morbidly, or which find it difficult to adjust to the rehabilitation process, are less likely to promote the patient's well- being and emotional functioning. However, the idea of family support needs to be expanded to include psychosocial integration as a whole. There is evidence that poor psychosocial reintegration into the wider community is related to depression. One of the frequent consequences of brain injury is that it is difficult or impossible for the brain-injured person to resume previous activities such as employment or leisure activities (Asikainen, Kaste, & Sarna, 1996). Individuals who find it difficult to successfully reintegrate with the community (often those with more severe injuries) describe lower levels of self-esteem (Tate & Broe, 1999) and report less satisfaction with life (Burghleigh, Farber, & Gillard, 1998; Tennant, Macdermott, & Neary, 1995). The experience of subsequent failure in the resumption of pre- existing roles has also been linked to depression (Ownsworth & Oei, 1998) and may contribute to the development of avoidance strategies as a means of coping. Social isolation is particularly common in individuals who experience personality changes and find it difficult to retain pre-morbid friendships (Weddell, Oddy, & Jenkins, 1980).

A final set of factors is the patient's reaction to their own difficulties and perceptions of the present and the future. In some individuals, depression may be understandable in terms of grief and the sense of loss following the brain injury (Rosenthal & Meyer, 1971). In others there may be a lack of insight, with unrealistic expectations and a catastrophic reaction to the experience of failure. Ownsworth and Oei (1998) cite a model developed by Moore and Stambrook, 1995, which states that, as the patient develops awareness of deficits, cognitive, behavioural and emotional consequences of TBI produce learned helplessness, deficits in coping and altered locus of control beliefs. Eventually individuals acquire self-limited belief systems and over-generalise the effects of the TBI into their daily lives. Understanding and managing such cognitions and belief-systems is central to modern approaches to the psychological management of depression (see below).

Psychological treatment of depression

Various studies (e.g., Morton & Wehman, 1995) have recommended that community rehabilitation services make psychological health of those with TBI a priority. However, there are few published studies that evaluate psychological interventions and to provide an evidence base to justify such an expansion of services.

Traditionally, psychological interventions in neurorehabilitation have taken a learning/behaviour theory approach to therapy (Schlund & Pace, 1999). Behaviour therapy (BT) aims to change maladaptive behaviour using techniques based on the principles of learning theory. In classical conditioning approaches the aim is to replace the old behaviour with new more adaptive responses (e.g., in systematic desensitisation) while in operant conditioning the aim is to selectively reinforce desired behaviours while discouraging the maladaptive responses (e.g., by using token economies). In neurorehabilitation BT has been effective in treating behavioural disturbances (Schlund & Pace, 1999), in social skills training (Brotherton, Thomas, Wisotzek, & Milan, 1988), and in cognitive remediation (Bellus, Kost, Vergo, & Dinezza, 1998).

Behavioural approaches also have a tradition in the treatment of depression, utilising the finding that, when pleasant events are increased, there is an associated improvement in mood (Lewinsohn, 1974). Relatively pure behavioural approaches to the treatment of depression have been developed and their effectiveness demonstrated (Jacobson et al., 1996) and behavioural activation is often used as the first phase of cognitive behaviour therapy (CBT). The individual is encouraged to increase activity levels, particularly of pleasant events, which it is assumed will be rewarding and result in improved mood.

The loss or restriction of opportunities for rewarding activity following brain injury, make such approaches appealing in the management of depression. However, to date, there is little in the way of direct evidence to argue their effectiveness specifically for the treatment of depression in the brain injury population. Nevertheless, positive results have been reported in other clinical groups. Teri, Logsdon, Umoto, and McCurry (1997) evaluated two types behavioural intervention, delivered through caregivers, to treat depression in older adults with Alzheimer's disease. The interventions consisted of nine weekly sessions with both the patient and caregiver participating to varying degrees. The "pleasant events" intervention was highly structured, with time spent at the outset helping participants to understand the treatment model. The initial sessions involved the caregiver identifying, planning, and increasing pleasant events. The mid-stage of the programme focused on depression, stress, anger, and carer burden, with caregivers encouraged to increase pleasant events for themselves and to develop support systems. The final sessions consisted of functional analysis, whereby incidents of behavioural disturbance were identified, together with antecedents and consequences, so that ways of modifying these behaviours could be explored. A second comparison intervention was less flexible, and trained caregivers in effective problem solving. Both intervention groups showed significant reductions in depression, in comparison with typical care and waiting list control groups, with almost two thirds maintaining these gains at 6-month follow up.

Such results, however, need to be balanced against some negative findings suggesting that a pure behavioural approach may not always work. Drummond and Walker (1996) evaluated the effectiveness of a leisure rehabilitation programme on functional performance and mood for stroke individuals, for 6 months post-discharge. The programme, utilising the strategy of behavioural activation, was run by occupational therapists, and in addition to conventional occupational therapy provided practical and financial advice. They found that despite a significant (albeit short-lived) improvement in mobility and responses to a psychological well being assessment, levels of depression remained unchanged.

Behavioural approaches based on reward and pleasant events may also be limited where individuals show an organic deficit (i.e., disrupted biological mechanisms) in their responsiveness to reinforcement (Wood & McMillan,

2000). Al-Adawi, Powell, and Greenwood (1998) used the Card Arranging Reward Responsivity Objectivity Test (CARROT) to demonstrate that individuals with brain injury were less responsive to financial incentives. Interestingly, treatment with bromocriptine (a drug that affects dopaminergic circuitry), led to an improvement in measures of reward responsivity, suggesting that pharmacotherapy may be useful as an adjunct to behaviour approaches where there are problems with motivation and drive. Pharmacotherapy in brain injury, including the role of bromocriptine, is discussed elsewhere in this special edition.

Cognitive behaviour therapy

As already indicated, personal reactions, thoughts, and expectations can play a central role in the aetiology and maintenance of depression. These are not addressed directly by behaviour therapy, but are the primary target of the most commonly used approaches to the treatment of depression: cognitive therapy or cognitive behaviour therapy (CBT; Clark, Beck, & Alford, 1999).

CBT is derived from both the cognitive model of depression (Beck, 1970) and learning/behaviour theory. The cognitive model considers that people make sense of the world and plan and evaluate behaviour according to belief systems, derived from early experience and significant others. Individuals are held to have a set of "core beliefs" about themselves, others, and the world, that are operationalised as conditional assumptions, ("if–then" statements) or rules for living (Fennell, 1999). These conditional assumptions can be very helpful in some instances. For example, the assumption, "If I am to be worthwhile then I must be successful at work" might encourage one to work hard. While success at work is possible, the individual feels worthy. The potentially problematic core belief, "I am unworthy" is suppressed. But what if a person perceives that s/he has lately been less successful at work? Will the individual then believe that s/he is unworthy? In fact, where conditional assumptions are extreme and inflexible, they are termed "dysfunctional assumptions", as their very nature does indeed render the individual potentially vulnerable in circumstances where the rule is likely to be broken. When a critical incident, such as a brain injury occurs, the inability to keep up with the standards set up in the conditional assumptions activates the latent, possibly depressogenic core beliefs. These then trigger the production of "negative automatic thoughts" (NATs). This is the negative internal dialogue, or, self-talk associated with the unpleasant affect, behaviours and physiological responses that contribute to and maintain depression. Figure 1 illustrates the cognitive model of depression. As can be seen, the early experiences and underlying cognitions, together with the critical incident, interact to cause the complex maintenance cycle of NATs, behaviours, and mood. These have a bi-directional association with the environment (all possible interactions are not shown in this diagram).

Past Events & Predisposing Factors

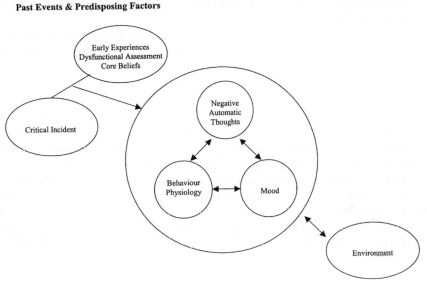

Figure 1.   The cognitive model of depression.

CBT aims to break into the negative cycle maintaining depression. It focuses on the here-and-now, rather than the past, and combines elements of cognitive theory and learning theory. A process of "functional analysis" attempts to provide an operational definition of problems, the related causal and mediating variables, the relationships between these variables, the identification of goals and the measurement and evaluation of change (Persons & Tompkins, 1997). The main goal of CBT is to help individuals, families or couples bring about effective coping and, by changing thinking and behaviour, improve mood. Intervention is driven by working hypotheses (formulations) developed jointly by patient and therapist from the assessment information. Change is brought about by a variety of possible interventions, including the practice of new behaviours, analysis of faulty thinking patterns, and learning more adaptive and rational self-talk skills. The reader is referred to Hawton, Salkovskis, Kirk, and Clark (1989) for a thorough review of CBT techniques for depression. What follows is a brief summary of some of the main tools (see Table 1).

Most treatments begin by socialising individuals into the cognitive model. This means, to explain the rationale behind the therapy and to demonstrate the links between thoughts, mood, behaviours, and physiology in a way that is meaningful for the client. The aim of this is to ensure the client understands the approach to therapy and to foster a sense of collaboration in therapy, between the client and therapist. Collaboration in therapy is deemed essential to engaging the client in CBT.

Behavioural strategies, for example activity scheduling, are then employed. The purpose of these is to monitor and generally increase the number of meaningful and enjoyable activities in which the person engages (House, 1992).

The next stage is typically negative automatic "thought catching" in order to explore the personal meaning of the brain injury and its consequences to the individual. This can be facilitated with Socratic questioning, and mood diaries are helpful for monitoring mood changes, their precipitants and consequences. Self-monitoring often increases awareness of depressive thoughts as they occur, for exploring how dysfunctional schema have built up over a lifetime and how they influence day-to-day thinking. The depressed person should be offered a forum in which to express and process grief reactions to the losses that have occurred.

Since depressed individuals are prone to distorted beliefs with regard to self, the world, and the future, the individual is taught how to examine the basis for the depressive thoughts by reality testing, selecting tasks which help test out the truth of depressive thoughts, and replacing the maladaptive thoughts with more constructive ones. This is termed cognitive restructuring.

Where individuals have suffered a catastrophic and life-changing event such as a brain injury, it may be useful to teach the individual alternative coping strategies. Examples of these include stress management, problem-solving skills, which are directed at increasing self-efficacy and helping the individual to move away from measuring themselves against their premorbid achievements, and to re-evaluate themselves in terms of their achievements post-injury (Ponsford, Sloan, & Snow, 1995).

Finally, the possibility of relapse is addressed and the likely scenarios where mood may deteriorate are generated. Possible management strategies for relapse prevention are learned and a blueprint (i.e., summary) of therapy is created, for use if relapse does occur.

Table 1 shows an example of a CBT treatment programme.

CBT and brain injury

CBT has an intuitive appeal in the management of depression following brain injury (1) it accommodates and seeks to tackle the many personal and social sequelae that may contribute to psychological morbidity both acutely and chronically, (2) it provides the therapist with a wide range of tools with which to work, and (3) is inherently flexible with the potential for accommodating differences in individual circumstances and limitations. However, despite its apparent potential, there is a paucity of research on the CBT in patients with brain injury. However, the few published studies provide enough supporting evidence for the use of CBT in depression in brain injury to justify further

TABLE 1
Example of a CBT treatment programme

Strategy	Aim
Assessment and formulation	Identification of goals for therapy and salient factors that may need to be addressed in intervention
Socialisation into CBT model	Engage client, increase collaboration
Behavioural activation	Increase activity and lift mood
Thought catching	Identify NATs, dysfunctional assumptions and core beliefs
Cognitive restructuring	To reduce/eliminate cognitive distortions
Problem solving and adaptive coping strategies	To increase client's sense of self-efficacy
Relapse management	To prepare client and foster a sense of independence

research and clinical trials (see Table 2). Lincoln, Flannaghan, Sutcliff, and Rother (1997) carried out a small uncontrolled study evaluating CBT in the treatment of post-stroke depression. Participants were recruited from a stroke register and depression was measured by the Beck Depression Inventory and Hospital Anxiety and Depression Scale. After a baseline period of 4 weeks, 19 individuals received an average of 8.4 sessions of CBT, including activity scheduling and cognitive restructuring. Although mean improvement was slight there were encouraging trends in the data. Cognitive strategies were reported to be harder to apply but individuals could identify negative automatic thoughts (NATs) and apply techniques to control them.

Another source of supportive evidence for the use of CBT in brain injury comes from the treatment of depression in individuals with multiple sclerosis (MS). Larcombe and Wilson (1984) found that just six weekly sessions of CBT was beneficial for the treatment of depression in MS, in comparison with a waiting list control condition, Mohr et al. (2001) compared individual CBT, supportive-expressive group therapy, and the antidepressant sertraline in 63 individuals with major depressive disorder. After 16 weeks, significant improvement was found in all groups, particularly those receiving CBT or sertraline.

Finally, Montgomery (1995) presented a brief case study of a 3rd year male college student who had suffered a basilar skull fracture. Deficits included fatigue, disturbed sleep, neck pain, and recurrent headaches. The diagnosis was adjustment disorder with depression. Assessment revealed that periods of relative disability were associated with fatigue and increased headaches, to which the patient responded with anger and depressive thinking. The intervention initially focused on reframing situations in order to reduce distracting and self-defeating cognitions. This was reported to be successful so that the patient became more receptive to activity scheduling, time management and relaxation

TABLE 2

Summary of research evidence for the use of cognitive and behavioural interventions for the treatment of depression in brain injury

Study	Study sample	N	Intervention	Results
Drummond and Walker, 1996	Stroke, at 6 months post-discharge	21 in each treatment group	Behavioural activation	Short-lived improvement in mobility and self-report ratings of well-being compared with waiting list controls. Depression unchanged
Teri et al., 1997	Alzeimer's disease	Total = 72	9 weekly sessions of BT, delivered either directly with clients or through their carers vs. typical care vs. waiting list control	Both groups showed improvements in depression, compared with controls, maintained at 6 month follow-up
Larcombe and Wilson, 1984	Multiple sclerosis	20	6 weekly sessions of CBT vs. waiting list control	Improvement in self- report depression scores, compared with controls, which was maintained at 1 month follow-up
Lincoln et al., 1997	Stroke	19	Average of 8.4 CBT sessions. No control group	Trend towards increased mobility
Mohr et al., 2001	Multiple sclerosis	63	16 weeks of individual CBT vs. supportive–expressive group therapy vs. sertraline	Improvements in all groups particularly CBT and sertraline
Montgomery, 1995	TBI	1	CBT	Decrease in negative thinking, improved coping strategies and ability to cope at college

strategies. Following treatment the patient was more able to cope at college, and reported a decreased frequency of dysfunctional thinking. Additionally, there was reduced stress, tension, fatigue, and less pain.

Delivering CBT to clients with brain injury

Assessment and formulation.   As indicated at the start of this paper, depression may present atypically in individuals with brain injury. There may also be overlap in the symptoms of brain injury and depression complicating diagnosis and management. For example, difficulties with expressing and understanding emotion may be due to a premorbid lack of psychological thinking, non-specific motor effects impairing the expression of emotion, or difficulties in the perception of emotion (House, 1992). Similarly, apathy, which is a decrease in goal-related activity because of diminished motivation, may be difficult to differentiated from the loss of interest found in depression (Marin, 1997).

Therefore, it is essential that the assessment and formulation is client-centred rather than rigidly applying diagnostic categories developed for a non-brain injured population. The information gained from the assessment can then be used to develop a formulation, or case conceptualisation, which is essentially a hypothetical map describing the presenting problems and factors involved in their aetiology and maintenance and which guides the intervention. This individual formulation should delineate the presenting problems, identify the extent of their impact on function and enable the intervention to be tailored according to the needs of the individual. It is important to recognise all the current problems that the patient is experiencing and information about precipitants and activating situations should be identified (Ponsford et al., 1995). It is also essential to consider pre-morbid factors, such as significant life-events that have occurred and how the individual coped with these. Finally, it is particularly important to try to identify the individual's appraisal of the brain injury, and the events surrounding it, so that core beliefs and dysfunctional assumptions can be accessed. The following list summarises the key features in the assessment and formulation of depression in individuals with brain injury:

- It should be client-centred.
- It should clearly delineate the presenting problems.
- It should identify the extent of their impact on function.
- It should identify precipitants and activating situations.
- It should consider pre-morbid factors.
- It should identify the individual's appraisal of the brain injury.

Neuropsychological testing can also play an important role. The assessment situation can provide a useful sample of behaviour and a way of assessing the client's response to challenges and possible failures, and their expectations and perceptions about their own performance. The definition of cognitive problems may also guide the most effective way of delivering therapy to maximise the chance of successful outcome.

Adapting CBT to accommodate cognitive problems. CBT is a highly structured therapy, with concrete goal-setting and an emphasis on working with specific behaviours and thoughts. Such a focused approach is essential where there are multiple complex difficulties as is general in most neurorehabilitation strategies. At the same time, however, CBT is a collaborative and dynamic approach enabling therapy to be adapted to suit cognitive limitations. Although there is some reason to suppose that CBT may be a useful approach to therapy in brain injury, however, as yet, evidence showing exactly how CBT can be/has been adapted to accommodate cognitive limitations is scarce. The next few sections contain some ideas addressing these issues, although there is a need for future work to establish the efficacy and effectiveness of these strategies.

Where memory is impaired, memory aids such as written summaries and cue cards can easily be incorporated (Ponsford et al., 1995), and in some cases it may be helpful for the patient to have an audiotape of the sessions. If concentration and attention are particularly impaired, it may be beneficial to shorten the length of each session and perhaps increase the frequency of sessions.

Therapeutic techniques such as summarising, ordinarily used to show empathy, may be used to refocus the individual who is tangential within a conversation. Additionally it is sometimes advantageous, as in more general neurorehabilitation, to involve a family member to act as a memory prompter between sessions or to assist the individual to carry out homework tasks. At times the therapist may need to be more directive, particularly in clients with dysexecutive syndrome, characterised by deficits in planning and organisation and problem solving.

A potential limitation to the delivery of CBT is the presence of deficits in verbal skills and communication difficulties. This may limit the scope of treatment and restrict attention to the more concrete and accessible techniques of CBT such as behavioural activation and thought-catching.

Finally, as with behaviour therapy, motivation may be a key limiting factor. During the initial period of therapy it is important to spend time building a therapeutic alliance, particularly where the client has had their brain injury for a number of years and has grown tired of the hospital system, or feels particularly hopeless about the possibility of future change.

The following list is a summary of useful techniques which aid the delivery of CBT in the context of cognitive difficulties:

- Use memory aids—written notes, cue cards, audio tapes.
- Shorten the length of individual sessions.
- Increase frequency of sessions.

- Involve a family member/close friend to help remind/reinforce therapy strategies and to assist with homeworks—e.g., behavioural activation.
- Use techniques such as summarising, or even agreeing hand signals, to refocus tangential clients.

Developing insight.   Clinical experience suggests that individuals and their carers often find it extremely difficult to grasp the consequences of brain injury, particularly some of the more subtle but still disabling cognitive and emotional changes (House, 1992). As already noted, some individuals may have unrealistic expectations of themselves and then experience failure. Others, particularly those without significant physical difficulties, may find that they have to live with the unrealistic expectations of others. Families may find the behaviour of their brain-injured relative bewildering and frustrating, and may even consider that their injured relative is being wilfully difficult.

Clear information about the physical, emotional, and behavioural consequences of the individual's brain injury and mood disturbances is a vital component of therapy and should be provided for both the patient and carers. Information can be presented in a variety of media, and charitable organisations often offer a wide range of information leaflets, and organise meetings. These may help to normalise the situation and help to reduce a possible sense of alienation. However, research in the field of chronic disease suggests that education simply about the pathophysiology of the disease is not enough by itself to facilitate an improvement in symptoms, and may even be associated with a short-term worsening of mood (e.g., Godfrey, Partridge, Knight, & Bishara, 1993; Wallace & Bogner, 2000). Increasing insight may be associated with depression as the client develops a more accurate, but sometimes more pessimistic, view of the likely future and chance of recovery. The issue of insight in brain injury is tackled elsewhere in this special edition.

Finally, education about the treatment itself is also important (Mazzuca, 1982), and CBT theory requires that the patient should be socialised into the model with the links between cognitions and affect being clearly demonstrated by the therapist. In non-brain injured clients, failure to understand and assimilate the basic cognitive model is associated with poor outcome to therapy. This may limit the applicability of CBT in some individuals with brain injury unless novel ways can be found to teach the basis of the cognitive model.

Conclusions and future questions

Various articles in the present volume are evidence of the growing interest in the management of psychological problems following brain injury. More specifically, there is a growing demand for empirical evidence to guide the delivery of CBT to the range of emotional problems seen in brain injury, including anxiety disorders and anger as well as depression. The development of holistic approaches to brain injury rehabilitation (e.g., Wilson, 1997), is consistent with the idea of addressing the issue of emotional functioning. However, while there have been many advances in the neuroscience of emotions and their disorder, this understanding has had little impact on the area of rehabilitation of brain injury. There are some indications that CBT may well be valuable in the treatment of depression in brain injury. Additionally, evidence implies that successful treatment of depression in brain injury may improve outcome from a neuropsychological perspective. However to date, no large studies have been carried out to establish an evidence base. At a practical level we need to determine the relative efficacies of different psycho-therapeutic approaches, in different patient groups and at different phases of recovery. We need to establish which components of effective therapies are responsible and their optimum modes of delivery. Given the scarcity of CBT therapists it is also important to determine the indicators of successful outcome, as well as ways of broadening access to other currently difficult to treat client groups.

REFERENCES

al-Adawi, S., Powell, J. H., & Greenwood, R. J. (1998). Motivational deficits after brain injury: A neuropsychological approach using new assessment techniques. *Neuropsychology, 12*, 115–124.

Angst, J. (1996). Comorbidity of mood disorders: A longitudinal prospective study. *British Journal of Psychiatry—Supplement, 30*, 31–37.

Asikainen, I., Kaste, M., & Sarna, S. (1996). Patients with traumatic brain injury referred to a rehabilitation and re-employment programme: Social and professional outcome for 508 Finnish patients 5 or more years after injury. *Brain Injury, 10*, 883–899.

Asvall, J. E. (2001). Can we turn the table on depression? In A. Tylee (Ed.), *Depression: Social and economic timebomb: Strategies for quality care: Proceedings of an international meeting organised by the World Health Organisation in collaboration with the international federation of health funds, Harvard Medical School and the Sir Robert Mond Memorial Trust.* London: BMJ Publishing Group.

Beck, A. T. (1970). Cognitive therapy: Nature and relation to behavior therapy. *Behaviour Therapy, 1*, 184–200.

Bellus, S. B., Kost, P. P., Vergo, J. G., & Dinezza, G. J. (1998). Improvements in cognitive functioning following intensive behavioural rehabilitation. *Brain Injury, 12*, 139–145.

Bernstein, D. M., & de Ruiter, S. W. (2000). The influence of motivation on neurocognitive performance long after traumatic brain injury. *Brain and Cognition, 44*, 50–66.

Bowen, A., Chamberlain, M. A., Tennant, A., Neumann, V., & Conner, M. (1999). The persistence of mood disorders following traumatic brain injury: A 1 year follow-up. *Brain Injury, 13*, 547–553.

Brotherton, F. A., Thomas, L. L., Wisotzek, I. E., & Milan, M. A. (1988). Social skills training in the rehabilitation of patients with traumatic closed head injury. *Archives of Physical Medicine & Rehabilitation, 69*, 827–832.

Brown, R., Scott, L., & Bench, C. (1994). Cognitive function in depression, its relationship to the presence and severity of intellectual decline. *Psychological Medicine, 24*, 829–847.

Burghleigh, S. A., Farber, R. S., & Gillard, M. (1998). Community integration and life satisfaction after traumatic brain injury: Long-term findings. *American Journal of Occupational Therapy*, *52*, 45–52.

Chisholm, D. (2001). The economic consequences of depression. In A. Tylee (Ed.), *Depression: Social and economic timebomb: Strategies for quality care: Proceedings of an international meeting organised by the World Health Organisation in collaboration with the international federation of health funds, Harvard Medical School and the Sir Robert Mond Memorial Trust.* London: BMJ Publishing Group.

Clark, D. A., Beck, A. T., & Alford, B. A. (1999). *Scientific foundations of cognitive theory and therapy of depression.* New York: Wiley.

Coyne, J. C., Pepper, C. M., & Flynn, H. (1999). Significance of prior episodes of depression in two patient populations. *Journal of Consulting & Clinical Psychology*, *67*, 76–81.

Curran, C. A., Ponsford, J. L., & Crowe, S. (2000). Coping strategies and emotional outcome following traumatic brain injury: A comparison with orthopedic patients. *Journal of Head Trauma Rehabilitation*, *15*, 1256–1274.

Davis, G. R., Armstrong, H. E., Donovan, D. M., & Temkin, N. R. (1984). Cognitive–behavioral treatment of depressed affect among epileptics: Preliminary findings. *Journal of Clinical Psychology*, *40*, 930–935.

Drummond, A., & Walker, M. (1996). Generalisation of the effects of leisure rehabilitation for stroke patients. *British Journal of Occupational Therapy*, *59*, 330–334.

Fann, J. R., Uomoto, J. M., & Katon, W. J. (2001). Cognitive improvement with treatment of depression following mild traumatic brain injury, *Psychosomatics*, *42*, 48–54.

Fennell, M. (1999) *Overcoming low self-esteem—a self-help guide using cognitive behavioral techniques*. London: Robinson Publishing.

Finset, A., & Andersson, S. (2000). Coping strategies in patients with acquired brain injury: Relationships between coping, apathy, depression and lesion location. *Brain Injury*, *14*, 887–905.

Fleming, J. M., Strong, J., & Ashton, R. (1998). Cluster analysis of self-awareness levels in adults with traumatic brain injury and relationship to outcome. *Journal of Head Trauma Rehabilitation*, *13*, 39–51.

Godfrey, H. P. D., Partridge, F. M., Knight, R. G., & Bishara, S. (1993). Course of insight disorder and emotional dysfunction following closed head injury: A controlled cross-sectional follow-up study. *Journal of Clinical & Experimental Neuropsychology*, *15*, 503–515.

Guth, P. E. (2000). The effects of depression in head injured adults as related to educational level, gender, and activity level. *Dissertation Abstracts International: Section B: the Sciences & Engineering*, *61*, 1803, US: Univ Microfilms International.

Hawton, K., Salkovskis, P. M., Kirk, J., & Clark, D. M. (1989). *Cognitive behaviour therapy for psychiatric problems: A practical guide*. Oxford: Oxford Medical Publications.

Hoofien, D., Gilboa, A., Vakil, E., & Donovick, P. J. (2001). Traumatic brain injury (TBI) 10–20 years later: A comprehensive outcome study of psychiatric symptomatology, cognitive abilities and psychosocial functioning. *Brain Injury*, *15*, 189–209.

House, A. (1992). Management of mood disorder in adults with brain damage: Can we improve what psychiatry has to offer? In K. Hawton, & P. J. Cowen (Eds.), *Practical problems in clinical psychiatry* (pp. 51–62). New York: Oxford University Press.

Jacobson, N. S., Dobson, K. S., Traux, P. A., Addis, M. E., Koerner, K., Gollan, J. K., Gortner, E., & Prince, S. E. (1996). A component analysis of cognitive–behavioural treatment for depression. *Journal of Consulting & Clinical Psychology*, *64*, 295–304.

Jean-Bay, E. (2000). The biobehavioral correlates of post-traumatic brain injury depression. *Journal of Neuroscience Nursing*, *32*, 169–176.

Kersel, D. A., Marsh, N. V., Havill, J. H., & Sleigh, J. W. (2001). Psychosocial functioning during the year following severe traumatic brain injury. *Brain Injury*, *15*, 683–696.

Kreutzer, J. S., Seel, R. T., & Gourley, E. (2001). The prevalence and symptom rates of depression after traumatic brain injury: A comprehensive examination. *Brain Injury*, *15*, 563–576.

Larcombe, N. A., & Wilson, P. H. (1984). An evaluation of cognitive behaviour therapy for depression in patients with multiple sclerosis. *British Journal of Psychiatry*, *145*, 366–371.

Leung, M. (1997). Post stroke depression: An investigation into the relationship between epidemiological data, neuroanatomical correlates and intellectual abilities as well as subjective ratings of own impairment and disability: Unpublished Psych D thesis, University of Surrey. Cited in A. Skelly (Ed.) (2002). *Clinical Psychology*, *10*, 2002. Psychological effect of stroke and the repertory grid.

Lewinsohn, P. M. (1974). A behavioural approach to depression. In R. J. Friedman & M. M. Katz (Eds.), *The psychology of depression: Contemporary theory of research*. Washington DC: Winston.

Lincoln, N. B., Flannaghan, T., Sutcliff, L., & Rother, L. (1997). Evaluation of cognitive behavioural treatment for depression after stroke: A pilot study. *Clinical Rehabilitation*, *11*, 114–122.

Linn, R. T., Allen, K., & Willer, B. S. (1994). Affective symptoms in the chronic stage of traumatic brain injury: A study of married couples. *Brain Injury*, *8*, 135–147.

Lishman, W. A. (1987). *Organic psychiatry, second edition*. Oxford: Blackwell Scientific Publications.

Malia, K., Powell, J., & Torode, S. (1995). Coping and psychosocial function after brain injury. *Brain Injury*, *9*, 607–618.

Marin, R. S. (1997). Differential diagnosis of apathy and related disorders of diminished motivation. *Psychiatric Annals*, *27*, 30–33.

Mazzuca, S. A. (1982). Does patient education in chronic disease have therapeutic value? *Journal of Chronic Diseases*, *35*, 521–529.

Mohr, D. C., Boudewyn, A. C., Goodkin, D. E., Bostrom, A., & Epstein, L. (2001). Comparative outcomes for individual cognitive–behavior therapy, supportive–expressive group psychotherapy, and sertraline for the treatment of depression in multiple sclerosis. *Journal of Consulting & Clinical Psychology*, *69*, 942–949.

Montgomery, G. K. (1995). A multi-factor account of disability after brain injury: Implications for neuropsychological counselling. *Brain Injury*, *9*, 453–469.

Moore, A. D., & Stambrook, M. (1995). Cognitive moderators of outcome following traumatic brain injury: A conceptual model and implications for rehabilitation. *Brain Injury*, *9*, 109–130.

Morton, M. V., & Wehman, P. (1995). Psychosocial and emotional sequelae of individuals with traumatic brain injury: A literature review and recommendations. *Brain Injury*, *9*, 81–92.

Ohayon, M. M., Priest, R. G., Guilleminault, C., & Caulet, M. (1999). The prevalence of depressive disorders in the United Kingdom. *Biological Psychiatry*, *45*, 300–307.

Ownsworth, T. L., & Oei, T. P. (1998). Depression after traumatic brain injury: Conceptualization and treatment considerations. *Brain Injury*, *12*, 735–751.

Parikh, R. M., Robinson, R. G., Lipsey, J. R., Starkstein, S. E., Fedoroff, J. P., & Price, T. R. (1990). The impact of poststroke depression on recovery in activities of daily living over a 2-year follow-up. *Archives of Neurology*, *47*, 785–789.

Perino, C., Rago, R., Cicolini, A., Torta, R., & Monaco, F. (2001). Mood and behavioural disorders following traumatic brain injury: Clinical evaluation and pharmacological management. *Brain Injury*, *15*, 139–148.

Persons, J. B., & Tompkins, M. A. (1997). Cognitive-behavioral case formulation. In T. D. Eells (Ed.), *Handbook of psychotherapy case formulation*. New York: The Guildford Press.

Piccinelli, M., & Wilkinson, G. (1994). Outcome of depression in psychiatric settings. *British Journal of Psychiatry*, *164*, 297–304.

Pohjasvaara, T., Vataja, R., Leppavuori, A., Kaste, M., & Erkinjuntti, T. (2001). Depression is an independent predictor of poor long-term functional outcome post-stroke. *European Journal of Neurology*, *8*, 315–319.

Ponsford, J. L., Sloan, S., & Snow, P. (1995). *Traumatic brain injury: Rehabilitation for everyday adaptive living*. Hove, UK: Psychology Press.

Raskin, S. A., & Stein, P. N. (2000). Depression. In S. A. Raskin (Ed.), Mateer, NY: Oxford University Press.

Reischies, F. M., & Neu, P. (2000). Comorbidity of mild cognitive disorder and depression—a neuropsychological analysis. *European Archives of Psychiatry and Clinical Neuroscience, 250*, 186–193.

Rosenthal, T. L., & Meyer, V. (1971). Case report: Behavioural treatment of clinical abulia. *Conditional Reflex, 6*, 22–29.

Sandin, K. J., Cifu, D. X., & Noll, S. F. (1994). Stroke rehabilitation: IV. Psychological and social implications. *Archives of Physical Medical Rehabilitation, 75*, 52–55.

Satz, P., Forney, D. L., Zaucha, K., Asarnow, R. R., Light, R., McCleary, C., Levin, H., Kelly, D., Bergsneider, M., Hovda, D., Martin, N., Namerow, N., & Becker, D. (1998). Depression, cognition, and functional correlates of recovery outcome after traumatic brain injury. *Brain Injury, 12*, 537–553.

Schlund, M. W., & Pace, G. (1999). Relations between traumatic brain injury and the environment: Feedback reduces maladaptive behaviour by three persons with traumatic brain injury. *Brain Injury, 13*, 889–897.

Tate, R. L., & Broe, G. A. (1999). Psychosocial adjustment after traumatic brain injury: What are the important variables? *Psychological Medicine, 29*, 713–725.

Tennant, A., Macdermott, N., & Neary, D. (1995). The long-term outcome of head injury: Implications for service planning. *Brain Injury, 9*, 595–605.

Teri, L., Logsdon, R. G., Umoto, J., & McCurry, S. M. (1997). Behavioural treatment of depression in dementia patients: A controlled trial. *Journal of Gerontology, 52B*, 159–166.

Wallace, C. A. (2000). Unawareness of deficits: Emotional implications for patients and significant others. *Dissertation Abstracts International: Section B: the Sciences & Engineering, 60*, 4257, US: Univ Microfilms International.

Wallace, C. A., & Bogner, J. (2000). Awareness of deficits: Emotional implications for persons with brain injury and their significant others. *Brain Injury, 14*, 549–562.

Watkins, E., & Brown, R. G. (2002). The effects of induced rumination on the suppression of habitual responses in depression. *Journal of Neurology, Neurosurgery and Psychiatry, 72*, 400–402.

Weddell, R., Oddy, M., & Jenkins, D. (1980). Social adjustment after rehabilitation: A two year follow–up of patients with severe head injury. *Psychological Medicine, 10*, 257–263.

Wilson, B. A. (1997). Cognitive rehabilitation: How it is and how it might be. *Journal of the International Neuropsychological Society, 3*, 487–496.

Wood, R. L., & McMillan, T. (2000.). *Neurobehavioural disabilities and social handicap following traumatic brain injury*. Hove, UK: Psychology Press.

The relevance of emotional
and psychosocial factors
in aphasia to rehabilitation

Chris Code[1,2] and Manfred Herrmann[3]

[1]Department of Psychology, University of Exeter, England,
[2]School of Communication Sciences and Disorders,
University of Sydney, Australia, and
[3]Centre for Cognitive Sciences, University of Bremen, Germany

In this paper we review the relationship between the impact of aphasia and emotional well-being. Depression is one of several types of emotional response that has been researched most and we examine the different causes of depression for people with aphasia. We discuss the relationships between recovery and emotional state and the clinical and psychosocial implications of these relationships. We examine methods for assessment of emotional response and psychosocial evaluation and review implications for rehabilitation. We discuss briefly issues of drug treatment for depression in aphasic people. We conclude that the emotional impact of aphasia can have a marked negative impact on recovery, response to rehabilitation, and psychosocial adjustment.

INTRODUCTION

This paper examines what we know about the causes of emotional and psychosocial change for people with aphasia, how they impact on recovery and how an improved understanding is being incorporated into rehabilitation.

Left and/or right hemisphere brain damage can have a wide range of effects on communication, and it is not the aim of this paper to review these. We can note, however, that stroke, traumatic brain injury and progressive neurological and neuropsychological deterioration of various kinds, can cause impairments

---

Correspondence should be addressed to Chris Code, PhD, School of Psychology, Washington Singer Laboratories, Exeter University, Perry Road, Exeter, EX4 4QG, UK. Tel: ++ 44 (0) 1392 264642, Fax: ++ 44 (0) 1392 264623, Email: c.f.s.code@exeter.ac.uk

This paper was completed while the first author was a Fellow at the Hause Institute for Advanced Study, Delmenhorst, Germany.

---

and disabilities in speech and voice production and perception and language processing. However, very little research has been conducted into the relationship between emotional and psychosocial factors and communication problems in this wide range of conditions, or the probable impact of these problems on recovery or response to rehabilitation. An exception is aphasia where research has been carried out into its emotional and psychosocial impact and has addressed the difficulties of assessment within a context of impaired language. This research has concentrated mainly on the relationship between depression and the site and nature of brain damage, but also on "reactive" depression in people with aphasia and in their relatives. Progress has been made too in efforts to address issues of adjustment in more chronically disabled aphasic people, using mainly psychosocial approaches. Therefore, we limit our discussion in this paper to the area of aphasia.

Aphasia can affect all modalities of language processing; expression and comprehension of speech, reading and writing, gesture and pantomime. It can be relatively mild, where the individual might have a word-finding difficulty to global where all modalities are severely impaired producing a significant disability. Aphasia can result from cerebrovascular accident (CVA), mainly to the left hemisphere, and progressive disorders like Altzeimer's disease and Parkinson's disease. Traumatic brain injury (TBI) too can cause aphasia, although the language processing difficulties following TBI most often affect the pragmatic and social uses of language (McDonald, Togher, & Code, 1999), mainly because of the pathodynamics and the primarily frontal nature of the brain damage, at least in road traffic accidents as the major cause of TBI.

Aphasia is a cognitive disorder; it results from damage to the architecture supporting the cognitive system, and a major research effort has focused on the examination of the nature of the processing deficits. However, there is a growing interest in the impact of aphasia on the social use of language, and the reintegration of aphasic people into community life. The importance of intact communication in the development and maintenance of social relationships and roles is well established. Most of our happiness and sadness comes from our interactions with others, whether directly or indirectly, and how we perceive this is what determines the quality of our life experiences. Our psychosocial life is grounded in our emotional experience within a social context (Code, Hemsley, & Herrmann, 1999). Emotional experience essentially defines our existence; it is what makes us human, and our personal sense of well-being emerges from our current experience of life (Campbell, 1976).

Our understanding of what causes the emotional changes that aphasic people often show, how to assess them and how these impact on language recovery and psychosocial reintegration is improving. This paper aims to present an overview of our current understanding. We discuss emotional and psychosocial issues separately, although, as implied above, the relationship between them is causal. We first examine the emotional impact of aphasia.

EMOTIONAL RESPONSES TO APHASIA

Aphasia following stroke impacts significantly on emotional state. The range of emotional reactions that can accompany aphasia were reviewed by Starkstein and Robinson (1988) and these are adapted and outlined in Table 1. There is a wide range of emotional reactions covering nearly the whole field of neuropsychiatric disorders although the interpretation of the pathodynamics differs widely in people engaged in aphasia rehabilitation. Positive emotional symptoms (e.g., mania, delirium) and negative symptoms (e.g., depression, anxiety, loss of interest) are often observed in aphasic people.

The experience of aphasia brings with it a sudden and catastrophic inability to function in many of the activities of everyday life; cognitive, behavioural,

TABLE 1
Abnormal positive and negative emotional states accompanying aphasia (adapted from and based on Starkstein & Robinson, 1988)

Abnormal emotional responses	Authors
Negative responses	
Generalised anxiety disorders	Robinson, et al., 1984a
Depression	Robinson, et al., 1984a; Sinyor et al., 1986b; Robinson, et al., 1987; Starkstein, Robinson & Price, 1987
Pathological crying	Andersen, 1997
Paranoid states	Benson, 1979
Psychotic states	Peroutka, et al., 1982; Price & Mesulam, 1985; Berthier & Starkstein, 1987
Obsessional disorders	Laplane, Baulac, Windlocher, & Dubois, 1984
Positive responses	
Manic syndromes	Starkstein, Pearlson, Boston & Robinson, 1987; Robinson, Bolduc & Price, 1987
Delirium	Mesulam, Waxman, Geschwind, & Sabin, 1976
Aprosodic states characterised by an inability to express and/or comprehend emotional intonation	Heilman, Scholes, & Watson, 1975; Ross, 1981
Apathetic states characterised by undue cheerfulness but with a loss of drive or motivation	Damasio & Van Hoesen, 1983
Disorders associated with an inability to recognise events, objects and states, such as denial, neglect, anosognosia	Cutting, 1978; Gainotti, 1972; Heilman, 1979;

leisure, occupational, social, and family activities are affected. Depression is a frequent reaction for both the person with aphasia as well as for those close to them. In fact, depression is the most widely investigated mood state accompanying brain damage, and the main focus of this paper. Severe depression is more than a transient unhappiness and manifests as a lasting decline in normal mood. It extinguishes joy, laughter, empathy, happiness and love; it impacts on contact with the outside world, leaving the individual alone and isolated (Browning, 1995). However, what causes depression following brain damage is still a matter for ongoing controversy.

Depression following stroke

Other papers in this Special Issue focus on various aspects of the organic and reactive causes of depression in neurological conditions (see Fleminger, Oliver, Williams, & Evans, this volume; Williams, Evans, & Fleminger, this volume; and Khan-Bourne & Brown, this volume). Post-stroke depression (PSD), is defined by the presence of clinically significant depressive state, as, for example, defined and diagnosed by the *Diagnostic and Statistical Manual of Mental Disorders* (*DSM*) of which the current version is the DSM-IV (American Psychiatric Association, 1994).

Most studies agree that PSD is very common, although the reported figures vary from 50–60% (Lipsey et al., 1985; Starkstein & Robinson, 1988) to 5–11% (House et al., 1990). This is at least partially due to the complexity of comparing studies, each using different sample selection criteria, operationalisation of emotional-mood disorders, as well as different ways of measuring depression (Herrmann & Wallesch, 1993).

When depression is present it very often persists in stroke survivors well into chronic stages. Åstrom, Adolfsson, and Asplund (1993) found major depression in 25% of stroke survivors during acute stages which rose to 31% at three months post-stroke. Clinically significant depression reduced to 16% at 12 , but increased again over the next two years to 29%; a level higher than at 3 months post-onset. At this time, reduced life satisfaction and reduced involvement in activities of daily living were present. However, PSD appears to have more than one possible cause.

Causes of depression in aphasia.   People with aphasia can be faced with depression, communicative and social isolation, and reduced involvement in everyday living and leisure activities (Code, submitted; Code & Muller, 1992; Friedland & McColl, 1987; Gainotti, 1997; Herrmann & Wallesch, 1989; Taylor Sarno, 1993, 1997). There is now converging evidence that emotional disorders can be directly caused by the nature, severity and site of brain damage, affecting the neuronal processes and neurobiochemical pathways underlying normal emotion (Starkstein & Robinson, 1988), but depression has also been characterised as a natural and reactive response to physical impairment and disturbances in communication functions (Fisher, 1961; Tanner, 1980; Tanner & Gerstenberger, 1988).

A range of studies suggest an organic aetiology for PSD (Beblo, Wallesch, & Herrmann, 1999a; Finkelstein et al., 1982; Folstein, Maiberger, & McHugh, 1977; Herrmann, Bartels, & Wallesch, 1993; Herrmann, Bartels, Schumacher, & Wallasch, 1995; Robinson et al., 1984a; Robinson & Price, 1982; Sinyor et al., 1986b). Robinson and Benson (1981) compared fluent, non-fluent and global aphasic speakers with matched controls on physical and cognitive impairments, several months post-brain damage and found that non-fluent aphasic speakers with more frontal damage had a significantly higher frequency and severity of depression. Degree of depression was not found to increase with increasing severity of cognitive impairment, so results were not attributable to awareness of disability, but rather suggested that the site of the lesion was the cause (Starkstein & Robinson, 1988).

Studies have also found a significant positive correlation between adjacency of left hemisphere lesions to the frontal pole and increasing frequency and severity of depression. Conversely, euphoric reaction, or abnormally positive affect, has been linked with more posterior, and right hemisphere lesions (Finkelstein et al., 1982; Sinyor et al., 1986b; Starkstein & Robinson, 1988). Other studies found depressive disorders after stroke significantly associated with lesions to left basal ganglia structures (Beblo et al., 1999a; Herrmann et al., 1993, 1995; Lauterbach et al., 1997) and the "left frontal lobe" hypothesis of PSD was interpreted as an epiphenomenon of the underlying vascular pathology. However, there are some limitations to the research concerning the neurobiochemical background of PSD and in the ways that depression is assessed in aphasic people (Stern, 1999). The problems of assessment of depression in aphasic speakers is discussed further later.

Lipsey, Spencer, Rabins, and Robinson (1986) showed that symptom clusters noted in the DSMIII-R were almost identical for patients suffering from PSD and functional or reactive depression without neurological damage. Criteria for diagnosis, however, specifically suggest that organic factors should not initiate or maintain the disturbance. However, the validity of using DSM criterion to identify PSD has been challenged because changes in levels of energy, weight, appetite and sleeping patterns following stroke can result from other neurological and neuropsychological deficits associated with stroke as well as depression (Herrmann & Wallesch, 1993). In addition, and importantly, neurological impairments can affect the expression of emotion through facial expression, motor speech and prosody, erroneously suggesting the presence of depression (Code & Muller, 1992; see Stern, 1999, and paper 3 in this Special Issue for fuller discussion of these issues). Research indicates that clinicians may not be very good at judging mood state and their interpretations of the mood of the people they work with often do not coincide with the individual's own internal mood state (Egelko et al., 1988; Stern & Bachman, 1994). In fact, in a study by Stern and Bachman (1994), the clinicians (i.e., neurologists, neurology nurses, neuropsychologists) based their interpretation, in large part, on the outward affective expression and on neurobehavioural signs and symptoms, such as emotional lability and motor slowing. However, taken together, there is good evidence that depression in an aphasic individual, at least in the post-acute stage, can have an organic basis.

A model of depression in aphasia.   It appears that a range of factors are involved in determining presence of depression in aphasic people, and that causation may vary as a function of progress through different phases of recovery (Gainotti, 1997; Herrmann, Bartels, & Wallesch, 1993; Herrmann & Wallesch, 1993). Depression in the acute stage appears to be most related to site of lesion for many, rather than degree of cognitive and physical impairment or quality of psychosocial support (Robinson, Bolduc, & Price, 1987). In the 6 months following stroke, however, the relationship between depression and cognitive and physical impairment increases to become almost as significant as lesion location (Robinson et al., 1984b). So while the presence of post-stroke depression depends to a large extent on the location of the lesion, there is an important interaction between impairment and depression (Starkstein & Robinson, 1988, p. 13).

Research suggests that depression can also emerge in stroke survivors as a reactive form. These have been termed *primary* and *secondary*, respectively. Herrmann and his colleagues (Herrmann & Wallesch, 1993) have added a third separate form *tertiary*; each appear to be related to different stages of recovery and rehabilitation. These terms "primary", "secondary", and "tertiary", however, mainly reflect the time of occurrence of depression in aphasia treatment and rehabilitation and do not necessarily indicate the pathophysiological basis of the type of depression. The relationship between them is illustrated in Figure 1.

On this model "primary depression" characterises the acute stage (0–3 months post-stroke) resulting directly from the brain damage. It is caused by structural lesions leading to neurobiochemical changes, although pre-morbid disposition to depression (psychiatric history, alcohol abuse, dementia), site of lesion, and configuration of lesion also contribute. People with middle cerebral artery infarction (causing damage to the major part of the frontal lobe and basal ganglia) appear to be especially vulnerable. During the acute period, there is apparently only a minor relationship between natural emotional reactions to loss and degree of depression.

As time passes, however, a reactive or secondary depression to psycho-social, neuropsychological and functional impairment and disability may develop, usually within the first six months of the chronic stages. Lazarus (1993) proposed that people react to particular negative life events through a

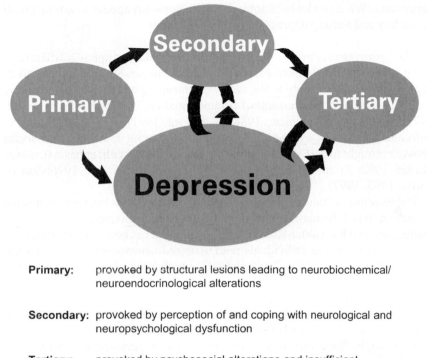

Primary: provoked by structural lesions leading to neurobiochemical/ neuroendocrinological alterations

Secondary: provoked by perception of and coping with neurological and neuropsychological dysfunction

Tertiary: provoked by psychosocial alterations and insufficient coping strategies

Figure 1. A model of different periods after brain lesions where patients seemed to be especially vulnerable to develop depression (modified from Herrmann & Wallesch, 1993).

subjective interpretation and evaluation of the event and its meaning for them. Herrmann and Wallesch suggest that there are two types of people specifically at risk for secondary reactive depression: those who "denied the consequences of stroke in the initial period and are now confronted with the whole spectrum of their functional, neurological and neuropsychological disabilities, or, those who primarily hoped for rapid restitution and reintegration and now realise that they may suffer from their disabilities for a long period of time" (Herrmann & Wallesch, 1993; p. 62).

On Herrmann and Wallesch's model, a "tertiary" depression can emerge during the transition from in-patient to out-patient. This may develop as people and their relatives begin to realise the psychosocial implications of their disabilities when they attempt to reintegrate into their pre-stroke social structure. The individual's social role changes from that of "patient" to "disabled" with all its negative connotations (Herrmann & Wallesch, 1993; p. 63). This role change may cause tertiary depression, or increase already existing depression. We consider next some of the factors that appear to interact with secondary and tertiary depression in aphasic people.

The "grieving process".   People respond to stroke and aphasia differently, and it is important to focus on each individual as unique. Severity of "reactive" depression relates strongly to the value and meaning attached to language by the individual in their pre-morbid occupational and familial roles (Benson, 1973; Starkstein & Robinson, 1988; Wahrborg, 1991). Also contributing to individual responses will be the coping style, coping resources and social network brought to bare when readjusting to, and living with, aphasia (Code & Muller, 1992; Friedland & McColl, 1987; Hemsley & Code, 1996; Taylor Sarno, 1993, 1997).

The response of aphasic people to secondary depression has been examined in the context of the classic grief model developed to characterise reaction to losing a loved one (Kubler-Ross, 1969). This model has been widely applied in many areas, including individuals with acquired neurogenic communication disorder (Tanner, 1980; Tanner & Gerstenberger, 1988). Tanner and Gerstenberger describe grieving as a natural and expected reaction for the individual faced with loss which they describe as a "complex progression of emotional and intellectual adjustments to separation from something or someone valued" (Tanner & Gerstenberger, 1988; p. 80).

They apply three dimensions of loss to the experience of people with aphasia. These are loss and separation involving person, self and object. These dimensions of loss are viewed symbolically; providing meaning associated with the losses experienced. Symbolic representations of loss include loss of role, prestige and identity, and are unique to each individual (Tanner & Gerstenberger, 1988).

Loss of person results from separation of the aphasic person from immediate family or social and community networks resulting in psychological isolation and is a consequence of reduced abilities to take part in verbal communication with those close to you. A *loss of self* results from the perception that some feature of physical or psychological integrity has been lost. This can result from loss of self as a communicator where there may be a realisation of differences in pre- and post-stroke abilities, which is confounded by contrasting self with others in functional, social, and occupational tasks (Brumfitt, 1993). *Loss of object* entails loss of use or ownership of significant possessions related directly to disability, such as loss of a job, an income, a hobby or an interest.

The grieving process is described as a series of stages—denial, anger, bargaining, depression, and acceptance which, according to the model, necessarily occur in the same order and reflect different psychodynamic properties of the grieving process. Acceptance is an end stage, reached when the process is worked through positively and successfully. It is reached when the person is emotionally removed from loss, accepting the way things are, given the limitations imposed by their disabilities. The non-organic form of denial conceived in the model may involve complete or partial lack of awareness of the presence, severity or permanence of aphasia. It is seen as acting as a psychological buffer between the self and reality, involving avoidance until disabilities can be more easily faced and dealt with. The next stages are anger and bargaining and Tanner and Gerstenberger (1988) suggest that frustration may manifest as anger or bargaining with health professionals, with some deity, or with self. In contrast to denial, frustration is caused by full awareness of disability and the feeling of powerlessness to significantly change the course of events and a distressing reality.

As awareness of the nature and permanence of deficits increases, a majority of people will experience a (secondary) depression, emerging from the full realisation of the value of the losses of person, self and object. As noted above, this reaction may last for weeks or months, but on the model can become fixated within the individual for years. The model sees depression as a necessary stage of emotional recovery that must be worked through successfully before acceptance can be achieved.

The model might explain some of the emotional and psychosocial fallout from aphasia, but researchers have noted that it falls short when explaining emotional disorders associated with lesions to the central nervous system. One problem critics have is that the grieving process is seen in static "stages", failing to reflect the dynamic nature of emotional response to aphasia (Gordon, Hibbard, & Morganstein, 1988; Jackson, 1988). Clinically significant depressive states often occur in the very early stage after stroke with aphasia, as noted above, and there is little evidence that they necessarely follow a psychodynamic line of coping as proposed by Tanner and Gerstenberger. Furthermore, stages like denial or anger do not inevitably occur as part of a grieving process, but might reflect independent neuropsychological or neuropsychiatric disorders associated with stroke (e.g., anosognosia or anosodiaphoria). While the stages of grief—denial, anger, depression, etc., are emotions that brain-damaged people experience, it is far from transparent that these reactions are inevitable, occur in stages, or are sequentially related to each other. The model was not developed for brain damage and aphasia and it is unable to deal with the observation that the same emotional states can also have neurobiological causes.

Herrmann and Wallesch (1993) suggests that we may be able to distinguish between a primary and secondary initiated depression (on the basis of the features of depression, reviewed earlier). We need to be able to distinguish, for instance, between primary and secondary depression and between denial which has a neurobiological cause, with denial which is caused by psychological protective mechanisms, a secondary denial in order that we develop appropriate approaches to rehabilitation and reintegration.

ASSESSING EMOTIONAL STATE IN APHASIA

The most reliable method of gaining information on the emotional state of someone seems to be to ask them (Starkstein & Robinson 1988), and language plays a crucial role in identifying and measuring mood. Clearly there are problems in using this approach with individuals with language problems. Language is our interface with the world and we make sense of the experience that life brings through language. It functions to express both emotional and intellectual messages between cognitive and emotional domains within the individual, as well as between individuals and the environment. Language is so important to life that when it is impaired the complete being is affected.

Studies of depression in brain-damaged people have used measures of behaviour symptomatic of depression. Factors utilised in widely used questionnaires designed to measure depression aim to identify problems like impaired patterns of sleeping and eating, restlessness, agitation and crying. However, as indicated earlier, it is not always clear whether these factors may be caused by physical illness, anxiety, hospitalisation, or a variety of other influences directly unrelated to underlying mood state (Herrmann & Wallesch, 1993; Starkstein & Robinson 1988). Communicative disability is additionally confounding because mood states express themselves externally through linguistic, paralinguistic and nonverbal communicative behaviour. A large literature demonstrates that facial expression, voice quality, rate and amount of speech, gesture and posture, as well as linguistic expression and comprehension can be variously affected in impaired mood (for review see Ellgring, 1989, and Fleminger, Oliver, Williams, & Evans, this issue). But these behaviours can also be affected by neurological damage. Below we examine the available methods of assessing emotional and psychosocial state in aphasic people.

Depression questionnaires

Popular self-report depression questionnaires include the Zung Self-Rating Depression Scale (Zung, 1965) and the Beck Depression Inventory (Beck et al., 1977). Both are short self-report questionnaires in the sense that the individual reads the questions and chooses a rating from a 1–4 scale. The questions aim to determine the presence within the recent past of the major symptoms of depression—appetite, sleep patterns, suicidal thoughts, etc.

Using self-report depression questionnaires with brain-damaged individuals raises well-known problems (see Wahrborg, 1991 for review) in addition to the obvious limitations of attempting to draw out precise information through verbal questioning with aphasic people, particularly those with significant comprehension problems and right-hemisphere damaged individuals. The latter often present with impairments in the expression and comprehension of emotional language (Bryan, 1989; Borod, Bloom, & Haywood, 1998; Code, 1987; Ross, 1981). Research suggests that emotional impairments can be dissociated from, and are independent of, language impairments, for both left-(Starkstein & Robinson, 1988) and right-hemisphere-damaged individuals (Bryan, 1989; Borod et al., 1998).

The 28-item Scaled Version of the General Health Questionnaire (GHQ; Goldberg & Hillier, 1979) is a self-assessment questionnaire of general psychological and psychosocial well-being that has been used with aphasic people and their relatives (Hemsley & Code, 1996; Rice, Paull, & Muller, 1987). It covers four scales (A somatic symptoms, B anxiety, C social dysfunction, D severe depression) which allows examination of relationships between these factors.

Hemsley and Code (1996) found that more mildly impaired aphasic people with good comprehension can understand the questions but even more severely impaired people can complete the questions with the tester providing help. The reliability of the "self" assessment with significant tester involvement will depend on the skill of the tester in avoiding assuming or supplying answers to questions.

Assessment of depression can also be achieved through standardised structured clinical interview where the tester asks the questions. Such measures as the Hamilton Rating Scale of Depression (HRSD; Hamilton, 1960) and the recently developed Cornell Depression Scale (CDS; Alexopoulos, Abrams, Young, & Shamoian, 1988) have the advantage that they can be used with people who have significant reading difficulties, but sufficient comprehension to be able to understand the tester's questioning. Here the tester completes the assessment through a process of standardised questioning and observation. Relatives and friends can also be asked to help verify the accuracy of observations.

For both the CDS and the HRSD the investigator uses a rating scale to assess the presence and severity of symptoms in the same major areas. For instance, on a 3-point scale, the Cornell rates: *mood-related signs* (e.g., sadness, anxiety), *behavioural disturbances* (e.g., loss of interest, agitation), *physical signs* (e.g., appetite and weight loss, lack of energy), *cyclic functions* (variation of mood, sleeping difficulties), *ideational disturbances* (e.g., pessimism, delusions, suicidal wishes or attempts). The CDS was developed originally for use with the elderly with dementia and Alexopoulos et al., (1988, p. 272) note that questionnaires pose particular problems for people with dementia as they are likely to have impairments in concentration, memory and judgement that can affect their responses. Most existing psychometrically robust depression scales are either designed for self-completion or clinical interview. Having said this, a range of studies have shown that comprehension and reading problems are a factor. Less severely impaired people who do not have impairments in reading can use self-assessment questionnaires and those with impaired language comprehension can be aided to understanding using nonverbal methods (Code & Muller,1992; Hemsley & Code, 1996).

Visual Analogue Mood Scales (VAMS)

One route to sampling the inner feelings of people with significant language problems is to use the nonverbal Visual Analogue Mood Scale (VAMS; Stern, 1997). Visual analogue scales were developed to address some of the problems of examining mood state in people with neurological conditions. First described by Aitken (1969), visual analogue scales are simple measures of mood state frequently used in psychiatric and behavioural research (Ahearn, 1997).

The standard visual analogue scale is simply a 5 cm line on a card with some bipolar abstract noun at each end like *happy/unhappy*. The task of the examinee is to dissect the line at a point between the bipolar ends which reflects their feelings. This simple procedure has been shown to be a reliable and valid method for gaining insight into the feelings of individuals with a range of psychiatric conditions, including depression, mania, schizophrenia, neurosis and personality disorders (Stern & Bachman, 1991).

The procedure can be made more meaningful to severely aphasic people by substituting schematic faces for words, as in the examples of the VAMS developed by Stern and colleagues (Stern, 1999). The visual analogue scales have been presented horizontally, often with the negative pole in the left field. This may present problems for people with visual field defects or unilateral neglect. The VAMS were specifically designed for use with neurological disorders, and with people with aphasia and other communication disorders, in particular (Stern, 1997; Stern et al., 1997). They consist of eight individual scales measuring the mood states: sad, happy, tense, afraid, confused, tired, energetic, angry. Each scale involves a "neutral" schematic face on the top of a 100 mm *vertical* line, and a specific mood face on the bottom together with the appropriate mood words above (i.e., "neutral") and below (e.g., "sad") the faces. The testee simply indicates how he or she is currently feeling by placing a mark across the vertical line. The VAMS are scored 0–100 for each scale, with 0 representing the complete lack of the mood state and 100 representing the extreme presence of the mood.

Normative data have been collected on over 400 healthy controls, aged 18–94 (Nyenhuis et al., 1997; Stern, 1997) and validation studies have been conducted on a variety of samples, including the same 18–94-year-old, psychiatrically and neurologically healthy individuals (Nyenhuis et al., 1997; Stern et al., 1997), psychiatric in-patients and out-patients, patients with dementia and acute and post-acute stroke in-patients. These studies have shown that the VAMS have excellent convergent and divergent validity (Stern, 1997).

Facial expression is a direct method of communicating emotion (e.g., Ekman, Friesen, & Ellsworth, 1982) and an ability that should be preserved in most unilaterally left-hemisphere damaged people with aphasia, for both the expression and comprehension of facial expressions. Bipolar schematic faces representing happy/sad, fear/neutral and anger/neutral and others can be substituted for the relevant words.

Because there is no learning effect, the VAMS can be repeatedly completed at any time. The VAMS can be interpreted more fully if a simple numeric rating scale is applied to the scale. To represent an individual's mood changes over time, for instance, graphs can be drawn up using the numeric information to ease understanding for the aphasic person and their relatives. Presenting information for discussion in this visually very meaningful way, can contribute to discussion and counselling.

Personal construct therapy

The techniques of personal construct therapy (PCT) have been used to explore the dynamics of psychological response to brain damage and aphasia within the framework of the grief model (Brumfitt, 1985). Kelly (1955) proposed that we adopt core roles in order to construct and maintain a sense of self and to be able to construe our place in the world. Brain damage brings many changes in an individual's life and can cause a breakdown of the core roles of self leading to invalidation of implications and the need to reconstruct the self.

Brumfitt (1985) suggests that the impact of becoming aphasic is seen as an event of such magnitude as to affect the way core-roles are construed (p. 93) and that the grief for the loss of the essential element of oneself as a speaker leads to an awareness that core constructs are in the process of change through loss of the essential elements.

A major technique of investigation in PCT is the analysis of an individual's repertory grid, and, like other approaches to the investigation of emotional states, completion of repertory grids ordinarily entails a verbally complex procedure. Brumfitt used a combination of photographs depicting human conditions and verbal cuing (e.g., "a person who smiles and laughs a lot is . . ."), to elicit constructs from seven moderately to severely aphasic people. Analysis of the grids revealed, not surprisingly perhaps, that all construed themselves differently in the present as compared to the past. Three construed their *past selves* as their *ideal selves* which, Brumfitt suggests, supports the grief model notion of searching for the lost self. It also supports the notion that depression can result initially from negative comparison of one's real with one's ideal situation.

The participants in Brumfitt's (1985) interesting study were all constricted construers, so It is difficult to know to what extent the inner world we get a glimpse of through adapted PCT techniques is truly representative, or whether the limited range of construct labels these constricted construers were able to produce are a reflection of a severely impaired expression.

Summary.   Normally the best way to find out how someone is feeling is to ask them. Gaining insight into someone's emotional and psychosocial state is hampered by communication impairments and disabilities. However, there are a range of options available for asking people how they feel and comprehension and reading abilities determine to a large extent the reliability of any of them. These include questionnaires, standardised clinical interviews and specially modified repertory grids, visual analogue mood scales and observation.

THE EFFECTS OF EMOTIONAL FACTORS ON RECOVERY AND RESPONSE TO REHABILITATION

The dramatic and disabling effects of physical impairment accompanying stroke often take priority in treatment. This emphasis reflects the dominance of the medical model in our health-care systems (Taylor Sarno, 1993); emotional experience and personal perspectives, social roles and psychosocial perceptions are neither objective nor easy to measure and are not traditionally seen as well suited to experimental investigation. Consequently, issues of personal experience are often neglected in rehabilitation. While emotional and psychosocial adjustment may be passively acknowledged, too few rehabilitation programmes entail significant assessment or make sufficient effort to incorporate emotional and psychosocial factors into reablement.

Emotional state has a significant impact on motivation, physical performance and cognitive and language processing (Beblo et al., 1999b; Oatley & Johnson-Laird, 1987; Power & Dalgleish, 1997; Tucker, 1981). Motivation increases and language and cognitive performance improves with positive mood and well-being. Cognitive performance can decline, however, when emotional balance is disrupted (Cohen et al., 1982; Stromgreen,1977). Mood state probably plays a major role in recovery (Hemsley & Code, 1996; Code, 2001) but still does not receive the attention it deserves in rehabilitation, although evidence suggests that attention to these factors has a significant impact on rehabilitation outcome. People with positive mood states respond better to therapy than those who are depressed. Robinson, Lipsey, Rao, and Price (1986) conducted a longitudinal study of post-stroke mood disorders, and concluded that depression, if present, interacted with disability and had negative effects on rehabilitation outcome. Similarly, Sinyor et al. (1986a) compared rehabilitation outcome in depressed and non-depressed stroke survivors, and found that depressed individuals were less likely to progress, frequently reducing functional status during the first month post-onset (where non-depressed people showed slight increases or no change in functional status). Starkstein and Robinson (1988) concluded that depressed aphasic individuals show a lower rate of recovery and significantly greater cognitive impairment. Similarly, Herrmann and Wallesch (1993) conclude that the success of rehabilitation may depend on early diagnosis and adequate therapy for depression.

Hemsley and Code (1996) examined the relationships between recovery from aphasia and emotional and psychosocial changes at 3 months and 9 months post-stroke in five individuals and their closest relative. They used the Scaled GHQ and the Western Aphasia Battery and found wide individual variability. There appeared to be a relationship between degree of awareness of the reality of the situation, perception of severity of the problems and degree of optimism for the future. For one there was a decline in well-being after 9 months but with marked improvement on the aphasia tests in comprehension and awareness of the nature of the deficits. For one spouse there was a decline in well-being at 9 months as she began to realise that improvement was going to be limited and slow. One mildly impaired aphasic person was severely depressed, while another more severely impaired showed no depression. One aphasic person was not depressed but his wife was significantly depressed. Relatively high optimism for the future, which was a feature for several at 3 months post-onset, was reduced at 9 months.

Summary.   We know very little about the impact of emotional and psychosocial factors on recovery and response to therapy in aphasia, and research is clearly needed. What data there are suggest an important association but significant individual variability. In the final section we consider how emotional reactions and psychosocial adjustment to aphasia have been incorporated into rehabilitation and the problems of living with aphasia. While there are increasing indications that rehabilitation efforts are incorporating such factors, again research is needed to examine the impact of such effort on outcome.

Incorporating emotional reactions and psychosocial adjustment into rehabilitation

There is now clear acceptance that emotional factors must be addressed in rehabilitation and that rehabilitation programmes based purely on the bio-medical model are simply not adequate or appropriate. However, what is also becoming clear is that emotional response to aphasia is complex and seems to be highly individualistic, although, as indicated above, there are strong indications that emotional and psychosocial issues will be different at different times post-onset. Emotion probably interacts with other factors as well as the individual's own perceptions of their problems and their significance. Comprehensive rehabilitation must therefore include a significant social frame of reference which converges on emotional and psychosocial factors (Brumfitt, 1993; Code & Muller, 1992; Parr, Byng, Gilpin, & Ireland, 1997; Taylor Sarno, 1993, 1997).

Pharmacotherapeutic intervention for depression following brain damage has been shown to be successful and different antidepressant drugs have been trialed. The effects of the classic tricyclic antidepressant, nortryptiline (Balunov, Sadov, & Alemasova, 1990; Finklestein, Weintraub, & Karmouz, 1987; Lipsey et al., 1984), selective serotonin re-uptake inhibitors (Andersen, 1997; Andersen, Veestergard, & Lauritzen, 1994), and dextroamphetamine or methylphenidate (Johnson, Roberts, Ross, & Witten, 1992; Lazarus et al., 1992; Masand & Chaudhary, 1994; Masand, Murray, & Pickett, 1991) have been examined. Studies indicate that treatment with antidepressant drugs can improve the emotional state of depressed stroke survivors and has a positive affect upon daily life activities (Reding et al., 1986). However, different approaches to intervention may be indicated at acute and post-acute stages. Physicians have been reluctant to prescribe antidepressants for aphasic people, partly perhaps because they may have believed the depression was of a reactive form, as well as a recognition of the unacceptable side effects (Andersen, 1997). However, trials have shown, for instance, that the SSRI citalopram is well tolerated and has only mild side effects (Andersen et al., 1994). We need to investigate further how drug therapy, counselling and psychotherapy may be combined at appropriate times post-stroke and in different ways for different individuals. Small (2001) discusses those drugs often prescibed for the range of medical conditions accompanying stroke, that can impact negatively on rehabilitation and response to therapy in aphasic people, and suggests alternatives with less adverse effects. For fuller discussion of the application of drugs to depression in aphasic people see Wallesch, Müller, and Herrmann (1996) and Andersen (1997). Some workers take the position that drugs should be avoided, but others suggest incorporating drugs (Code et al., 1999) and psychotherapy (Brumfitt, 1995), with drugs perhaps being more appropriate at early stages to counter primary effects, and psychotherapy and counselling later when the individual is more ready to deal with their present and their future. Comparative research is urgently needed to evaluate the contribution of both broad approaches.

Because aphasia affects others too, it has implications for the individual's whole social network, especially the immediate family, and the perceptions of the likely recovery of aphasia differ between aphasic people, their closest relatives and the professionals involved with them (Code & Muller, 1992). The *value-dimensions* in our lives, like health, sexuality, career, creativity, marriage, intelligence, money, family, etc., contribute to our quality of life and are markedly affected for the aphasic person (Hinckley, 1998) and their relatives, who experience considerable disruption to professional, social and family life, reductions in social contact, depression, loneliness, frustration, and aggression (Herrmann & Wallesch, 1989). The ultimate aim of rehabilitation for persistent communication disabilities is psychosocial adjustment and reintegration and the development of autonomy. The individual's experience of disability as they engage in social exchange and interaction, rather than the impairment itself, is the focus of a psychosocial approach. Simmons-Mackie (1998) argues that the general aim of authentic rehabilitation should be to prepare and assist people to integrate into a community and stresses the importance of social affiliation as a means of maintaining and developing self-identity. Facilitating participation in the community entails passing responsibility to the individual over a gradual period in order to develop autonomy, to enhance self-esteem and to take greater ownership of the issues that face people. The importance of involving the aphasic individual fully is highlighted by Parr et al. (1997).

As time passes, and psychological healing begins to occur, individuals have to face the problems of reintegrating themselves into their social and community networks (Code, submitted). This is a significant step, and many aphasic people do not have the opportunity to make it. Psychosocial reintegration for aphasic people increasingly includes community based work and support from not-for-profit organisations, support groups, and self-help groups. A range of psychosocial concerns have been addressed, dealing with: depression and other emotions; social reintegration; the development of autonomy and self-worth; and the impact of aphasia on family and friends. Workers in the field are agreed that the aphasic person's family and other carers need to be involved as much as possible in rehabilitation and that this needs to go beyond formal discharge (Code et al., 1999; Hersh, 1998; Parr et al., 1997). Hersh (1998) argues that at discharge from formal aphasia therapy we particularly need to take account of the ongoing management of psychosocial adjustment.

Self-esteem and self-worth are complex constructs tied to psychosocial activity that workers suggest should be central to psychosocial rehabilitation As noted above, the role of perception of self has been examined by Brumfitt (1993) using personal construct techniques and incorporated into counselling. "Talking therapies" are dependent on communication, but individual (Cunningham, 1998) and group counselling for aphasic people (Elman & Bernstein-Ellis, 1999) and their relatives (Johannsen-Horbach, Crone, & Wallesch, 1999) have been shown to be effective, and aphasic people themselves have recently become involved as counsellors (Ireland & Wotton, 1996). Studies have shown the potential benefits of family therapy and including people who are close to the aphasic person in rehabilitation (Wahrborg & Borenstein, 1989). Nichols, Varchevker, and Pring (1996) found positive changes in two families following family therapy.

Returning to work remains a constant concern for many aphasic people of working age. Work and other purposeful activity is an important value-dimension central in the development and maintenance of self-worth and autonomy. Parr et al. (1997) report that only one person in their study in work at the time of the stroke returned to the same employment. A few found part-time work and the rest became unemployed or retired. Garcia, Barrette, and Laroche (2000) studied perceived barriers to work and found therapists focused on personal and social barriers, employers on organisational ones, and aphasic people themselves on all levels.

A range of not-for-profit and charitable organisations offer long-term support for psychosocial well-being, and provide community-based pro- grammes for aphasic people and their families, including training for relatives and professionals to become better conversation partners (see Appendix for details). Using trained volunteers as communication partners results in notable gains in psychological well-being and communication among aphasic partici- pants and their relatives (Lyon et al., 1997). Volunteers figure increasingly in efforts to develop social reintegration, providing a valuable resource, and helping establish, facilitate and maintain self-help and support groups.

The contribution of self-help groups is becoming established and evaluated (Coles & Eales, 1999; Code et al., 2001, in press), where the aphasic members decide on the purpose and aims of the group and take responsibility for running the group. Taking a significant role in the group (e.g., Chair, Secretary) is seen as contributing to the development of independence and autonomy. The network of self-help groups in the UK attracts mainly younger and the less severely impaired people and uses little in the way of statutory resources (Code et al., 2001). Work by Wahrborg et al. (1997) and Elman (1998) has demon- strated a number of the benefits that can occur through integrating individuals with aphasia into educational organisations and programmes. Parker, Gladman, and Drummond (1997) have presented the case for leisure learning programmes to be included in the rehabilitation process and offer important insight into the role of leisure in rehabilitation.

CONCLUSIONS

Taken together the research suggests an obligation to closely monitor the effects of emotional changes, their impact on psychosocial reintegration, and the way in which they interact with the ability of the aphasic people we work with to respond to rehabilitation and to adjust to the changes in their lives. We end with the time-honoured call for research. While methods of assessment have been developed which attempt to take account of communication impair- ments, there is still a need for sensitive methods that aid our understanding of the personally relevant world of people with aphasia. Clinical trials are required to determine the effectiveness of drugs and their appropriate combination with rehabilitation and psychosocial reintegration. In this sub-field of neuro- psychology research methodology has been, and will continue to be, mixed, with single case studies and group studies and quantitive and qualitative methods combining to increase our understanding and form the foundation for research-based rehabilitation.

REFERENCES

Ahearn, E. P. (1997). The use of visual analog scales in mood disorders: A critical review. *Journal of Psychiatric Research, 31*, 569–579.

Aitken, R. C. B. (1969). Measurement of feelings using visual analogue scales. *Proceedings of the Royal Society of Medicine, 62*, 989–993.

Alexopoulos, G. S., Abrams, R. C., Young, R. C., & Shamoian, C. A. (1988). Cornell scale for depression in dementia. *Biological Psychiatry, 23*, 271–284.

American Psychiatric Association (1994). *Diagnostic and statistical manual of mental disorders, Fourth Edition.* Washington, DC: American Psychiatric Association.

Andersen, G. (1997). Post-stroke depression and pathological crying: Clinical aspects and new pharmacological approaches. *Aphasiology, 11*, 651–664.

Andersen, G., Veestergard, K., & Lauritzen, L. (1994). Effective treatment of poststroke depression with the selective serotonin reuptake inhibitor citalopram. *Stroke, 25*, 1099–1104.

Åström, M., Adolfsson, R., & Asplund, K. (1993). Major depression in stroke patients— A 3-year longitudinal study. *Stroke, 24*, 976–982.

Balunov, O. A., Sadov, O. G., & Alemasova, A. Yu. (1990). Therapy of depressions in post-stroke patients. *Alaska Medicine, 32*, 27–29.

Beblo, Th., Baumann, B., Bogerts, B., Wallesch, C. W., & Herrmann, M. (1999b). Neuropsychological correlates of major depression: A short term follow-up. *Cognitive Neuropsychiatry, 4*, 333–341.

Beblo, Th., Wallesch, C. W., & Herrmann, M. (1999a). The crucial role of frontostriatal circuits for depressive disorders in the post-acute stage after stroke. *Neuropsychiatry, Neuropsychology, and Behavioral Neurology, 12*, 234–246.

Beck, A. T., Ward, C. H., Mendelson, M., Mock, J., & Erbaugh, J. (1977). *An inventory for measuring depression.* New York: Biometric Research.

Benson, D. F. (1973). Psychiatric aspects of aphasia. *British Journal of Psychiatry, 123*, 555–566.

Benson, D. F. (1979). *Aphasia, alexia, agraphia.* New York: Churchill Livingstone.

Berthier, M. L., & Starkstein, S. E. (1987). Acute atypical psychosis following a right hemisphere stroke. *Acta Neurologica Belgica, 87*, 125–131.

Borod, J. C., Bloom, R. L., & Haywood, C. S. (1998). Verbal aspects of emotional communication. In M. Beeson & C. Chiarello (Eds.), *Right hemisphere language comprehension: Perspectives from cognitive neuroscience.* Mahwah, NJ: Lawrence Erlbaum Associates, Inc.

Browning, M. A. (1995). Depression. In M. O. Hogstel (Ed.), *Geropsychiatric nursing.* St Louis: Mosby Year Book.

Brumfitt, S. (1985). The use of repertory grids with aphasic people. In: N. Beail (Ed.), *Repertory grid technique and personal constructs.* London: Croom-Helm.

Brumfitt, S. (1993). Losing your sense of self: What aphasia can do. *Aphasiology, 7*, 569–574.

Brumfitt, S. (1995). Psychotherapy and aphasia. In C. Code & D. J. Muller (Eds.), *Treatment of aphasia: From theory to practice.* London: Whurr.

Bryan, K. (1989). Language prosody and the right hemisphere. *Aphasiology, 3*, 285–299.

Campbell, A. (1976). Subjective measures of well being. *American Psychologist, 31*, 117–124.

Code, C. (1987). *Language, aphasia and the right hemisphere.* Chichester, UK: John Wiley.

Code, C. (1999). Meeting expectations. *Speech and Language Therapy and Communication in Practice.*

Code, C. (2001). Multifactorial processes in recovery from aphasia: Developing the foundations for a multileveled framework. *Brain & Language, 77*, 25–44.

Code, C. (in press). The quantity of life for people with chronic aphasia. *Neuropsychological Rehabilitation*.

Code, C., Eales, C., Pearl, G., Conan, M., Cowin, K., & Hickin, J. (2001). Profiling the membership of self-help groups for aphasic people. *International Journal of Language and Communication Disorders, 36*, 41–45 (Supplement).

Code, C., Eales, C., Pearl, G., Conan, M., Cowin, K., & Hickin, J. (in press). Supported self-help groups for aphasic people; development and research. In I. Papathanasiou & Ria de Bleser (Eds.), *The science of aphasia*. North-Holland: Elsevier.

Code, C., Hemsley, G., & Herrmann, M. (1999). The emotional impact of aphasia. *Seminars in Speech & Language, 20*, 19–31.

Code, C., & Muller, D. J. (1992). *The Code–Muller protocols: Assessing perceptions of psychosocial adjustment to aphasia and related disorders*. London: Whurr.

Cohen, R. M., Weingartner, H., Smallberg, S. A., Picker, D., & Murphy, D. L. (1982). Effort and cognition in depression, *Archives of General Psychiatry, 39*, 593–597.

Coles, R., & Eales, C. (1999). The aphasia self-help movement in Britain: A challenge and an opportunity. In R. J. Elman (Ed.), *Group treatment of neurogenic communication disorders: The expert clinician's approach*. Woburn, MA: Butterworth-Heinemann.

Cunningham, R. (1998). Counselling someone with severe aphasia: An explorative case study. *Disability & Rehabilitation, 20*, 346–354.

Cutting, R. (1978). A study of anosognosia. *Journal of Neurology, Neurosurgery and Psychiatry, 41*, 548–555.

Damasio, A. R., & Van Hoesen, G. W. (1983). Emotional disturbances associated with focal lesions of the limbic frontal lobe. In K. M. Heilman & P. Satz (Eds.), *Neuropsychology of human emotion*. New York: Guildford Press.

Egelko, S., Gordon, W. A., Hibbard, M. R., Diller, L., Lieberman, A., Holliday, R., Ragnarsson, K., Shaver, M. S., & Orazem, J. (1988). Relationship among CT scans, neurological exam, and neuropsychological test performance in right-brain-damaged stroke patients. *Journal of Clinical and Experimental Neuropsychology, 10*, 539–564.

Ekman, P., Friesen, W. V., & Ellsworth, P. (1982). What emotion categories or dimensions can observers judge from facial behaviour. In P. Ekman (Ed.), *Emotions in human face* (2nd ed.). Cambridge: Cambridge University Press.

Ellgring, H. (1989). Facial expression as a behavioral indicator of emotional states. *Pharmacopsychiatry, 22*, 23–28 (Suppl).

Elman, R. J. (1998). Memories of the "plateau": Health care changes provide an opportunity to redefine aphasia treatment and discharge. *Aphasiology, 12*, 227–231.

Elman, R. J., & Bernstein-Ellis, E. (1999). Psychosocial aspects of group communication treatment: preliminary findings. *Seminars in Speech & Language, 20*, 65–72.

Finklestein, S., Benowitz, L. J., Baldessarini, R. G., Arana, G. W., Levine, D., Woo, E., Bear, D., Moya, K., & Stoll, A. L. (1982). Mood, vegetative disturbance and dexamethasone suppression test after stroke. *Annals of Neurology, 12*, 463–468.

Finklestein, S. P., Weintraub, R. J., & Karmouz, N. (1987). Antidepressant drug treatment for post-stroke depression: A retrospective study. *Archives of Physical Medicine & Rehabilitation, 68*, 772–776.

Fisher, S. (1961). Psychiatric considerations of cerebral vascular disease. *American Journal of Cardiology, 7*, 379.

Folstein, M. F., Maiberger, R., & McHugh, P. R. (1977). Mood disorders as a specific complication of stroke. *Journal of Neurology, Neurosurgery, and Psychiatry, 41*, 470–473.

Friedland, J., & McColl, M. (1987). Social support and psychosocial dysfunction after stroke: buffering effects in a community sample. *Archives of Physical Medicine and Rehabilitation, 68*, 475–480.

Gainotti, G. (1972). Emotional behavior and hemispheric side of the lesion. *Cortex, 8*, 41–55.

Gainotti, G. (1997). Emotional, psychological and psychosocial problems of aphasic patients: An introduction. *Aphasiology*, *11*, 635–650.

Garcia, L. J., Barrette, J., & Laroche, C. (2000). Perceptions of the obstacles to work reintegration for persons with aphasia. *Aphasiology*, *14*, 269–290.

Goldberg, D., & Hillier, V. (1979). A scaled version of the General Health Questionnaire. *Psychological Medicine*, *9*, 139–145.

Gordon, W. A., Hibbard, M. R., & Morganstein, S. (1988). Response to Tanner and Gerstenberger. *Aphasiology*, *2*, 85–87.

Hamilton, M. A. (1960). A rating scale for depression. *Journal of Neurology, Neurosurgery, and Psychiatry*, *23*, 56–62.

Heilman, K. M. (1979). Neglect and related disorders. In K. M. Hcilman & E. Valenstein (Eds.), *Clinical neuropsychology*. New York: Oxford University Press.

Heilman, K. M., Scholes, R., & Watson, R. T. (1975). Auditory affective agnosia: Disturbed comprehension of affective speech. *Journal of Neurology, Neurosurgery and Psychiatry*, *38*, 69–72.

Hemsley, G., & Code, C. (1996). Interactions between recovery in aphasia, emotional and psychosocial factors in subjects with aphasia, their significant others and speech pathologists. *Disability & Rehabilitation*, *18*, 567–584.

Herrmann, M., Bartels, C., Schumacher, M., & Wallesch, C. W. (1995). Poststroke depression: Is there a patho-anatomical correlate for depression following the post-acute stage of stroke? *Stroke*, *26*, 850–856.

Herrmann, M., Bartels, C. & Wallesch, C. W. (1993). Depression in acute and chronic aphasia— Symptoms, pathoanatomo-clinical correlations, and functional implications. *Journal of Neurology, Neurosurgery, and Psychiatry*, *56*, 672–678.

Herrmann, M., & Wallesch, C. W. (1989). Psychosocial changes and psychosocial adjustment with severe aphasia. *Aphasiology*, *3*, 513–526.

Herrmann, M., & Wallesch, C. W. (1993). Depressive changes in stroke patients. *Disability and Rehabilitation 15*, 55–66.

Hersh, D. (1998). Beyond the 'plateau': discharge dilemmas in chronic aphasia. *Aphasiology*, *12*, 207–243.

Hinckley, J. (1998). Investigating the predictors of lifestyle satisfaction among younger adults with chronic aphasia. *Aphasiology*, *12*, 509–518.

Hoen, B., Thelander, M., & Worsley, J. (1997). Improvement in psychosocial well-being of people with aphasia and their families: Evaluation of a community-based programme. *Aphasiology*, *11*, 681–691.

House, A., Dennis, M., Warlow, C., Hawton, K., & Molyneux, A. (1990). Mood disorders after stroke and their relation to lesion location—A CT scan study. *Brain*, *113*, 1113–1129.

Ireland, C., & Wotton, G. (1996). Time to talk: Counselling for people with dysphasia. *Disability and Rehabilitation*, *18*, 585–591.

Jackson, H. F. (1988). Brain, cognition and grief. *Aphasiology*, *2*, 89–92.

Johannsen-Horbach, H., Crone, M., & Wallesch, C.-W. (1999). Group treatment for spouses of aphasic patients. *Seminars in Speech & Language*, *20*, 73–83.

Johnson, M. L., Roberts, M. D., Ross, A. R., & Witten, C. M. (1992). Methylphenidate in stroke patients with depression. *American Journal of Physical Medicine and Rehabilitation*, *71*, 239–241.

Kagan, A. (1998). Supported conversation for adults with aphasia: Methods and resources for training conversation partners. *Aphasiology*, *9*, 816–831.

Kelly, G. (1955). *The psychology of personal constructs*. New York: Norton.

Kubler-Ross, E. (1969). *On death and dying*. New York: Macmillan.

Laplane, D., Baulac, M., Windlocher, D., & Dubois, B. (1984). Pure psychic akinesia with bilateral lesions of basal ganglia. *Journal of Neurology, Neurosurgery and Psychiatry*, *47*, 377–385.

Lauterbach, E. C., Jackson, J. G., Wilson, A. N., Dever, G. E., & Kirsh, A. D. (1997). Major depression after left posterior globus pallidus lesions. *Neuropsychiatry, Neuropsychology, and Behavioral Neurology, 10*, 9–16.

Lazarus, R. (1993). Coping theory and research: past present and future. *Psychosomatic Medicine, 55*, 234–247.

Lazarus, L. W., Winemiller, D. R., Lingam, V. R., Neyman, I., Hartman, C., Abassian, M., Kartan, U., Groves, L., & Fawcett, J. (1992). Efficacy and side effects of methylphenidate for poststroke depression. *Journal of Clinical Psychiatry, 53*, 447–449.

Lipsey, J. R., Robinson, R. G., Pearlson, G. D., Rao, K., & Price, T. R. (1984). Nortriptyline treatment of post-stroke depression: A double blind treatment trial. *Lancet, 1*, 297–300.

Lipsey, J. R., Robinson, R. G., Pearlson, G. D., Rao, K., & Price, T. R. (1985). The dexamethasone suppression test and mood following stroke. *American Journal of Psychiatry, 142*, 318–323.

Lipsey, J. R., Spencer, W. C., Rabins, P. V., & Robinson, R. G. (1986). Phenomenological comparison of post-stroke depression and functional depression. *American Journal of Psychiatry, 143*, 527–529.

Lyon, J. G., Cariski, D., Keisler, L., Rosenbek, J., Levine, R., Kumpula, J., Ryff, C., Coyne, S., & Blanc, M. (1997). Communication partners: Enhancing participation in life and communication for adults with aphasia in natural settings. *Aphasiology, 11*, 693–708.

McDonald, S., Togher, L., & Code, C. (1999). *Traumatic brain injury and communication disorders*. Hove, UK: Psychology Press.

Masand, P., & Chaudhary, P. (1994). Methylphenidate treatment of poststroke depression in a patient with global aphasia. *Annals of Clinical Psychiatry, 6*, 271–274.

Masand, P., Murray, G. B., & Pickett, P. (1991). Psychostimulants in post-stroke depression. *Journal of Neuropsychiatry and Clinical Neurosciences, 3*, 23–27.

Mesulam, M. M., Waxman, S. G., Geschwind, N., & Sabin, T. D. (1976). Acute confusional states with right middle cerebral artery infarctions. *Journal of Neurology, Neurosurgery, and Psychiatry, 39*, 84–89.

Nichols, F., Varchevker, A., & Pring, T. (1996). Working with people with aphasia and their families: an exploration of the use of family therapy techniques. *Aphasiology, 10*, 767–781.

Nyenhuis, D. L., Stern, R. A., Yamamoto, C., Luchetta, T., & Arruda, J. E. (1997). Standardization and validation of the Visual Analog Mood Scales. *Clinical Neuropsychologist, 11*, 407–415.

Oatley, K., & Johnson-Laird, P. N. (1987). Towards a cognitive theory of emotions. *Cognition and Emotion, 1*, 29–50.

Parker, C. J., Gladman, J. R. F., & Drummond, A. E. R. (1997). The role of leisure in stroke rehabilitation. *Disability and Rehabilitation, 19*, 1–5.

Parr, S., Byng, S., Gilpin, S., & Ireland, C. (1997). *Talking about aphasia*. Buckingham, UK: Open University Press

Peroutka, S. J., Sohmer, B. H., Kumar, A. J., Folstein, M. F., & Robinson, R. G. (1982). Hallucinations and delusions following a right temporoparietooccipital infarction. *Johns Hopkins Medical Journal, 151*, 256–273.

Power, M., & Dalgleish, T. (1997). *Cognition and emotion: From order to disorder*. Hove, UK: Psychology Press.

Price, B. H., & Mesulam, M. M. (1985). Psychiatric manifestations of right hemisphere infarctions. *Journal of Nervous and Mental Disease, 173*, 610–614.

Reding, M. J., Orto, L. A., Winter, S. W., Fortuna, I. M., DiPonte, P., & McDowell, F. N. (1986). Antidepressant therapy after stroke: A double-blind trial. *Archives of Neurology, 43*, 763–765.

Rice, B., Paull, A., & Müller, D. J. (1987). An evaluation of a social support group for spouses and aphasic adults. *Aphasiology, 1*, 247–256.

Robinson, R. G., & Benson, D. F. (1981). Depression in aphasic patients: Frequency, severity, and clinical-pathological correlations. *Brain and Language, 14*, 282–291.

Robinson, R. G., Bolduc, P. L., & Price, T. R. (1987). A two year longitudinal study of post-stroke mood disorders: diagnosis and outcome at one and two years. *Stroke, 18*, 837–843.

Robinson, R. G., Kubos, K. L., Starr, L. B., Rao, K., & Price, T. R. (1984a). Mood disorders in stroke patients: importance of location of lesion. *Brain, 107*, 81–93.

Robinson, R. G., Lipsey, J. R., Rao, K., & Price, T. R. (1986). A two-year longitudinal study of poststroke mood disorders: Comparison of acute-onset with delayed-onset depression. *American Journal of Psychiatry, 143*, 1238–1244.

Robinson, R. G., & Price, T. R. (1982). Post stroke depressive disorders: A follow up study of 103 patients. *Stroke, 13*, 635–641.

Robinson, R. G., Starr, L. B., Lipsey, J. R., Rao, K., & Price, T. R. (1984b). A two-year longitudinal study of post-stroke disorders: Dynamic changes in associated variables over the first six months of follow-up. *Stroke, 15*, 510–517.

Ross, E. D. (1981). The aprosodias: Functional-anotomic organization of the affective components of language in the right hemisphere. *Archives of Neurology, 38*, 561–569.

Simmons-Mackie, N. (1998). A solution to the discharge dilemma in aphasia: Social approaches to aphasia management. *Aphasiology, 12*, 231–239.

Sinyor, D., Amato, P., Kaloupek, D. B., Becker, R., Goldenberg, M., & Coppersmith, H. M. (1986a). Post-stroke depression: Relationship to functional impairment, coping strategies, and rehabilitation outcome. *Stroke, 17*, 1102–1107.

Sinyor, D., Jacques, P., Kaloupek, D. B., Becker, R., Goldenberg, M., & Coopersmith, H. M. (1986b). Post-stroke depression and lesion location: An attempted replication. *Brain, 109*, 537–546.

Small, S. L. (2001). Biological approaches to the treatment of aphasia. In A. Hillis (Ed.), *Handbook on adult language disorders: Integrating cognitive neuropsychology, neurology, and rehabilitation*. Philadelphia: Psychology Press.

Starkstein, S. E., Pearlson, G. D., Boston, J., & Robinson, R. G. (1987). Mania after brain injury: A controlled study of causative factors. *Archives of Neurology, 44*, 1069–1073.

Starkstein, S. E., & Robinson, R. G. (1988). Aphasia and depression. *Aphasiology, 2*, 1–20.

Starkstein, S. E., Robinson, R. G., & Price, T. R. (1987). Comparison of cortical and subcortical lesions in the production of poststroke mood disorders. *Brain, 110*, 1045–1059.

Stern, R. A. (1997). *Visual Analog Mood Scales: Professional manual*. Odessa, FL: Psychological Assessment Resources.

Stern, R. A. (1999). Assessment of mood states in aphasia. *Seminars in Speech & Language, 20*, 33–51.

Stern, R. A., Arruda, J. E., Hooper, C. R., Wolfner, G. D., & Morey, C. E. (1997). Visual Analogue Mood Scales to measure internal mood state in neurologically impaired patients: Description and initial validity evidence. *Aphasiology, 11*, 59–71.

Stern, R. A., & Bachman, D. L. (1991). Depressive symptoms following stroke. *American Journal of Psychiatry, 148*, 351–356.

Stern, R. A., & Bachman, D. L. (1994). Discrepancy between self-report and observer rating of mood in stroke patients: Implications for the differential diagnosis of post-stroke depression [abstract]. *Journal of Neuropsychiatry and Clinical Neurosciences, 6*, 319.

Stromgreen, L. S. (1977). The influence of depression on memory. *Acta Psychiatrica Scandinavica, 56*, 109–128.

Tanner, D. C. (1980). Loss and grief: Implications for the speech-language pathologist and audiologist. *Journal of the American Speech and Hearing Association, 22*, 916–928.

Tanner, D. C., & Gerstenberger, D. L. (1988). The grief response in neuropathologies of speech and language. *Aphasiology, 2*, 79–84.

Taylor Sarno, M. (1993). Aphasia rehabilitation: psychosocial and ethical considerations. *Aphasiology, 7*, 321–334.

Taylor Sarno, M. (1997). Quality of life in aphasia in the first post-stroke year. *Aphasiology, 11*, 665–679.

Tucker, D. M. (1981). Lateral brain functions, emotion, and conceptualisation. *Psychological Bulletin*, *89*, 19–46.

Wahrborg, P. (1991). *Assessment and management of emotional and psychosocial reactions to brain damage and aphasia*. London: Whurr.

Wahrborg, P., & Borenstein, P. (1989). Family therapy in families with an aphasic member. *Aphasiology*, *3*, 93–98.

Wahrborg, P., Borenstein, P., Linell, S., Hedberg-Borenstein, E., & Asking, A. (1997). Ten year follow-up of young aphasic participants in a 34-week course at a Folk High School. *Aphasiology*, *11*, 709–715.

Wallesch, C. W., Müller, U., & Herrmann, M. (1997). Aphasia: role of pharmacotherapy in treatment. *CNS-Drugs*, *7*, 203–213.

Zung, W. W. K. (1965). A self-rating depression scale. *Archives of General Psychiatry*, *12*, 63–70.

APPENDIX

References and contact details to not-for-profit organisations providing therapy, psychosocial support, self-help groups, counselling and conversation training in North America and the United Kingdom.

North America

Pat Orato Aphasia Centre, 53 The Links Rd, North York, Ontario, Canada M2P 1T7. Tel: 416 226 3636. Http://www.aphasia.on.ca (Hoen et al., 1997; Kagan, 1998).
Aphasia Center of California, 3996 Lyman Rd, Oakland, CA 94602. USA. Tel: 570 336 0112.
Email: RJElman@aol.com (Elman et al., 1998).

UK

Speakability, 1 Royal St, London, SE1 7LL. Tel: 0207 261 9572.
Email: speakability@speakability.org.uk (Code et al., 2001; Code et al., in press).
Connect Network,16–18 Marshalsea Rd, London SE1 1HL. Tel: 0200 7367 0840.
Email: info@ukconnect.org

NEUROPSYCHOLOGICAL REHABILITATION, 2003, *13* (1/2), 133–148

Neurorehabilitation and cognitive–behaviour therapy of anxiety disorders after brain injury: An overview and a case illustration of obsessive–compulsive disorder

W. H. Williams

School of Psychology, University of Exeter, Exeter, UK

J. J. Evans

Oliver Zangwill Centre for Neuropsychological Rehabilitation, Ely, UK

S. Fleminger

Lishman Brain Injury Unit, Maudsley Hospital, London, UK

Survivors of acquired and traumatic brain injuries may often experience anxiety states. Psychological reactions to neurological trauma may be caused by a complex interaction of a host of factors. We explore how anxiety states may be understood in terms of a biopsychosocial formulation of such factors. We also review the current evidence for the presence of specific anxiety disorders after brain injury. We then describe how cognitive–behaviour therapy (CBT), a treatment of choice for many anxiety disorders, may be integrated with cognitive rehabilitation (CR), for the management of anxiety disorders in brain injury. We illustrate how CBT and CR may be delivered with a case of a survivor of traumatic brain injury (TBI) who had developed obsessive compulsive disorder and health anxiety. We show how CBT plus CR allows a biopsychosocial formulation to be developed of the survivor's concerns for guiding a goal-based intervention. The survivor made significant gains from intervention in terms of goals achieved and changes on clinical measures. We argue that large-scale research is needed for developing an evidence base for managing emotional disorders in brain injury.

Correspondence should be addressed to Dr Huw Williams, Lecturer in Clinical Psychology, School of Psychology, Washington Singer Laboratories, University of Exeter, Exeter, UK. Phone 1: +44 1392 264661, Phone 2: +44 1392 264626, Fax: +44 1392 264623, Email: w.h.williams@exeter.ac.uk

© 2003 Psychology Press Ltd

http://www.tandf.co.uk/journals/pp/09602011.html   DOI:10.1080/09602010244000417

INTRODUCTION

Survivors of brain injury are at particular risk of developing mood disorders. Psychological reactions to neurological trauma may be caused by a complex interaction of a host of factors. Cognitive–behaviour therapy (CBT) is advocated as being a treatment of choice for many anxiety disorders, and has an extensive evidence base. There is a limited, albeit growing, literature on the use of CBT with people with brain injury. In this paper we address how brain injury survivors may experience anxiety disorders, and a case of a traumatic brain injury (TBI) survivor is provided to illustrate the integration of cognitive rehabilitation with CBT for the management of obsessive–compulsive disorder and health anxiety.

Assessment of anxiety disorders

Anxiety disorders are the most commonly diagnosed group of mental health disorder in general mental health settings. They are suspected to be very common after brain injury, although possibly under-diagnosed due to difficulties in identifying symptoms in the context of other issues (see Scheutzow & Wiercisiewski, 1999). As we have described elsewhere (see Williams, in press), there are a host of factors that may contribute to the development of mood disorders in brain injured groups. Principal factors include the following: The nature and severity of the neurological injury; the pre-injury history of the survivor; the survivor's adjustment and coping systems; the type and nature of the emotional trauma of the event suffered; and the presence of additional stresses (such as pain, divorce, and/or sleep problems). In addition, the forms of support available and the length of time elapsed since the injury need to be considered. One crucial issue is that people with severe brain injuries may not be able to voice their anxiety, or indeed be aware of its origins. One of the current authors was involved in the care of a patient with very limited communication who suffered high levels of agitation and aggression, particularly when in his room with the window open. He refused to go outside. This behaviour was partly explained by his family who noted that before the injury he had always been phobic of wasps. This panic attack was a major block to his rehabilitation.

A biopsychosocial account is advocated for understanding psychosocial outcome in TBI (see Macmillan, Martelli, Hart, & Zasler, 2002). It is important to be able to give a formulation of anxiety symptoms that is able to take account of the various aetiological processes involved on the one hand, and the consequences of the anxiety on the other. With regard to the aetiological factors it must, though, be remembered that anxiety is a normal reaction to stress, and that indeed many well-adjusted people suffer significant anxiety symptoms in day-to-day life. However, following brain injuries, survivors are likely to be exposed to much greater symptoms, which may become incapacitating and prejudice full recovery. Indeed, we note that Lishman (1988) proposed that anxiety symptoms play a fundamental role in the development of chronic post concussion syndrome. Others may go on to develop a well-defined anxiety disorder meeting DSM IV criteria, little different from that to be found in those without a brain injury; i.e., the brain injury may have acted as a non-specific stressor. Anxiety may also be associated with premorbid factors which may bring a community reintegration programme to a standstill.

Diagnsotic criteria.   DSM IV (American Psychiatric Association, 1994) and the recent DSM IV revised text (American Psychiatric Association, 2000) provide five domains for a multi-axial assessment of mental health disorders, and is purported to provide a biopsychosocial perspective on such disorders. Clinical disorders arc represented on Axis I. Anxiety disorders on this axis include: generalised anxiety disorder (GAD), phobias (including social phobia), panic disorder (with or without agoraphobia), obsessive–compulsive disorder (OCD), post-traumatic stress disorder (PTSD), and acute stress disorder. Personality disorders are listed on Axis II, and some have anxiety-related symptoms as diagnostic criteria, such as avoidant or dependent types. A change in personality may be noted to have been occasioned by organic injury, and be specified as, for example, "labile" or "disinhibited". On Axis III general medical conditions that may have lead directly, or indirectly, to Axis I or Axis II disorders may be specified. Axis IV contains examples of the psychosocial pressures that may lead to clinical symptoms (such as negative life events, losses and lack of social support, etc.). On Axis V an overall rating may be given to the person's psychosocial functioning.

Neurological considerations.   Damage to the brain will have an impact on the processing of anxiety and fear reactions. Neurological disorders associated with anxiety were reviewed by Wise and Rundell (1999). Lesions affecting temporo-limbic areas, in particular the amygdala, basal ganglia and frontal cortex, in particular cingulate gyrus, have all been implicated in the development of anxiety disorders, including obsessive compulsive disorder. Right-sided lesions are perhaps more likely to produce anxiety reactions. These findings are consistent by and large with functional imaging studies demonstrating increased cerebral metabolism during provocation of anxiety in vulnerable patients in orbitofrontal and insular cortex, and basal ganglia (Rauch et al., 1997). Chronic anxiety may itself have neurotoxic effects on the brain as suggested by the finding of smaller hippocampi in people with chronic PTSD (Bremner et al., 1995) and in animals exposed to high levels of glucocorticoids (Sapolsky, Uno, Rebert, & Finch, 1990). It would not be surprising if people with traumatic brain injury were particularly vulnerable to such effects. It is also worth noting that some commentators have suggested that conditions such as OCD may have a neurological basis, with the frontal system being implicated (see Bradshaw, 2001).

Neurobehavioural syndromes.   As TBI leads to complex forms of emotional disturbance, and is often associated with cognitive-affective disorders, such as a dysexecutive or amnesic syndrome, it is more likely that a person with TBI would suffer a syndrome of neurological-emotional reactions than a singular form of emotional disturbance (Berrios, personal communication). Within these reactions, as indicated above, sometimes the neurological factors are more prominent, and at other times the emotional reaction is more prominent. A crucial element of the process of assessment of a mood disorder following TBI is that of establishing the level of insight the person has into their functioning. This has been described in detail in other papers in this special issue (see Prigatano and Johnson, this issue, and Fleminger, Oliver, Williams, & Evans, this issue). However, we may note that in the assessment process it is important to gain an understanding of survivors' awareness of the consequences of their injuries, their appreciation of "realistic" goals, and awareness of any emotional issues they may experience.

Measures.   The assessment of anxiety disorders in TBI is further complicated as there is a lack of appropriate measures of psychiatric/mental health status for TBI groups. Measures in use have usually been developed for other, non-brain injured groups, and may lack validity when used with ABI groups (see Bowen et al., 1998; Williams, Evans & Wilson, 1999). Moreover, it important to note that, due to these issues, false-positive and false-negative findings, on psychiatric or mood measures, may be common in TBI practice (see Pender & Fleminger, 1999, for a discussion of neuropsychiatric ratings scales and self-rated measures).

Differential diagnoses.   Within this context, it is important to consider the differential diagnosis of symptoms of anxiety disorder in patients with brain injury. For example, obsessive–compulsive symptoms need to be distinguished from "organic orderliness"; brain injured people often have a tendency to rigidity in their behaviour and a lack of tolerance to disruption to routines. In some cases this is manifest by a need to have everything tidy and well ordered. This can often be understood as a way of helping them manage memory impairment and being overwhelmed by dysexecutive symptoms. Also, for example, panic disorder may need to be distinguished from temporal lobe epilepsy (TLE), particularly as depersonalisation/derealisation is common to both TLE and brain injury. Reliance, then, on "routine" screening measures, is particularly problematic in TBI, and, as such, care needs to be taken to undertake assessment from different perspectives (the client's, the partner's, and/or significant others') with a range of techniques (interviews, cognitive tests, mood measures, behavioural checklists and observation). From such assessments it may become possible to understand how a mood disorder may represent elements of a person's overall neurobehavioural syndrome. In terms of rehabilitation, a clinical formulation of elements that contribute to an anxiety disorder can inform areas for intervention, such as the symptoms a survivor is most troubled by and/or for which goals may be set.

   Clinical formulation.   For many survivors of TBI, anxiety may be associated with a complex set of biopsychosocial factors which require careful assessment prior to diagnoses being provided. For some there may be a pattern of anxiety that "fits" a reactive anxiety disorder, although there may be organic and illness-related issues, for others the anxiety states may well be much more organic in nature, for others it may be more to do with environmental issues and losses. Therefore, although, it must be acknowledged that, while categorical features of classification may be helpful (in so far as the "medical condition" is relevant to particular forms of functioning, for example), diagnoses are best viewed as multi-factorial and dynamic. This view is consonant with the position that mental health may be seen as belonging on a set of continua (see Eells, 1997, regarding categorical versus dimensional models of mental health). This also gives the advantage for assessment purposes that a person's symptomology may, if it does not meet full criteria, be represented as subclinical. Indeed, it may be argued that a diagnosis may be best seen as a clinical formulation that "holds" information along such axes in such a way as to guide treatment and allow for re-formulation as intervention progresses—that is "working hypotheses" to be tested by intervention.

Anxiety disorders following TBI

With the above considerations and caveats in mind regarding the assessment of anxiety in TBI, a review of the existing evidence reveals that emotional disturbance of various forms is very common following TBI. The seminal work of Brooks and colleagues (1987) revealed how the emotional and behavioural consequences of brain injury were more common and distressing for carers than purely cognitive problems. More recently, Bowen et al. (1998), using the Wimbledon Self-report Scale for Mood Disorders, found a 38% rate of "caseness" for mood disorders in 77 survivors 6 months after injury. Hibbard et al. (1998) investigated patterns of mood disorders in TBI with the Structured Clinical Interview for DSM-IV. They found that the most frequent diagnoses were major depression and specific anxiety disorders and that comorbidity was high, with 44% of individuals having two or more diagnoses.

   Specific anxiety disorders have been identified following TBI. Generalised anxiety disorder has been reported, and is often associated with depression (see Jorge, Robinson, Starkstein & Arndt, 1993). Scheutznow and Wiercisiewski

(1999) described the case of a TBI survivor assessed as having a panic disorder who presented with clear health anxiety symptoms, with avoidance of activities due to a fear of suffering a heart attack. Phobic reactions are infrequently reported in the literature, although, clinically, patients are often found to have stress responses in reaction to particular stimuli. Such reactions might be best understood within the literature on PTSD (see McMillan, Williams, & Bryant, this issue, on PTSD). In brief, PTSD is characterised by intrusive experiences, hyper-vigilance, anxiety, fear, and avoidance of particular activities. If left untreated it may severely limit a person's ability to function. Williams, Evans, and Wilson (in press) showed that PTSD was evident in 18% of a representative sample of community-based survivors of TBI. OCD was considered rare in brain injured groups, although there is increasing evidence of it occurring (see Lishman, 1998). OCD is characterised by symptoms of either recurrent intrusive thoughts and/or compulsive repetitive behaviours. It tends to present in the context of an affective disorder with symptoms of tension, rumination, self-doubt, indecision and compulsive preoccupation. Recent research with non-neurological groups has suggested that persons with OCD may well have memory deficits and that these set up doubt and consequent checking rituals (see Zitterl et al., 2001; and see Tallis, 1997). McKeown, McGuffin, and Robinson (1984) found three of a sample of 25 survivors of mild brain injury, and a further individual from a twin study, to have severe OCD. There was an absence of any premorbid features in three of the four cases. Berthier, Kulisevsky, Gironell and Lopez (2001) reported a study of 10 people with TBI who had OCD. They noted that the patterns of OCD symptoms (such as a high frequency of obsessions regarding contamination, somatic symptoms, need for symmetry, and compulsions such as cleaning and checking) were relatively well specified. They noted that patterns of cognitive deficits and magnetic resonance imaging (MRI) findings suggested dysfunction of frontal-subcortical circuits.

Pharmacological therapy for anxiety after brain injury

Psychological treatments are the mainstay of the management of anxiety in those with a brain injury, as they are in those without brain injury (see Lishman, 1998). With severe symptoms, or symptoms that do not respond to psychological treatment, medication is worth trying, with a view to augmenting the pharmacological strategy with a psychological approach when possible. When it comes to choosing which drug to use there is no good evidence for choosing one class of anxiolytics over another. Often it is the potential side-effects of the anxiolytics that may dictate which drug is chosen.

There have been some studies on buspirone in TBI; it seems well tolerated and mechanisms have been explored for such action (for example, see Holzer,

1998). Antidepressants are worth trying, particularly if depression is also present. Selective serotonin reuptake inhibitors are a reasonable first choice. Antidepressants with sedative properties are valuable in some patients with anxiety, and may also help the insomnia which is often present. Trazodone has the advantage of being quite sedative and with less anti-cholinergic side-effects which might exacerbate cognitive impairment. Benzodiazepines should be avoided in those with chronic symptoms or in those with evidence of substance abuse, but may be useful in the acute situation. Propranolol may be helpful. Zafonte, Cullen, and Lexell (2002) provide a review of the mechanisms, efficacy, and side effects of serotonin agents in traumatic brain injury for the treatment of depression, and for panic disorder, obsessive–compulsive disorders, agitation, sleep disorders, and motor dysfunction.

Caution must be exercised with the use of psychotropic medication with brain injured groups. Many psychotropics may produce slight derealisation, or a feeling of being strange and detached. Given that derealisation/depersonalisation is common after head injury and is seen in those with anxiety, those with anxiety after TBI are particularly vulnerable to this side-effect. Care must also be taken to ensure that clients are aware of the risks and contraindications of use of such psychotropics. For example, Spinella and Eaton (2002) reported a case in which hypomania was induced by herbal and pharmaceutical psychotropic medicines being used in combination following mild traumatic brain injury, and that the hypomanic state was relieved by the discontinuation of the herbal remedies.

CR and CBT

Neurorehabilitation is concerned with supporting survivors in achieving meaningful goals, which are self-sustaining, self-actualising, and rewarding. For example, being in a job that is manageable and that one likes, or being able to take care of one's children, or to socialise with friends. Holistic forms of rehabilitation (be they cognitive and/or humanistic in background) are increasingly seen as appropriate systems for engaging survivors in reclaiming such social roles. However, referrals to outpatient and outreach programmes are not usually made on the basis of a defined goal arising from a cognitive problem (to compensate for a memory problem to regain employment), but usually on the basis of a combination of reduced insight, development of mood problems, chemical dependency, or threatened (or actual) family disintegration (see Harris, 1997). With such issues being key factors for either management for their own sake, and/or for their management such that a person could be enabled to develop a social role. Given the need for systems and strategies for managing mood-related issues, there is a need to develop evidence on which to base practice in this area.

CBT has been shown to be highly effective for the management of a range of mood disorders in the general mental health groups (see Roth & Fonaghy, 1996). CR and CBT both have an emphasis on enabling survivors to gain skills, record progress, challenge pessimism, and promote self-efficacy. CBT appears particularly well-suited for integration with CR as it provides systems and strategies for structuring interventions for people with cognitive disabilities (Manchester & Woods, 2001; Ponsford, 1995; Williams & Jones, 1997). CBT for OCD includes behavioural exposure, response prevention and management of negative intrusive thoughts. The behavioural components of CBT have been shown to be effective for the management of OCD symptoms (see March, Mulle, & Herbel, 1994). Davey and Tallis (1994) described additional features for a CBT treatment for OCD, including attentional strategies for managing self-doubt. CBT has shown to be effective, in general, for OCD and in the preventation of relapse (Roth & Fonagy, 1996). CBT has also been utilised extensively in health related issues (see Salkovskis & Warwick, 2001).

In describing the following case we hope to illustrate how CBT and CR are particularly well suited for TBI. First, both approaches share common philosophical roots and are philosophically consonant. Second, strategies from each may be developed in a complementary manner for assisting the other. Such as, one might learn (by role play and practice) relaxation skills, which might help manage intrusive thoughts, that clears space in working memory for processing other information. Or, for example, one might learn to use diaries and palm-tops that might help with predicting what to do and when, but might also serve for recording and challenging negative automatic thoughts.

CASE STUDY
DC: CBT and neuro-rehabilitation for OCD and health anxiety

DC was seen at a centre for cognitive rehabilitation. He was diagnosed as having an OCD and health concerns in the context of general neuropsychological deficits.

Assessment process. Assessment consisted of neuropsychological evaluation, multidisciplinary therapy assessment interviews, clinical psychology and neuropsychiatric evaluations, administration of mood and behaviour inventories, and self and observer ratings of cognitive, mood and behavioural symptoms over a 2-week period (for further details see Williams, Evans, & Wilson, 1999). Mood and psychiatric assessments followed DSM-IV guidelines for diagnoses of psychiatric disorders (American Psychiatric Association, 1994).

Pre-injury history, neuropsychological status, and mood state.   DC was a security system officer at the time of injury. He had suffered a TBI in an road traffic accident (coma of 4 weeks, PTA of 2–3 months). He also suffered orthopaedic injuries. He was seen 2 years post-injury. His family had become concerned over his withdrawn state, lack of purpose, and low mood. He had a dense retrograde amnesia and a poor anterograde memory. He exhibited a range of compulsive behaviours, involving tidying (kitchen areas, living room, etc.), and checking (doors, cookers, etc.). He did not have any premorbid psychological or psychiatric history of note.

DC's premorbid and current IQ were in at least the average range, which did not suggest any significant loss of intellectual ability or processing speed. His problem-solving, excecutive and sustained attention skills were also intact. His recognition memory also appeared intact. His ability to sustain divided attention, and switch attention, was impaired. His memory for immediate and delayed recall for verbal information was also impaired. His memory for the immediate recall for visual information was intact while his memory for and delayed recall of visual information was impaired.

DC noted that he did not "trust" himself to remember activities, of which there were few—he had a limited daily routine. He often "tidied up", and on rare trips from the house, checked that the cooker was off and that the doors were locked, up to 20 times. He socialised with difficulty, "checking himself" for personal possessions "constantly". He believed himself to be "a mess" (in terms of physical appearance) and therefore socially unacceptable. He also had fears over harming his legs if he engaged in any physical activities, such as playing football or swimming. His scores on the Hospital Anxiety and Depression Scale (HADS; Zigmond & Snaith, 1983) were in the moderate and mild ranges for anxiety and depression, respectively. At interview, he was assessed as being at risk of suicidal depression in the longer term. His responses on the Maudsley Obsessive–Compulsive Inventory (MOCI; see Hodgson & Rachman, 1977) were elevated.

Formulation.   DC had a dense amnestic disorder with attentional difficulties consequent to his TBI. He was also noted to have an OCD (Axis I) as an indirect consequence of organic injury (Axis III). It was also noted that he had maladaptive health behaviours affecting recovery of physical function (see DSM IV regarding "other conditions of clinical attention"). DC's OCD symptoms appeared to be related to the following: (1) cognitive disorders triggering self-doubt and rumination with checking as an overcompensation for poor memory; (2) checking and tidying providing a means of controlling aspects of his immediate environment and sense of safety in the absence of other, more meaningful, activities; (3) behaviours being negatively reinforced by avoidance (the behaviour "saved" him from social demands); (4) distorted self-image being maintained, and exacerbated, by avoidance of activities, with core negative self-beliefs leading to negative automatic thoughts; (5) health fears contributing to general avoidance behavioural pattern; and (6) problems being maintained and exacerbated by a lack of opportunity for developing adaptive responses. It was noted that DC's symptoms could not be understood solely in terms of a organic orderliness condition. It was also noted that DC had a number of strengths in terms of intact visual recall ability, family support, and an ability to identify personal goals.

Rehabilitation programme

The rehabilitation programme consisted of five components: (1) goal-setting procedures; (2) co-ordinating therapists for facilitating survivor's understanding of intervention and goals; (3) intervention on awareness of impairments and emotional reactions; (4) therapeutic group milieu for encouraging awareness and acceptance and use of strategies; and (5) supported social reintegration for follow-through of strategy use in home or work settings. For each survivor, individualised programmes contained an intensive rehabilitation phase followed by a community reintegration phase (attending the centre on 1–2 days per week, for example). Family members, partners and/or friends of the participant were invited to attend a support group for facilitating their understanding of the participant and to derive mutual emotional support. In "cognitive groups" survivors were encouraged to develop their understanding of their brain injury and its consequences, and how to manage and compensate for cognitive problems, for example, in a memory group. In "mood groups" survivors learn about their cognitive–behavioural reactions to trauma and their coping responses, and are facilitated to adopt strategies for managing their mood, and provided with a forum for mutual support.

General intervention.   DC was provided with support for developing an external memory system which included: filofax for long-term memory; voice organiser for supporting delayed memory; and an electronic organiser for prospective memory/reminding. He was also supported in developing stress management skills, including: relaxation skills; management of negative automatic thoughts (NATs); and attentional skills for "burning in" what he had "just done". A graded exposure programme was developed based on his least to most worrisome situations in three domains: social–leisure; community–mobility; and physical activities (see Table 1 for hierarchies of anxiety-provoking situations). He was asked to rate situations as "not involving much anxiety" (0–3), involving some anxiety, but usually manageable (4–6), and involving much anxiety and would be avoided (7–10). Over a period of 8 months, DC was provided with a programme that progressed from developing basic emotional and cognitive control skills through to integrating their use in functional situations (see Table 1 for "worries" and "coping strategies"

TABLE 1

Sample items from hierarchies of anxiety-provoking situations
(rated 0 (not anxious) to 10 (extremely anxious)) at Assessment (A) and Discharge (B)

		Worries (W) and Coping Strategies (CS)	A	B
Community mobility				
1. Local shop at home	W	What to buy/how much money/leaving house safe	3	3
	CS	List/associations (picture what I need)/listen to "door-click"		
2. Walking to Gym/pool near hospital	W	As above and how to get there/take what I need	8	4
	CS	Visual imagery/checklist		
3. Shopping in local town, e.g., for music	W	What I can afford/have already/what if see someone/too many people	5	3
	CS	Relaxation/visual image of what I have at home		
4. Shopping in main town with brother	W	What size/what I have already/too many people/get lost	7	2
	CS	List e.g. size/check "impulse buy", breathing exercise		
4. Shopping in main town by self	W	What bus to tak/where ticket is/getting lost/too many people	9	6
5. Travelling by bus by self	CS	Planning for it, not rushing/ticket in wallet/find quiet place on bus	6	5
Socialising				
1. Phone call to a friend to "catch up"	W	Only "putting up" with	7	5
	CS	List chat items/pad for notes who-what-when-where/breathing exercises		
1. Phone call to a friend to plan going out			8	5
2. Meeting friends in a pub	W	Unable to keep track of belongings/conversation	7	6
	CS	Visualise belongings (at home?)/find quiet area/check breathing		
3. Going to a club with friends	W	Too many people/pushing etc./losing friends and not getting self home	9	6
	CS	Breathing/picture where things are/make arrangements early		
Physical leisure				
1. Pool near hospital (quiet) with carer	W	Preoccupation with belongings/self-image and health	3	2
1. Pool near hospital (quiet) by self, quiet time	CS	Associations for locker number/picture what's in locker/relaxation	5	4
1. Pool near hospital (quiet) by self, moderately busy		As above	7	6
2. Pool, near home, with friend	W	Being hurt (pins in legs)	4	3
3. Football exercises, with friend	CS	Do warm ups/avoid hard tackling/catch negative thoughts	4	2

for anxiety-provoking situations). He was provided with specific clinical psychology input to develop his integrated use of such skills, with interdisciplinary input across all areas of his hierarchies.

Specific interventions.   For socialising, DC had a hierarchy that included the following situations, and associated negative automatic thoughts: calling a friend ("They're only putting up with me", "Anyway, I'll forget what we talked about"); going to a pub, and staying for 40 minutes ("I'll repeat myself", "I'll look a mess") and going to a club ("I'll get pushed and hurt my legs"). Over the course of the intervention, DC became skilled at using relaxation to prepare for situations and answer NATs, and became engaged in activities. For example, for making a call, he had a plan of using breathing exercises and getting a notepad for questions to ask and noting responses. On "checking the evidence" for "being a nuisance" to friends, he found that, when reviewing his mood diary on his organiser, he had examples of friends asking his advice, joking, and making joint plans. Regarding his physical health worries, he was supported in identifying and managing catastrophic NATs. For example, he was supported in re-contacting his consultant orthopaedic surgeon for feedback and advice on re-engaging in activities (such as, whether swimming or playing 5-a-side soccer would involve greater "risk" or "improve recovery"). Information gained was entered onto his personal organiser for checking when he felt signs of anxiety.

For socialising and community mobility, DC initially needed to develop his skills for leaving the house. This included "over-attending" to indications that the door was locked (when closing the door, he was instructed to listen to the click of the lock, and the serrated key making a scraping sound when coming out of the lock). He also practised making a visual image of where things were before leaving the house, so he could be more confident that he could "recreate" the image later ("I left the phone on the tabletop, picture it, don't worry"). When socialising he used his voice-recorder to note any future plans (where to meet later, for example), and relaxation skills if needed.

Outcome.   DC reported increased confidence in integrating such skills to achieve his goals. As can be seen in Figure 1, at discharge from the programme his scores on the HADs were significantly reduced, for anxiety and depression, to the non-clinical range, and his score on the MOCI scale was also reduced. He was asked to re-rate his anxiety for situations on his hierarchies. As can be seen in Figures 2, 3, and 4, his responses indicated that he had made progress in all areas, with significant improvements in social activities and community mobility, and some improvement in physical functioning. His self-report— corroborated by family members—indicated that not only were his anxiety levels reduced, he was engaging in previously avoided activities. He said: "I've

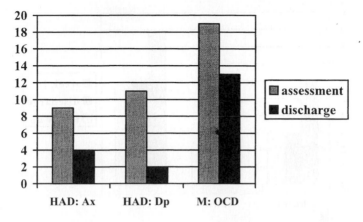

Figure 1.   Scores on mood measures—HADS and Maudsley OCD scale.

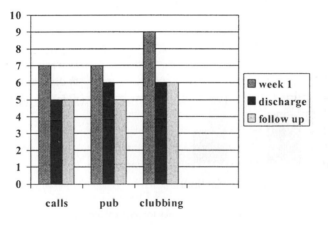

Figure 2.   Anxiety ratings for social hierarchy.

had my life back", "I spent all the time since the accident at home watching TV, afraid that if I do something I'd look foolish" "[I'm now with out with friends or] using [memory and emotional control strategies which] were confusing for a while but over time you get used to the new habits, and what technique to use where and when, and you get to trust it and [you] get confident [but] you've got to watch for that vicious cycle, of withdrawal". DC had maintained his progress at a 6-month review.

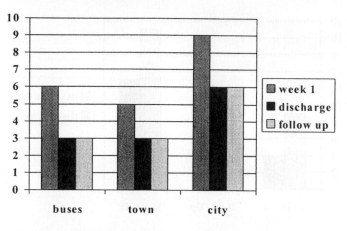

Figure 3.   Anxiety ratings for community mobility hierarchy.

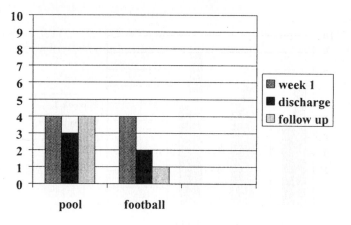

Figure 4.   Anxiety ratings for physical hierarchy.

CONCLUSIONS

Anxiety disorders may well be under-diagnosed in brain injured groups. However, clinical practice and existing evidence suggests that such disorders are probably common. Anxiety disorders may exist per se, but may also be in combination with a neuropsychiatric–behavioural syndrome. There is a need to develop effective assessment and treatment measures and strategies for such disorders for brain injury survivors.

In this paper we have illustrated how cognitive rehabilitation, in combination with CBT, provide systems and strategies for understanding and managing cognitive and emotional disorders for a TBI survivors. Although such themes were peripheral to the scope of this review, we have also discussed how neurological and neuropsychological factors may play a role in the aetiology of mental health problems in non-neurological groups.

It is recommended that there is continued integration of theory and practice between those in the fields of clinical neurosciences and mental health for addressing both the neurological aspects of mental health conditions and the mental health of neurological groups. One such level of integration is at that of therapeutic practice—such as in the use of CBT for neurological groups. Indeed, we believe that there are two crucial avenues for further research at present in TBI rehabilitation—to identify which TBI survivors may require CBT, and how CBT may be best delivered.

REFERENCES

American Psychiatric Association (1994). *Diagnostic and statistical manual—IV*. Washington, DC: American Psychiatric Association.

American Psychiatric Association (2000). *Diagnostic and statistical manual—IV* (4th edition). Washington, DC: American Psychiatric Association.

Berthier, M., Kulisevsky, J., Gironell, A., & Lopez, O. L. (2001). Obsessive–compulsive disorder and traumatic brain injury: Behavioural, cognitive and neuroimaging findings. *Neuropsychiatry, Neuropsychology & Behavioral Neurology, 14*, 23–31.

Bowen, A., Neumann, V., Conners, M., Tennant, A., & Chamberlain, M. A. (1998). Mood disorders following traumatic brain injury: Identifying the extent of the problem and the people at risk. *Brain Injury, 12*, 177–190.

Bradshaw, J. (2001). *Developmental disorders of the frontostriatal system: neuropsychological, neuropsychiatric, and evolutionary perspectives*. Hove: Psychology Press.

Bremner, J. D., Randall, P., Scott, T. M., Bronen, R. A., Seibyl, J. P., Southwick, S. M., Delaney, R. C., McCarthy, G., & Charney, D. S. (1995). MRI-based measurement of hippocampal volume in patients with combat related post traumatic stress disorder. *American Journal of Psychiatry, 152*, 973–981.

Brooks, N., Campsie, L., Symington, C., Beattie, A., & McKinley, W. (1987). The effects of severe head injury on patient and relative within seven years of injury. *Journal of Head Injury Rehabilitation, 2*, 1–13.

Davey, G. L., & Tallis, F. (1994). *New worrying: Perspectives on theory, assessment, and treatment*. New York: John Wiley.

Eells, T. D. (1997). Psychotherapy case formulation: History and current status. In T. Eells (Ed.), *Handbook of psychotherapy and case formulation*. New York: Guilford Press.

Harris, D. P. (1997). Outcome measures and a program evaluation model for postacute brain injury rehabilitation. *Journal of Outcomes Measurement, 1*, 23–30.

Hibbard, M. R., Uysal, S., Keple, K., Bogdany, J., & Silver, J. (1998). Axis I psychopathology in individuals with traumatic brain injury. *Journal of Head Trauma Rehabilitation, 13*, 24–39.

Hodgson, R., & Rachman, S. (1977). Obsessional–compulsive complaints. *Behaviour Research and Therapy, 15*, 389–395.

Holzer, J. C. (1998) Buspirone and brain injury. *Journal of Neuropsychiatry and Clinical Neurosciences, 10*(1), 113

Lishman, W. A. (1988). Physiogenesis and psychogenesis in the "post-concussional syndrome". *British Journal of Psychiatry, 153*, 460–469.

Lishman, W. (1998). *Organic psychiatry* (3rd ed.). Oxford: Blackwell Science.

Macmillan, P. J., Martelli, M. F., Hart, R. P., & Zasler, N. D. (2002). Pre-injury status and adaptation following traumatic brain injury. *Brain Injury, 16*, 41–49.

Manchester, D., & Woods, R. Ll. (2001). Applying cognitive therapy in neurobehavioural rehabilitation. In R. Ll. Woods & T. M. McMillan (Eds.), *Neurobehavioural disability and social handicap following traumatic brain injury*. Hove, UK: Psychology Press.

March, J., Mulle, K., & Herbel, B. (1994). Behavioural psychotherapy for children and adolescents with obsessive–compulsive disorder: An open trial of a new protocol-driven treatment package. *Journal of the American Academy of Child and Adolescent Psychiatry, 33*, 333–341.

McKeown, J., McGuffin, P., & Robinson, P. (1984). Obsessive–compulsive neurosis following head injury. A report of four cases. *British Journal of Psychiatry, 144*, 190–192.

Pender, N., & Fleminger, S. (1999). Outcome measures on inpatient cognitive and behavioural units: An overview. *Neuropsychological Rehabilitation, 9*, 345–361.

Ponsford, J., Sloan, S., & Snow, P. (1995). *Traumatic brain injury: Rehabilitation for everyday adaptive living*. Hove, UK: Psychology Press.

Rauch, S. L., Savage, C. R., Alpert, N. M., Fischman, A. J., & Jenike, M. A. (1997) The functional neuroanatomy of anxiety: A study of three disorders using positron emission tomography and symptom provocation. *Biological Psychiatry, 42*, 446–452.

Rosenthal, M., & Bond, M. R. (1990). Behavioural and psychiatric sequelae. In M. Rosenthal, E. R. Griffith, M. R. Bond, & J. D. Miller (Eds.), *Rehabilitation of the adult and child with traumatic brain injury* (2nd ed., pp. 179–192). Philadelphia: F. A. Davis.

Roth, A. D., & Fonagy, P. (1996). *What works for whom? A critical review of psychotherapy research*. New York: Guilford Press.

Scheutzow, M. H., & Wiercisiewski, D. R. (1999). Panic disorder in a patient with traumatic brain injury: A case report and discussion. *Brain Injury, 13*, 705–714.

Salkovskis, P. M., & Warwick, H. M. C. (2001) Meaning, misinterpretations, and medicine: A cognitive behavioural approach to understanding health anxiety and hypochondriasis. In V. Starcevic and D. R. Lipsitt (Eds.), *Hypochondriasis: Modern perspectives on an ancient malady*. Oxford: Oxford University Press.

Sapolsky, R., Uno, H., Rebert, C., & Finch, C. (1990). Hippocampal damage associated with prolonged glucocorticoid exposure in primates. *Journal of Neurosciences, 10*, 2897–2902.

Spinella, M., & Eaton, L. A. (2002). Hypomania induced by herbal and pharmaceutical psychotropic medicines following mild traumatic brain injury. *Brain Injury, 16*(4), 359–367.

Tallis, F. (1997). The neuropsychology of obsessive–compulsive disorder: A review and consideration of clinical implications. *British Journal of Clinical Psychology, 36*, 3–20.

Williams, W. H. (in press). Neuro-rehabilitation and cognitive behaviour therapy for emotional disorders in acquired brain injury. In B. A. Wilson (Ed), *Neuropsychological rehabilitation: Theory and practice* [In series Studies in neuropsychology: Development and cognition]. Sweets Verlag.

Williams, W. H., Evans J. J., & Wilson, B. A. (1999). Outcome measures for survivors of acquired brain injury in day and outpatient neurorehabilitation programmes. *Neuropsychological Rehabilitation, 9*, 421–436.

Williams, W. H., Evans J. J., & Wilson, B. A. (in press). Prevalence of post-traumatic stress disorder after severe traumatic brain injury in a representative community sample. *Brain Injury*.

Williams, W. H., & Jones, R. S. (1997). Teaching cognitive self-regulation of independence and emotion control skills. In B. S. Kroese, D. Dagnan, & K. Loumidis (Eds.), *Cognitive therapy for people with learning disabilities*. London: Routledge.

Wise, M. G., & Rundell, J. R. (1999) Anxiety and neurological disorders. *Seminars in Clinical Neuropsychiatry, 4*, 98–102.

Zafonte, R. D., Cullen, N., & Lexell, J. (2002) Serotonin agents in the treatment of acquired brain injury. *Journal of Head Trauma Rehabilitation, 17*(4), 322–334.

Zigmound A. S., & Snaith, R. P. (1983). The Hospital Anxiety and Depression Scale. *Acta Psychiatrica Scandinavica, 67*, 361–370.

Zitterl, W., Urban, C., Linzmayer I., Aigner, M., Demal, U., Semler, B., & Zitterl-Eglseer, K. (2001). Memory deficits in patients with DSM-IV obsessive–compulsive disorder. *Psychopathology, 34*, 113–117.

NEUROPSYCHOLOGICAL REHABILITATION, 2003, *13* (1/2), 149–164

Post-traumatic stress disorder and traumatic brain injury: A review of causal mechanisms, assessment, and treatment

Tom M. McMillan

University of Glasgow, UK

W. Huw Williams

University of Exeter, UK

Richard Bryant

University of New South Wales, Australia

In this paper we explore the evidence for post-traumatic stress disorder (PTSD) after traumatic brain injury (TBI). We examine its possible mediating mechanisms after brain injury, the evidence for its occurrence, risk, and protective factors, and the implications for intervention and service demands. In the first section we review the current literature relevant to cause, maintenance, and treatment of PTSD in general, before addressing issues associated with the assessment and management of PTSD after TBI. It is argued that PTSD may occur after a brain injury, and can be, relatively, a common disorder. However, explanatory mechanisms for its occurrence may be speculative. In this context, we argue, assessment and treatment need to be carefully considered, and comprehensive.

Emotional disorders seem common after brain injury (see Williams, Evans, & Fleminger, this issue). However, the psychological impact of the trauma event itself (as opposed to the brain injury), has only received attention relatively recently. In this paper we examine the prevalence of post-traumatic stress

---

Correspondence should be addressed to Tom McMillan, Department of Psychological Medicine, Academic Centre, Gartnavel Royal Hospital, 1055 Great Western Road, Glasgow G12 0XH, UK. Tel: (44) 141 211 3927, Email: t.m.mcmillan@clinmed.gla.ac.uk

http://www.tandf.co.uk/journals/pp/0960201l.html   DOI:10.1080/09602010244000453 disorder (PTSD) after traumatic brain injury (TBI), how it could be caused, the evidence for it occurring, risk factors, and implications for intervention and service demands. In the first section, we provide context in an overview of factors associated with cause, maintenance, and treatment of PTSD in general, before addressing issues associated with the assessment and management of PTSD after TBI.

PTSD: FEATURES, HISTORY, AND SYMPTOMS

There is a "presumed aetiology" of PTSD, involving direct experience or witnessing of an event during which someone died, and/or there was a threat either of death or to the physical integrity of self or others. It is expected that a survivor's initial response will involve fear, helplessness, and horror. Indeed, it is generally accepted that PTSD symptoms are most likely following experience of intense fear and helplessness during a traumatic event (see Diagnostic and Statistical Manual-IV, American Psychiatric Association, 1994; Breslau & Kessler, 2001). Traumatic events may also lie behind other mood and mental health disorders, although the links may be unclear (see Foa, Keane, & Friedman, 2000).

During the 20th century many labels have been given to people with complaints of severe distress after a traumatic event, including railway spine, shell shock, nervous shock, stress breakdown, post-Vietnam syndrome, traumatic neurosis, and rape trauma syndrome. The view that these were not symptoms specific to the events themselves, but were a pattern of normal reactions to abnormally horrifying events emerged partly as a result of the study of psychological complaints in Vietnam war veterans in the 1970s. By 1980 there was consensus that PTSD is a general anxiety disorder, as described in DSMIII (American Psychiatric Association, 1980). A key feature of PTSD is a change in how survivors construe the world and their place in it. Many survivors of trauma no longer feel in control of their lives, that the world is unpredictable and dangerous and they live in fear, often reporting a loss in trust in a "just world". Their memories of the trauma are frightening and they react by avoiding thoughts or situations that might trigger these memories and report feelings of emotional numbness and signs of blunted affect. The emotion is unresolved and invades daily life as flashbacks, intrusive thoughts and nightmares together with signs of hyperarousal such as enhanced startle. Acute stress disorder (ASD) is similar to PTSD conceptually (see Bryant & Harvey, 1997), and covers the first month after trauma, with greater emphasis on dissociative symptoms. If survivors develop ASD, there is significant risk of them developing PTSD.

Prevalence and risk factors

There is a lifetime prevalence rate for PTSD of 5% for males and 10% for females (see Foa, Keane, & Friedman, 2000). Women are four times more likely to develop PTSD than men given similar trauma. Symptom reporting can vary by gender. Men may under-report symptoms, or may mask symptoms, for example, through alcohol or drug misuse. Women may be more vulnerable because they are less able to buffer effects of anxiety as a result of social inequalities, such as being victims of domestic violence and having less economic power (see Resick, 2001). There may be an increased risk of PTSD in some individuals, for example, those with a premorbid history that includes early separation and/or a family history of general anxiety/PTSD (Resick, 2001).

The circumstances and nature of the traumatic event are also important. In terms of the event, "exposure level" and "controllability" are particularly salient in the genesis of PTSD. Exposure level refers to how personal the trauma was, how long the event was endured, the level of risk to the person, and the magnitude of horror they experienced. Controllability refers to the degree to which the person thinks they could have influenced the event. Litz et al. (1997) found that military personnel developed PTSD following high levels of exposure (such as being in the line of fire during patrol and witnessing comrades die), both in low and high risk groups, whereas in others with low exposure (e.g., being in a compound that was close to combat), PTSD was only associated with high risk groups. In essence, if the event is unanticipated and not preventable, involves actual or threatened fear of death, and is outside the person's control, then development of PTSD symptoms is likely.

Mechanisms of trauma

Biological and psychological factors converge to lead to PTSD, while social factors may put people more at risk for maintenance of the disorder.

Biological factors. It is widely accepted that evolutionary processes resulted in the "flight or fight" sympathetic nervous system for managing threat. The right frontal lobe and the limbic system seem particularly implicated in producing "alert, prepare, and act" responses to danger (see LeDoux, 1999). Physiological responses (adrenaline surge and associated cardiovascular and skeletal muscle effects) provide "emotional radar" for dealing with everyday life. However, the system may become overwhelmed if confronted with an abnormally powerful stressor. The survived event, and its internal register of the extreme stress reaction, can become associated with a cascade of psychological associations including fear, dread, and horror. Indeed stress-hormone levels, found to be elevated within a few hours of a traumatic event, might be associated with the development of PTSD (see Hawk et al., 2000; van der Kolk, 1994). Once the danger passes (or the body is too exhausted to cope) noradrenaline is released to restore body homoeostasis. When stress is severe, there may be a chronic stress response, shifting from hyper to hypo-aroused states, without periods of calm. Further complicating factors associated with the physiological response to trauma include production of higher levels of natural opiates, which may mask pain but may add to the blunted emotions associated with the condition (Resick, 2001); raised levels of cortisol during and following trauma may cause neuronal, including hippocampal, damage with consequent effects on memory (see Markowitsch, 1998). Reduced hippocampal volume, activation of the amygdala following symptom activation, and decreased activity in Broca's area have been reported in brain imaging studies of people with PTSD (Hull, 2002). In fact, reduced hippocampal volume has been reported in people with chronic PTSD (Bremner et al., 1995), but not soon after trauma (Bonne et al., 2001) suggesting that there may be a developmental process rather than a premorbid neuroanatomical vulnerability. Although further controlled studies are required here, it is possible that physiological reactions associated with trauma might cause brain impairment that in turn reduces the ability to cope with the aftermath of events.

Psychological.   There is a range of psychological reactions to trauma. Initial reactions are usually to perception of a major threat and can involve relief or remain unresolved. At semantic levels there are attributions, which, if particularly related to blame, may be associated with the development of PTSD. Following accidents, such as road traffic accidents (RTA), it seems that external attributions of causality are particularly associated with symptom complaints. Hickling et al. (1998) found that people with PTSD who blamed themselves had fewer symptoms and recovered more rapidly than those who blame others. Delahanty et al. (1997) also found that RTA survivors who reported others as "responsible" were likely to demonstrate greater distress 6 and 12 months post-accident. Williams, Williams, and Ghadiali (1998) found that external attribution of causality (e.g., believing that someone recklessly drove towards the survivor) was associated with anxiety and depression in TBI survivors. However, internal attributions may not always be accurate or related to better outcome. For example, it is common for survivors of assault or abuse to experience inappropriate self-blame (see Resick, 2001). This has been described as "responsibility distortion", which entails "the belief that one caused an event that is out of one's control" (Resick, 2001, p. 129). Underscoring this point, a prospective study of 157 crime victims found that the attributions of blame to oneself (shame) in relation to the trauma in the initial month predicted PTSD severity 6 months later—with elevated shame being associated with PTSD symptoms (Andrews, Brewin, Rose, & Kirk, 1998). It is therefore important to identify how survivors develop their attributions, and to consider the context, nature and type of survived event. Avoidance tends to be the longer term behavioural reaction to trauma material (e.g., places, images) and has further consequences for the symptom picture; a desire to avoid intrusions can result in avoidance of situational triggers, resulting in negative reinforcement (reduced frequency of fear response), which in turn increases the likelihood of further avoidance. Such behavioural factors may be associated with the development of negative cognitive schemata involving cognitive distortions about themselves, the world, and their future. For example, survivors may have very concrete "all or nothing" assumptions such as "I can't cope . . . I will always be like this". These distortions may indicate a perception of insecurity and difficulty that reflects reduced feelings of self-efficacy (sense of control in the world), reduced ability to predict events and outcomes, and hyper-vigilance for potential danger. Such themes are consonant with psychodynamic formulations of responses to trauma, where the survivor is considered to have experienced such an overwhelming degree of stress that they have difficulty in integrating and assimilating the trauma images and beliefs in a coherent self-narrative. Consequently, trauma material is repressed by a process of emotional numbing that protects the ego (Brewin, Dalgleish, & Joseph, 1996; Horowitz, Wilner, & Alvarez, 1979).

Maintenance, course and duration. If exposed to trauma, most people develop stress reactions. Despite the prevalence of acute stress reactions, there is evidence that the typical course of adaptation is to recover in the months following trauma exposure. For example, in one study 70% of women and 50% of men were diagnosed with PTSD at an average of 19 days after an assault; the rate of PTSD at 4-month follow-up dropped to 21% for women and zero for men (Riggs, Rothbaum, & Foa, 1995). Similarly, whereas 94% of rape victims displayed PTSD symptoms 2 weeks post-trauma, this rate dropped to 47% 11 weeks later (Rothbaum et al., 1992). Similarly, half of a sample meeting criteria for PTSD shortly after a motor vehicle accident had remitted by 6 months and two-thirds had remitted by 1 year post-trauma (Blanchard, et al., 1996). These patterns indicate that the normative response following trauma is initially to experience a range of PTSD symptoms but that the majority of these reactions will remit in the following months.

Comorbidity. PTSD is often comorbid with other mental health problems including panic disorder, phobic reactions, depression, somatisation, obsessive–compulsive disorder, and substance abuse (see DSMIV). PTSD is also associated with impairment in social and occupational functioning. Treatment is important not only to reduce distress, but for health-economy gains. PTSD may be overlooked, particularly in someone who presents with mood or behavioural difficulties.

Faking symptoms of PTSD.   This can be a consideration particularly in cases pursuing litigation to obtain compensation, and faking has been reported (Lynn & Belza, 1984). Existing studies on lay people suggest that they have a limited knowledge at recall of symptoms of PTSD when presented with a vignette relating a traumatic event (Burges & McMillan, 2000), but are able to *recognise* symptoms from a checklist (Burges & McMillan, 2001; Lees-Haley & Dunn, 1994). The implication is that assessors of claimants should be cautious in their use of questionnaires as they can be "faked by untrained lay people" (Burges & McMillan, 2000).

PTSD AND TRAUMATIC BRAIN INJURY

Some have argued that PTSD cannot develop after TBI because the coma and organic amnesia associated with TBI interfere with or prevent the genesis of traumatic experience, and hence an anxiety state based on re-experience cannot develop (Bontke, Rattok, & Boake, 1996; Sbordone, 1992). Consistent with this, Sbordone and Liter (1995) found no evidence for PTSD in a post-concussional symptom group and none for postconcussional syndrome in people without TBI and diagnosed with PTSD. These authors appropriately warn about the overlap of symptoms between the two conditions (e.g., problems with concentration, sleep, and temper). However, a difficulty with this study is that it was retrospective and non-blind. There is mounting evidence that PTSD can occur in the context of minor or severe TBI, underpinned by a more complex and comprehensive account of potential mechanisms (Bryant, 2001; McMillan, 1996).

PTSD and mild TBI

Mild TBI involves loss of consciousness for up to 30 minutes and post-traumatic amnesia of less than 24 hours (American Congress of Rehabilitation Medicine, 1993). Several studies on minor brain injury show that PTSD can occur despite a loss of consciousness during the event.

Controlled studies.   Bryant and Harvey (1995) found acute stress disorder in 27% of 38 people with "mild" TBI and in 43% of 38 non-TBI controls. A prospective study on minor TBI found acute stress disorder in 15% of 48 cases (Harvey & Bryant, 1998). In a later paper on 63 people with mild TBI and 71 people with no TBI, there was an incidence of PTSD of approximately 25% in both groups at 6-month follow-up (Bryant & Harvey, 1999). Mayou, Black, and Bryant (2000) investigated 1441 RTA survivors, of whom 2% had definitely been unconscious, 4% probably and the remainder not (severe TBI cases were excluded). At 3 months 48% of the definite and 23% of the probable minor TBI groups had PTSD compared with 23% of the non-TBI group. At one year 33% of the definite and 14% of the probable TBI group had PTSD compared to 17% of the non-TBI group. This reversed their earlier view, based on a study of 188 consecutive RTA cases, where PTSD was not found in a sub-group with mild TBI (Mayou, Bryant, & Duthie, 1993).

Uncontrolled studies. Middleboe, Andersen, Birket-Smith, and Friis (1992) carried out a prospective study on mild TBI; 51 of 118 people partici-pated, and one was thought to have PTSD on the basis of Impact of Events Scale (IES; Horowitz et al., 1979) scores and interview. Grigsby and Kaye (1993) reported PTSD in one third of patients who had whiplash or an undefined range of severity of TBI. Hickling et al. (1998) found that 36% of 107 motor vehicle accident survivors with mild brain injury developed PTSD; 16 of their sample had lost consciousness, and 9 of these had symptoms of PTSD. At least 8 single case reports also attest to the development of PTSD after minor TBI (Horton, 1993; Layton & Wardi-Zonna, 1995; McGrath, 1997; Silver, Rattock, & Anderson, 1997).

PTSD and severe TBI

Severe traumatic brain injury involves a period of coma of at least 6 hours and/or a period of post-traumatic amnesia of at least one day (McMillan and Greenwood, 2003).

Controlled studies. No controlled studies on severe TBI were identified.

Uncontrolled studies. In a retrospective study of clinical cases, using interview and the IES, McMillan (1996) found that 10 of 312 patients with TBI had PTSD. At least 9 other single case reports of PTSD after severe TBI have been published (Bryant, 1996; King, 1997; Layton & Wardi-Zonna, 1995; McMillan, 1991; McNeil & Greenwood, 1996; Silver et al., 1997; Williams, Evans, & Wilson, 2002).

In terms of single group studies, Bryant et al. (2000) reported a 6-month follow-up of 96 patients admitted to a brain injury unit. They found that 27% satisfied diagnostic criteria for PTSD using an interview schedule based on DSMIII criteria. In this study the sample was not fully representative of severe TBI because participants were not randomly selected and survivors with low Glasgow Coma Scale scores were excluded. Ohry, Rattock, and Solomon (1996) found that 33% of a mixed group of 24 people with brain injury met the criteria for PTSD; information about the severity of the TBI is not given, but as they were accepted for inpatient rehabilitation the TBI was likely to be severe. Warden et al. (1997) report 47 military personnel with severe TBI, none of whom had PTSD according to DSMIII-R criteria, although 14% had avoidance and arousal symptoms. Hibbard et al. (1998) considered psychopathology generally in a retrospective study on 100 people with TBI, and in whom the brain injury was severe in 61%; PTSD was reported in 19% of whom 2% had this diagnosis before the brain injury. Williams, Evans, Needham, and Wilson (2002) reported a prevalence of PTSD of 18% (6% had severe PTSD) in a representative, post-acute community sample of 66 survivors of severe TBI. Given the elevated risk of false-positive diagnoses of psychiatric problems in people with TBI (McMillan, 2001) they only took scores on the IES that were above the mild range to indicate the presence of PTSD symptoms.

PTSD and TBI in children

Although documented, "reliable estimation of the prevalence of PTSD in children and adolescents is extremely difficult" (Yule, Perrin, & Smith, 1999, p. 33). Following Hurricane Hugo in South Carolina, the incidence of PTSD in children varied with exposure to the event; 5% if no exposure, 10% if mild, 16% if moderate, and 29% in a high exposure group (Lonigan, Shannon, Finch, & Daugherty, 1991). Levi, Drotar, Yeates, and Taylor (1999) examined PTSD symptoms in 6–12 year old children with severe TBI, moderate TBI, or ortho-paedic injuries. Using a self-rating scale and a structured interview, they found that the numbers of children with moderate to severe PTSD symptomatology (self-rating) was 42% at 6 months and 49% at 12 months for those with severe TBI ($n = 29$) compared to 18% and 21%, respectively, for those with moderate TBI ($n = 31$), and 22% and 29% for the orthopaedic group ($n = 36$). Carer/parent ratings confirmed this general pattern of symptomatology. Gerring et al. (2002) studied 95 children with severe TBI and amnesia for the event prospectively for one year. On the basis of interviews with parents and child, 13% (12) of children were diagnosed with PTSD at one year, and predictors of symptom severity were premorbid factors including psychosocial adversity and anxiety, injury severity, early post-injury symptoms of depression, and non-neurotic psychiatric diagnosis.

Summary

Over the past decade an increasing number of papers have been published on PTSD after TBI, which overall support the case that PTSD can develop after minor or severe TBI in children and adults, despite loss of consciousness and post-traumatic amnesia. Some caution is required when comparing studies, given that different assessments of PTSD have been used, the severity of brain injury is not always clear, several studies are retrospective, and because relatively few are well controlled and none incorporate assessment of PTSD that is "blind" to group membership.

The genesis of PTSD after TBI

Although it is increasingly accepted that PTSD can occur after TBI, the mechanisms underlying its development remain speculative and accounts have to consider the context of neurological injury and neuropsychological deficits. A key issue is memory and attribution, which are now considered.

Declarative memory.   The duration of retrograde amnesia after severe TBI is variable, after minor TBI is brief, and in some survivors of TBI there is a complete or patchy recall up to, or a few seconds before impact. Memory for events shortly before a TBI might therefore provide a source for the development of PTSD; for example the terror associated with "a lorry emerging from a side road on a collision course" (McMillan, 1996). It is widely accepted that there are often "islands" of memory during post-traumatic amnesia. For this reason its end is defined as a return of continuous memory for day-to-day events (Russell and Smith, 1961), and assessors must take care not to define the end point of PTA as the first event recalled after coma (McMillan, 1997). These "islands" of memory for a traumatic event can form a substrate for intrusive experiences, for example, "of being trapped in a vehicle . . . of the distress of others involved in the accident" (McMillan, 1996), thinking "the car was going to blow . . . and going to be burned" (Silver et al., 1997). There may be upsetting memories after the survivor leaves the scene of the accident; for example, the journey to hospital by ambulance, or a first recollection on regaining consciousness in hospital with "no recollection of how they had sustained their injuries" (McMillan, 1996). Recently, Williams et al. (2002) found that of 66 TBI survivors 18 had an island of memory for their events. They found that having a memory for the event was not necessarily associated with the development of PTSD. Indeed, mean scores on the IES did not differ between those who did and those who did not have declarative memories. However, the nature of the experience on which the memory is based may be relevant. One survivor, who had a high IES score, remembered his girlfriend dying in the accident and feeling he was about to die, before becoming comatose. Another, with a low IES score remembered rescue workers saying he would be free shortly before losing consciousness. Hence, peri-traumatic experience might influence the risk of developing PTSD (Grey, Holmes, & Brewin, 2001), although other factors (e.g., bereavement) may be important.

Implicit memory.   Recent theories have recognised that traumatic memories may be encoded and stored at an implicit level. This view has been most thoroughly described by Brewin and colleagues in their dual representation theory of PTSD (Brewin et al., 1996). This theory posits that traumatic experiences can be encoded and stored either as verbally accessible memories

(VAMs) or as situationally accessible memories (SAMs). Whereas VAMs are defined as verbal or visual memories that can be intentionally retrieved, SAMs are conceptualised as subconsciously generated memories. The latter may be experienced as flashbacks, a sense of reliving a trauma, or somatic sensations that are reminiscent of the traumatic experience. It is possible that during periods of impaired consciousness associated with TBI, people may encode features of their experience that are not consciously elaborated on. That is, despite disruption to areas of the brain that store declarative memories, implicit memories may be accessed during exposure to situations similar to those in which the original trauma occurred. For example, McNeil and Greenwood (1996) describe the case of a survivor of attempted murder who had no memory for the event in which assailants attempted drive into him, but he nevertheless avoided carrying out mobility exercises that took him near urban roads. This perspective is consistent with considerable evidence that memories can be encoded outside of awareness and that these memories can influence ongoing emotions and behaviours (for a review, see Schacter, Chiu, & Ochsner, 1993). In terms of PTSD, this perspective can explain findings that PTSD following severe TBI is mediated more by psychological distress or physiological reactivity than by declarative memories of the traumatic event (Bryant et al., 2000).

Confabulation, reconstructed and repressed memories. Intrusive thoughts and images might not be veridical accounts of events. They may have emotional pain but not have a discursive memory of the event. Survivors may retain emotional traces of their events, and a need to create a "unified script". Reported "memories" may be a narrative consistent with their emotional state, which is a reconstruction of events containing information given to them by others as well as their own imaginings (Bryant et al., 1998; Bryant, Marosszeky, Crooks, & Gurka, 2000; McMillan, 1996). Harvey and Bryant (2001) found that 40% of mild TBI patients who reported significant memory loss in the first month after their trauma reported that they had full recall for the event when they were re-assessed 2 years later. For example, a man with no awareness of an accident, 10 months later said "he imagined the wreck of the car and saw himself bleeding in the front seat" (Bryant, 1996). The amnesic gap itself may provide a source for rumination that might itself become traumatic or be misconstrued as such (McMillan, 2001). Furthermore, a rumination may be established in part because of pre-injury thoughts, tendencies or circumstances, which are expressed more readily, or be emotionally "reawakened", as a result of brain injury if there is reduced capacity to manage ruminative material (see also Berthier, Posada, & Puentes, 2001).

Neurological and neuropsychological variables as protective and risk factors

It has been argued that the amnesic gap (retrograde amnesia, coma and post-traumatic amnesia) may protect against the development of PTSD (Sbordone & Leiter, 1995). There is not strong evidence for this, although several authors note that intrusive re-experience may be less frequent, less vivid, and less severe in people with brain injury (McMillan, 1996; Turnbull, Campell, & Swann, 2001; Warden et al., 1997). Generally, the situation is likely to be more complex given that PTSD seems to occur in people with a wide range of severity of TBI as measured by durations of coma and PTA. Further, no clear relationship between severity of TBI and severity of PTSD has been found (Feinstein et al., 2002). It may be that a combination of factors such as recall of the trauma, new learning, insight, executive ability, and coping strategies play a role. Hence, incomplete representations of the trauma could be less effective in fuelling ruminations or alternatively could provide a drive to fill the "amnesic gap" (McMillan, 2001). Greater severities of brain injury are more likely to result in greater likelihood of severe cognitive deficits, which in turn will reduce abilities to consider, reflect on, and report experiences. Survivors with severe memory disorders may not recall their current experiences well enough to make accurate reports about symptoms of disturbed mood, and those with dysexecutive disorders may lack insight into difficulties with making realistic judgements about their mood state or have difficulty in forming or developing appropriate coping strategies. Cognitive impairments may reduce the likelihood of symptom complaints associated with PTSD being distinguished from more non-specific malaise after TBI. Indeed, it is often assumed that reduced insight protects against mood disorder after TBI (Ownsworth & Oei, 1998) although there is little empirical evidence to support this proposition. Williams, Evans, Needham, and Wilson (2002) found no relationship between reporting of PTSD symptoms and severity of TBI, but did find that intensity of PTSD symptoms correlated with responses on a measure of insight (i.e., those with apparently lower insight reported less intense symptoms than those with more intact insight). However, the authors noted that although poorer insight might protect against PTSD symptom complaints in some cases, this does not mean that such survivors are not vulnerable to the disorder. Indeed, poor insight may make a survivor vulnerable to being "trapped" by intrusions if associated with other dysexecutive problems such as concreteness and rigidity of thinking. The finding that disorganisation of memory is a predictor of ASD would support this view (Harvey & Bryant; 1999).

There are a number of parallels in terms of predictors of ASD or PTSD in cases with and with no TBI. These include avoidant coping (Harvey & Bryant, 1998), external attributions of causality/blame (Williams et al., 1998, 2002), fear of death or belief in survival, and loss of control at the time of the event. Depression has not been consistently associated with PTSD after TBI (Harvey & Bryant, 1998, Levin et al., 2001).

TREATMENT

Cognitive–behaviour therapy (CBT) is widely accepted as a treatment for PTSD (Foa, Keane, & Friedman, 2000) and case studies support a use for it in patients with PTSD after TBI (McGrath, 1997; McMillan, 1991; McNeil & Greenwood, 1996; Middleboe et al., 1992). In fact CBT may be of particular value to people with cognitive disability because it is structured, educative, and interactive (Manchester & Wood, 2001; Ponsford, Sloan, & Snow, 1995; see Williams, Evans, and Fleminger this issue).

McMillan (1991) described the first treatment case of PTSD after TBI, with successful use of a behavioural approach in managing intrusive and avoidant symptoms in a survivor of a severe head injury with complete amnesia for the event. McGrath (1997) described the use of a CBT approach in a mild head injured survivor with PTSD. It was noted that changes in "personality", originally believed to be due to brain damage, were mediated by stress and were modified by treatment. McNeil and Greenwood (1996) used CBT in a survivor of severe TBI with amnesia for the event (attempted murder) which achieved a reduction in IES score, frequency of nightmares and irritability, and re-engagement in previously avoided activities. Williams, Evans, and Wilson (2003) describe two survivors of TBI with PTSD; for KE, an island of memory for the event, coupled with fear conditioning to similar situations, was related to the development of core PTSD symptoms. CM survived a severe penetrating head injury without disturbance of consciousness, and there was a clear congruency between the event survived and PTSD experienced. Both had persisting cognitive impairments (primarily attention and memory), selective visual impairments, and suffered significant loss of social role. In common with many PTSD sufferers, there were comorbid problems with alcohol and depression, respectively. Cognitive rehabilitation was provided to help with their cognitive and social problems and to enable them to engage in CBT for their PTSD symptoms—which included use of stress inoculation and graded exposure to avoided situations and trauma re-experiences. Both reported improvement in managing mood state and in re-developing social roles. Bryant, Moulds, Guthrie, and Nixon (in press) used five sessions of CBT or supportive counselling in 24 cases of ASD after mild TBI, with the aim of preventing PTSD from developing. A better outcome was found for the CBT group post-treatment and at 6-month follow-up, suggesting that PTSD after mild TBI may be prevented by early provision of CBT.

CONCLUSIONS

There is a growing body of evidence that suggests that PTSD can occur after TBI in children or adults, even if the brain injury has been severe and there is little or no recall of the event that caused the injury. The incidence remains uncertain, with wide variations reported between studies. There is a need for further well-controlled studies that carefully consider diagnostic assessment issues and risk factors in people who have brain injury. Further research is required on ways in which PTSD might develop in people who are amnesic for the traumatic event and this may inform treatment techniques, which may need to be adapted to account for brain injury factors that might be important in the genesis and maintenance of symptoms.

REFERENCES

American Congress of Rehabilitation Medicine (1993). Definition of mild traumatic brain injury. *Journal of Head Trauma Rehabilitation, 8*, 86–87.

American Psychiatric Association (1980). *Diagnostic and Statistical Manual of Mental Disorders* (4th ed.). Washington, DC: American Psychiatric Association.

American Psychiatric Association (1994). *Diagnostic and Statistical Manual of Mental Disorders* (4th ed.). Washington, DC: American Psychiatric Association.

Andrews B., Brewin C. R., Rose, S., & Kirk, M. (2000). Predicting PTSD in victims of violent crime: The role of shame, anger and blame. *Journal of Abnormal Psychology, 109*, 69–73.

Berthier, M. L., Posada, A., & Puentes, C. (2001). Dissociative flashbacks after right frontal injury in a Vietnam veteran with combat-related posttraumatic stress disorder. *Journal of Neuropsychiatry and Clinical Neuroscience, 13*, 101–105.

Blanchard, E. B., Hickling, E. J., Taylor, A. E., Loos, W. R., Forneris, C. A., & Jaccard, J. (1996). Who develops PTSD from motor vehicle accidents. *Behaviour Research and Therapy, 34*, 1–10.

Bonne, O., Brandes, G., & Golboa, A. (2001). Longitudinal study of hippocampal volume in trauma survivors with PTSD. *American Journal of Psychiatry, 158*, 1248–1251.

Bontke, F., Rattok, J, & Boake, C. (1996). Do patients with mild brain injury have posttraumatic stress disorder too? *Journal of Head Trauma Rehabilitation, 11*, 95–102.

Bremner, J. D., Randall, P., Scott, T. M., Bronen, R. A., Seibyl, J. P., Southwick, S. M., Delaney, R. C., McCarthy, G., Charney, D. S., & Innis, R. B. (1995). MRI-based measures of hippocampal volume in patients with combat related post traumatic stress disorder. *American Journal of Psychiatry, 152*, 973–981.

Breslau, N., & Kessler, R. C. (2001). The stressor criterion in DSMIV post traumatic stress disorder: An empirical investigation. *Biological Psychiatry, 50*, 699–704.

Brewin, C. R., Dalgleish, T., & Joseph, S. (1996). A dual representation theory of posttraumatic stress disorder. *Psychological Review, 103*, 670–686.

Bryant, R. (1996). Post traumatic stress disorder, flashbacks and pseudomemories in closed head injury. *Journal of Traumatic stress, 9*, 621–629.

Bryant, R. A. (2001). Posttraumatic stress disorder and traumatic brain injury: Can they co-exist? *Clinical Psychology Review, 21*, 931–945.

Bryant, R. A., & Harvey, A. G. (1995). Acute stress response: A comparison of head injured and non-head injured patients. *Psychological Medicine, 25*, 869–873.

Bryant, R. A., & Harvey, A. G. (1997). Acute Stress Disorder: A critical review of diagnostic issues. *Psychological Review, 17*, 757–773, 1995.

Bryant, R. A., & Harvey, A. G, (1999). The influence of traumatic brain injury on acute stress disorder and post traumatic stress disorder following motor vehicle accidents. *Brain Injury*, *13*, 15–22.

Bryant, R. A., Marosszeky, J. E., Crooks, J., & Gurka, J. A. (2000). Posttraumatic stress disorder after severe traumatic brain injury. *American Journal of Psychiatry*, *157*(4), 629–631.

Bryant, R. A., Moulds, M. L., Guthrie, R., & Nixon, R. D. V. (in press). Treating acute stress disorder after mild brain injury. *American Journal of Psychiatry.*

Burges, C., & McMillan, T. M. (2001). The ability of naive participants to report symptoms of post-traumatic stress disorder . *British Journal of Clinical Psychology*, *40*, 209–214.

Delahanty, D. L., Herberman, H. B., Craig, K. J., Hayward, M. C., Fullerton,C. S., Ursano, R. J., & Baum, A. (1997). Acute and chronic distress and posttraumatic stress disorder as a function of responsibility for serious motor vehicle accidents. *Journal of Consulting and Clinical Psychology*, *65*, 560–567.

Feinstein, A., Hershkop, S., Ouchterlony, D., Jardine, A., & McCullagh, S. (2002). Post traumatic amnesia and recall of a traumatic event following traumatic brain injury. *Journal of Neuropsychiatry and Clinical Neurosciences*, *14*, 25–30.

Foa, E. B., Keane, T. M., & Friedman, M. J. (2000). Introduction to "Guidelines for Treatment of PTSD", *Journal of Traumatic Stress*, *13*, 4.

Gerring, J. P., Slomine, B., Vasa, R. A., Grados, M., Chen, A., Rising, W., Christensen, J., Denckla, M., & Ernst, M. (2002). Clinical predictors of post traumatic stress disorder after closed head injury in children. *Journal of American Academy of Child and Adolescent Psychiatry*, *41*, 157–165.

Grey, N. H., Holmes, E., & Brewin, C. R. (2001). Peritraumatic emotional "hot spots" in memory. *Behavioural and Cognitive Psychotherapy*, *29*, 367–372.

Grigsby, J., & Kaye, K. (1993). Incidence and correlates of depersonalisation following head trauma. *Brain Injury*, *7*, 507–513.

Harvey, A. G., & Bryant, R. A. (1998). Predictors of acute stress following mild traumatic brain injury. *Brain Injury*, *12*, 147–154.

Harvey, A. G., & Bryant, R. A. (1999). A qualitative investiagation of the organisation of traumatic memories. *British Journal of Clinical Psychology*, *38*, 401–405.

Harvey, A. G., & Bryant, R. A. (2001). Reconstructing trauma memories: A prospective study of amnesic trauma survivors. *Journal of Traumatic Stress*, *14*, 277–282.

Hawk, L. W., Dougall, A. L., Ursano, R. J., & Baum A. (2000). Urinary catecholamines and cortisol in recent-onset posttraumatic stress disorder after motor vehicle accidents. *Psychosomatic Medicine*, *62*(3), 423–434.

Hibbard, M. R., Uyssal, S., Kepler, K., Bogdany, J., & Silver, J. (1998). Axis I symptomatology in individuals with traumatic brain injury. *Journal of Head Trauma Rehabilitation*, *13*, 24–39.

Hickling, E. J., Gillen, R., Blanchard, E. B., Buckley, T. C., & Taylor, A. E. (1998). Traumatic brain injury and PTSD: A preliminary investigation of neuropsychological test results in PTSD secondary to motor vehicle accidents. *Brain Injury*, *12*, 265–274.

Horowitz, M., Wilner, N., & Alvarez, W. (1979). Impact of events scale: A measure of subjective stress. *Psychosomatic Medicine*, *41*, 209–218.

Horton, A. M., Jr. (1993). PTSD and mild head trauma. *Perceptual Motor Skills*, *76*, 243–246.

Jennett, B., & MacMillan, R. (1981). Epidemiology of head injury. *British Medical Journal*, *282*, 101–104.

Hull, A. M. (2002). Neuroimaging findings in post traumatic stress disorder. *British Journal of Psychiatry*, *181*, 102–110.

King, N. S. (1997). Post traumatic stress disorder and head injury as a dual diagnosis: "islands" of memory as a mechanism. *Journal of Neurology Neurosurgery Psychiatry*, *62*, 82–84.

Layton, B. S., & Wardi-Zonna, K. (1995). Post traumatic stress disorder with neurogenic amnesia for the traumatic event. *The Clinical Neuropsychologist*, *9*, 2–10.

LeDoux, J. (1999). The power of emotions. In R. Conlan (Ed.), *States of mind: New discoveries about how our brains make us who we are.* New York: Wiley.

Lees-Hayley, P. R., & Dunn, J. T. (1994). The ability of naïve subjects to report symptoms of mild brain injury, post-traumatic stress disorder, major depression and generalised anxiety disorder. *Journal of Clinical Psychology, 50,* 252–256.

Levi, R. B., Drotar, D., Yeates, K. O., & Taylor, H. G. (1999). Postraumatioc stress symptoms in children following orthopaedic or traumatic brain injury. *Journal of Clinical Child Psychology, 28,* 232–243.

Levin, H. S., Brown, S. A., Song, J. X., McCauley, S. R., Boake, C., Contant, C. F., Goodman, H., & Kotrla, K. J. (2001). Depression and post traumatic stress disorder at three months after mild to moderate traumatic brain injury. *Journal of Clinical Experimental Neuropsychology, 23,* 754–769.

Litz, B. T., Orsillo, S. M., Friedman, M. J., Ehlich, P. J., & Batres, A. R. (1997). Posttraumatic stress disorder associated with peacekeeping duty in Somalia for U.S. military personnel. *American Journal of Psychiatry, 54*(2), 178–184.

Lonigan, Shannon, Finch, & Daugherty, (1991). Stress symptoms in children following orthopedic or traumatic brain injury. *Journal of Clinical Psychotherapy, 28,* 232–243.

Lynn, E. J., & Belza, M. (1984). Factitious posttraumatic stress disorder: The veteran who never got to Vietnam. *Hospital and Community Psychiatry, 35,* 697–701.

Manchester, D., & Wood, R. Ll. (2001). Applying cognitive therapy in neurobehavioural rehabilitation. In R. Ll. Wood & T. M. McMillan, *Neurobehavioural disability and social handicap following acquired brain injury,* (pp 157–174). Hove, UK: Psychology Press.

Markowitsch, H. I (1999). Cognitive neuroscience of memory. *Neurocase, 4,* 429–435.

Mayou, R. A., Black, J., & Bryant, B. (2000). Unconsciousness, amnesia and psychiatric symptoms following road traffic accident injury. *British Journal of Psychiatry, 177,* 540–545.

Mayou, R., Bryant, B., & Duthie, R. (1993). Psychiatric consequences of road traffic accidents. *British Medical Journal, 307,* 647–651.

McGrath, J. (1997). Cognitive impairment associated with post traumatic stress disorder and minor head injury: A case report. *Neuropsychological Rehabilitation, 7,* 231–239.

McMillan, T. M. (1991). Post-traumatic stress disorder and severe head injury. *British Journal of Psychiatry,* 159, 431–433.

McMillan, T. M. (1996). Post traumatic stress disorder following minor and severe head injury: 10 single cases. *Brain Injury, 10,* 749–758.

McMillan, T. M. (1997). Minor head injury. *Current Opinion in Neurology, 10,* 479–483.

McMillan, T. M. (2001). Errors in diagnosing PTSD after traumatic brain injury. *Brain Injury, 15,* 39–46.

McMillan, T. M., & Greenwood, R. J, (2003). Head injury. In R. J. Greenwood, M. Barnes, T. M. McMillan, & C. Ward (Eds.), *Handbook of neurological rehabilitation* (pp. 465–486). Hove, UK: Psychology Press.

McNeil, J. E., & Greenwood, R. (1996). Can PTSD occur with amnesia for the precipitating event? *Cognitive Neuropsychiatry, 1,* 239–246.

Middelboe, T., Andersen, H. S., Birket-Smith, M., & Friis, M. L. (1992). Psychiatric sequelae of minor head injury, a prospective follow-up study. *European Psychiatry, 7,* 183–189.

Norris, F. (1992). Epidemiology of trauma: Frequency and impact of different potentially occurring events on different demographic groups. *Journal of Consulting Clinical Psychology, 60,* 409–418.

Ohry, A., Rattok, J., & Solomon, Z. (1996). Post traumatic stress disorder in brain injury patients. *Brain Injury, 10,* 687–695.

Ownsworth, T. L., & Oei, T. (1998). Depression after traumatic brain injury: Conceptualization and treatment considerations. *Brain-Injury, 12,* 735–751.

Ponsford, J., Sloan, S., & Snow, P. (1995). *Traumatic brain injury: Rehabilitation for everyday adaptive living.* Hove, UK: Psychology Press.

Resick, P. A. (2001). *Stress and trauma.* Hove, UK: Psychology Press.

Riggs, D. S., Rothbaum, B. O., & Foa, E. B. (1995). A prospective examination of symptoms of posttraumatic stress disorder in victims of nonsexual assault. *Journal of Interpersonal Violence, 10,* 201–213.

Rothbaum, B., Foa, E., Riggs, D., Murdock, T., & Walsh, W. (1992). A prospective examination of post-traumatic stress disorder in rape victims. *Journal of Traumatic Stress, 5,* 455–475.

Russell, W. R., & Smith, A. (1961). Post traumatic amnesia after closed head injury. *Archives Neurology, 5,* 16–29.

Sbordone, R. J. (1992). Distinguishing brain injury from post traumatic stress disorder. Neurolaw Letters, 3 May.

Sbordone, R. J., & Liter, J. C. (1995). Mild traumatic brain injury does not produce post-traumatic stress disorder. *Brian Injury, 9,* 405–412.

Schacter, D. L., Chiu, C. Y. P., & Ochsner, K. N. (1993). Implicit memory: A selective review. *Annual Review of Neuroscience, 16,* 159–182.

Silver, J. M., Rattock, J., & Anderson, K. (1997). Post traumatic stress disorder and brain injury. *Neurocase, 3,* 151–157.

van der Kolk, B. A. (1994). The body keeps the score: Memory and the emerging psychobiology of post traumatic stress. *Harvard Review of Psychiatry, 1,* 253–265.

Warden, D. L., Labbate, L. A., Salazar, A. M., Nelson, R., Sheley, E., Staudenmeier, J., & Martin, E. (1997). Post traumatic stress disorder in patients with traumatic brain injury and amnesia for the event? *Journal of Neuropsychiatry and Clinical Neurosciences, 9,* 18–22.

Williams, W. H., Evans, J. J., Needham, P., & Wilson, B. (2002). Neurological, cognitive and attributional predictors of posttraumatic stress symptoms after traumatic brain injury. *Journal of Traumatic Stress, 15,* 397–401.

Williams, W. H., Evans, J. J., & Wilson, B. A. (2002). Prevalence of posttraumatic stress disorder after severe traumatic brain injury in a representative community sample. *Brain Injury, 16,* 673–679.

Williams, W. H., Evans, J. J., & Wilson, B. A. (2003). Neurorehabilitation for two cases of post-traumatic stress disorder following traumatic brain injury. *Cognitive Neuropsychiatry, 8,* 1–18.

Williams, W. H., Williams, J. M. G., & Ghadiali, E. J. (1998). Autobiographical memory in traumatic brain injury: Neuropsychological and mood predictors of recall. *Neuropsychological Rehabilitation, 8,* 43–60.

Yule, W., Perrin, S., & Smith, P. (1999). Post-traumatic stress disorder in children and adolescents. In W. Yule (Ed.), *Post-traumatic stress disorder: Concepts and therapy.* Chichester: Wiley.

NEUROPSYCHOLOGICAL REHABILITATION, 2003, *13* (1/2), 165–188

Traumatic brain injury and substance abuse: A review and analysis of the literature

Laura A. Taylor, Jeffrey S. Kreutzer, Sarah R. Demm, and Michelle A. Meade

*Virginia Commonwealth University Health System,
MCV Hospitals and Physicians, Richmond, Virginia, USA*

Traumatic brain injury (TBI) is a leading cause of death and disability world-wide. Accidents are a major cause of brain injury, and many accidents are alcohol or drug related. Evidence indicates that a vast majority of victims test positive for alcohol or illicit drugs at the time of hospital admission. Research also suggests that a majority of TBI survivors were moderate to heavy drinkers pre-injury. This manuscript reviews literature on pre- and post-injury substance use patterns, abuse risk factors, and dangers of post-injury use. Assessment is discussed in detail with information provided on the need for quantitative assessment, records review, corroboration, and long-term monitoring. Information is also provided on critical features of treatment, prevention, and education, and on the role of psychologists in substance abuse assessment and treatment. The manuscript concludes with a section addressing issues, questions, and concerns commonly encountered by clinicians.

INTRODUCTION

Traumatic brain injury (TBI) is a significant health problem and a major cause of disability and death (Marion, 1998). Substance abuse is a major problem for individuals with TBI, occurring more frequently than in the general population (Kolakowsky-Hayner et al., 1999; Kreutzer, Marwitz, & Witol, 1995). Young adult males have the highest incidence of TBI (Abrams, Barker, Haffey, &

Correspondence should be addressed to Jeffrey S. Kreutzer, Professor and Director, Division of Rehabilitation Psychology and Neuropsychology, Virginia Commonwealth University Health System, PO Box 980542, Richmond, Virginia 23298-0542, USA; Email: jskreutz@hsc.vdu.edu

This work was partly supported by Grants #H133P970003 and #H133A980026 from the National Institute on Disability and Rehabilitation Research (NIDRR), Office of Special Education and Rehabilitative Services (OSERS), Department of Education, Washington, DC.

---

http://www.tandf.co.uk/journals/pp/09602011.html   DOI:10.1080/09602010244000336

Nelson, 1993; Kolakowsky-Hayner & Kreutzer, 2001) and the highest incidence of substance abuse (Johnson et al., 1977; Miller & Cisin, 1983). A comprehensive review study (Corrigan, 1995) indicated that approximately two thirds of individuals with TBI have a history of substance abuse pre-injury, and one third to one half of individuals hospitalised are intoxicated at the time of injury. Research suggests that those who were intoxicated at the time of injury are more likely to be heavier drinkers both pre- and post-injury (Kreutzer et al., 1996b).

Given the extent of substance abuse within the TBI population and the associated dangers, rehabilitation professionals are strongly encouraged to develop assessment, prevention, and treatment skills. The primary purposes of this paper are as follows: (1) review the literature on pre- and post-injury substance abuse and intoxication at the time of injury; (2) discuss the relationship between substance abuse and neurological, neurobehavioural, vocational, and life-satisfaction outcomes; (3) provide an overview of commonly used assessment techniques; (4) identify subtle signs of abuse and abuse risk factors; (5) provide treatment and prevention recommendations; and (6) address issues, questions, and concerns frequently identified by clinicians.

PRE-INJURY SUBSTANCE USE

A number of investigators have examined pre-injury substance abuse rates. Research indicates that between 44% and 79% of people with TBI have a history of alcohol abuse (Bogner et al., 2001; Corrigan, 1995; Corrigan et al., 2001; Kolakowsky-Hayner et al., 1999; Kreutzer, Witol, & Marwitz, 1996a; Ruff et al., 1990), and 21–37% report a history of illicit drug use (Kolakowsky-Hayner et al., 1999; Kreutzer et al., 1996a; Kreutzer et al., 1991b; Ruff et al., 1990).

Ruff and colleagues (1990) questioned TBI patients and their relatives about pre-injury substance use, using a four-point scale (none, occasional, regular, excessive). History of illicit drug and alcohol use was known for 464 and 414 patients, respectively. Approximately 79% denied pre-injury drug abuse, while 5% of the sample reported regular use and 8% excessive use. Although nearly 30% of the subjects denied alcohol history, 27% endorsed occasional use, 24% regular use, and 20% excessive use. A history of alcohol abuse was associated with intoxication at the time of injury.

Kreutzer and colleagues (1991b) studied substance use in 74 patients with TBI, using the General Health and History Questionnaire (GHHQ), Quantity–Frequency–Variability Index (QFVI), and the Brief Michigan Alcohol Screening Test (B-MAST). Results revealed that 20% of patients reported abstinence pre-injury, while 12% endorsed infrequent/light, 30% moderate, and 38% heavy use. Pre-injury drug use was described by 37% of patients, who cited marijuana as the drug of choice.

Drubach, Kelly, Winslow, and Flynn (1993) assessed substance abuse rates among 322 patients with TBI, using DSM-III-R criteria (American Psychiatric Association, 1987). Approximately 33% met criteria for a history of alcohol abuse, 8% for drug abuse, and 29% for alcohol/drug abuse. Substance abuse history was associated with fewer years of education and history of prior TBI. Violent injuries were more likely among patients with a drug/alcohol abuse history.

A comparison of pre-injury substance use patterns among 26 patients with TBI and 26 matched patients with spinal cord injuries (SCI) revealed that 81% of TBI patients and 96% of SCI patients reported pre-injury alcohol use (Kolakowsky-Hayner et al., 1999). Pre-injury, 42% of TBI patients and 57% of SCI patients were classified as heavy drinkers. Abstinence within the year before injury was reported by 19% of the TBI sample and 4% of the SCI sample. Compared to the general population, twice as many TBI patients reported moderate drinking and three times as many reported heavy drinking. Illicit drug use within the year pre-injury was described by 30% of the TBI sample and one third of the SCI sample. Marijuana use predominated for both groups.

Bogner and colleagues (2001) studied 351 patients with TBI, utilising an interview based upon DSM-IV criteria (American Psychiatric Association, 1994) to establish substance abuse history. Nearly 60% of the entire sample and 79% of patients with violence-related TBI reported a history of substance abuse. A history of substance abuse was more likely among patients who were male, lacked post-high school education, and were unmarried and not productive at the time of injury.

In summary, pre-injury alcohol abuse was reported by as many as 79% of TBI patients. A history of alcohol abuse was associated with lacking post-high school education, violence-related aetiology, and being male, unmarried, and unemployed at the time of injury. Pre-injury alcohol use was higher than the general population. Pre-injury illicit drug use, less prevalent than alcohol abuse, was described by up to 37% of TBI patients studied.

INTOXICATION AT THE TIME OF INJURY

Several studies have examined alcohol use at the time of injury. Literature reviews suggest that one to three quarters of TBI survivors are likely to be intoxicated at the time of injury (Corrigan, 1995; Corrigan et al., 2001; Kreutzer et al., 1991b). Rimel, Giordani, Barth, and Jane (1982) studied 1248 patients admitted for hospitalisation with TBI. Alcohol was detectable in the blood of 73% of the sample, with 53% having blood alcohol levels (BAL) beyond the legal limit. The moderate TBI group was found to have a higher incidence of pre-injury alcohol abuse.

Klonoff, Snow, and Costa (1986) investigated 78 patients 2–4 years after closed head injury. Alcohol use at the time of injury was reported by 40% of the sample. In a later study of 2649 patients who were hospitalised or died secondary to TBI (Kraus et al., 1989), BALs were obtained for 44% of patients. Of those tested, 43% had a negative BAL, and 49% had a BAL above the legal limit. Positive BALs were obtained from two thirds of patients injured in motor vehicle accidents and 60% of those assaulted.

Sparadeo and Gill (1989) retrospectively reviewed records of 102 patients hospitalised for TBI. Approximately two thirds of patients had a positive BAL, and half were legally intoxicated. Alcohol history was 10 times more likely in patients with a positive BAL than those without. Gurney and colleagues (1992) studied 520 patients admitted to the emergency department for acute TBI and found that approximately 37% of patients were intoxicated on admission. Another 10% had positive BALs below the legal limit.

Kreutzer and colleagues (1996b) studied intoxication rates of 56 TBI patients. The majority of patients showed positive BAL on admission, and half were intoxicated. Individuals with higher admission BAL and younger persons were more likely to be classified as heavy drinkers. A later study (Corrigan et al., 2001) found 23% of TBI patients with available admission BAL (81% of the 218 patients) had a BAL beyond the legal limit.

Wagner and colleagues (2000) investigated 2637 patients with TBI referred to a Level I trauma centre. Approximately one third of patients reported illicit drug use and about half endorsed alcohol use at the time of the injury. Nearly 20% of injuries were described as self-inflicted. Substance use was found to be associated with self-inflicted injury.

Overall, research suggests that up to three quarters of TBI patients have a positive admission BAL and approximately half are intoxicated on admission. A positive admission BAL was common among patients sustaining injuries in motor vehicle accidents, in assaults, and by self-inflicted means. A history of alcohol abuse was significantly more likely among patients with a positive BAL than those without.

POST-INJURY SUBSTANCE USE PATTERNS

A number of studies have been conducted investigating post-injury substance abuse patterns among TBI patients. Kreutzer and colleagues (1990a) studied rates of pre- and post-injury alcohol use among 87 TBI patients, using the GHHQ, QFVI, and B-MAST. Results revealed that problematic and heavy drinking declined post-injury, while abstinence rates increased. Nearly three quarters of patients scored within the range suggesting no evidence of alcohol abuse or dependence post-injury on the B-MAST, while 14% obtained scores suggestive of abuse or dependence.

Kreutzer and colleagues (1991b) explored substance abuse and crime patterns among 74 TBI patients referred for supported employment, using the GHHQ, QFVI, and B-MAST. Results revealed increased alcohol abstinence rates and decreased quantity and frequency of alcohol use post-injury. Similarly, illicit drug use was found to decrease post-injury. Pre-injury, 20% of the sample had been arrested, while only 10% reported post-injury arrests. Drug and alcohol convictions predominated. Later, Kreutzer and colleagues (1995) studied 327 outpatients with TBI. Pre-injury abstinence rates were reportedly comparable to the general population, while post-injury abstinence rates were nearly twice that of the general population.

In a study of 211 patients referred to a community-based treatment pro-gramme for patients with TBI and substance abuse problems (Corrigan, Rust, & Lamb-Hart, 1995b), 61% of the entire sample and 71% of assault victims described injuries as substance use-related. Pre-injury substance use rates were higher than national averages, while post-injury use was comparable with national averages. Use reportedly increased with time post-injury, and the sample evidenced low return-to-work rates. In contrast, a retrospective, 10-year follow-up study of 20 TBI patients revealed that substance abuse decreased significantly immediately post-injury and did not return to pre-injury levels (Sbordone, Liter, & Pettler-Jennings, 1995).

A pattern of increasing alcohol consumption was observed among 73 people with TBI studied in a prospective, longitudinal multicentre study of alcohol use (Kreutzer et al., 1996b). Higher levels of disability on the Disability Rating Scale were associated with lower alcohol consumption rates, suggesting that impaired patients are likely to drink less that patients with fewer impairments.

Similarly, Kreutzer, Witol, and Marwitz (1996a) investigated substance use patterns among 87 16- to 20-year-olds with TBI. The majority of patients (73%) reported drinking pre-injury, with half reporting moderate to heavy use. Upon initial follow-up (Mean = 8 months post-injury), 58% of patients reported abstinence and 25% moderate to heavy use. Similarly, during the second follow-up evaluation (Mean = 28 months post-injury), 49% were clas-sified as abstinent and 35% as moderate to heavy drinkers. Pre-injury illicit drug use was reported by 29% of patients, while at both initial and second follow-up appointments, more that 90% of patients endorsed abstinence.

In a study of outcomes at 5-year follow-up, Corrigan, Smith-Knapp, and Granger (1998) interviewed 95 patients with TBI. Results revealed that during the first 2 years post-discharge, no subjects were found to abuse alcohol or illicit drugs. However, approximately 25% of patients in subsequent time periods were found to have substance abuse problems.

Kolakowsky-Hayner and colleagues (in press) compared post-injury substance use patterns of 30 TBI patients and a matched sample of 30 SCI patients at 1-year follow-up. Comparable rates of alcohol use were found in both groups, with 50% of patients endorsing abstinence post-injury. Among those acknowledging alcohol consumption, 43% of the TBI sample reported moderate to heavy use. The SCI sample was more likely than the TBI sample to report daily alcohol consumption. Post-injury consumption rates differed from pre-injury rates for both groups. Significant differences in rates of illicit drug use were found such that a greater percentage of patients with SCI reported drug use within the past 6–12 months (20.7% vs. 3.3%). Marijuana use was predominant in both groups, followed by poly-drug, cocaine, and opiate use. Post-injury drug use declined for both groups.

In summary, research revealed that alcohol and illicit drug use decline after injury. Long-term patterns of alcohol use are characterised by increasing use as time post-injury elapses. Evidence suggests that patients with fewer impairments are more likely to drink post-injury than impaired patients.

SUBSTANCE USE AS MEDIATING FACTORS IN OUTCOME

Questions have emerged about the relationship between substance abuse and outcome after brain injury. Four outcome categories, neurological, neurobehavioural, vocational, and life-satisfaction, have received considerable attention.

Neurological outcome

Several studies have been conducted investigating the neurological outcomes associated with pre-injury substance abuse. Literature review reveals that history of substance abuse has been found to be related to higher mortality rates, poorer neuropsychological outcome, increased chance of second injury, and late deterioration (Corrigan, 1995). Ruff and colleagues (1990) questioned patients with TBI and their close relatives about pre-injury substance use. Results suggested no association between history of illicit drug use and outcome as measured by the Glasgow Outcome Scale. In contrast, there was a strong association between a history of alcohol use and outcome, such that excessive users had higher mortality rates and lower probability of good outcome. More than 40% of excessive alcohol users died, while mortality rates for TBI patients with no, occasional, or regular alcohol use ranged from 13% to 23%. Positive outcome was observed for 32–42% of patients with non-excessive alcohol use, while only 13% of excessive alcohol users had a good outcome.

Ronty and colleagues (1993) explored the relationship between alcohol abuse and cerebral trauma in 56 patients with TBI. Fifteen patients met DSM-III-R criteria for alcohol abuse (American Psychiatric Association, 1987). Compared to non-abusers, alcohol abusers evidenced significantly greater volumes of intracranial haemorrhage, weaker quantitative EEG improvement, and more pronounced local brain atrophy at 1-year follow-up.

In contrast, Drubach and colleagues (1993) studied 322 patients with moderate to severe TBI and found no differences between alcohol abusers, drug abusers, alcohol/drug abusers, and non-abusers regarding injury severity or required treatment. The four groups also had comparable admission GCS scores, mean length of post-traumatic amnesia, duration of acute hospitalisation, and length of rehabilitation. Individuals who reported abuse of drugs or drugs/alcohol were more likely to have sustained violent injuries than those who reported alcohol abuse alone or denied substance abuse.

Research has also been conducted to explore the relationship between neurological outcome and intoxication at the time of injury. Alcohol intoxication at injury has been found to be associated with acute complications, longer hospital stays, and poorer discharge status (Corrigan, 1995). Klonoff and colleagues (1986) found that injury severity and mortality rates were inversely related to BAL, likely reflecting lower rates of BAL testing with mild injuries. Among those with severe injuries, BAL was positively associated with discharge diagnoses of neurological impairments and longer length of hospitalisation.

Later, Sparadeo and Gill (1989) showed that a positive BAL was associated with longer hospital stays, increased duration of agitation, and lower global cognitive status on the Rancho Los Amigos Scale. There was no difference between intoxicated and non-intoxicated patients in terms of neurosurgical procedures.

Gurney and colleagues (1992) compared outcomes of TBI patients who were intoxicated at injury to those who were not. A greater proportion of intoxicated patients required intubation, developed pneumonia, experienced respiratory distress, and required intracranial pressure monitor placement. No significant differences between the groups were found regarding length of hospital stay, TBI severity, or necessity of head CT scan or intracranial surgery.

Neurobehavioural outcome

Several investigators have studied the neurobehavioural outcomes associated with a history of pre-injury substance abuse. Dunlop and colleagues (1991) studied 34 TBI patients showing evidence of emotional or cognitive deterioration 6 months or more after TBI and 34 TBI patients showing signs of improvement. Patients were matched for severity of initial neuropsychiatric impairment. The deterioration group was more likely to have a history of alcohol abuse, been involved in assaults, and sustained a skull fracture. Symptoms most likely to worsen included agitation, hostility, apathy, depression, and emotional lability or withdrawal.

Kreutzer and colleagues (1995) investigated pre- and post-injury substance abuse and crime patterns among 327 TBI out-patients who were at least 6 months post-injury, using the GHHQ and QFVI. In comparison to those who were never arrested, a higher proportion of arrested patients were moderate to heavy drinkers pre- and post-injury. Compared to the general population, the proportion of arrested patients with TBIs who were moderate to heavy drinkers was more than three times greater. Post-injury abstinence rates increased two-fold among patients without an arrest record and three-fold for arrested patients.

In a study of military personnel who were discharged from duty, Ommaya and colleagues (1996) compared discharge rates within the total discharge population ($N = 1,879,724$) to those of military personnel with mild ($N = 1778$), moderate ($N = 174$), and severe ($N = 274$) TBI. In comparison to the general discharge population, relative risk for discharge secondary to behavioural problems, substance use, criminal conviction, and medical problems was significantly greater for military personnel with TBI. Findings revealed that behavioural discharge rates were highest for those with mild TBI, and medical discharge rates were highest for those with severe TBI. Discharge for substance use or criminal conviction was highest for those with moderate TBI.

Jong, Zafonte, Millis, and Yavuzer (1999) compared TBI patients with positive admission cocaine screens to those who had negative drug screens. There were no significant differences between the two groups on the Disability Rating Scale or the Functional Independence Measure on admission or discharge. Eleven cocaine-positive patients and 14 drug-free patients completed a comprehensive neuropsychological battery. Significant differences were found only for the total score on the Rey Auditory Verbal Learning Test, with cocaine-positive patients performing more poorly than no-drug patients.

Pre-injury crime rates, substance abuse, and neurobehavioural functioning were studied by Kolakowsky-Hayner and Kreutzer (2001) in a sample of 211 patients with TBI. Alcohol abusers were defined as those who reported moderate or heavy use on the QFVI, and non-abusers reported abstinence or light/infrequent use. Results revealed that 30% of subjects were classified as abusers. Abusers tended to be younger males, and they were more likely to have been injured in assaults and have a history of psychological treatment. Abusers were also significantly more likely to have severe injuries than non-abusers. Non-abusers endorsed problems with greater severity across all scales on the Neurobehavioural Functioning Inventory (NFI), while heavier drinkers reported fewer problems with aggression, somatic symptoms, and motor problems on the NFI. No significant differences were found with regard to illicit drug abuse.

Employment outcome

Research has consistently shown that unemployment is a persistent, costly consequence of TBI (Abrams et al., 1993; Oddy & Humphrey, 1980; Sander, Kreutzer, & Fernandez, 1997). Although substance abuse has been thought to impact negatively on vocational status, few studies have explored the impact of substance abuse on employment. Ronty and colleagues (1993) found that TBI patients who met DSM-III-R criteria for history of alcohol abuse were less likely to return to work post-injury. Only 40% of those who misused alcohol returned to work after injury, whereas 73% of non-abusers returned to work.

Sander and colleagues (1997) studied the employment status, neuro-behavioural functioning, and substance abuse rates among 138 individuals with TBI. Approximately 33% of the sample was employed at the time of evaluation (56% full-time, 44% part-time). Results revealed that nearly twice as many employed subjects reported moderate/heavy use (46%) and light/infrequent (20%) alcohol use than the unemployed subjects (26% and 12%, respectively). However, the proportion of abstainers among unemployed subjects was nearly twice as great as among the employed subjects (62% vs. 34%). Employed persons may drink more because they are less likely to be supervised and have greater financial and transportation resources. Less than 6% of patients reported post-injury drug use within either group, and no significant differences were found between groups based upon drug use.

Sherer, Bergloff High, and Nick (1999) investigated the long-term employment outcome of 76 patients with TBI. Pre-injury substance use was obtained through collateral reports, with ratings of none or minimal use, significant use, and history of substance abuse treatment or use-related life problems. Forty-three subjects were reported to have no history of use, 17 a history of significant use, and 16 a history of treatment or life problems. Pre-injury substance was predictive of long-term productivity outcome. Patients without a history of substance use were more than eight times as likely to be working at follow-up as patients who used substances pre-injury.

In a prospective study, Wagner and colleagues (2002) explored the relationship between return to productive activity (RTPA) and substance use among 105 patients with TBI. RTPA was defined as return to work, full-time education, or homemaking that was comparable to pre-injury status. Pre-injury alcohol and illicit drug use was reported by 35% and 6% of patients, respectively. Logistic regression revealed a relationship between RTPA and history of substance use. Among patients with RTPA, 71% denied a history of alcohol use, and 97% denied a history of drug use. In contrast, 52% of patients without RTPA reported a history of alcohol use, and 14 % endorsed a history of drug use.

Life satisfaction outcome

Two published studies have been conducted exploring the relationship between life satisfaction outcomes and substance abuse among TBI patients. Bogner and colleagues (2001) conducted telephone and mail surveys with 351 patients, using the Satisfaction with Life Scale (SWLS) and the Community Integration Questionnaire (CIQ). Substance abuse proved to be a strong predictor of life satisfaction and productivity at 1-year follow-up. Those with a history of substance abuse reported lower life-satisfaction and productivity levels. On the CIQ, those with higher social integration scores were less likely to report a history of substance abuse.

In a prospective, longitudinal study, Corrigan and colleagues (2001) studied 218 patients with TBI 1–2 years post-injury. A history of substance abuse was established through interview and observation by social work and psychology staff based upon DSM-IV criteria. Follow-up assessments included measures of life satisfaction (SWLS) and community integration (CIQ) as well as a three-question depression screen. Life satisfaction was associated with maintaining a healthy lifestyle and productivity. Pre-injury substance abuse history and unemployment at follow-up were associated with lower life satisfaction 1–2 years post-injury. Change in life satisfaction was typically associated with marital status and depression 2 years post-injury.

Summary

In summary, a history of pre-injury alcohol abuse has been associated with post-injury emotional or cognitive deterioration, military discharge from duty, decreased likelihood of return to work or other productive activity, and lower life satisfaction. Additionally, research revealed an association between a history of alcohol abuse and numerous negative neurological outcomes, including higher mortality rates, increased risk of re-injury, late deterioration, lower probability of good outcome, greater volume of intracranial haemorrhage, weaker quantitative EEG improvement, and local brain atrophy. Intoxication at the time of injury has also been found to be associated with negative neurological outcomes such as acute illness and complications, longer hospital stays, poorer discharge status, increased duration of agitation, and required procedures. Few studies have evaluated the effects of pre-injury illicit drug use on outcome, and findings are equivocal.

ASSESSMENT

Problems with drug and alcohol use can be identified using a number of screening tools, including biological measures (such as blood alcohol levels and toxicology screening for illicit drugs) and structured interviews and questionnaires for patients and family members. For comprehensive assessment, review of records, clinical interviews with patients and their family, and administration of standardised measures should be conducted. Abuse risk factors and subtle signs of abuse should be considered during the evaluation process.

Record review

Review of the medical, psychological, criminal, employment, and educational records is a critical component of the assessment process. Medical and psychological records often contain information about risk factors, history of use, previous substance abuse diagnoses, and medical problems or injuries associated with prolonged or excessive use. Criminal records may reveal information about drug or alcohol-related arrests and convictions. Work and school attendance and productivity are often good indicators of mental health and the behavioural effects of substance abuse. In many cases, few records are available, limiting the quality of such a review.

Assessment instruments

Measures designed to assess substance abuse in the general population are often used to assess pre- and post-injury substance use in persons with TBI. Assessment measures frequently used include the Michigan Alcoholism Screening Test (MAST), Brief Michigan Alcoholism Screening Test (B-MAST), CAGE, Quantity–Frequency–Variability Index (QFVI), Addiction Severity Index (ASI), and Substance Abuse Subtle Screening Inventory (SASSI). More than one test may be used, and research indicates that composite measures are helpful in diagnosing and treating substance abuse problems in TBI populations (Cherner, Temkin, Machamer, & Dikmen, 2001).

Several screening measures are widely used to assess alcohol problems in both clinical and research settings. The MAST is a 25-item questionnaire that focuses on lifetime problems and consequences of drinking, including social, vocational, and family problems (Selzer, 1971). The B-MAST is an easily administered, shortened version of the MAST, containing 10 of the original 25 MAST items. Correlations between MAST and B-MAST scores range from .95 to .99 (Pokorny, Miller, & Kaplan, 1972). Fuller, Fishman, Taylor, and Wood (1994) demonstrated the utility of the B-MAST in detecting alcohol abuse problems in TBI populations.

The CAGE, a mnemonic for a four-question screening tool with a yes/no format, is highly effective in detecting alcohol abuse problems in the general population (Ewing, 1984) and in individuals with TBI (Fuller et al., 1994). Easily administered and scored, two or more positive responses suggest an alcohol problem.

The QFVI is a useful self-report measure that classifies individuals' drinking behaviour in one of five categories: abstinent, infrequent, light, moderate, or heavy (Cahalan & Cisin, 1968a, 1968b). Research by Kreutzer et al., (1990a) supports the use of quantity-frequency measures in assessing pre- and post-injury alcohol use among TBI survivors. Concordance rates between patients' and family members' reports have been shown to exceed 90% (Sander, Witol, & Kreutzer, 1997).

Two measures are widely used to detect the presence of illicit drug and alcohol use problems, the ASI and the SASSI. The ASI is widely used in clinical and research settings to assess recent and lifetime substance use difficulties (McLellan, Luborsky, O'Brien, & Woody, 1980). In addition to measuring substance use, information is obtained regarding legal status and medical, vocational, and family/social functioning. The ASI has been shown to have good reliability and validity (McLellan et al., 1985). Research on the ASI and TBI populations is very limited, and future studies are needed to determine the utility of the instrument among neurologically impaired individuals.

The SASSI is a 78-item, empirically based, self-report questionnaire used to identify alcohol and drug abuse problems. Although the SASSI has high sensitivity and specificity when used with the general population, the measure appears to be less effective in assessing TBI populations (Arenth, Bogner, Cowigan, & Schmidt, 2001). Overall, research indicates that the SASSI and ASI are more time-consuming and less effective than the CAGE or B-MAST in assessing alcohol use in TBI populations (Fuller et al., 1994).

Although self-report and collateral measures are easily administered and relatively inexpensive, there is a risk of under-reporting because of their reliance upon individuals' willingness and ability to disclose information accurately. Family reports may be influenced by minimisation, denial of problems, personal substance abuse history, or lack of information regarding the patient's abuse (Arenth et al., 2001). Injury-related problems, including limited self-awareness and memory deficits, may hinder patients' abilities to describe themselves accurately (Sander, Kreutzer, & Fernandez, 1997). For these reasons, some have suggested that accurate assessment is nearly impossible if one relies predominantly on information provided by one source. Soliciting information from a variety of informants and corroboration with records review often helps to compensate for the limitations of self-report and collateral measures

Risk factors

Research and clinical experience have helped identify risk factors for substance abuse, which are applicable to survivors of TBI. Awareness of these risk factors is critical for early recognition of substance abuse problems. Early recognition facilitates the development of treatment plans and recommendations to address substance abuse problems. Table 1 depicts risk factors that should be considered when reviewing records and interviewing patients and their families.

TABLE 1
Factors associated with higher risk of post-injury abuse

- Pre-injury history of alcohol or drug abuse
- Intoxication at the time of injury
- History of legal problems related to substance use
- Substance abuse problems among family members and/or friends
- Denial of or lack of knowledge about dangers associated with substance abuse
- Age less than 25 years
- Physically healthy with income and transportation access

Subtle signs of abuse

When reviewing records and interviewing patients, clinicians must be alert to subtle signs that signal substance abuse. Subtle signs include the following:

- Irregular vocational or educational history such as frequent job changes, excessive tardiness or absenteeism, particularly after weekends.
- Frequent participation in social activities involving alcohol or drug use and/or held in drinking establishments.
- Denial or minimisation of substance abuse problems.
- Mentioning the need to cut down their use.
- Guilt surrounding substance use.
- Becoming upset when others ask questions or express concern about their substance use.
- Early morning substance use.
- Frequently telling stories about or steering conversation towards alcohol or drug-related issues.

Summary

When developing an assessment approach, professionals are encouraged to recognise and consider carefully the needs of patients and the nature of their setting. Factors such as the amount of time available to conduct assessments, availability of collateral informants, and survivors' reading abilities and cognitive impairments should be considered. Effective substance abuse assessment requires a combination of data collection methods, including review of records, clinical interview, and administration of standardised measures. Risk factors and subtle signs of abuse should be considered. Whenever possible, information should be gathered from multiple sources to ensure accuracy. Since alcohol use patterns have been shown to change over time, repeated assessment and monitoring are critical to developing valid conclusions.

PREVENTION AND TREATMENT

Education and prevention

Education is a key component in promoting abstinence and preventing substance abuse. Patients and their family members and friends should be given information about the substance abuse policies of their rehabilitation programme, signs of abuse, risk factors, and treatment alternatives (Kreutzer et al., 1991a). In addition, education about the effects of and dangers associated with alcohol consumption and drug use after TBI is essential (Kreutzer, Marwitz, & Wehman, 1991a). Dangers that should be emphasised include: (1) increased risk of injuries and seizures (Kelly, 1995; Kreutzer, Leninger, Sherron, & Groah, 1990b); (2) exacerbation of cognitive, behavioural, and emotional difficulties (Kreutzer et al., 1990b; Seaton & David, 1990); (3) potential interaction with prescribed medications (Kreutzer et al., 1990b); (4) diminished benefits of rehabilitation (Kolakowsky-Hayner et al., in press); (5) decreased level of consciousness as evidenced by depressed GCS scores (Kelly, 1995); and (6) poorer nutritional status which is necessary for optimal recovery (Kreutzer et al., 1990).

Family involvement in treatment

After discharge from the hospital or rehabilitation programme, many survivors of TBI return home to live with family, placing family members in the role of caring for the injured relative. Research indicates that survivors with a history of pre-injury abuse run the risk of resuming substance use after discharge, particularly as time post-injury increases (Kreutzer et al., 1996b). Family members are in a unique position to help survivors maintain abstinence. For this reason, rehabilitation professionals should involve families in assessment, treatment, and discharge planning. Family members should be made aware of the subtle signs of abuse and the dangers associated with substance use following TBI, and they should be encouraged to support the patient's abstinence. In an effort to promote a non-abusing social support system, family members should encourage survivors to engage in activities that do not involve substance use and develop relationships with non-abusing individuals (Kreutzer et al., 1990b).

Seaton and David (1990) assert that effective family intervention requires that family members be encouraged to drop enabling roles and urge survivors to accept responsibility for their behaviour. However, the authors acknowledge that this may be difficult in cases involving co-morbid TBI. The authors recommend referral to Alcoholics Anonymous (AA), Narcotics Anonymous (NA), or other therapeutic support agencies that encourage survivors to accept responsibility for their behaviour, thereby helping families disengage from their enabling roles. Family members should be encouraged to seek out their own support and become involved in programmes such as Al-Anon and Alateen. The authors further suggest that rehabilitation professionals educate family members about how to separate problems associated with substance abuse from those associated with TBI.

Langley, Lindsay, Lam, and Priddy (1990) encourage educating family members to identify high-risk situations and use relapse prevention strategies to prepare survivors for these situations. Additionally, family members should be taught to identify warning signs of relapse and deal with relapse. The authors further assert that family members should be made aware of the impact of their own use on survivors and be encouraged to refrain from use themselves.

Referrals

Rehabilitation professionals often lack comprehensive training in substance abuse treatment. Although this education would likely prove beneficial, gaining expertise in multiple areas is often not feasible. Rehabilitation professionals should strive to be aware of their limitations and make referrals to outside agencies when appropriate. When referring TBI patients for outside treatment, a number of factors should be considered. First, treatment programmes should be evaluated for their receptiveness to experience working with TBI survivors, willingness to learn about TBI, and their proximity and accessibility. Patients should be referred to programmes with expertise whenever possible. However, if such programmes are unavailable, rehabilitation professionals should consider educating staff about TBI (Kreutzer et al., 1990b), helping with the development of treatment plans, and consulting if behavioural or cognitive problems interfere with treatment.

Second, rehabilitation professionals are often asked to recommend the mode of treatment: in-patient, out-patient, or community-based support services. In determining the appropriate modality, the extent of pre-injury substance abuse, family history of substance abuse, history of substance abuse-related problems, and availability of support systems should be considered. Patients with chronic, severe problems often benefit from in-patient treatment, with subsequent out-patient services. Out-patient services or support groups may be more appropriate for those patients who have less severe substance abuse problems, are unwilling to consider in-patient treatment, or lack access to in-patient services. The nature and severity of problems will likely change over time, and thus, regular monitoring is beneficial.

Finally, many professionals question whether substance abuse problems preclude rehabilitation. Typically, it is appropriate for rehabilitation professionals to provide their services in conjunction with substance abuse treatment provided by another trained professional. Regular communication between treating professionals will likely improve treatment effectiveness and aid in treatment planning. In some situations where substance abuse is severe and impedes rehabilitation efforts, substance abuse treatment may be a pre-requisite for providing other rehabilitation services. The rehabilitation treatment team should meet to weigh these options.

Models of treatment

Langley and colleagues (1990) presented a comprehensive alcohol abuse treatment programme for TBI survivors. Assessment of alcohol-related problems through screening measures and criteria-based interviews were strongly encouraged. Treatment strategies included the following: patient and family education; altering alcohol beliefs; promoting lifestyle changes; enhancing commitment to, motivation for, and maintenance of behaviour change; reduction and management of cravings; and support of family members. No data were presented evaluating this model.

Corrigan, Lamb-Hart, and Rust (1995a) described a community-based model of intervention called the Traumatic Brain Injury and Substance Abuse Vocational Rehabilitation Centre, or TBI Network, which provides services for individuals with co-morbid TBI and substance abuse problems. The TBI Network seeks to enhance existing services within survivors' communities, using an interdisciplinary team of professionals with expertise in vocational rehabilitation, TBI, and substance abuse treatment. Services provided include: comprehensive substance abuse and neuropsychological assessment and monitoring; integrated service planning and co-ordination; monitoring; outreach to identify clients needing treatment; client, family, and employer education; job development, placement, and maintenance; support in accessing resources; social and emotional support; and advocacy to increase awareness and policies of service providers.

Following their programme description, Corrigan and colleagues (1995b) presented a study of 37 patients who proceeded to the 6-month monitoring in the TBI Network. Results provided support for the effectiveness of the programme as findings revealed that patients reported increased abstinence rates and decreased frequency and quantity of alcohol consumed. At 6-month follow-up, 30% more subjects were employed than on initial assessment. Similarly, Bogner and colleagues (1997) investigated the effectiveness of the TBI Network among 72 survivors of TBI monitored for at least 1 year. Significantly improved vocational status and increased abstinence rates were observed. Involvement of a community team was related to decreased substance use. A trend was observed for decreased substance abuse among those referred within three months post-injury.

Delmonico, Hanley-Peterson, and Englander (1998) described a group psychotherapy model for in-patients and out-patients with co-morbid TBI and substance abuse problems based upon the "harm reduction" philosophy. A rehabilitation psychologist with expertise in substance abuse and TBI facilitated the group, which was interpersonal in nature and met weekly for 1 hour. The group was open and welcomed individuals who were not yet abstinent. Treatment goals included the following: identifying substance abuse problems, maladaptive coping styles, and triggers; recognising the consequences of use; and developing effective relapse prevention and coping strategies. Group members were provided with written didactic materials and encouraged to take notes. The authors presented indicators of treatment success, including reduced clinic visits, fewer emergency calls for substance abuse-related health problems, and increased stability in housing and relationships.

Critical features of substance abuse treatment for patients with TBI

In summary, for optimal recovery and progress post-injury, rehabilitation professionals should assist in identifying and treating substance abuse problems. Based upon available research and clinical experience, the components listed in Table 2 appear to be beneficial in treating co-morbid substance abuse and TBI in rehabilitation settings.

Rehabilitation providers are encouraged to consider developing on-site substance abuse support groups or provide meeting space for AA or NA, welcoming in-patients and out-patients to attend meetings. In-house support groups facilitate contacts with mentors and role models who have experience with long-term sobriety (Pires, 1989).

ISSUES, QUESTIONS, AND CONCERNS COMMONLY ENCOUNTERED BY CLINICIANS

A number of issues, questions, and concerns arise repeatedly in clinical settings. The most common are addressed below.

How does post-injury substance abuse influence long-term prognosis? While many survivors live outside of institutional settings, relatively few are able to work post-injury. Continuing substance use increases the risk of unemployment and job termination, decreases the likelihood of advancement, and, in the long-term, reduces income. Post-injury substance abuse increases the risk of re-injury and exacerbates injury-related cognitive problems. Furthermore, alcohol endangers health, relationships, and the ability to participate fully in community activities.

Which patients are at greatest risk for continuing abuse? Patients who have a history of substance abuse pre-injury, including intoxication at the time of injury, are at greatest risk. In danger are people who have close friends and family members who use or abuse alcohol or drugs and those who are uninformed about or unwilling to acknowledge the dangers of abuse. People

TABLE 2
Critical features of substance abuse treatment for patients with TBI

- Identify abuse risk factors, subtle signs of abuse, use patterns, treatment needs, available resources, and challenges to recovery
- Monitor substance use over time with routine assessments, especially for patients at risk
- Assist patients in recognising substance abuse problems and encourage them to take responsibility for their behaviour
- Involve family members and friends in assessment and treatment
- Educate patients and family members about substance use dangers, relapse prevention, and treatment alternatives. Distinguish between substance abuse-related and TBI-related problems
- Be proactive. Emphasise education and prevention as much or more than treatment
- Encourage patients to seek treatment and recognise the positive aspects of choosing abstinence. Avoid treating harshly patients who make bad choices
- Help patients discuss the effects of substance use on their feelings, self-esteem, and relationships
- Use repetition and present information in a variety of modalities, such as role play, visual aids, peer modelling videotaping, and coaching, in order to promote learning
- Measure steps to recovery one day at a time. Offer praise for making good decisions and working toward goals
- Recognise and prepare for the relapses that are inevitable for many patients
- Help patients and families access local community resources including AA, NA, Al-Anon, and Alateen
- Encourage participation in alcohol and drug-free social and recreational activities
- Carefully weigh the pros and cons of referring for out-patient and in-patient substance abuse treatment programmes
- Provide information to community agencies and treatment programmes about the effects of TBI and the need for programme accommodations

---

who view alcohol use as a "right and privilege" that should not be given up by anyone, regardless of circumstance, are also susceptible to abuse.

What are the dangers for people who use medication and continue to use alcohol or illicit drugs? Dangerous interactions between alcohol, illicit drugs, and medication are common. Fainting, weakness, vision problems, hallucinations, and fatigue are commonly reported indications of dangerous interactions. Substances can also reduce the effectiveness of medication and increase the risk of seizures.

How important is substance abuse assessment in treatment planning? Alcohol or illicit drug-related health problems or reckless behaviours can undermine months or years of progress in recovery. Regardless of setting, substance abuse history, risk factors, and current use of substances are important considerations in treatment planning. Patients who have made considerable progress in recovery are often in danger of resuming use as they attempt to take up "normal" activities again, which often include using substances. To aid in prevention and early identification of problems, substance use monitoring should preferably be continued for several years post-injury.

What is the psychologist's role in substance abuse treatment and assessment? In both out-patient and in-patient rehabilitation settings, psychologists are capable of taking a lead role in addressing substance abuse issues. For example, many psychologists have assessment training and experience, including evaluation of substance use. Psychologists are typically effective interviewers, successful in gathering information from survivors, family members, and friends. They can also review records, administer standardised assessment approaches, help to identify patients at risk, and address problems with denial. Psychologists often serve as counsellors, helping patients make the first steps towards successful treatment and making referrals for out-patient services.

How do cognitive issues affect treatment? Neuropsychological impairments are common after TBI. Visual and reading impairments can affect a survivor's ability to read and comprehend educational materials. Attention, concentration, learning, memory, and language impairments can affect survivors' ability to learn and recall information presented in treatment. Frontal lobe injuries and disorders of executive functioning can decrease survivors' self-awareness and impair their abilities to anticipate consequences, inhibit behaviour, plan solutions to problems, and implement solutions effectively. Survivors' behavioural difficulties may be perceived as disruptive in traditional treatment settings. Several strategies are recommended to enhance treatment effectiveness. First, information should be presented in a variety of complementary modalities, written and oral. Second, teaching should proceed slowly, with paraphrasing and repetition of information encouraged. Third, survivors should be encouraged to attend group meetings where their special needs are recognised and understood, and their participation is welcomed. Effective group intervention for survivors often places greater emphasis on structured teaching and the application of behavioural principles.

What are the best ways to deal with resistance? Perhaps due to a combination of psychological denial and lack of awareness, people with TBI are often reluctant to report they have a substance abuse problem or enrol in treatment. Reluctance to acknowledge difficulties in the face of a significant problem is often a major obstacle to TBI recovery and resumption of productive living. No matter how resistant a patient seems, professionals can still take a number of steps to promote recognition of substance abuse problems and involvement in treatment. (1) Wherever possible, involve family members and significant others in assessment, treatment, education, and prevention efforts. They can encourage the patient to acknowledge problems and facilitate seeking help. (2) Conduct an assessment, and discuss the results with the survivor and others whom the patient wishes to involve. (3) Identify accessible treatment resources, and encourage the patient to visit them personally. (4) Encourage the patient to consider how drinking or illicit drugs will affect their ability to reach personal goals. (5) Recognise that treatment is a personal choice and that encouragement will facilitate progress far better than criticism or threats. (6) Discuss and examine potential barriers to enrolling in treatment and benefiting. (7) Be patient. Recognise that patients may be willing to seek help later despite unwillingness to do so now. Our efforts now can lay the groundwork for future treatment successes.

What is the role of families in treatment? In many cases, family members play a powerful role in patients' lives. They are often close observers of patients' behaviour and can exert a strong positive or negative influence. Family members can provide helpful information about the frequency, quantity, and impact of substance use on survivors' lives. Family members can help reinforce learning and positive behaviours and facilitate participation in alcohol and drug-free activities. On the other hand, family members can undermine successful treatment by using substances themselves, directly encouraging use, or downplaying the dangers of substance abuse. Whenever possible, clinicians should encourage family members to assume a positive role.

Do I provide rehabilitation to patients who deny having substance abuse problems? Some professionals assert that alcohol abuse treatment should precede rehabilitation, believing strongly that substance abuse undermines rehabilitation effectiveness. Research showing that alcohol use impairs cognitive functioning (Lezak, 1995; Loberg, 1986; Parsons, 1996) helps substantiate assertions that active substance abuse is a major obstacle to rehabilitation success. Concurrent substance abuse treatment and rehabilitation can be effective if patients are closely monitored and committed to abstinence and treatment. The pros and cons of restricting patients from receiving rehabilitation services must be carefully weighed from an ethical and legal perspective. Rehabilitation programmes are encouraged to develop clear policies regarding substance abuse and rehabilitation treatment. Patients should understand these policies before enrolling in rehabilitation. In some cases, patients' decisions to refrain from substance abuse treatment may concurrently be a decision to refrain from rehabilitation.

How do you separate the effects of alcohol abuse from those of brain injury? Neuropsychologists often endeavour to ascertain the extent to which post-injury cognitive impairments are a function of substance abuse or injury-related impairment. The likelihood that substance abuse has affected cognitive functioning is greatest in patients who:

- Are older, with a longer history of heavier drinking or drug use.
- Have a history of substance abuse-related medical problems, including kidney, liver, or stomach ailments.
- Have a history of overdose(s).

Research indicates that heavy abusers who remain abstinent show improvements in cognitive functioning. So, as the period of abstinence increases, there is a greater likelihood that cognitive impairments are injury-related.

SUMMARY AND CONCLUSIONS

Research has identified a clear relationship between substance abuse and TBI. First, survivors who abuse alcohol or illicit drugs are at high risk for injury. Second, many survivors continue to abuse alcohol post-injury, although there is evidence of significant declines in post-injury illicit drug use. Third, evidence indicates that improving functional and physical status increases the risk of post-injury alcohol use. Evidently, people who work and drive post-injury find that alcohol is readily accessible. Finally, post-injury substance abuse increases the risk of poor medical, neurobehavioural, vocational, and life-satisfaction outcomes.

Substance abuse is a major problem for people without TBI, and presents a greater challenge for people with TBI. Fortunately, psychologists have important training, skills, and sensitivity that enables them to have a leadership role in the interdisciplinary team, providing substance abuse prevention, education, assessment, and treatment programmes.

REFERENCES

Abrams, D., Barker, L. T., Haffey, W., & Nelson, H. (1993). The economics of return to work for survivors of traumatic brain injury: Vocational services are worth the investment. *Journal of Head Trauma Rehabilitation*, *8*(4), 59–76.

American Psychiatric Association (1987). *Diagnostic and statistical manual of mental disorders (3rd edition, revised) DSM-IIIR*. Washington, DC: American Psychiatric Association.

American Psychiatric Association (1994). *Diagnostic and statistical manual of mental disorders: DSM-IV* (4th ed.). Washington, DC: American Psychiatric Association.

Arenth, P. M., Bogner, J. A., Corrigan, J. D., & Schmidt, L. (2001). The utility of the Substance Abuse Subtle Screening Inventory-3 for use with individuals with brain injury. *Brain Injury*, *15*(6), 499–510.

Bogner, J. A., Corrigan, J. D., Mysiw, W. J., Clinchot, D., & Fugate, L. (2001). A comparison of substance abuse and violence in the prediction of long-term rehabilitation outcomes after traumatic brain injury. *Archives of Physical Medicine & Rehabilitation*, *82*(5), 571–577.

Bogner, J. A., Corrigan, J. D., Spafford, D. E., & Lamb-Hart, G. L. (1997). Integrating substance abuse treatment and vocational rehabilitation after traumatic brain injury. *Journal of Head Trauma Rehabilitation*, *12*(5), 57–71.

Cahalan, D., & Cisin, I. H. (1968a). American drinking practices: Summary of findings from a national probability sample. II. Measurement of massed versus spaced drinking. *Quarterly Journal of Studies on Alcohol*, *29*(3), 642–656.

Cahalan, D., & Cisin, I. H. (1968b). American drinking practices: Summary of findings from a national probability sample: I. Extent of drinking by population subgroups. *Quarterly Journal of Studies on Alcohol*, *29*, 130–151.

Cherner, M., Temkin, N. R., Machamer, J. E., & Dikmen, S. S. (2001). Utility of a composite measure to detect problematic alcohol use in persons with traumatic brain injury. *Archives of Physical Medicine & Rehabilitation, 82*(6), 780–786.

Corrigan, J. D. (1995). Substance abuse as a mediating factor in outcome from traumatic brain injury. *Archives of Physical Medicine & Rehabilitation, 76*(4), 302–309.

Corrigan, J. D., Bogner, J. A., Mysiw, W. J., Clinchot, D., & Fugate, L. (2001). Life satisfaction after traumatic brain injury. *Journal of Head Trauma Rehabilitation, 16*(6), 543–555.

Corrigan, J. D., Lamb-Hart, G. L., & Rust, E. (1995a). A programme of intervention for substance abuse following traumatic brain injury. *Brain Injury, 9*(3), 221–236.

Corrigan, J. D., Rust, E., & Lamb-Hart, G. L. (1995b). The nature and extent of substance abuse problems in persons with traumatic brain injury. *Journal of Head Trauma Rehabilitation, 10*(3), 29–46.

Corrigan, J. D., Smith-Knapp, K., & Granger, C. V. (1998). Outcomes in the first 5 years after traumatic brain injury. *Archives of Physical Medicine & Rehabilitation, 79*(3), 298–305.

Delmonico, R. L., Hanley-Peterson, P., & Englander, J. (1998). Group psychotherapy for persons with traumatic brain injury: Management of frustration and substance abuse. *Journal of Head Trauma Rehabilitation, 13*(6), 10–22.

Drubach, D. A., Kelly, M. P., Winslow, M. M., & Flynn, J. P. (1993). Substance abuse as a factor in the causality, severity, and recurrence rate of traumatic brain injury. *Maryland Medical Journal, 42*(10), 989–993.

Dunlop, T. W., Udvarhelyi, G. B., Stedem, A. F., O'Connor, J. M., Isaacs, M. L., Puig, J. G., & Mather, J. H. (1991). Comparison of patients with and without emotional/behavioural deterioration during the first year after traumatic brain injury. *Journal of Neuropsychiatry & Clinical Neurosciences, 3*(2), 150–156.

Ewing, J. A. (1984). Detecting alcoholism, The CAGE questionnaire. *JAMA, 252*(14), 1905–1907.

Fuller, M. G., Fishman, E., Taylor, C. A., & Wood, R. B. (1994). Screening patients with traumatic brain injuries for substance abuse. *Journal of Neuropsychiatry & Clinical Neurosciences, 6*(2), 143–146.

Gurney, J. G., Rivara, F. P., Mueller, B. A., Newell, D. W., Copass, M. K., & Jurkovich, G. J. (1992). The effects of alcohol intoxication on the initial treatment and hospital course of patients with acute brain injury. *Journal of Trauma-Injury Infection & Critical Care, 33*(5), 709–713.

Johnson, P., Armour, D., Polich, S., & et al. (1977). *U.S. adult drinking practices: Time, trends, social correlations, and sex roles. Draft report for the National Institute on Alcohol Abuse and Alcoholism under contract no. (ADM) 281–76-0200.* Santa Monica, CA: Rand Corporation.

Jong, C. N., Zafonte, R. D., Millis, S. R., & Yavuzer, G. (1999). The effect of cocaine on traumatic brain injury outcome: A preliminary evaluation. *Brain Injury, 13*(12), 1017–1023.

Kelly, D. F. (1995). Alcohol and head injury: An issue revisited. *Journal of Neurotrauma, 12*(5), 883–890.

Klonoff, P. S., Snow, W. G., & Costa, L. D. (1986). Quality of life in patients 2 to 4 years after closed head injury. *Neurosurgery, 19*(5), 735–743.

Kolakowsky-Hayner, S. A., Gourley, E. V., III, Kreutzer, J. S., Marwitz, J. H., Cifu, D. X., & McKinley, W. O. (1999). Pre-injury substance abuse among persons with brain injury and persons with spinal cord injury. *Brain Injury, 13*(8), 571–581.

Kolakowsky-Hayner, S. A., Gourley, E. V., III, Kreutzer, J. S., Marwitz, J. H., Meade, M. A., & Cifu, D. X. (in press). Post-injury substance abuse among persons with brain injury and persons with spinal cord injury. *Brain Injury.*

Kolaskowsky-Hayner, S. A., & Kreutzer, J. S. (2001). Pre-injury crime, substance abuse, and neurobehavioural functioning after traumatic brain injury. *Brain Injury, 15*(1), 53–63.

Kraus, J. F., Morgenstern, H., Fife, D., Conroy, C., & Nourjah, P. (1989). Blood alcohol tests, prevalence of involvement, and outcomes following brain injury. *American Journal of Public Health*, *79*(3), 294–299.

Kreutzer, J. S., Doherty, K. R., Harris, J. A., & Zasler, N. D. (1990a). Alcohol use among persons with traumatic brain injury. *Journal of Head Trauma Rehabilitation*, *5*(3), 9–20.

Kreutzer, J. S., Leininger, B. E., Sherron, P. D., & Groah, C. H. (1990b). Managing psychosocial dysfunction. In P. H. Wehman & J. S. Kreutzer (Eds.), *Vocational rehabilitation for persons with traumatic brain injury*. Rockville, MD: Aspen Publications.

Kreutzer, J. S., Marwitz, J. H., & Wehman, P. H. (1991a). Substance abuse assessment and treatment in vocational rehabilitation for persons with brain injury. *Journal of Head Trauma Rehabilitation*, *6*(3), 12–23.

Kreutzer, J. S., Marwitz, J. H., & Witol, A. D. (1995). Interrelationships between crime, substance abuse, and aggressive behaviours among persons with traumatic brain injury. *Brain Injury*, *9*(8), 757–768.

Kreutzer, J. S., Wehman, P. H., Harris, J. A., Burns, C. T., & Young, H. F. (1991b). Substance abuse and crime patterns among persons with traumatic brain injury referred for supported employment. *Brain Injury*, *5*(2), 177–187.

Kreutzer, J. S., Witol, A. D., & Marwitz, J. H. (1996a). Alcohol and drug use among young persons with traumatic brain injury. *Journal of Learning Disabilities*, *29*(6), 643–651.

Kreutzer, J. S., Witol, A. D., Sander, A. M., Cifu, D. X., Marwitz, J. H., & Delmonico, R. (1996b). A prospective longitudinal multicenter analysis of alcohol use patterns among persons with traumatic brain injury. *Journal of Head Trauma Rehabilitation*, *11*(5), 58–69.

Langley, M. J., Lindsay, W. P., Lam, C. S., & Priddy, D. A. (1990). A comprehensive alcohol abuse treatment programme for persons with traumatic brain injury. *Brain Injury*, *4*(1), 77–86.

Lezak, M. D. (1995). *Neuropsychological assessment* (3rd ed.). New York: Oxford University Press.

Loberg, T. (1986). Neuropsychological findings in the early and middle phases of alcoholism. In I. Grant & K. M. Adams (Eds.), *Neuropsychological assessment of neuropsychiatric disorders* (pp. 415–440). New York: Oxford University Press.

Marion, D. W. (1998). Head injury and spinal cord injury. *Neurology Clinics*, *16*, 485–502.

McLellan, A. T., Luborsky, L., Cacciola, J., Griffith, J., Evans, F., Barr, H. L., & O'Brien, C. P. (1985). New data from the Addiction Severity Index. Reliability and validity in three centers. *Journal of Nervous & Mental Disease*, *173*(7), 412–423.

McLellan, A. T., Luborsky, L., Woody, G. E., & O'Brien, C. P. (1980). An improved diagnostic evaluation instrument for substance abuse patients. The Addiction Severity Index. *Journal of Nervous and Mental Disease*, *168*(1), 26–33.

Miller, J. D., & Cisin, I. H. (1983). *Highlights from the National Survey on Drug Abuse: 1982* (DHHS publication no. ADM 83–1277). Washington, DC: US Government Printing Office.

Oddy, M., & Humphrey, M. (1980). Social recovery during the year following severe head injury. *Journal of Neurology, Neurosurgery & Psychiatry*, *43*(9), 798–802.

Ommaya, A. K., Salazar, A. M., Dannenberg, A. L., Chervinsky, A. B., & Schwab, K. (1996). Outcome after traumatic brain injury in the US military medical system. *Journal of Trauma-Injury Infection & Critical Care*, *41*(6), 972–975.

Parsons, O. A. (1996). Alcohol abuse and alcoholism. In R. L. Adams, O. A. Parsons, J. L. Culbertson, & S. J. Nixon (Eds.), *Neuropsychology for clinical practice: Etiology, assessment, and treatment of common neurological disorders* (pp. 175–202). Washington, DC: American Psychological Association.

Pires, M. (1989). Substance abuse: The silent saboteur in rehabilitation. *Nursing Clinics of North America*, *24*(1), 291–296.

Pokorny, A. D., Miller, B. A., & Kaplan, H. B. (1972). The brief MAST: A shortened version of the Michigan Alcoholism Screening Test. *American Journal of Psychiatry*, *129*(3), 342–345.

Rimel, R. W., Giordani, B., Barth, J. T., & Jane, J. A. (1982). Moderate head injury: Completing the clinical spectrum of brain trauma. *Neurosurgery, 11*(3), 344–351.

Ronty, H., Ahonen, A., Tolonen, U., Heikkila, J., & Niemela, O. (1993). Cerebral trauma and alcohol abuse. *European Journal of Clinical Investigation, 23*(3), 182–187.

Ruff, R. M., Marshall, L. F., Klauber, M. R., Blunt, B. A., Grant, I., Foulkes, M. A., Eisenberg, H., Jane, J., & Marmarou, A. (1990). Alcohol abuse and neurological outcome of the severely head injured. *Journal of Head Trauma Rehabilitation, 5*(3), 21–31.

Sander, A. M., Kreutzer, J. S., & Fernandez, C. C. (1997). Neurobehavioural functioning, substance abuse, and employment after brain injury: Implications for vocational rehabilitation. *Journal of Head Trauma Rehabilitation, 12*(5), 28–41.

Sander, A. M., Witol, A. D., & Kreutzer, J. S. (1997). Alcohol use after traumatic brain injury: Concordance of patients' and relatives' reports. *Archives of Physical Medicine & Rehabilitation, 78*(2), 138–142.

Sbordone, R. J., Liter, J. C., & Pettler-Jennings, P. (1995). Recovery of function following severe traumatic brain injury: A retrospective 10-year follow-up. *Brain Injury, 9*(3), 285–299.

Seaton, J. D., & David, C. O. (1990). Family role in substance abuse and traumatic brain injury rehabilitation. *Journal of Head Trauma Rehabilitation, 5*(3), 41–46.

Selzer, M. L. (1971). The Michigan alcoholism screening test: The quest for a new diagnostic instrument. *American Journal of Psychiatry, 127*(12), 1653–1658.

Sherer, M., Bergloff, P., High, W., Jr. & Nick, T. G. (1999). Contribution of functional ratings to prediction of longterm employment outcome after traumatic brain injury. *Brain Injury, 13*(12), 973–981.

Sparadeo, F. R., & Gill, D. (1989). Effects of prior alcohol use on head injury recovery. *Journal of Head Trauma Rehabilitation, 4*(1), 75–81.

Wagner, A. K., Hammond, F. M., Sasser, H. C., & Wiercisiewski, D. (2002). Return to productive activity after traumatic brain injury: Relationship with measures of disability, handicap, and community integration. *Archives of Physical Medicine & Rehabilitation, 83*(1), 107–114.

Wagner, A. K., Sasser, H. C., Hammond, F. M., Wiercisiewski, D., & Alexander, J. (2000). Intentional traumatic brain injury: Epidemiology, risk factors, and associations with injury severity and mortality [erratum appears in *J. Trauma* 2000 Nov. 49(5):982.]. *Journal of Trauma-Injury Infection & Critical Care, 49*(3), 404–410.

NEUROPSYCHOLOGICAL REHABILITATION, 2003, *13* (1/2), 189–210

Pain following traumatic brain injury: Assessment and management

Stephen Tyrer and Amy Lievesley

University of Newcastle-upon-Tyne, UK

Traumatic brain injury is frequently associated with painful complaints immediately after injury and subsequently. Early assessment of possible painful conditions can be made at the time of physical examination in those who are unable to give a history. Non-verbal signs of pain, including withdrawal of a painful limb or body part, irritability or tears should draw the attention of the assessing physician to a peripheral painful site. Treatment of conditions giving rise to pain can be made at this stage.

Persistent pain may arise from a combination of physical and psychological factors and is best managed in a multidisciplinary pain clinic. Contributions from physicians in pain management, psychologists, physiotherapists and clinical nurse specialists enable a rehabilitation programme to take place. Treatments include analgesic drugs, graded exercise, cognitive–behavioural therapy, and transcutaneous electrical nerve stimulation. Rehabilitation of people who have a head injury and pain takes longer than usual and separate pain management facilities should be developed for this population.

INTRODUCTION

This paper is confined largely to the assessment and management of pain following traumatic brain injury (TBI) but the information is also applicable to the assessment of those with brain damage arising from other sources.

What is pain?

Pain is a subjective experience and is closely linked to psychological factors as well as physical input. Pain has been defined by the Taxonomy Committee of the International Association for the Study of Pain as "an unpleasant sensory

Correspondence should be sent to Stephen Tyrer, Pain Management Unit, Royal Victoria Infirmary, Newcastle-upon-Tyne, NE1 4LP.

The authors wish to thank the Royal College of Psychiatrists for permission to reproduce material from a paper published in the *British Journal of Psychiatry* (1992, *160*, 733–741).

© 2003 Psychology Press Ltd
http://www.tandf.co.uk/journals/pp/09602011.html   DOI:10.1080/09602010244000381

and emotional experience associated with actual and potential tissue damage, or described in terms of such damage". The Committee refined this definition by stating that "activity induced in the nociceptive pathways by a noxious stimulus is not pain, which is always a psychological state. . ." (Merskey, 1979). Pain can affect mood, behaviour and cognition with consequences on self-esteem and coping ability. It needs to be treated to alleviate patient discomfort, to allow rehabilitation programmes to be implemented with optimal effect, and to reduce associated psychological and physiological distress. In the case of brain injured patients, the perception of pain can be altered by the severity of the injury and cognitive level. Both can affect patients' ability to relay information about pain, thus making treatment decisions complex.

It is necessary to distinguish between acute and chronic pain. Acute pain is pain that arises from damage to organs and tissues at the time of trauma, including pain that is generated from nociceptors, i.e., peripheral sense organs, during injury and in the process of subsequent healing. This type of pain "enables the organism to sense impending damage and thus avoid harm and prolong survival" (Sternbach, 1984). It acts as a warning sign that something is wrong.

Chronic pain is pain that is maintained after the healing process has been completed. It nearly always occurs after an acute painful episode when the behavioural and autonomic signs that characterise acute pain have receded. It is associated with depression, lassitude and lack of motivation.

Epidemiology of pain and injuries to the head

Factors affecting pain experience in TBI

In people who sustain a TBI and who also have pain there is an incomplete relationship between tissue damage and complaint of pain. There are a number of reasons for this:

Level of cognitive awareness.   In patients who have severe brain damage there is associated reduction in cognitive capacity. Indeed, the Glasgow Coma Scale (Teasdale & Jennett, 1974), a widely used measure in the assessment of consciousness following brain injury, includes the response to a painful stimulus in the assessment of degree of coma. In severe brain injuries there is often no response to a painful stimulus, such as squeezing tightly the Achilles tendon. In such injuries severe tissue damage can occur at a time when the patient is unconscious or has diminished cognitive functioning to such an extent that perception is profoundly affected.

Circumstances of accident/damage.   Weir Mitchell, in the American Civil War of 1861–65 (1872), and Beecher (1946) showed clearly the relationship between the degree of pain experienced and the circumstances surrounding the injury and resulting consequences. Beecher showed how external events affect both the severity of pain and behaviour associated with this. Beecher was a surgeon accompanying the American forces during the D-Day landings. Caring for soldiers severely wounded at this time, he was surprised that only one in three taken into combat hospitals complained of sufficient pain to warrant receipt of morphine. The relief of being away from battle with a likely return home was a sufficient analgesic to reduce pain. This contrasted with the experience of similar people who received wounds in the normal course of events in civilian life. These individuals complained of much more severe pain and requested morphine in over 80% of cases.

Subjective differences in tolerance of pain.   There are considerable differences between people from different cultures in their response to pain as well as ethnic, gender, and age differences. These differences are outside the scope of this article. The particular issues that affect women with TBI are covered in a recent review (Bell & Pepping, 2001).

Incidence of pain following TBI

The incidence of pain following TBI varies according to the interval of time following brain injury. Headache is reported as occurring in 80% of patients at some stage during the recovery process whereas 20% complain of pain in the limbs more than 6 months after injury (Gellman, Keenan, & Botte, 1996). Although, as a general rule, the greater the extent of tissue damage the greater the degree of pain in the acute stages, the relationship between complaint of pain and organic pathology is much less apparent subsequently.

Acute pain often accompanies the initial stages of brain damage, particularly in more severe cases of TBI, as multiple injuries may be present. Attention may be focused on injuries to the limbs or body, particularly in those who sustain a closed head injury. Conversely, injuries to the head may be missed in an acute setting owing to clinicians' initial concerns for patients' medical stability and impaired consciousness (Killen & Huntoon, 1997). Garland and Bailey (1981) found that in 254 patients admitted to an adult head injury unit, there was an 11% incidence of missed fractures and dislocations, both possible causes of pain. These included one patient with a fracture dislocation of the thoracic spine and nine patients each with undetected ulnar and peroneal nerve neuropathies. Three brachial plexus injuries were missed.

In 60 children with TBI, 27% had undetected soft tissue trauma shortly after starting rehabilitation that was only identified after total body scan (Sobus, Alexander, & Harcke, 1993). Three quarters of the children thus identified had previously shown behaviour problems or co-operated poorly with treatment because of pain occurring during rehabilitation procedures.

Characteristics and pain syndromes following head injury

It is evident that the site and nature of pain following injury will depend on the type of injury sustained. If a skull fracture has occurred, subsequent painful symptoms are probably more common than in closed head injuries but the literature is scanty on this subject. Headache is very common as a presenting symptom and is almost universal at some time in the course of those who sustain a mild TBI, irrespective of whether a fracture has occurred. There are, however, a number of other painful syndromes that are manifest in many cases, some of which are not apparently related to focal damage.

Postconcussional syndrome

A syndrome, comprising diffuse headache, irritability, loss of concentration, dizziness, and disturbance of smell and vision that occurs shortly after head injury in which there is loss of consciousness, is referred to as the postconcussional or postconcussive syndrome (Kay, Kerr, & Lassman, 1971). Loss of consciousness is necessary for this term to be used. There is debate about the use of this term, many preferring to use the term, post-traumatic headache. In some cases headache is persistent and is associated with either cognitive and somatic symptoms or emotional and vegetative symptoms or both (Bohnen, et al., 1994; Martelli, Grayson, & Zasler, 1999). Some refer to this collection of symptoms as persistent postconcussive syndrome (Alexander, 1995). This syndrome is more common in those of female sex, those of lower social class status, subjects who have had a previous TBI, those with previous headaches, in those individuals who have associated severe systemic injury, or if there is a compensation claim in progress.

There is also evidence to show that patients who have pain at the time of injury (Alexander et al., 1992; Ettlin et al., 1992; Radanov et al., 1999) are more likely to develop such symptoms. However, *severity* of headache within the first few weeks does not necessarily presage chronic headache later (Gualtieri, 1995; Jagoda & Riggio, 2000).

How far such a pain syndrome is psychologically or organically determined remains undetermined. Alexander (1995) posits that persistent PCS is not likely to have a neurological basis because of the lack of both physical signs and neuropsychological impairment in these less severely injured patients. For instance, in the study of Ettlin et al. (1992) none of the patients had lost consciousness. However, in some patients with more severe mild head injury with loss of consciousness for up to 15 minutes, impairment of the special senses is apparent (Kay et al., 1971) and migraine and cluster headache are recognised sequelae (Alexander, 1995), suggesting vascular changes resulting from the TBI. Furthermore, the effect of pain in reducing attention, memory, speed of processing and executive functioning—neuropsychological deficits that also occur in head injury—suggest that chronic pain is a factor that increases and maintains persistent PCS (Nicholson, 2000b; Nicholson, Martelli, & Zasler, 2001).

Cervical-injury related headaches

Damage to the cervical nerve roots is classically caused by a hyperextension injury of the neck, the so-called whiplash syndrome. The diagnosis is suspected when unilateral neckache and headaches occur following neck injury. Associated symptoms include visual disturbances, dizziness, fatigue, depression and cognitive impairment. There are signs of focal muscle tenderness over the back of the neck and scalp on the affected side. A reduced range of motion of the neck is noted characteristically, persistence of which is closely related to subsequent handicap (Kasch, Bach, & Jensen, 2001). Computed tomography and magnetic resonance imaging do not show abnormalities and are not normally carried out except in cases of neurological deficit, suspected disc or spinal cord damage, or fracture.

Early active mobilisation is of benefit in less severe cases (Anon 1998a; Borchgrevink et al., 1998). Predictors of poor physical and psychological outcome include initial severity of injury (Radanov et al., 1999), duration of symptoms, older age, radiation of symptoms to the upper limb, spinal pain, previous psychological problems, and chronic social difficulties (Mayou & Radanov, 1996). Specific psychological treatment strategies are not well supported by the evidence (Mayou & Radanov, 1996).

Spasticity

Loss of upper motor neurone control following brain damage may lead to muscle spasticity and contractures. The imbalance between agonist and antagonist muscles can lead to severe pain. Treatment with muscle relaxant drugs that inhibit spinal transmission, such as baclofen and tizanidine, is normally the first choice if increased tone is persistent and cannot be overcome by passive stretching (Elovic, 2001). Botulinum toxin injections are of particular value in severe spasticity and can allow physiotherapeutic measures which would otherwise be impossible (Davis & Barnes, 2000).

Heterotopic ossification

Heterotopic ossification refers to a process in which there is development of bone in tissues other than the skeleton. The most frequent site for this abnormal bone formation in those with TBI is in the muscles of spastic limbs, usually in the hips, knees, shoulders or elbows. Movement of the affected limbs can give rise to severe pain. Diagnosis is made by radiographic examination of the affected joint, which should be carried out if movement of the joint is difficult or painful. Treatment usually involves surgical excision after prior treatment with diphosphonate drugs and/or non-steroidal anti-inflammatory agents (Ayers, 2002). The prognosis is not good because subsequent exercise may promote the development of further ectopic bone.

Complex regional pain syndromes

The term, complex regional pain syndrome, is now used to describe what used to be called reflex sympathetic dystrophy. It was thought that these syndromes were due to damage to sympathetic nerves, often from only minor trauma, resulting in sympathetic overactivity associated with continuous burning pain. Opinion is divided on the extent of peripheral autonomic nerve involvement in this condition and central mechanisms may predominate. However, there is no doubt about the separate nature of this condition and other causes of sympathetically mediated pain. In the first stages there is vasodilatation, increased sweating of the affected area, and oedema. Later there is reduced blood supply to the affected part, sensitivity to cold, decreased temperature of the area, and atrophy of the skin and soft tissues, but usually no diminution in pain.

Diagnosis used to depend on the response to a local sympathetic block but there is scepticism about the use of this measure. Three-phase bone scanning has some diagnostic significance and shows increased activity in the delayed phase in affected patients (Gellman et al., 1996). Early physiotherapy is often recommended in mild cases. Drug treatment with tricyclic antidepressants or anticonvulsants relieves pain to an extent and there have been recent trials illustrating benefits of diphosphonates and spinal cord stimulation (Bogduk, 2001).

Neuropathic pain

Pain that occurs in the absence of detectable damage to the nervous system yet in which there is presumptive evidence of nerve injury, is known as neuropathic pain. The characteristics of neuropathic pain include abnormal burning or tingling sensations (dysaesthesiae), pain in a region of sensory deficit (often numbness) and pain arising from stimuli that would not normally cause pain, e.g., touch. The structures that are affected include the peripheral nerve, the dorsal root ganglion or dorsal root, and the central nervous system itself. Damage to these structures frequently accompanies TBI.

Mechanisms of pain after brain injury

It is often difficult to explain why patients complain of pain following injury to the brain itself. The brain does not have nociceptors or other sensory receptors so how can painful sensations be experienced by a damaged brain? We have already seen that neuropathic pain can occur from damage to neural tissue. This can arise from anywhere within the nervous system, including the peripheral nerves. Such damage occurring in the brain or spinal cord is commonly known as central pain. Central pain does not require stimulation of nociceptors, it results from abnormal somatosensory function and is related directly to the site of such malfunction. On the evidence of the site of brain damage in those who subsequently develop central pain states, it has been postulated that lesions of the spinothalamic cortical pathways or their trigeminal equivalents are necessary for brain central pain to develop (Boivie, Lcijon, & Johansson, 1985). Central pain resulting from damage to the brain often has a delayed onset, may occur in the absence of clinically detectable sensory loss and is characteristically associated with hyperaesthesia, hyperpathia, or allodynia.

These terms need to be defined. Hyperaesthesia is increased sensitivity to any stimulation, hyperpathia refers to an abnormally painful and exaggerated reaction to a stimulus, especially a repetitive one, and allodynia is the provocation of pain from a stimulus that does not usually cause pain.

Central pain does not follow characteristic dermatomal patterns and is generally ill-localised. It is usually caused by vascular damage and is more common in patients with strokes than in those with TBI. The suggested mechanisms for the origin of such pain include denervation neuronal hypersensitivity, and disinhibition of related structures because of the loss of function of a neural pathway (Boivie et al., 1985).

It has been conjectured that ill-defined pain syndromes such as fibromyalgia and atypical pain states could result from central pain mechanisms (Nicholson, 2000a). This is an interesting suggestion, but has not yet been substantiated by evidence of disordered neural function as demonstrated on electrophysiological or neuroimaging procedures.

Outcome and predictors of patients with TBI and pain

Pain that is still present in patients six months or more following brain injury is common. Lahz and Bryant (1996) found that 52% of moderate/severe TBI patients and 58% of mild TBI patients who later attended a tertiary brain injury clinic, reported chronic pain. Uomoto and Esselman (1993) performed a retrospective survey on TBI patients referred to an outpatient brain injury rehabilitation clinic. They found that 89% of patients with a mild TBI reported headache, with a lesser frequency of neck/shoulder, back, and other painful sites. This compares with a much lower frequency of 18% of patients with moderate/severe TBI. Beetar, Guilmette, and Sparadeo (1996), in a similar retrospective study of patients referred for neuropsychological assessment at a medical centre, found that 59% of TBI subjects reported pain on at least one occasion compared with 22% of general neurological patients referred to the same facility. Sleep difficulties were reported significantly more often in those patients with mild TBI who complained of pain. As in other surveys there was a greater incidence of pain in those with mild injuries—70% compared with 40% of those with moderate/severe injuries.

These results suggest approximately half of patients who sustain a TBI and who are referred to specialist clinics are likely to have a chronic painful complaint subsequently. The frequency of pain is much lower when one considers all patients who have a TBI—this figure refers to those referred to specialist clinics, presumably because their problems are more intractable. More reliance should be placed on the figures from the prospective survey by Lahz and Bryant (1996), although the results probably cannot be applied to all patients with TBI as the patients involved were selectively referred to a clinic.

The finding that those with milder degrees of injury are more likely to complain of pain appears paradoxical. Depression and concerns about change in occupational and functional status can amplify painful symptoms (Merskey & Chandarana, 1992). In those who are more severely injured there may be less concern about issues in the future because of attention to immediate problems. Patients who attend brain injury clinics are likely to focus on reporting symptoms associated with the brain injury itself. Patients may not report pain because it is not the primary reason for their attendance at the clinic. Cognitive impairment may also limit patients' insight into pain and its role in their functional and emotional disturbance (Lahz & Bryant, 1997; Uomoto & Esselman, 1993).

Identification of both TBI and pain

On the other hand, patients referred to a pain management service may not have adequate assessment of the problems sustained at the time of head injury. Chronic pain in TBI patients and TBI in chronic pain patients can be very difficult to identify as the symptoms of each are very similar and confound each other. Both populations present with a range of symptoms including anxiety, depression, impaired attention and concentration and a fixation on their injuries/pain.

Andary et al. (1997) found 18.5% of patients referred to an out-patient university-based rehabilitation medicine centre for chronic pain were found to have a history and symptoms that indicated previously undiagnosed/untreated mild TBI.

Anderson, Kaplan, and Fesenthal (1990) found that 11% of patients referred to a pain rehabilitation programme also showed signs of concomitant brain injury. Mild head injury may not be identified during standard physical examination or patients may appear to recover fully enough to warrant no further medical attention. In addition, secondary complications such as hypoxia, or cerebral ischaemia may cause difficulties after the patient is thought to be well. Furthermore, the effects of mild TBI may not be morphologically identifiable until after some delay, which means any mental state changes may not be noted at the acute stage (Anderson et al., 1990).

Warning features of TBI include memory and concentration problems, pain in the head and upper limbs and extensive unsuccessful treatments, particularly if the patient has been involved in a motor vehicle accident (Andary et al., 1997). Anderson et al. (1990) identified parts of the mental state examination that are more helpful in identifying previously undiagnosed mild TBI. Digit and word recall, constructional testing, proverb interpretation and conceptual series completion tasks appeared to offer specific benefit in establishing the presence of TBI.

ASSESSMENT

Assessment of acute pain

Assessment of pain at the acute stage depends upon the level of consciousness and the site and extent of the injury. Careful physical examination is vital at this stage, as this will affect subsequent place of transfer. Pain must be suspected if there is severe injury and the patient is groaning and/or is attempting to rub or guard the affected part. As severity of injury and time spent unconscious increases, the ability to self-report pain decreases. In such cases the physician has to determine from objective assessment how much the patient is in pain. Often the only indication that a patient is in pain is a rapid withdrawal of any area that is touched or moved. Physical signs of a painful area may be indicated by slight increase in temperature relative to the areas surrounding it or by mild swelling (Gellman et al., 1996).

Assessment of pain is important as treatment with analgesic measures at this stage minimises later complaints of pain (Mollmann & Auf der Landwehr, 2000).

Assessment of chronic pain

Patients with chronic pain accompanying head injury require a detailed physical and psychological assessment. Ideally they should be seen at least once in a multidisciplinary pain unit, which is accepted as the best way to manage chronic pain (Loeser, 2001). The aims of assessment are to discover the origin, site and intensity of the pain. Both physical and psychological factors affect the perception and behavioural consequences of long-standing pain.

The intensity of pain is normally assessed by asking the patient to estimate the degree of pain experienced at the time of interview on a scale of 0 to 10, where a score of 0 represents no pain whatsoever whereas 10 is the worst pain imaginable (Seymour, Simpson, & Charlton, 1985). Alternatively, or in addition, the patient may mark the perceived intensity of pain on a 10 cm visual analogue scale using the same end-points. These scales are also useful to compare intensity over time and in different conditions. When patients are in distress from physical or psychiatric factors they tend to rate the intensity of their pain as higher than when they are in an euthymic state (Price, Gracely, & Bennett, 1995).

An indication of the degree of contribution of psychological factors to the perception of pain can be assessed by using the McGill Pain Questionnaire (Melzack, 1975). A shorter version of this questionnaire may be more appropriate (Melzack, 1987). The McGill pain questionnaire is a checklist of 78 words that describe different pain states. Three main major classes of words have been found to describe pain: sensory, affective, and intensity. Words used to describe pain in the sensory category include burning, crushing, sharp, sore, and throbbing. Affective words include agonising, dreadful, exhausting, punishing, and sickening. Intensity is described by words such as weak, moderate, strong, intense, severe, and excruciating. Patients with a significant psychological component to perception of pain use a greater number of affective words proportionally to others. The total number of words selected on the McGill pain questionnaire is most closely associated with the intensity of the pain.

The history from the patient of the development of pain, coupled with the findings from the examination of the patient, usually provide the most heuristic information about the nature of the patient's pain. Questions that should be asked include the following:

- When did your pain first start?
- Where do you feel your pain?
- How intense is your pain?
- How does it change throughout the day?
- What is the effect of movement and change in posture on your pain?
- What other factors make your pain (a) better, or (b) worse?
- What do you now do less frequently and what do you do more frequently since you developed the pain?
- Does your mood affect your pain?
- What effect do drugs have on your pain?

Pain that is accurately localised in specific dermatomes, that is described by adjectives such as sore, boring, and nagging, that is intensified considerably by certain movements, and which is sufficient enough to wake patients from sleep is likely to be associated with an organic cause (Tyrer, 1992a). The converse does not apply to the same degree but regional description of pain, lack of variability during the day and emotional descriptors of pain are features that are over-represented in patients with non-organic contributions to pain.

In those with very severe injuries and in patients with post-traumatic confusion it is difficult to assess pain adequately. It has been shown that when children who are unable to communicate effectively are in pain, they are more irritable, seek comfort from others, screw up their eyes, are less active and are more inclined to cry (Breau et al., 2001). Two other items in the questionnaire that the carers of the children were given, gesturing to the painful area and gasping, were reduced during painful episodes. The authors believed that reasons for this were related to these manoeuvres leading to increased pain, although cognitive difficulties might be related.

Although this study was based on children with mainly cerebral palsy and seizure disorder, some of the subjects had suffered from TBI and this investigation provides some indication of what signs to look for if patients are unable to communicate verbally.

A physical examination should be carried out in all cases. Signs that have been linked to non-organic pathology include over-reaction to examination (excessive pain behaviour in response to examination), superficial tenderness, and production of pain when manoeuvres are tested that patients think will cause pain but in fact do not affect body mechanics, for example pressure on the head (Waddell, McCulloch, Kummell, & Vennell, 1980).

By this stage, the clinician should have a reasonable idea of the level of organic contribution to the pain, and how pain and related symptoms are affecting the patient's life. Several questions are useful to ask at this point:

- Is there evidence of existing physical disease or past tissue damage?
- If so, has pain persisted beyond the time that healing would have been expected to take place?
- Is there evidence of psychiatric illness, and if present is it primary or secondary?
- Are there any emotional conflicts or psychosocial problems that were associated with the onset of pain or with its continued maintenance?
- Is there any suggestion of intentional production or feigning of symptoms?

Most patients with chronic pain have organic, psychiatric, personality and sociocultural contributions towards their pain problem. The skill of the therapist is in evaluating the extent of each factor and providing the best treatment for each patient after assessment of these factors (Tyrer, 1992a).

Confounders in assessment of pain

Depression

The prevalence of depression following TBI varies from 5% to 25% depending on the population studied (Fleminger, 2001). It has been shown that depression after head injury is a predictor of later disability status (Ericsson et al., 2002). In patients with persistent pain depression is more frequent. The greater the degree of comorbidity the greater the impairment. In patients with both depression and pain it is important to find out the nature of the circumstances that gave rise to the TBI. It is also helpful to determine the beliefs of the patient about his or her condition. The focus for patients who wish for pain relief should be to reduce pain, directly or indirectly. Those who are clearly depressed should be treated for this condition.

It is important to distinguish feelings of depression from depressive illness. Patients who sustain TBI are often not able to carry out activities which they found previously enjoyable. This handicap leads to depressed feelings but it is only if there is persistent lack of enjoyment from most activities, in particular those where there is no reason to suppose the injury has altered the ability to carry these out, that a depressive illness should be diagnosed. It is helpful to ask the patient whether he or she still derives pleasure from his or her favourite television programme. If lack of pleasure is accompanied by interrupted sleep or early morning wakening, coupled with loss of appetite and weight a major depressive illness is likely. Most people who sustain a TBI have reduced energy and concentration and the presence of these symptoms are not valuable in contributing to a diagnosis of depression in this population.

It is also important to explain to the patient what has happened, the existing physical and mental problems, and how these are going to be managed. A likely timescale for change should be given as far as possible even though there is considerable variation from person to person in the pace of recovery. The premorbid personality and psychiatric history of the person should be obtained from a close informant in all cases. Mental state abnormalities detected following a TBI may have been present before injury. Premorbid alcohol and drug misuse should be identified.

Post-traumatic stress disorder

Head injuries frequently occur in circumstances which are extremely threatening. It is therefore not surprising that post-traumatic stress disorder (PTSD) is common and would probably be more frequently found if it were not for the anterograde amnesia that accompanies severe head injuries (see McMillan, Williams, & Bryant, this issue). Although pain is not a necessary feature of PTSD for diagnosis it is a common accompaniment of this condition and was recorded in almost one quarter of patients at a Veteran's Hospital in the USA (White & Faustman, 1989). Patients with accident-related pain and high PTSD symptoms reported both higher levels of pain and affective disturbance than patients involved in an accident who did not have such symptoms (Geisser, Roth, Bachman, & Eckert, 1996). Pain is a symptom occurring in PTSD about which enquiry should be made and which may need specific attention in its own right (Schreiber & Galai-Gat, 1993).

TREATMENT

Medication-based treatments

Acute pain

The choice of analgesic drug used in acute painful states depends on the extent of injury and respiratory function. In many traumatic injuries without extensive damage, intravenous ketamine, an NMDA antagonist drug, is used in subanaesthetic doses (0.2–0.5 mg) (Mollmann & Auf der Landwehr, 2000). The drug is of advantage to patients in shock as it raises blood pressure. The non-steroidal anti-inflammatory drugs have also been used in acute painful injuries because they do not affect respiration. Ketorolac has been shown to be cost-effective compared with morphine in such conditions (Rainer et al., 2000).

Opiate drugs are still the mainstay of treatment in most units. Morphine is widely used but the agent sometimes favoured is pethidine, especially in visceral pain, because of its lesser sedative effect and shorter duration of action compared to morphine. However, in more severe injuries, morphine is likely to be required, although it may be necessary to intubate and ventilate the patient if respiratory depression supervenes (Colvin, Healy, & Samra, 1998). Combinations of analgesic drugs, both with each other and with other non-analgesic drugs, are often employed as they provide better pain relief with fewer side-effects (Haetzman & Stickle, 1999). This practice offers particular benefit to those who have sustained a brain injury, as the injury may put them at increased risk of adverse effects, particularly those that affect cognition.

Chronic pain

Drugs that are used in patients with TBI and chronic pain are shown in Table 1.

If the pain is not severe, paracetamol is the drug of choice. This drug is very safe as long as it is given in doses of not more than 4g per day. It should normally be administered on a regular drug schedule or in advance of when pain is expected. The non-steroidal anti-inflammatory drugs are useful if there is evidence of an inflammatory process but are not indicated if there is traumatic damage as these drugs can prolong coagulation time (Killen & Huntoon 1997). When these agents are given it is often necessary to administer prophylactic ulcer-healing drugs such as the proton-pump inhibitors, e.g., lansoprazole or prostaglandin analogues such as misoprostol.

Antidepressants are valuable in the treatment of chronic pain and the effects of these drugs in pain is achieved through a different mechanism than their use in depression. Their analgesic effects are thought to be due to their effects on blocking sodium channels in peripheral nerves. The tricyclic antidepressants, such as amitriptyline or dothiepin, administered in substantially lower doses than are used in depression are valuable. The evidence is compelling. A

TABLE 1
Drugs used in the management of patients with head injury and chronic pain

Drug type	Examples of drug	Mode of analgesic action	Advantages	Disadvantages
Opioids	Codeine Diamorphine Methadone Morphine	Inhibits nociceptive input from peripheral nerves Modulates nociceptive input from spinal cord Affects emotional response to pain	Highly effective No ceiling effect for morphine	Possible respiratory depression Mood alteration (for the stronger opioids) Sedative effects
Psycho-stimulants	Amphetamine Methylphenidate	Activates inhibitory pathways by increasing dopamine and noradrenaline	Can enhance analgesic effect of opioids Reduces excessive sedation	Possible anxiety Agitation
Anti-convulsants	Carbamazepine Sodium Valproate Gabapentin	Sodium channel blockers acting as a local anaesthetic on damaged nerve fibres	Fewer side effects May be beneficial for mood and cognition	Can also affect intellectual functioning, concentration and memory
Anti-depressants	Amitriptyline Dothiepin Lofepramine Venlafaxine SSRI drugs, e.g. fluoxetine	Blockade of nerve sodium channels Block reuptake of serotonin	Lack of tolerance Very little abuse potential Aid sleep	Slight sedative effects but not a problem at usual low dosage Limited benefit in affecting pain
Non-steroidal anti-inflammatory drugs	Ibuprofen Diclofenac Piroxicam Celecoxib Ketorolac	Decrease levels of inflammation	Low level of cognitive side-effects	Can affect renal functioning Less suitable for elderly
Muscle relaxants	Baclofen Diazepam Dantrolene	Decrease muscle spasms	Good in associated musculoskeletal disorders	Sedation Tolerance Abuse potential

systematic review showed that the number of patients needed to be treated by these agents (NNT) to enable one extra patient to benefit was 2.3–3, depending on the nature of the condition treated (McQuay et al., 1996). Dothiepin has also been found to be helpful in the treatment of atypical facial pain (Feinmann, Harris, & Cawley, 1984). The selective serotonin re-uptake inhibitor group of drugs do not have the same consistent benefits (Anon, 1998a).

Anticonvulsants, e.g., carbamazepine and gabapentin, were also found to be of value in neuropathic pain in a further systematic review (Collins, Moore, McQuay, & Wiffen, 2000). The effectiveness of these drugs in pain arising from TBI has not been evaluated. However, in neuralgic pain the NNT is of a similar magnitude to that achieved with antidepressants.

At present there is no convincing evidence to suggest whether anti-convulsants could be preferred to antidepressants as a first-line treatment in neuropathic pain, either because of greater degree of benefit or lower adverse affects. A randomised comparison of an antidepressant with an anticonvulsant in central pain showed greater benefit with amitriptyline compared with carbamazepine (Leijon & Boivie, 1989).

The value of both antidepressants and anticonvulsants in pain arising other than from damage to nerve structures is not established.

If pain is more severe, opioid drugs should be given. Their use in patients with chronic pain shows that the dangers of dependence are low (McQuay, 1999). Nevertheless, they should be avoided in those with an antisocial or dependent personality disorder and in those with evidence of previous dependence on alcohol or benzodiazepines. Morphine is the mainstay of treatment. The drug should be started in the form of a short acting preparation in the first instance to determine response. It should be given in a low dose, 5–10 mg every 4–6 hours depending on response and adjusted according to pain intensity. Drug doses should be decreased substantially if creatinine clearance is less than 30 ml/min (McQuay, 1999). Longer acting preparations such as sustained relief morphine are recommended if there is benefit. The maintenance dose is calculated by titration over a few days, and then the drug is given regularly, without waiting for the pain to return. The initial reactions of nausea or dizziness commonly diminish. Constipation may remain and laxatives may be needed. If pain starts to increase, the dose is increased. Alternatively, psychostimulants such as methylphenidate or dexamphetamine can be given with the opioid drug to potentiate its effect and reduce sedation.

Other treatments

Pain clinics

A multidisciplinary approach is generally accepted as the most effective process in treating chronic pain (Ashburn & Staats, 1999; Linton, Hellsing, & Andersson, 1993; Loeser, 2001). This is usually carried out in a Pain Clinic. Pain Clinics were first started almost 50 years ago to provide a service from the many agencies that are involved in those with persistent painful complaints. These clinics involve health-care providers from several disciplines, each of whom specialises in different features of treatment (Loeser, 2001). A typical team involves a pain management physician (usually an anaesthetist in the UK), a psychologist, a clinical nurse specialist, a physiotherapist, and a pharmacist.

Vocational advisers may assist. Patients are seen on an out-patient clinic basis or in a more intensive pain management programme. Pain management programmes combine all the above therapist input plus patient education, vocational training and physiotherapy over a set period of time. The value of such programmes has been shown consistently and is reflected in an extensive meta-analysis (Flor, Fydrich, & Turk, 1992). The aim of treatment is to reduce illness behaviour and employ self-help strategies to help in managing the standard activities of daily life rather than focusing on diminishing pain itself (Tyrer, 1997). Pain management programmes are only offered to patients after all relevant medical interventions have been tried or are not considered appropriate.

Management of chronic pain for patients with TBI focuses largely on the same problems as management for chronic pain for patients without brain injury. There may be scope for more improvement in those with TBI. A comparison between patients with pain and TBI and those with pain alone showed that the TBI group had less control over pain than those without TBI (Lahz & Bryant, 1997). This is likely related to the cognitive defects found in those with TBI and strategies may be required to address this problem. TBI patients should be given separate attention from those with pain from other causes because of their cognitive difficulties (Nicholson, 2000a). There are few studies on the rehabilitation of this group but Andary et al. (1997) found that patients with TBI took a significantly longer time to complete a pain management treatment programme than a comparison group without TBI.

Although this is a preliminary study it seems sensible to treat patients who have both head injury and pain separately from those with chronic pain alone. Although most cities in the developed world have at least one pain management programme there are few if any that are concerned only with those who have a TBI. There would be advantages in such clinics being developed because of the slower pace of rehabilitation in this group.

In addition to medication the following strategies should be considered for all patients

- Physiotherapy.
- Occupational therapy.
- Stimulation-produced analgesia.
- Cognitive–behavioural therapy.
- Relaxation/hypnosis.
- Anaesthetic nerve blocks.

Physiotherapy

Early mobilisation and activity have been shown to be of value in patients with neck pain following a road traffic accident (Anon, 1998b). More intensive physiotherapy will be required later in those with more severe injuries. Assessment of strength, flexibility, and physical endurance is made at the outset followed by education on active physical coping skills. In those who have avoided movements because of pain and in whom there is no medical contra-indication to exercise, passive physical therapy techniques may be used, although there is insufficient data to show that these techniques improve long-term outcome. Reduction of pain by anaesthetic blocks and muscle relaxants such as botulinum toxin enables physiotherapeutic measures to be taken while the patient is pain free; these may be indicated in selective sites (Davis & Barnes, 2000).

Occupational therapy

Assessment by an occupational therapist early in treatment can help to focus where interventions should be aimed. If pain is hindering treatment other strategies, e.g., drugs, anaesthetic blocks, or physiotherapy should be considered.

Stimulation-produced analgesia

The three techniques of stimulation-produced analgesia that are normally used in patients with TBI and pain are transcutaneous electrical nerve stimulation (TENS), acupuncture, and dorsal column stimulation.

TENS is administered by a battery-operated stimulator that is attached to electrodes that are sited over sensory nerves close to the site of pain or at the level where the painful afferent fibres enter the dorsal horn of the spinal cord. The resulting barrage of touch and vibration stimuli from the TENS machine blocks the slow-moving pain messages along C nerve fibres. TENS should be widely used. It reduces pain measurably in patients attending pain clinics (Fishbain et al., 1996), although there is debate about its value in patients with chronic back pain (Anon, 2001). It is a very safe treatment and there are very few contraindications. TENS machines are now cheap and reliable and can be purchased from many retail outlets.

Acupuncture is widely used and produces transient benefits in many cases. However, the evidence base for its use is meagre (Ter Riet, Kleijnen, & Knipschild, 1990).

Dorsal column stimulation involves the implantation of electrodes very close to the dorsal horn of the spinal cord to modulate the transmission of pain. It is not usually recommended unless all other treatment remedies have been exhausted.

Cognitive–behavioural therapy (CBT)

This treatment in patients with TBI is covered in Khan-Bourne and Brown (this issue). However, there are issues in patients with persistent pain that need addressing.

Many patients who develop pain following TBI adopt behaviours that are not always of long-term benefit. These include reluctance to carry out physical exercise because of concern that pain will become worse, over-reliance on others and behavioural benefits accruing from the sickness role (Tyrer, 1986).

Treatment is based on the assumption that pain is a handicap only if it leads to behavioural impairments. Improvement in activity and daily living functions leads to improvement in self-esteem despite pain. Cognitive coping strategies that are used in patients with chronic pain include increasing tolerance to pain, stress management techniques, pacing (carrying out activities in short stages and resting between these), and diverting attention away from pain by use of imagery or focusing on other body sensations such as warmth (Tyrer, 1997). Plans to take a rest from behavioural programmes if there is an increase in pain for either physical or emotional reasons are permitted, but the criteria for employing these should be scheduled in advance.

In patients with chronic pain alone there is evidence that CBT is of value. Comparison with alternative active treatments revealed that CBT produced significantly greater reduction in the behavioural expression of pain, and an increase in cognitive coping and appraisal measures (Morley, Eccleston, & Williams, 1999).

Relaxation/hypnosis

Relaxation techniques have been shown to be effective in the treatment of chronic pain (NIH Technology Assessment Panel, 1996). There are significant benefits from inducing relaxation in the clinic compared to explanation alone (Dahabra, Blennerhasset, Charlton, & Tyrer, 1996). Biofeedback techniques provide the patient with information on physiological functions to help in the relaxation process. Hypnotic techniques can help induce states of direct relaxation (Tyrer, 1992b).

Anaesthetic nerve blocks

Anaesthetic nerve blocks are primarily used for diagnostic purposes although they are employed to give pain relief at a time that other manoeuvres can be employed to aid motor function, e.g., physiotherapy.

Epidural and intrathecal drug delivery systems have been used effectively for the treatment of some patients with intractable chronic pain.

CONCLUSION

Pain is a common accompaniment of TBI, and patients with both conditions need attention to both. Assessment of the extent of both brain injury and pain should be carried out at an early stage to help decide on appropriate treatment strategies. Acute pain is generally more identifiable than chronic pain and management focuses on pharmacotherapy. In more persistent pain the value of psychological strategies are more apparent although improvement is slow. A combined treatment programme involving physicians, psychologists, nurses, occupational therapists and pharmacists provides the best means of managing these patients.

REFERENCES

Alexander, M. P. (1992). Neuropsychiatric correlates of persistent postconcussive syndrome. *Journal of Head Trauma Rehabilitation, 7*, 60–69.

Alexander, M. P. (1995). Mild traumatic brain injury. *Neurology, 45*, 1253–1260.

Andary, M. T., Crewe, N., Ganzel, S. K., Haines-Pepi, C., Kulkarni, M. R., Stainton, D. F., Thompson, A., & Yosef, M. (1997). Traumatic brain injury/chronic pain syndrome: A case comparison. *Clinical Journal of Pain, 13*, 244–250

Anderson, J. M., Kaplan, M. S., & Fesenthal, G. (1990). Brain injury obscured by chronic pain: A preliminary report. *Archives of Physical Medicine and Rehabilitation, 71*, 703–708.

Anon (1998a). Continuing to engage in normal activities after neck-sprain injury led to fewer symptoms than immobilisation and sick leave. *Evidence-Based Medicine, 3*, 110.

Anon (1998b). Selective serotonin reuptake inhibitors are effective for mixed chronic pain. *ACP Journal Club, 128*, 3.

Anon (2001). TENS is not effective for chronic low-back pain. *ACP Journal Club, 135*, 99.

Ashburn, M. A., & Staats, P. S. (1999). Management of chronic pain. *Lancet, 353*, 1865–1869.

Ayers, A. W. (2002). Heterotopic ossification. *Trauma, 43*, 5–26.

Beecher, H. K. (1946). Pain in men wounded in battle. *Bulletin of United States Army Medical Department, 5*, 445–454.

Beetar, J. T., Guilmette, T. J., & Sparadeo, F. R. (1996). Sleep and pain complaints in symptomatic traumatic brain injury and neurologic patients. *Archives of Physical Medicine and Rehabilitation, 77*, 1298–1302.

Bell, K. R., & Pepping, M. (2001). Women and traumatic brain injury. *Physical Medicine & Rehabilitation Clinics of North America, 12*, 169–182.

Bogduk, N. (2001). Complex regional pain syndrome. *Current Opinion in Anaesthesiology, 14*, 541–546.

Bohnen, N., Van Zutphen, W., Twijnstra, A., Wijnen, G., Bongers, J., & Jolles, J. (1994). Late outcome of mild head injury. *Brain Injury, 8*, 701–708.

Boivie, J., Leijon, G., & Johansson, I. (1985). Central post-stroke pain: A study of the mechanisms through analyses of the sensory abnormalities. *Pain, 37*, 173–185.

Borchgrevink, G. E., Kaasa, A., McDonagh, D., Stiles, T. C., Haraldseth, O., & Lereim, I. (1998). Acute treatment of whiplash neck sprain injuries: A randomized trial of treatment during the first 14 days after a car accident. *Spine, 23*, 25–31.

Breau, L. M., McGrath, P. J., Camfield, C., Rosmus, C., & Finley, G. A. (2001). Measuring pain accurately in children with cognitive impairments: Refinements of a caregiver scale. *The Journal of Pediatrics, 138*. 721–727.

Collins, S. L., Moore, R. A., McQuay, H. J., & Wiffen, P. (2000). Antidepressants and anti-convulsants for diabetic neuropathy and postherpetic neuralgia: A quantitative systematic review. *Journal of Pain & Symptom Management, 20*, 449–458.

Colvin, M. P., Healy, M. T., & Samra, G. S. (1998). Early management of the severely injured patient. *Journal of the Royal Society of Medicine. 91*, 26–29.

Dahabra, S., Blennerhasset, R., Charlton, J. E., & Tyrer, S. P. (1996). Induction of relaxation improves cognitive control of pain compared to delivery of relaxation tape alone. *Abstracts, VIIIth International Association of the Study of Pain Triennial Meeting, Vancouver, 513.*

Davis, E. C., & Barnes, M. P. (2000). Botulinum toxin and spasticity. *Journal of Neurology, Neurosurgery & Psychiatry, 69,* 143–147.

Elovic, E. (2001). Principles of pharmaceutical management of spastic hypertonia. *Physical Medicine & Rehabilitation Clinics of North America, 12,* 793-816.

Ericsson, M., Poston, W. S. C., Linder, J., Taylor, J. V., Haddock, C. K., & Foreyt, J. P. (2002). Depression predicts disability in long-term chronic pain patients. *Disability and Rehabilitation, 24,* 334–340.

Ettlin, T. M., Kischka, U., Reichmann, S., Radii, E. W., Heim, S. A., Wengen, D., & Benson, D. F. (1992). Cerebral symptoms after whiplash injury of the neck: A prospective clinical and neuropsychological study of whiplash injury. *Journal of Neurology, Neurosurgery, & Psychiatry, 55,* 943–948.

Feinmann, C., Harris, M., & Cawley, R. (1984). Psychogenic facial pain: Presentation and treatment. *British Medical Journal, 288,* 436–438.

Fishbain, D. A., Chabal, C., Abbott, A., Heine, L. W., & Cutler, R. (1996). Transcutaneous electrical nerve stimulation (TENS) treatment outcome in long-term users. *Clinical Journal of Pain, 12 ,* 201–214.

Fleminger, S. (2001). Accidents, burns and other trauma. In M. G. Gelder, J. J. Lopez-Ibor Jr, & N. C. Andreason (Eds.), *The New Oxford Textbook of Psychiatry.* Oxford; Oxford University Press.

Flor, H., Fydrich, T., & Turk, D. C. (1992). Efficacy of multidisciplinary pain treatment centers: A meta-analytic review. *Pain, 49,* 221–230.

Garland, D. E., & Bailey, S. (1981). Undetected injuries in head-injured adults. *Clinical Orthopaedics and Related Research, 155,* 162–165.

Geisser, M. E., Roth, R. S., Bachman, J. E., & Eckert, T. A. (1996). The relationship between symptoms of post-traumatic stress disorder and pain, affective disturbance and disability among patients with accident and non-accident related pain. *Pain, 66,* 207–214.

Gellman, H., Keenan, M., & Botte, M. J. (1996). Recognition and management of upper extremity pain syndromes in the patient with brain injury. *Journal of Head Trauma Rehabilitation, 11,* 23–30.

Gualtieri, C. T. (1995). The problem of mild brain injury. *Neuropsychiatry, Neuropsychology and Behavioral Neurology, 8,* 127–136.

Haetzman, M., & Stickle, B. (1999). Epidural analgesia for postoperative pain. *Current Anaesthesia and Critical Care, 10,* 140–146.

Jagoda, A., & Riggio, S. (2000). Mild traumatic brain injury and the postconcussive syndrome. *Emergency Medicine Clinics of North America, 18,* 355–363.

Kasch, H., Bach, F. W., & Jensen, T. S. (2001). Handicap after acute whiplash injury. A 1-year prospective study of risk factors. *Neurology, 56,* 1637-1643.

Kay, D. W. K., Kerr, T. A., & Lassman, L. P. (1971). Brain trauma and the postconcussional syndrome. *Lancet, 2,* 1052–1055.

Killen, S. A., & Huntoon, E. (1997). Drugs for Pain Management. *Physical Medicine and Rehabilitation, 8,* 695-705

Lahz, S., & Bryant, R. A. (1996). Incidence of chronic pain following traumatic brain injury. *Archives of Physical Medicine and Rehabilitation, 77,* 889–891.

Lahz, S., & Bryant, R. A. (1997). Pain coping strategies following traumatic brain injury. *Journal of Head Trauma Rehabilitation, 12,* 85–90.

Leijon, G., & Boivie, J. (1989). Central post-stroke pain—A controlled trial of amitriptyline and carbamazepine. *Pain, 36,* 27–36.

Linton, S. J., Hellsing, A. L., & Andersson, D. (1993). A controlled study of the effects of an early intervention on acute musculoskeletal pain problems. *Pain, 54,* 353–359.

Loeser, J. D. (2001). Multidisciplinary pain programs. In J. D. Loeser (Ed.), *Bonica's management of pain,* Philadelphia: Lippincott, Williams & Wilkins.

Martelli, M. F., Grayson, R. L., & Zasler, N. D. (1999). Posttraumatic headache: Neuropsychological and psychological effects and treatment implications. *Journal of Head Trauma Rehabilitation, 14*, 49–69.

Mayou, R., & Radanov, B. P. (1996). Whiplash neck injury. *Journal of Psychosomatic Research, 40*, 461–474.

McQuay, H. (1999). Opioids in pain management. *Lancet, 353*, 2229–2232.

McQuay, H. J., Tramer, M., Nye, B. A., Carroll, D., Wiffen P. J., & Moore R. A. (1996). A systematic review of antidepressants in neuropathic pain. *Pain, 68*, 217–227.

Melzack, R. (1975). The McGill Pain Questionnaire; major properties and scoring methods. *Pain, 1*, 277–299.

Melzack, R. (1987). The short-form McGill Pain Questionnaire. *Pain, 30*, 191–197.

Merskey, H. (1979). Pain terms—a list with definitions and notes on the usage—Recommended by the IASP Sub-Committee on Taxonomy. *Pain, 6*, 249–252.

Merskey, H., & Chandarana, P. (1992). Chronic pain problems and psychiatry. In S. P. Tyrer (Ed.), *Psychology, psychiatry and chronic pain*. Oxford: Butterworth-Heinemann.

Mitchell, S. W. (1872). *Injuries of nerves and their consequences* (1st edition). New York: Dover Publications.

Mollmann, M., & Auf der Landwehr, U. (2000). Treatment of pain in trauma patients with injuries of the upper limb. *Injury, 31*, 3–10.

Morley, S., Eccleston, C., & Williams, A. (1999). Systematic review and meta-analysis of randomized controlled trials of cognitive behaviour therapy and behaviour therapy for chronic pain in adults, excluding headache. *Pain, 80*, 1–13.

Nicholson, K. (2000a). An overview of pain problems associated with lesions, disorder or dysfunction of the central nervous system. *Neurorehabilitation, 14*, 3–13.

Nicholson, K. (2000b). Pain, cognition and traumatic brain injury. *Neurorehabilitation, 14*, 95–103.

Nicholson, K., Martelli, M. F., & Zasler, N. D. (2001). Does pain confound interpretation of neuropsychological test results? *Neurorehabilitation, 16*, 225–230.

NIH Technology Assessment Panel (1996). Integration of behavioral and relaxation approaches into the treatment of chronic pain and insomnia. *JAMA, 276*, 313–318.

Price, D. D., Gracely, R. H., & Bennett, G. J. (1995). The challenge and the problem of placebo in the assessment of sympathetically maintained pain. In W. Janig & M. Stanton-Hicks (Eds.), *Reflex sympathetic dystrophy: A reappraisal*. Seattle: IASP Press.

Radanov, B. P., Bicik, I., Dvorak, J., Antinnes, J., Von Schulthess, G. K., & Buck, A. (1999). Relation between neuropsychological and neuroimaging findings in patients with late whiplash syndrome. *Journal of Neurology, Neurosurgery & Psychiatry, 66*, 485–489.

Rainer, T. H., Jacobs, P., Ng, Y. C., Cheung, N. K., Tam, M., Lam, P. K. W., Wong, R., & Cocks, R. A. (2000). Cost effectiveness analysis of intravenous ketorolac and morphine for treating pain after limb injury: Double blind randomised controlled trial. *British Medical Journal, 321*, 1247–1251.

Schreiber, S., & Galai-Gat, T. (1993). Uncontrolled pain following physical injury as the core-trauma in post-traumatic stress disorder. *Pain, 54*, 107–110.

Seymour, R. A., Simpson, J. M., & Charlton, J. E. (1985). An evaluation of length and end-phrase of visual analogue scales in dental pain. *Pain, 21*, 177–185.

Sobus, K. M. L., Alexander, M. A., & Harcke, H. T. (1993). Undetected musculoskeletal trauma in children with traumatic brain injury or spinal cord injury. *Archives of Physical Medicine and Rehabilitation, 74*, 902–904.

Sternbach, R. E. (1984). Acute versus chronic pain. In P. D. Wall & R. Melzack (Eds.), *Textbook of pain* (1st ed.). Edinburgh: Churchill Livingstone.

Teasdale, G., & Jennett, B. (1974). Assessment of coma and impaired consciousness: A practical scale, *Lancet, 2*, 81–84.

Ter Riet, G., Kleijnen, J., & Knipschild, P. (1990). Acupuncture and chronic pain: A criteria-based meta-analysis. *Journal of Clinical Epidemiology, 43,* 1191–1199.

Tyrer, S. P. (1986). Learned pain behaviour. *British Medical Journal, 292,* 1–2.

Tyrer, S. P. (1992a). Psychiatric assessment of chronic pain. *British Journal of Psychiatry, 160,* 733–741.

Tyrer, S. P. (1992b). Hypnosis. In S. P. Tyrer (Ed.), *Psychology, psychiatry and chronic pain.* Oxford: Butterworth-Heinemann.

Tyrer, S. P. (1997). Management of chronic pain. *Advances in Psychiatric Treatment, 3,* 86–93.

Uomoto, J. M., & Esselman, P. C. (1993). Traumatic brain injury and chronic pain: Differential types and rates by head injury severity. *Archives of Physical Medicine and Rehabilitation, 74,* 61–64.

Waddell, G., McCulloch, J. A., Kummell, E., & Venner, R. M. (1980). Non-organic physical signs in low back pain. *Spine, 5,* 117–125.

White, P., & Faustman, W. (1989). Coexisting physical conditions among inpatients with post-traumatic stress disorder. *Military Medicine, 154,* 66–71.

NEUROPSYCHOLOGICAL REHABILITATION, 2003, *13* (1/2), 211–240

Contemporary approaches to the management of irritability and aggression following traumatic brain injury

Nick Alderman

St Andrew's Hospital, Northampton, UK

In this paper, the principal means of managing irritability and aggression following traumatic brain injury (TBI) will be briefly reviewed. The paper will initially consider the prevalence of irritability, what it is and some of the likely causes that drive the condition. Aggression will then be similarly contemplated. Prior to a discussion regarding those methods most regularly employed in their management, the attention of the reader will be directed to a range of methodological issues that need to be considered in relation to reporting treatment efficacy, including lack of homogeneity and the need to use standardised assessment tools. Three principal management approaches will then be described and appraised, these being pharmacology, psychotherapy, and behaviour therapy. Within the discussion of psychotherapeutic methods, special mention will be made with regard to use of cognitive behaviour therapy, and two detailed case studies will be employed to illustrate issues relating to both cognitive behaviour therapy and behaviour therapy.

INTRODUCTION

It is now well established that survivors of TBI potentially experience a wide range of physical, functional, cognitive, behavioural, and psychosocial problems. Many people report a range of symptoms that collectively constitute what has become known as the post-concussional syndrome (PCS). The core symptoms are headache, dizziness, and intolerance of noise; however, problems with concentration and memory, fatigue, depressed mood, and irritability are among a wider range of complaints associated with PCS (Eames, 2001).

Correspondence should be addressed to Dr N. Alderman, Kemsley Division, St Andrew's Hospital, Northampton, NN1 5DG, UK.

© 2003 Psychology Press Ltd
http://www.tandf.co.uk/journals/pp/09602011.html   DOI:10.1080/09602010244000327

These difficulties may persist far longer than severity of injury, as measured by duration of post-traumatic amnesia, would suggest (Weddell, Oddy, & Jenkins, 1980).

Outcome studies show that irritability is one of a constellation of symptoms most frequently reported during the first few weeks following trauma by patients who have sustained mild head injuries. Haboubi, Long, Koshy, and Ward (2001) found that it was the third most cited complaint in a large cohort of patients when assessed up to 6 weeks after injury. Studies are in general agreement that about a third of patients with mild head injuries report irritability. However, this symptom also remains a persistent complaint in the longer term. Two recent studies reported by Deb, Lyons, and Koutzoukis (1998, 1999) found that 30–35% of people with mild head injury still described irritability one year after injury; furthermore, this was the most frequently cited neurobehavioural symptom elicited. Van der Naalt, van Zomeren, Sluiter, and Minderhoud (1999) investigated prevalence of cognitive and neurobehavioural complaints a year post-injury among a sample comprising both mild and moderate head injuries. Patients were followed up four times within a 12-month period. A similar proportion of survivors complained of irritability one year after trauma (32%). However, severity of injury did not affect the prevalence of this (or other) symptoms, a finding also reported by Hayes, Smith, and Berker (1997). Furthermore, while the frequency of most other complaints decreased or stabilised over time, reports of irritability increased between six months and a year after insult.

While the proportion of patients with mild and moderate head injuries who complain of irritability is similar, findings regarding those with severe head injury are variable. For example, 33.3% of the mixed severity head injury group investigated by Kim, Manes, Kosier, Baruah, and Robinson (1999) complained of irritability at some point within the first 12 months after trauma. However, complaints were disproportionally represented within the mild and moderate severity subgroups, and were significantly less evident among those with severe head injury. Alternatively, in a well-known study by Brooks et al. (1987), who investigated outcome in a large sample of patients with severe head injury, prevalence of irritability was found to be much higher. Irritability (as reported by family members) was present in 67% of patients 1 year after injury; however, it was as prevalent amongst a separate sample that was 5 years post-injury (64%).

WHAT IS IRRITABILITY?

While outcome studies routinely address the presence or absence of irritability, what does this term actually mean? The *Oxford Advanced Learners' Dictionary* illustrates a methodological problem in that "irritable" reflects both an internal subjective state ("getting annoyed easily") and behaviour arising from this ("showing your anger, an irritable gesture"). This causes some difficulties as not all studies necessarily report irritability in the same way. For example, some people may experience subjective feelings of irritability but not reflect this in their behaviour. Alternatively, some overt behaviours may be erroneously attributed to underlying irritability. Different studies elicit information regarding irritability using various methodological tools, which can also lead to inconsistency in what is meant by the term. These include self-report, family report, behavioural observation, and questionnaires. Kim et al. (1999) used a modified version of the Present State Exam (PSE: Robinson et al., 1983; Wing, Cooper, & Sartorius, 1974) to help determine presence of irritability. However, as Kim et al. stated, the PSE only rates irritability as present if the patient subjectively experiences it independent of behaviour. In addition to PSE results, these authors also required patients to both acknowledge feeling irritable and demonstrate behaviours consistent with this during interview, or for a family member to confirm they had observed defined behaviours consistent with this.

A further methodological consideration concerns a point made earlier, that behaviours symptomatic of irritability are not in themselves evidence that this condition is present. For example, Kim et al. (1999) judged irritable mood to exist if relatives reported repeated observation of "uncooperative, angry, hostile, shouting, or antagonistic language or behavior" (p. 329). Of course, any of these behaviours could be accounted for by means other than as an expression of irritation, and an informed decision taken regarding their origin should ordinarily be preceded by appropriate assessment.

Causes of irritability

With respect to this last point, an understanding of the mechanisms underlying irritability will help inform whatever assessment is undertaken. It is well known that TBI patients do not form a homogeneous group. Pre-morbid factors mean that no two brains are identical; similarly no two brains are damaged in exactly the same way (Mateer & Ruff, 1990). As a consequence, sequelae of brain injury are potentially variable and extensive and it is a mistake to believe irritability has a single cause. Instead, it is thought to have multiple origins, including both environmental and biological factors (Slagle, 1990). These include neuroanatomical correlates, and psychosocial and psychopathological factors. Gualtieri (1991) correlated irritability with damage to orbitofrontal or anterior temporal lobes. Eames (1990) stressed the former, attributing increased irritability (in part) to specific orbitofrontal lesion, or through disruption of the connections between frontal and limbic systems. Starkstein and Robinson (1991) elaborated further the contribution made by damage to these connections, specifically to the orbito-temporal-limbic feedback loop, in which the inhibitory function of the cortex over the amygdala is disrupted thereby depriving the cognitive functions of any ability to suppress instinctive emotional reactions. Long and Web (1995) highlighted impaired cortical function (for example, difficulties with concentration) as being a further determinant of irritability. McLean, Dikmen, and Temkin (1993) illustrated the contribution made by psychosocial factors (for example, job loss, social isolation), while Rohrbaugh, Siegal, and Giller (1988) stressed psychopathology by linking depression with irritability.

The point at which irritability becomes evident following trauma may be a function of different underlying causal agents. For example, Kim et al. (1999) discriminated between acute onset and delayed onset irritability in their sample of TBI patients. They found frequency of cortical lesions was highest among irritable patients in comparison to those for whom this was not a complaint. However, acute onset irritability patients had a significantly higher incidence of left-sided cortical lesions, while delayed onset irritability was associated with poorer social functioning, impairment in activities of daily living, and depressed mood. On the basis of these results, Kim et al. suggested that acute onset irritability was primarily attributable to organic dysfunction, which indicated pharmacological treatment, while late onset irritability was secondary to a mood disorder arising from poor adjustment to physical and social impairment. Consequently, these authors suggested the latter might respond to use of social and rehabilitation interventions.

Eames (2001) also differentiated irritability on the basis of temporal onset. First, he described the qualities of outburst behaviours attributable to post-traumatic and frontal irritability. Such behaviours are characterised by what he called "pervasive 'snappiness'" (p. 39) that is present immediately after recovery of consciousness. They tend to be symptomatic of almost any stress or frustration, but show a tendency to improve over time. Patients are usually aware they engage in these behaviours; furthermore, they display a tendency to justify them by circumstances. In contrast, Eames defined a second category of later onset irritability. This differs from the acute form in that: there is a delay (days, months, even years) between injury and outburst behaviour; the outbursts are brief, clear-cut, and "out of character"; triggers are unpredictable and trivial; outbursts persist or even worsen over time; and they are followed by remorse (even with amnesia for events). This form of irritability is believed to be attributable to the episodic dyscontrol syndrome (EDS), one of the post-traumatic tempero-limbic disorders. These are all characterised by paroxysmal changes and reflect behavioural sequelae of electrophysiological disturbance in the brain. As a consequence, anti-convulsant medication is believed by some authors to have special relevance in treatment (for example, see Foster, Hillbrand, & Chi, 1989; Lewin & Sumners, 1992; Mattes, 1990; Monroe, 1989; Stein, 1992).

AGGRESSION

Aggressive behaviour may be a clear reflection of irritability. Although less well documented than irritability, it has been especially highlighted because of the impact it has on families (Brooks et al., 1987) and the special challenges its presence creates within rehabilitation centres, particularly when it takes the form of physical assaults on others. Physical aggression compromises the safety of patients and staff, increases the vulnerability of the person who engages in it, and may prevent the individual from achieving their full rehabilitation potential (Burke, Wesolowski, & Lane, 1988). Aggressive behaviour may exclude the individual from some rehabilitation programmes altogether (Prigatano, 1987). When this happens, survivors of brain injury may gravitate to placements for management purposes; unfortunately, such establishments are rarely equipped to meet their rehabilitation needs (Alderman, 2001; Eames & Wood, 1985a; Wood & Worthington, 2001a, 2001b).

Causes of aggressive behaviour

It is probably not unreasonable to attribute behavioural expressions of anger, such as aggression, to irritability when this occurs in people whose mood is low, and when the behaviour is clearly spontaneous rather than a premeditated act. However, there are many reasons, other than mood, as to why neurological patients are aggressive. Miller (1994) summarised three of the most frequently cited explanations in the literature. First, it may be the product of EDS. Second, damage to frontal brain structures (or more specifically, disruption to the connections between frontal and limbic structures) results in a decreased ability to inhibit and regulate emotional responses, leading to a lower threshold for aggressive behaviour in circumstances in which the patient experiences frustration. Third, a tendency has been reported that brain injury may exacerbate negative pre-morbid personality traits: People who were aggressive prior to insult are likely to be more so after injury.

Aggressive behaviour may also be the product of poor insight and reduced awareness of deficit, and through learning. Reduced insight and awareness following brain injury is not uncommon (see Manchester & Wood, 2001) to the extent that motivation to engage in the rehabilitation process is compromised (Prigatano, 1991; Sazbon & Groswasser, 1991; Wood, 1988). Attempts to coerce such patients to engage in rehabilitation may elicit spontaneous bouts of aggressive behaviour (especially when frontal-limbic connections have been disrupted rendering poor control over the ability to inhibit emotional responses). When nurses and therapists withdraw, this behaviour may be inadvertently reinforced as it leads to avoidance of, or escape from, rehabilitation activities (see Alderman, 1991, 2001; Alderman, Shepherd, & Youngson, 1992). Aggressive behaviour may also be a learned response within environments that lack consistent positive contingencies for desirable conduct (see Alderman, 2001, pp. 190–191).

Aggression following neurological insult is likely to have multiple causes. While 'irritability' may precede aggression, aggressive behaviour also has multiple determinants as it may be organic, pre-morbid, a response to the psychological status of the individual, or any combination of these factors. Non-organic factors (such as reactive mood disorder) may more easily antago-nise aggressive behaviour when inhibitory controls and frustration-tolerance threshold are low. While the presence of irritability may initially explain the presence of aggression, continuation of this behaviour may be because of other reasons, such as new learning.

TREATMENT OF IRRITABILITY AND AGGRESSION

The problem of evaluation

Lack of homogeneity among people with acquired brain injury and the multivariate aetiology of behaviour disorders creates problems in the evalua-tion of treatment methods that aim to reduce irritability and aggression (see Alderman, 2002). Alderman, Knight, and Morgan (1997) highlighted a number of issues regarding the literature on treatment of post-brain injury aggressive behaviour disorders. Despite the prevalence and potentially catastrophic impact of aggression, relatively little had (at that time) been written about treat-ment. A review of a sample of the literature indicated medication was the most frequent intervention. However, the review highlighted a range of methodolog-ical and other problems that hindered inter-study comparisons and created difficulties for clinicians wishing to gauge whether treatments could be extrap-olated and used with their own patients. For example: information concerning type and severity of aggressive behaviour being treated was generally absent; use of scientific methodologies as a means of objectively measuring efficacy were not routinely used, the emphasis being on retrospective descriptions of cases; and antecedents that preceded aggressive behaviour were rarely described.

Alderman et al. (1997) suggested that some of these inconsistencies could be addressed, and evidence-based outcome determination of treatments enhanced, if a standardised means of recording and quantifying observations of aggressive behaviour was universally adopted. They consequently described the Overt Aggression Scale—Modified for Neurorehabilitation (OAS-MNR) as a tool that could be employed for this purpose. This was a modification of the original Overt Aggression Scale (OAS) created by Yudofsky et al. (1986), devised for use with psychiatric populations. The nature of the changes and additions made to the OAS were intended to increase its usefulness within post-acute neurological rehabilitation environments, as well as promote greater consistency in reporting treatment of challenging behaviour in the brain injury literature. The OAS-MNR has proved to be a valid measure of aggressive behaviour with good inter-rater reliability (Alderman et al., 1997). Accounts regarding its clinical utility have subsequently begun to appear and its usefulness at several different levels illustrated (clinical audit, applied research, and treatment outcomes; see for example: Alderman, Bentley, & Dawson, 1999a; Alderman & Burgess, 2002; Alderman, Knight, & Henman, 2002; Alderman, Davies, Jones, & McDonnell, 1999b; Watson et al., 2001). In addition, it has also been argued it is necessary to utilise appropriate methodological paradigms in order that treatment efficacy be objectively assessed; to this end, single case experimental designs ideally should be employed with a minimum criteria in which data are captured regarding aggressive behaviour before and during treatment (Alderman, 2002; Alderman et al., 1999a). Examples of how the OAS-MNR and methodologies borrowed from single-case experimental design may be incorporated in routine clinical practice in an effort to determine evidence-based outcomes of treatment for irritability and aggression will be presented in the course of this paper.

Range of treatments available

A variety of treatment options that have emerged from a broad range of different conceptual frameworks have been described within the literature: These include both pharmacological and rehabilitative interventions (Rao & Lyketsos, 2000). Lack of homogeneity among people with acquired brain injury, and the complex range of factors that underlie behaviour disturbance, highlight two important issues: first, that in order to plan treatment that is likely to be effective individual assessment is an absolute necessity; and second, because irritability and aggression do not have a single cause, different treatment approaches are unlikely to be equally efficacious for all patients.

It is beyond the scope of this paper to attempt a comprehensive review of all treatment methods reported in the applied literature. However, principal mainstream approaches will be briefly considered.

Pharmacological intervention.   There is little doubt that there is considerable scope for successful pharmacological intervention, especially when it can be demonstrated that irritability and aggressive behaviour disorders are primarily driven by organic factors (see Eames, 2001; Rao & Lyketsos, 2000). Unfortunately, despite a considerable number of accounts regarding drug therapies in the literature, there are a number of constraints that raise questions about both efficacy and suitability. The first, lack of sufficient methodological rigour to enable objective evaluation of efficacy, has already been mentioned and is certainly not limited to pharmacological intervention (Rao & Lyketsos, 2000; Alderman et al., 1997).

A second constraint highlighted by practitioners, including Eames (1990, 2001) is that symptoms of organic brain injury can sometimes be mistaken as evidence of mental illness and thus lead to administration of an inappropriate and ineffectual drug regime. To avoid this it is essential that an assessment is made by an experienced neuropsychiatrist who has expert skills to differentiate neurobehavioural difficulties from symptoms that truly reflect the presence of a functional illness. Unfortunately, within the UK at least, few experienced practitioners are available (Alderman, 2001). This is reflected in the fact that within the Royal College of Psychiatrists (the professional and educational body for this branch of medicine in the UK and Republic of Ireland) a special interest group in neuropsychiatry has only been formed very recently (2001). There is almost certainly a long way to go before enough interest and numbers of practitioners are available to justify the establishment of neuropsychiatry as a fully fledged sub-specialism and as a faculty within the college with equivalent status and influence to long-established ones representing, for example, forensic, and child and adolescent psychiatry.

A third constraint discussed by Alderman (2001) is that of sedation. Administration of sedating medication is an appealing option in the management of aggression as the benefits in reducing risk imposed by this behaviour previously highlighted by Burke et al. (1988) are substantially reduced within a short time period. However, while this may sometimes be appropriate as an emergency measure, it is not acceptable as a long-term solution with the majority of patients. In most cases, imposition of pharmacological restraint will not purposefully target those factors underlying irritability and aggression; and neither will it enable adequate assessment of causal factors to be undertaken. A further drawback is that sedation is not specific in suppressing aggressive behaviour; all behaviour will be affected, including that which is appropriate. Another unwelcome consequence will be to depress impaired cognitive functioning further, thereby placing yet more obstacles to new learning (including the acquisition of adaptive behaviours). Finally, neurological patients are very sensitive to medication, and undesirable side-effects can in themselves prove debilitating: for example, while psychostimulants are used in the treatment of distractibility and impulsivity, especially methylphenidate and dextroamphetamine, a potential side-effect is increased irritability (Rao & Lyketsos, 2000).

Despite these constraints, pharmacological intervention clearly has a potentially important role to play in the management of irritability and aggression. Successful reports of dopaminergic agents have appeared in the literature: for example, amantadine has been shown to be beneficial in the treatment of a range of neurobehavioural sequelae, including aggression (Gualtieri, 1991; Nickels, Schneider, Dombovy, & Wong, 1994). Anticonvulsants are especially relevant in the treatment of EDS (as well as other paroxysmal mood disorders) and thus in the management of irritability and aggression arising through this. There are certainly accounts in the literature that report reduction of aggressive behaviour using anticonvulsants, albeit within the constraints of the method-ological issues highlighted earlier (Giakas, Seibyl, & Mazure, 1990; Hirsch, 1993; Mooney & Hass, 1993). Carbamazepine appears to have special rele-vance (Azouvi et al., 1999; Foster et al., 1989; Mattes, 1990). Eames (1988) and Wood (1987) recommend a combination of carbamazepine and behaviour modification methods as providing the optimal route for the treatment of aggression secondary to EDS. They argue that while medication exerts control over underlying seizure activity, behaviour modification methods are used to teach adaptive forms of behaviour and new skills (for an example of this see patient MD described by Alderman et al., 1999b). Valproic acid is also commonly used and reported to be equally as beneficial as carbamazepine; however, outcome remains poorly informed as no large-scale controlled studies examining efficacy of these drugs have been undertaken (Rao & Lyketsos, 2000).

Psychotherapy.   This is a broad and multiply defined concept (Jackson & Gouvier, 1992) that encompasses various therapies that have arisen from different models of psychopathology (Patterson, 1986). Certainly, successful outcomes have been reported which have led to positive psychosocial outcomes: well-known and successful programmes have been reported by Ben-Yishay et al. (1985) and Prigatano (Prigatano, 1986; Prigatano et al., 1984). However, applicability of therapies falling under this umbrella for neurological patients who have aggressive behaviour disorders is questionable; indeed, some commentators have argued that people with serious behaviour problems are usually excluded from participation in such therapies because of intransigent problems with insight and motivation (Burgess & Wood, 1990; Sazbon & Groswasser, 1991), and because the severity of the challenging behaviour they exhibit is too great (Wood, 1987). Wood and Worthington (2001a) argued that these programmes can only be employed with articulate patients with less debilitating handicaps.

Cognitive therapy.   A specific form of psychotherapy is that of cognitive therapy. These approaches are subsumed within the wide variety of treatment procedures that fall under the heading of cognitive behaviour modification (Meichenbaum, 1986) and, more popularly, cognitive behaviour therapy (CBT; Hawton, Salkovskis, Kirk, & Clark, 1989). These are fundamentally concerned with information processing: How people perceive and interpret their experience, and how this in turn alters and shapes behaviour. Events are processed through pre-existing cognitive schema (beliefs, knowledge and prepositions) that effectively bias interpretation of experience. Emotional disorders can arise through cognitive distortion; underlying schema process experience in a way that reflects the nature of these schema. For example, in depression, events are processed through schema that reflect hopelessness, helplessness and failure (Beck, 1976) while in anxiety they are concerned with threat (Clark, 1989). Furthermore, bias in interpretation of experience maintains these maladaptive schema that are evident from the automatic thoughts triggered by events. Cognitive therapies attempt to help the patient understand the link between beliefs, thinking and behaviour, identify their own thinking distortions, and help them generate more rational interpretations of events. Patients are helped to become their own "therapist" and encouraged to test the validity of their automatic thoughts through participation in behavioural experiments. Cognitive distortions are transformed or replaced altogether by altering underlying belief systems that generate them through this process of hypothesis testing. Therapy is very much a collaborative venture between the cognitive therapist and the patient. In this way dysfunctional emotions and behaviour that are shaped by the perception of experience are successfully modified to the benefit of the individual. Behaviour therapy techniques may also be incorporated (Beck, Rush, Shaw, & Emery, 1979). Approaches within CBT also incorporate strategies that aim to directly change behaviour; for example, it has proven effective in the case of depressed patients whose negative expectations are challenged through behavioural change using such techniques as scheduling, mastery and pleasure, graded task assignment and role play (Haaga & Davison, 1986).

Cognitive therapies continue to be successfully employed with many clinical populations, covering a broad range of disorders (Scott, 1997), and represent the preferred and most efficacious intervention available in some cases (for example see Clark et al., 1994). Reports in the literature demonstrate they have a beneficial role to play in the reduction of aggression among children and adolescents (for example see Gibbs, Potter, Barriga, & Liau, 1996; Sukhodolsky, Solomon, & Perine, 2000), within a psychiatric context (Reeder, 1991), and with people who have mild-to-moderate learning disabilities (Jahoda, Trower, Pert, & Finn, 2001). Treating people in groups has obvious benefits for resource allocation, including costs. Attempting to relieve irritability and reduce aggressive behaviour among people with TBI using group-based cognitive therapy is an attractive proposition.

Given their success, cognitive therapies have an inherent appeal regarding reduction of irritability and aggression among people with acquired brain injury. However, lack of awareness, poor insight, and an inability to participate in therapy because of the severity of behaviour disturbance create a special challenge to be overcome when using cognitive therapy.

A second obstacle to participation in cognitive therapy is impairment of those cognitive functions necessary to engage in the hypothesis-testing process that is central to it. Attention, monitoring skills, memory, the ability to think abstractly, and to generate alternatives are crucial. Yet deficits in memory and executive functioning are almost routine following brain injury. Manchester and Wood (2001) acknowledge these difficulties and highlight the role of procedural learning. They advocate employing brief, highly structured, repetitive sessions within which role-play is used to encourage assimilation of new, adaptive automatic thoughts. Concrete, inflexible thinking may also impede progress. Within cognitive therapy, the process of subjecting maladaptive automatic thoughts that drive behaviour is undertaken by the patient, facilitated by the therapist. Once these have been identified, it is the patient who appraises these and seeks to generate more rational alternatives. When the ability to think in abstract terms and generate alternatives is grossly impaired, techniques will have to be employed within therapy sessions to circumvent these difficulties. For example, Kinney (2001) reports methods that enable CBT to be adapted for use with brain-injured clients whose problems with memory, self-monitoring and ability to engage in therapy, would otherwise exclude them from participating in this form of psychotherapy.

An example of successful reduction in irritability/aggression using CBT. A case will now be briefly described which illustrates how some of the challenges imposed by TBI may be overcome so that cognitive therapy can be successfully employed.

The patient concerned, PL, had previously sustained a very severe traumatic brain injury as a result of a road traffic accident. While he made a good physical and functional recovery, problems with irritability and aggression rendered placement within both the community and the family home untenable. He was consequently admitted to a locked ward within a specialised neurobehavioural rehabilitation service for assessment and treatment of his aggressive behaviour disorder. In the weeks that followed, staff observed that PL was intolerant, easily provoked and lost his temper rapidly. He was frequently aggressive, both verbally and physically, towards staff and patients. Neuropsychological assessment reflected memory impairment and the presence of a dysexecutive syndrome, which included difficulties with monitoring and abstraction.

PL intensely disliked placement within a locked ward, to the extent that the negative emotion provoked by this was a major antagonist for aggressive behaviour. For example, on one occasion he made threats to kill staff while they were locking the main door to the ward. When he was given feedback about his behaviour a few minutes later, PL became instantly enraged and launched a physical assault on staff of such severity it was necessary to place him in seclusion. It became apparent later that he found the sight and sound of keys highly provoking as they reminded him of the constraints to his liberty while in hospital.

Following assessment, PL was offered CBT with the stated aim of helping to reduce irritability and aggression. While he was highly motivated to leave the locked ward, it had been previously explained to him that his aggressive behaviour prevented admission to the open pre-community discharge ward of the neurobehavioural service. PL wanted to transfer to this ward, so he agreed to participate in therapy. Despite his desire to engage in treatment, PL's insight regarding his behaviour was poor. For example, when he completed the Dysexecutive Questionnaire (Burgess et al., 1996), he assigned the item "I lose my temper at the slightest thing" the lowest possible rating ("never") on the 5-point Likert scale used for this purpose. By contrast, staff gave him the highest possible rating ("very often").

A four-stage approach to CBT was undertaken: enhancing monitoring skills; cognitive appraisal; teaching coping strategies; and graded task assignment with increasing demands. In addition, therapy was further modified in an effort to circumvent cognitive impairments that might otherwise prevent engagement. For example, because of PL's poor memory he was seen for two formal sessions during the week, and daily checks were made on his homework assignments. In the first stage of therapy, PL was encouraged to understand the relationship between maladaptive thoughts, attributions and behaviour. While he was able to perceive this link regarding other people, he failed to appreciate how it might apply to his own case. In order to try and improve insight regarding his behaviour and improve self-monitoring skills (essential if he was to successfully employ coping strategies later in therapy) PL was given a simple diary to complete whenever he felt irritable or was aggressive. This contained columns in which he was prompted to fill in the date and time of an incident, its antecedent, his behaviour, and its consequences. Staff also recorded times when he was aggressive. Within sessions, PL's records were compared with those made by staff and any inconsistencies addressed. As therapy progressed and PL's ability to monitor his own feelings (irritability) and behaviour (aggression) improved, diary columns were modified to encourage development of further awareness. For example, under "Behaviour" he was also asked to record physical symptoms and thoughts, while beneath "Consequences" he was required to write down any coping strategies used.

When PL became more consistent in making simple recordings, the diary sheet was replaced with a form that encouraged him to appraise dysfunctional automatic thoughts associated with irritability and aggression, and to generate more rational alternatives (see Clark, 1986, p. 288). Again, examples were worked on within formal sessions. Cognitive impairment, especially with abstraction, rendered this a slow and effortful process, requiring extensive facilitation from the two therapists. However, three assumptions were identified which PL agreed underlay much of his aggressive behaviour: first, he routinely blamed others when things went wrong; second, he always assumed the worst; and third, he habitually jumped to the wrong conclusion. Memory impairment further hindered progress. Most of the formal session time was taken up with re-establishing these assumptions; between sessions, PL could not recall them at all. As a consequence, he agreed that under the column on the form in which he was required to reappraise dysfunctional automatic thoughts, the three assumptions were printed as a reminder. This simple modification subsequently proved invaluable in moving therapy forward. PL proved able to recognise these assumptions were dysfunctional and learned to reappraise habitual thoughts experienced in situations associated with irritability and aggression. He was also taught some simple coping strategies, including breathing exercises intended to reduce arousal. Finally, a hierarchy of situations was identified, all of which enabled PL to spend increasingly more time out the locked ward pursuing designated activities by himself. Providing he accepted the limits imposed, and was not physically assaultative, he was permitted access to the next level after a week.

Figure 1 shows progress made by PL while participating in CBT. Although variable, staff recordings prior to treatment showed he had been physically aggressive towards people up to eight times a week. Following implementation of CBT, it can be seen that during the 22 weeks of treatment, frequency of staff recordings decreased: During the last 6 weeks, no aggression was observed. Figure 1 also shows the number of times PL recorded in his diary he had been aggressive or irritable. While, because of monitoring difficulties he did not always record all such instances, it is interesting to see that there were occasions when he experienced frustration that did not always result in overt aggression.

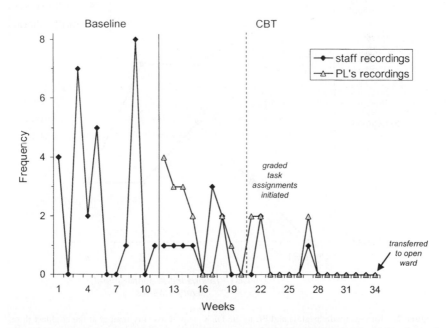

Figure 1.   Staff recordings of the frequency of PL's aggressive behaviour, and PL's own recordings of aggression and feeling irritable. Less frequent recordings were made following implementation of CBT, and as a consequence PL successfully transferred to an unlocked ward in week 34.

It is also interesting to note that participation in CBT improved insight and awareness. Both PL and staff repeated rating the item from the DEX "I lose my temper at the slightest thing" at 4-week intervals during therapy. Figure 2 shows that PL's rating increased, while that of staff decreased, as his control over his behaviour improved.

After 22 weeks, the reduction in physical aggression and acquisition of new behavioural controls led to PL being successfully transferred from the locked ward to the open pre-community discharge unit.

This brief account of PL's treatment highlights the fact that despite the presence of cognitive and others factors, CBT could nevertheless be applied and achieve a successful outcome. The particular challenges to therapy in this case were overcome as follows. First, it was apparent that PL initially had little insight regarding his behaviour or its consequences. However, it was possible to motivate him to engage in therapy by linking participation to possible attainment of a goal to which he aspired, that of moving to an unlocked ward. As a consequence, at the initial stage it was not necessary to directly address the issue of the need to change. Second, cognitive impairment meant the

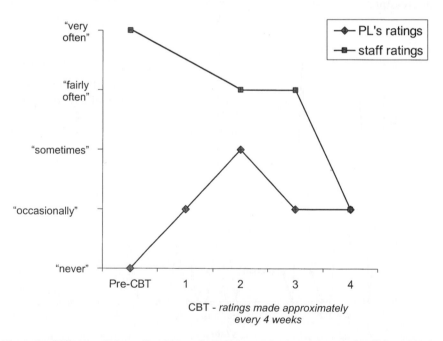

Figure 2. Ratings made by staff and PL to the DEX item "I lose my temper at the slightest thing" before and during the course of CBT. Staff ratings reflect the positive change they observed in PL as he acquired greater control over his irritable and aggressive behaviour. The change in PL's ratings suggests he gained greater insight and awareness of the problem being evaluated.

pragmatics of therapy had to be considerably modified. Poor memory necessitated frequent repetition of principles within sessions, while successive modification of recording forms proved necessary to circumvent some of the problems with recall. Problems with monitoring and abstraction meant that the process of identifying automatic dysfunctional thoughts had to be delayed until PL first acquired the habit of routinely recording simple information. Because of concrete thinking, intensive therapist facilitation was required to help him identify alternatives to these thoughts. However, because PL was poor at self-monitoring it may have been the case that this skill improved generally simply because it was a focus for therapy. Cognitive impairment meant the number of sessions required to progress was greater than the norm and necessitated a longer period (in excess of 40 sessions plus daily checks over a 22-week period, in contrast to one session a week for 10 weeks, see Sukhodolsky et al., 2000). To avoid therapist burnout because of the very demanding nature of the work two therapists were employed to avoid exhaustion. In addition, support from the rehabilitation team as a whole was utilised.

There are other challenges that may have to be circumvented when considering use of cognitive therapy among people with severe brain injuries who also present with behaviour disorders. Severely impaired patients whose poor awareness is a direct function of neurological damage may simply not be amenable to the sort of techniques described by Manchester and Wood (2001), or above, while those with very severe memory impairment and other cognitive deficits may be similarly excluded. The presence of language and communication problems may also prohibit a proportion of patients from accessing this type of treatment. Furthermore, the nature of underlying neurological damage may interfere with the presumed causal relationship between adaptive thinking and behaviour. For example, while it may be perfectly possible to replace dysfunctional automatic thoughts, damage to the orbito-temporal-limbic feedback loop, in which the inhibitory function of the cortex over the amygdala is disrupted will render the expression of spontaneous instinctive emotion (such as aggression) beyond the previously suppressing control of intellectual function (Starkstein & Robinson, 1991). When this is the case, the influence of thinking on behaviour is obviously more tenuous and the value of expending extensive amounts of time and resources into cognitive therapy questionable.

Because of the nature of TBI sequelae it may be that the proportion of people with severe brain injuries and behaviour disorders who can engage in and benefit from the cognitive therapies is somewhat less than other clinical populations. Unfortunately, this area remains poorly researched to date so conclusions cannot at this time be reliably drawn about efficacy (Manchester & Wood, 2001). However, there are at least two reasons to be optimistic about application of these clinically proven methods to TBI. First, there is potential to effectively integrate them into existing neurorehabilitation programmes (see Williams, Evans, & Fleminger, this issue; McMillan, Williams, & Bryant, this issue). Second, the cognitive therapies have been successfully applied to people with learning difficulties. This clinical population has much in common with TBI, although it must be acknowledged there are also important differences (Alderman, 2001). There is certainly a growing evidence base for employing cognitive therapy methods in helping people with not only mild and moderate, but also severe learning disability, from use of Socratic dialogues through to self-instruction. Methods are selected that best circumvent whatever language and cognitive handicaps clients present with in order to meet their particular needs. Similar rules for selecting what methods may work best according to the challenges set by these handicaps may also be possible for people with TBI (see Jones, Williams, & Lowe, 1993; Williams & Jones, 1997).

Behaviour therapy.   Treatment of behaviour problems among people with acquired brain injury using procedures developed from operant conditioning theory has seen considerable attention in the rehabilitation literature for the last two decades. Some of these have directly addressed aggressive behaviour disorders (for example, see Alderman et al., 1999b; Burke et al, 1988; Hegel & Ferguson, 2000; Wood, 1987) while others have been concerned with remediating behavioural symptoms of underlying irritability (for example see Alderman, 1991; Alderman & Knight, 1997; Burgess & Alderman, 1990). Unlike the cognitive therapies, behaviour therapy approaches are not directly concerned with modifying thoughts and beliefs that may (or may not) perform some mediating role in the evolution and maintenance of behaviour disorders. Instead, it attempts to change behaviour by modifying antecedents that normally elicit it. Alternatively, interventions based on this approach systematically alter contingencies that follow behaviour in a such a way as to encourage or discourage the probability it will happen again in future. While this approach may seem over-simplistic, many effective treatment techniques have evolved which have been successfully used with many diverse clinical populations (see Kanfer & Goldstein, 1986).

Behaviour therapy has many advantages (see Powell, 1981; Wilson, 1989), but there are particular reasons why it has special relevance to people with acquired brain injury, and ultimately to those who present with aggression or behaviours symptomatic of irritability. Behaviour therapy embraces the scientific approach to the study of behaviour. Problems caused by lack of homogeneity within this population, together with the multivariate and unique interactions between different factors that underlie clinical challenges presented by this group are well known. These problems lend themselves to a data-driven, objective and analytical approach to the investigation of causation: Behaviour therapy provides such a means of enquiry. Wood and Eames (for example see Wood, 1987, 1990; Wood & Eames, 1981) argued that problems caused by poor homogeneity are best addressed by casting the damaged brain in the role of the dependent variable and subjecting it to systematic and planned environmental manipulations. Observation of different cause-and-effect relationships, together with knowledge about individuals' cognitive and neurological status, enables informed inferences to be drawn regarding brain–behaviour relationships. These inferences inform the clinician about what factors drive observable behaviour and constitute hypotheses that may be tested through implementing relevant behaviour therapy interventions. Integration of principles from behaviour therapy, neuropsychology, and behavioural neurology in this way constitute what has become known as a *neurobehavioural paradigm* to rehabilitation; as well as targeting behaviour disorders, it also encompasses systems that address cognitive, emotional, and physical sequelae of brain injury (Wood, 1987; Wood & Worthington, 2001a, 2001b).

Behaviour therapy also lends itself well to behaviour problems that are attributable to underlying cognitive impairment. For example, behaviour disorders symptomatic of irritability can arise as a result of poor monitoring. Behaviour therapy interventions can provide a means of encouraging the development of monitoring skills by providing regular and systematic feedback about performance (see Alderman, 1996; Alderman, Fry, & Youngson, 1995).

It could be argued that behaviour therapy is not humanistic because it does not directly consider thoughts, beliefs and emotions: Instead, it reduces people to a mechanistic level where the brain is no more than a medium for facilitating cause-and-effect relationships. However, Alderman (2001) argued that many behaviour disorders seen among survivors of traumatic brain injury were probably maintained by those people charged with their care. It certainly remains the case that people with acquired brain injury are not popular with rehabilitation professionals because of their irritating, threatening, and embarrassing behaviour, as well as their general lack of motivation (Miller & Cruzat, 1981). As a consequence, Alderman argued there is a tendency to pay less attention to those people who are irritable and aggressive. Unfortunately, while behaviour disorders may be primarily attributable to irritability, there is a tendency to reinforce them further when an individual is within an environment in which opportunities for rewarding appropriate social behaviour are rarely available. However, Alderman pointed out that most behaviour therapy interventions have the effect of reversing these "naturalistic" contingencies, first by requiring staff to interact with patients who may previously have been ignored, and second, by ensuring social reinforcement is directed at desirable, rather than disadvantageous, behaviour. In this way behaviour therapy changes the behaviour of people working with, or caring for, irritable or aggressive brain injured patients and encourages the development of positive social relationships. When interaction between brain injured people and their environment can be shown to drive and maintain challenging behaviour, behaviour therapy provides an eminently "humanistic" therapeutic framework.

A final reason why behaviour therapy has special relevance to brain injured people concerns those for whom the challenge is too great for psychotherapy (Wood, 1987). However, the barriers that exclude people from verbal therapies falling under this umbrella do not necessarily constitute a barrier to the effective use of behaviour therapy. One advantage of this is that very severely impaired patients may benefit from its use.

The benefits of utilising behaviour therapy principles within a specialised service organised to enable the wider neurobehavioural paradigm to be operationalised are well established (for example see Eames & Wood, 1985a, 1985b; Eames et al., 1996). While dedicated neurobehavioural units have the potential to manage severe behaviour disorders it is possible to employ behaviour therapy principles to reduce less severe behavioural symptoms of irritability within non-specialised services (for example, see Davis, Turner, Rolinder, & Cartwright, 1994; Goll & Hawley, 1988; Johnston, Burgess, McMillan, & Greenwood, 1991; McMillan, Papadopoulas, Cornall, & Greenwood, 1990; Watson et al., 2001; Wood, 1988). Accounts of the successful treatment of aggression and behavioural symptoms of irritability are probably most pertinent to the majority of clinicians as many do not work within specialised neurobehavioural units, but are nevertheless faced with the challenge of managing these difficulties.

An example of successful reduction in irritability/aggression using behaviour therapy.   The following case illustrates how behaviour therapy principles may be used to help ease the difficulties caused by behaviours symptomatic of irritability, including overt aggression. Cognitive impairment prevented engagement in CBT. This account concerns NR, who sustained multiple injuries, which included a very severe traumatic brain injury, as a result of a road traffic accident. Unfortunately, no attempt had been undertaken to engage him in rehabilitation until 4 years later when he was admitted to a neurorehabilitation unit. Prior to this it had been reported that NR frequently demonstrated aggressive behaviour. NR was epileptic. Assessment of cognitive functioning was limited because of variable co-operation: However, it was clear that most aspects were severely impaired. NR was easily distracted, and he was poorly oriented for time. A mild comprehension deficit was evident, and verbal fluency was reduced. Executive function was severely impaired. While semantic and autobiographical memory was preserved, NR's ability to learn new information was very poor. He was perseverative and disinhibited.

During the course of the next year NR was reported by an independent expert to have made obvious improvements as a result of rehabilitation: However, he remained severely disabled. For example, despite physical improvement, abnormalities remained evident which affected the movement of both lower limbs, while the left upper limb was most severely impaired by the neurological damage. He remained dependent on others for nearly all aspects of care. While medical opinion was that NR had considerable rehabilitation potential to exploit, aggression and other behaviours arising through irritability prevented him fully accessing therapy.

The severity of NR's cognitive impairment prevented access to psychotherapy (including cognitive therapy). As a consequence, behaviour modification principles were employed in order to help him acquire greater control over his aggressive behaviour so that he could fully access rehabilitation and achieve his potential for recovery.

A range of behaviours was identified that prevented engagement in rehabilitation: Aggression and shouting were highlighted by staff as particular problems. Shouting comprised an urgent priority for management as it actively impeded NR's progress within therapy sessions. Frequent, loud shouting had rendered him unpopular with both staff and other patients. As a consequence he spent much of his time isolated. NR's ability to tolerate frustration was very poor. Assessment indicated he shouted more frequently when demands were placed on him, particularly when these involved physical tasks. Behavioural analysis also demonstrated significant inconsistency among staff: Different people interacted with and responded to him in different ways. When shouting, he was frequently asked not to do so. Staff also had varying expectations regarding his functional performance across most situations and varying beliefs concerning reasons as to why he shouted and was aggressive.

On the basis of assessment, it was concluded that NR shouted in high demand sessions in an effort to avoid or escape tasks, especially when these were physical. It was proposed that shouting was intermittently reinforced as staff either withdrew, or lowered their expectations regarding his performance. Thus, while increased irritability was originally responsible for this behaviour, NR had learned to use it purposefully to avoid, or escape from, rehabilitation activities he disliked. During low demand periods NR was generally ignored and appropriate behaviour went unheeded most of the time. However, some staff gave him attention when he shouted. As a consequence it was concluded that this behaviour was intermittently positively reinforced, as it was the principal means by which NR's social needs were met.

NR was not resident in a specialised neurobehavioural unit: accordingly, it was recognised it was not possible to obtain the degree of consistency necessary to implement a neurobehavioural programme throughout the entire day. Assessment had indicated NR shouted most when staff assisted him to wash and dress; his behaviour was therefore initially targeted during this activity.

First, it had been noted that any member of the clinical team had previously facilitated washing and dressing. By ensuring only a few specified staff carried out this task consistency was enhanced. It was decided that two staff would be present while NR washed and dressed: one was to facilitate him with these tasks, while the other recorded frequency of shouting. Recordings were made during a 3-week baseline period. Data indicated the average time it took to prepare NR for the day was 36.1 min, although this did take as long as 50 min. Shouting was frequent: The average number of shouts was 213.8, while on one occasion a total of 548 was recorded (to count as a separate incident, there had to be a minimum gap of at least 2 s between shouting episodes).

As had been noted, there was inconsistency in how staff interacted with and responded to NR. There was also considerable variation in the level of expectation held regarding his contribution to getting washed and dressed: Some team members did everything for him, while others expected him to do some things for himself. A behavioural intervention was consequently designed which aimed to help NR reduce shouting while washing and dressing. It was intended this goal be achieved by pursuing two aims.

The first was to increase staff consistency regarding expectations and interaction. In order to increase expectations and obtain consistency among staff, a hygiene programme was devised. Getting up, showering, and dressing were broken down into 32 individual task-parts. This followed the procedure described by Giles and Clark-Wilson (1988) in that each task-part was presented in the form of a verbal statement to NR immediately following completion of that which preceded it (for example, "wash your left arm"). A recording form was devised together with clear verbal instructions regarding what action staff should follow: Task-parts NR was expected to do himself versus those which required staff facilitation were specified. To increase consistency regarding how staff interacted with NR while carrying out the programme, a verbal mediation approach was used. Staff would state what the next task-part to be undertaken was and NR was asked to repeat this: If he did not, staff would do so on his behalf. The task-part was then executed. One advantage of a verbal mediation approach is its ability to enhance learning (Alderman & Ward, 1991). However, it also helped achieve consistency, as staff were instructed to give NR social praise after successful completion of any task-part, while avoiding reinforcing shouting by not commenting on this behaviour.

The second aim of the intervention was to directly encourage NR to exert greater behavioural control by specifically reinforcing less frequent shouting. A differential reinforcement programme (DRL) was implemented alongside the hygiene programme. A target number of shouts not to exceed was defined (initially, this was 300). If NR did not exceed this he earned a reward of his choice, and the target was reduced for the next day. The member of staff recording gave him feedback every 5 min regarding the number of times he had shouted, and the target not to exceed (see Alderman & Knight, 1997, for more information regarding differential reinforcement).

Following staff training the intervention was implemented. Outcome is shown in Figure 3. This clearly shows the benefit of the intervention with a significant reduction in the frequency of NR's shouting evident. He was noted to become more independent in execution of task-parts, and time to complete the hygiene programme decreased. DRL was subsequently withdrawn after approximately 20 weeks. The structure of the hygiene programme was retained, although it subsequently proved possible to reduce the number of task-parts as NR became more independent.

Frequency counts of shouting were periodically repeated following withdrawal of DRL. It is implied that learning occurred: Figure 3 shows the increased behavioural control was maintained. The last frequency count, conducted 36 months after DRL was withdrawn, confirmed the benefits of the intervention: The average number of shouts was just 13.2, while time taken to complete getting ready for the day had more than halved (17.2 min).

The same approach was subsequently used to reduce behavioural sequelae of irritability within physiotherapy sessions. This also comprised a high demand activity in which shouting had been reinforced as it led to escape from physical rehabilitation. Initially, sessions in which sitting-to-standing were practised were targeted. Prior to intervention NR shouted an average of 168.3 times during a 30-minute session (the highest number recorded was 309). After 80 sessions in which increased consistency and DRL had been implemented this had reduced to an average of just 5.42, with the most recorded being 15. Functional improvement was subsequently achieved as NR became independent in this task. As tolerance increased, further skills were successfully practised (rolling, sit-ups, and transfers) using the same approach.

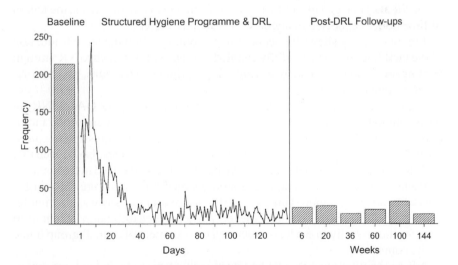

Figure 3.   Reduction in the frequency of NR's shouting while washing and dressing following implementation of a structured hygiene programme and DRL. Maintenance of increased behavioural control following withdrawal of DRL is also demonstrated up to three years later. (Follow-up data represents the mean frequency of shouting during the course of five successive occasions in which NR was observed to wash and dress.)

While NR made obvious benefits in terms of increased behavioural control and functional independence regarding hygiene and physiotherapy, the rehabilitation service was not organised sufficiently to enable the behaviour therapy approach to be used throughout the day. Consequently a facilitator was appointed whose task was to work with NR to: provide the necessary level of structure throughout the day; ensure a consistent approach to management which would enable treatment of other identified challenging behaviours; and to help ensure generalisation and maintenance of the gains made by NR in the long-term. The person appointed had previously worked with NR as a therapy aide and was thus already familiar with the principles of the approach used.

First, the facilitator discretely monitored and recorded the frequency of a range of target behaviours, including shouting (the most numerous) for 9 days. Following this, the facilitator introduced a consistent daily routine, which began at 08:00 with NR's hygiene programme, and continued until the late afternoon. This incorporated specific times for meals, rehabilitation sessions, and "free" time. Despite the label, the latter was nevertheless structured as various leisure activities were encouraged, for example, shopping trips. NR was encouraged throughout the day to participate. Reinforcement (both social and tangible) was available for appropriate behaviour, and withdrawn when it was not. A consistent approach that incorporated contingent reinforcement also included gradual exposure to increasingly higher expectations. For example, NR was noted to shout in group sessions. Expectations were reduced to begin with: NR attended groups for just 10 min. With increasing tolerance, the length of time he was expected to attend was gradually increased.

Figure 4 clearly shows the reduction in shouting following the introduction of the facilitator who successfully enabled a consistent approach to NR through contingent responses to his behaviour, appropriate expectations, and a structured routine to the day.

Figure 5 shows data regarding aggression recorded using the OAS-MNR, an observational tool referred to earlier, following the appointment of the facilitator. As with shouting, it can be seen that an increase in aggression occurred initially in response to increased expectations; likewise, it can also be seen that with consistent management, aggressive behaviour also reduced in frequency.

Reduction in shouting and aggression enabled NR to engage fully in his rehabilitation programme. Three years after behaviour therapy was first implemented, it was judged he had achieved sufficient rehabilitation potential to transfer successfully to the less-structured environment of a small group home in the community.

NR's rehabilitation potential had been compromised by behaviours symptomatic of irritability. However, his case helps illustrate the multivariate origins of such behaviour. While shouting and aggression were almost certainly organic in origin, as shouting and aggression were the behavioural products of irritability in high demand situations, NR had clearly learned to use

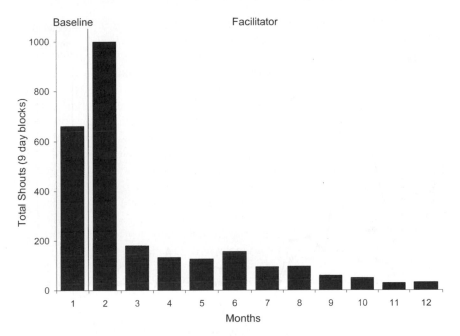

Figure 4.   Reduction in NR's shouting throughout the day following introduction of a personal facilitator. (Each bar represents the total number of shouts recorded over the course of nine days each month.)

them for both the purposes of escape, and securing attention within an environment devoid of appropriate social contact. His case also illustrates how such difficulties may be managed when cognitive impairment, and behaviour, exclude use of psychotherapy and cognitive therapy. Medication was also not used in this case because of concern that cognitive handicap would be exacerbated and further reduce learning potential.

NR's case is also of interest as it demonstrates successful use of behaviour therapy within a service that was not organised to manage challenging behaviour. However, there were some limitations. The first was that the process of addressing NR's behavioural problems was much slower than would have been the case had he been admitted to a specialised neurobehavioural unit. The main reasons for this were because expertise regarding intervention was only available to the unit 1 day a month, and a complete lack of experience among staff necessitated lengthy training. Consequently, four months elapsed before the first intervention was implemented. Second, NR's treatment plan remained vulnerable. The service was not organised sufficiently to enable a consistent approach to be used throughout the day. Although a facilitator was appointed to circumvent this problem, consistency was variable when she was away. Observational data collected when the facilitator was absent demonstrated

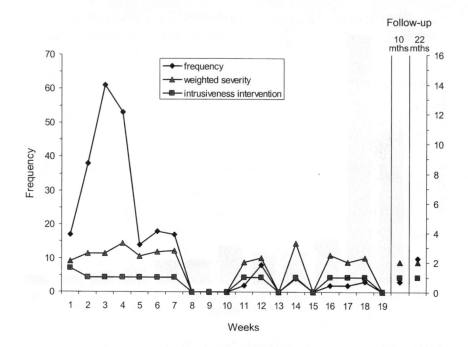

Figure 5.   Recordings made using the OAS-MNR regarding the frequency and weighted severity of all aggressive behaviour, and intrusiveness of interventions necessary to manage it, following introduction of NR's personal facilitator. Despite increased expectations, data reflect reduction in the frequency of aggression. Further recordings made over the course of a week 10 and 22 months later confirm that aggressive behaviour remained well controlled.

NR's irritable behaviour was initially more frequent in her absence. However, as time passed this discrepancy became less evident. This may have been because NR learned greater control that subsequently generalised to other times when his facilitator was absent. Alternatively, it may have been the case that the facilitator proved a successful role model for staff. It was certainly the case that staff regarded NR more positively as his irritable behaviour decreased and he became more engaged in the programme. A consequence of this was that the contingencies operating in the environment prior to intervention were reversed: Instead of shouting and aggression being socially reinforced, these contingencies became available for appropriate behaviour.

CONCLUSIONS

Irritability is a characteristic sequelae of traumatic brain injury. It is evident in about one-third of people with mild-to-moderate TBI within weeks of injury. Irritability is also persistent as it is as prevalent a year or more after injury;

indeed, there is some evidence that suggests incidence increases with time. It is also clear that irritability is not a unitary clinical phenomenon and that it has more than one underlying cause. There are also problems in determining its presence as a number of different, and possibly conflicting, clinical criteria have been used to identify it (self-report, report from significant others, questionnaire responses, and behavioural observation). Interestingly, some studies suggest irritability is less evident among people with severe TBI. However, this may reflect reduced insight within this group of patients, as reports from relatives reflect irritability is more prevalent and endures longer. Irritability may be the product of organic damage to the brain, the result of abnormal electrical discharge, or an emotional response to disabilities arising from neurological damage. Behaviour attributed to underlying irritability, including aggression, may have initially arisen as a consequence of any one of these primary causal factors, but may be sustained for other reasons (for example as learned behaviour).

It is therefore clear that treatment of irritability requires careful, detailed assessment by experienced clinicians in order to determine what factors underlie it if appropriate and effective treatment is to follow. In some cases behaviours that are assumed to be symptomatic of irritability need not be. Clinicians also need to be aware that irritability may be present even when patients deny this is the case. For most people, studies suggest that problems regarding irritability will resolve with time. However, for a significant minority they will not. There is a growing range of therapy options available for treatment of pervasive irritability. Psychotherapy may be appropriate for later onset irritability that reflects an emotional response to perception of handicap. Psychiatry also has a pertinent role to play in the management of adjustment-related mood disorders such as depression. Pharmacological intervention also has much to offer when it is suspected that irritability is primarily organic in origin. Cognitive therapies have proven beneficial in the treatment of a wide range of psychological problems. Little is known regarding its usefulness in the management of emotional disorders that either underlie or are the product of irritability, as well as behaviours arising from it such as overt aggression. Descriptions of individual cases suggest it may be beneficial, but systematic research on outcome remains a priority. Some people are excluded from participating in cognitive therapy (and other forms of verbal psychotherapy) as the challenge imposed by the severity of their cognitive impairment, poor insight and low awareness, and the presence of behaviour disorders arising from irritability is too great. When these difficulties cannot be circumvented, and for cases where medication is less appropriate, behaviour therapy may be helpful in encouraging patients to inhibit behaviour disorders that are secondary to irritability, including those that have been subsequently learned. While the range of treatment options for irritability and aggression among brain-injured survivors gives cause for optimism (Denmark & Gemeinhardt, 2002), this confidence must be tempered by the clinical reality that availability of services charged with delivering these (within the UK) remain limited (McMillan & Oddy, 2001).

REFERENCES

Alderman, N. (1991). The treatment of avoidance behaviour following severe brain injury by satiation through negative practice. *Brain Injury*, *5*, 77–86.

Alderman, N. (1996). Central executive deficit and response to operant conditioning methods. *Neuropsychological Rehabilitation*, *6*, 161–186.

Alderman, N. (2001). Management of challenging behaviour. In R. Ll. Wood & T. McMillan (Eds.), *Neurobehavioural disability and social handicap following traumatic brain injury*. Hove, UK: Psychology Press.

Alderman, N. (2002). Individual case studies. In S. Priebe & M. Slade (Eds.). *Evidence in mental health care*. London: Routledge.

Alderman, N., Bentley, J., & Dawson, K. (1999a). Issues and practice regarding behavioural outcome measurement undertaken by a specialised service provider. *Neuropsychological Rehabilitation*, *9*, 385–400.

Alderman, N., & Burgess, P. W. (2002). Assessment and rehabilitation of the dysexecutive syndrome. In R. Greenwood, M. P. Barns, T. McMillan, & T. Ward (Eds.). *Neurological rehabilitation*. Hove, UK: Psychology Press.

Alderman, N., Davies, J.A., Jones, C., & McDonnell, P. (1999b). Reduction of severe aggressive behaviour in acquired brain injury: Case studies illustrating clinical use of the OAS-MNR in the management of challenging behaviours. *Brain Injury*, *13*, 669–704.

Alderman, N., Fry, R. K., & Youngson, H. A. (1995). Improvement of self-monitoring skills, reduction of behaviour disturbance and the dysexecutive syndrome: Comparison of response cost and a new programme of self-monitoring training. *Neuropsychological Rehabilitation*, *5*, 193–221.

Alderman, N., & Knight, C. (1997). The effectiveness of DRL in the management and treatment of severe behaviour disorders following brain injury. *Brain Injury*, *11*, 79–101.

Alderman, N., Knight, C., & Henman, C. (2002). Aggressive behaviours observed within a neurobehavioural rehabilitation service: Utility of the OAS-MNR in clinical audit and applied research. *Brain Injury*, *16*, 469–489.

Alderman, N., Knight, C., & Morgan, C. (1997). Use of a modified version of the Overt Aggression Scale in the measurement and assessment of aggressive behaviours following brain injury. *Brain Injury*, *11*, 503–523.

Alderman, N., Shepherd, J., & Youngson, H. A. (1992). Increasing standing tolerance and posture quality following severe brain injury using a behaviour modification approach. *Physiotherapy*, *78*, 335–343.

Alderman, N., & Ward, A. (1991). Behavioural treatment of the dysexecutive syndrome: Reduction of repetitive speech using response cost and cognitive overlearning. *Neuropsychological Rehabilitation*, *1*, 65–80.

Azouvi, P., Jokic, C., Attral, N., Denys, P., Markabi, S., & Bussel, B. (1999). Carbamazepine in agitation and aggressive behaviour following severe closed-head injury: Results of an open trial. *Brain Injury*, *13*, 797–804.

Beck, A. T. (1976). *Cognitive therapy and the emotional disorders*. Madison, CT: International Universities Press.

Beck, A. T., Rush, A. J., Shaw, B. F., & Emery, G. (1979). *Cognitive therapy of depression*. New York: Guilford.

Ben-Yishay, Y., Rattock, J., Lakin, P., Piasetsky, E. B., Ross, B., Silver, S., Zide, E., & Ezrachi, O. (1985). Neuropsychologic rehabilitation: Quest for a holistic approach. *Seminars in Neurology*, *5*, 252–258.

Burgess, P.W., & Alderman, N. (1990). Rehabilitation of dyscontrol syndromes following frontal lobe damage: A cognitive neuropsychological approach. In R. Ll. Wood & I. Fussey (Ed.), *Cognitive rehabilitation in perspective*. Hove, UK: Psychology Press.

Burgess, P. W., Alderman, N., Emslie, H., Evans, J. J., & Wilson, B. W. (1996). The Dysexecutive Questionnaire. In B. A. Wilson, N. Alderman, P. W. Burgess, H. Emslie, & J. J. Evans (Eds.), *Behavioural assessment of the dysexecutive syndrome*. Bury St Edmunds, UK: Thames Valley Test Company.

Burgess, P. W., & Wood, R. Ll. (1990). Neuropsychology of behaviour disorders following brain injury. In R. Ll. Wood (Ed.), *Neurobehavioural sequelae of traumatic brain injury*. Hove, UK: Psychology Press.

Brooks, D. N., McKinlay, W., Symington, C., Beattie, A., & Campsie, L. (1987). The effects of severe head injury upon patient and relative within seven years of injury. *Journal of Head Trauma Rehabilitation*, *2*, 1–13.

Burke, H. H., Wesolowski, M. D., & Lane, I. (1988). A positive approach to the treatment of aggressive brain injured clients. *International Journal of Rehabilitation Research*, *11*, 235–241.

Clark, D. M. (1986). Cognitive therapy for anxiety. *Behavioural Psychotherapy*, *14*, 283–294.

Clark, D. M. (1989). Anxiety states: Panic and generalised anxiety. In K. Hawton, P. M. Salkovskis, J. Kirk, and D. M. Clark (Eds.), *Cognitive behaviour therapy for psychiatric problems: A practical guide*. Oxford: Oxford University Press.

Clark, D. M., Salkovskis, P. M., Hackmann, A., Middleton, H., Anastasiades, P., & Gelder, M. (1994). A comparison of cognitive therapy, applied relaxation and imipramine in the treatment of panic disorder. *British Journal of Psychiatry*, *164*, 759–769.

Davis, J. R., Turner, W., Rolinder, A., & Cartwright, T. (1994). Natural and structured baselines in the treatment of aggression following brain injury. *Brain Injury*, *8*, 589–597.

Deb, S., Lyons, I., & Koutzoukis, C. (1998). Neuropsychiatric sequelae one year after a minor head injury. *Journal of Neurology, Neurosurgery, and Psychiatry*, *65*, 899–902.

Deb, S., Lyons, I., & Koutzoukis, C. (1999). Neurobehavioural symptoms one year after a head injury. *British Journal of Psychiatry*, *174*, 360–365.

Denmark, J., & Gemeinhardt, M. (2002). Anger and its management for survivors of acquired brain injury. *Brain Injury*, *16*, 91–108.

Eames, P. (1988). Behavior disorders after severe brain injury: Their nature, causes and strategies for management. *Journal of Head Trauma Rehabilitation*, *3*, 1–6.

Eames, P. G. (1990). Organic bases of behaviour disorders after traumatic brain injury. In R. Ll. Wood (Ed.), *Neurobehavioural sequelae of traumatic brain injury*. Hove, UK: Psychology Press.

Eames, P. G. (2001). Distinguishing the neuropsychiatric, psychiatric, and psychological consequences of acquired brain injury. In R. Ll. Wood and T. McMillan (Eds.), *Neurobehavioural disability and social handicap following traumatic brain injury*. Hove, UK: Psychology Press.

Eames, P., Cotterill, G., Kneale, T. A., Storrar, A. L., & Yeomans, P. (1996). Outcome of intensive rehabilitation after severe brain injury: A long-term follow-up study. *Brain Injury*, *10*, 631–650.

Eames, P., & Wood, R. Ll. (1985a). Rehabilitation after severe brain injury: A follow-up study of a behaviour modification approach. *Journal of Neurology, Neurosurgery, and Psychiatry*, *48*, 613–619.

Eames, P., & Wood, R. Ll. (1985b). Rehabilitation after severe brain injury: A special-unit approach to behaviour disorders. *International Rehabilitation Medicine*, *7*, 130–133.

Foster, H. G., Hillbrand, M., & Chi, C. C. (1989). Efficacy of carbamazepine in assaultive patients with frontal lobe dysfunction. *Progress in Neuro-Psychopharmacology and Biological Psychiatry*, *13*, 865–874.

Giakas, W. J., Seibyl, J. P., & Mazure, C.M. (1990). Valporate in the treatment of temper outburst. *Journal of Clinical Psychiatry, 51*, 525.

Gibbs, J. C., Potter, G. B., Barriga, A. Q., & Liau, A. K. (1996). Developing the helping skills and prosocial motivation of aggressive adolescents in peer programs. *Aggression and Violent Behavior, A Review Journal, 1*, 283–305.

Giles, G. M., & Clark-Wilson, J. (1988). Functional skills training in severe brain injury. In I. Fussey & G. M. Giles (Eds.), Rehabilitation of the severely brain injured adult: A practical approach (1st ed.). London: Croom Helm.

Goll, S., & Hawley, K. (1988). Social rehabilitation: The role of the transitional living centre. In R. Ll. Wood & P. G. Eames (Eds.), *Models of brain injury rehabilitation*. London: Chapman Hall.

Gualtieri, C. T. (1991). *Neuropsychiatry and behavioral pharmacology*. New York: Springer-Verlag.

Haaga, D. A., & Davison, G. C. (1986). Cognitive change methods. In F. H. Kanfer & A. P. Goldstein (Eds.), *Helping people change: A textbook of methods*. New York: Pergamon Press.

Haboubi, N. H. J., Long, J., Koshy, M., & Ward, A. B. (2001). Short-term sequelae of minor head injury (6 years experience of minor head injury clinic). *Disability and Rehabilitation, 23*, 635–638.

Hawton, K., Salkovskis, P. M., Kirk, J., & Clark, D. M. (Eds.). (1989). *Cognitive behaviour therapy for psychiatric problems: A practical guide*. Oxford: Oxford University Press.

Hayes, N., Smith, A., & Berker, E. (1997). Emergence and persistence of symptoms comprising the post-traumatic syndrome in 322 patients with closed head injury. *Archives of Clinical Neuropsychology, 12*, 333–333.

Hegel, M. T., & Ferguson, R. J. (2000). Differential reinforcement of other behavior (DRO) to reduce aggressive behavior following traumatic brain injury. *Behaviour Modification, 24*, 94–101.

Hirsch, J. (1993). Promising drugs for neurobehavioural treatment. *Headlines, March/April*, 10–11.

Jackson, W. T., & Gouvier, W. D. (1992). Group psychotherapy with brain-damaged adults and their families. In C. J. Lang & L. K. Ross (Eds.), *Handbook of head trauma, acute care to recovery*. New York: Plenum Press.

Jahoda, A., Trower, P., Pert, C., & Finn, D. (2001). Contingent reinforcement or defending the self? A review of evolving models of aggressive people with mild learning disabilities. *British Journal of Medical Psychology, 74*, 305–321.

Johnston, S., Burgess, J., McMillan, T., & Greenwood, R. (1991). Management of adipsia by a behavioural modification technique. *Journal of Neurology, Neurosurgery and Psychiatry, 54*, 272–274.

Jones, R. S. P., Williams, H., & Lowe, F. (1993). Verbal self-regulation. In I. Fleming & B. Stenfert-Kroese (Eds.), *People with severe learning disability and challenging behaviour: New developments in services and therapy*. Manchester, UK: Manchester University Press.

Kanfer, F. H., & Goldstein, A. P. (1986). *Helping people change: A textbook of methods*. New York: Pergamon Press.

Kim, S. H., Manes, F., Kosier, T., Baruah, S., & Robinson, R. G. (1999). Irritability following traumatic brain injury. *Journal of Nervous and Mental Disease, 187*, 327–335.

Kinney, A. (2001). Cognitive therapy and brain injury: Theoretical and conceptual issues. *Journal of Contemporary Psychotherapy, 31*, 89–102.

Lewin, J., & Sumners, D. (1992). Successful treatment of episodic dyscontrol with carbamazepine. *British Journal of Psychiatry, 161*, 261–262.

Long, C. J., & Web, W. L. (1995). Psychological sequelae of head trauma. In M. D. Lezak (Ed.), *Neuropsychological assessment* (3rd ed.). New York: Oxford University Press.

Manchester, D., & Wood, R. Ll. (2001). Applying cognitive therapy in neuropsychological rehabilitation. In R. Ll. Wood & T. M. McMillan (Eds.), *Neurobehavioural disability and social handicap following traumatic brain injury*. Hove, UK: Psychology Press.

Mateer, C. A., & Ruff, R. M. (1990). Effectiveness of behavioral management procedures in the rehabilitation of head-injured patients. In R. Ll. Wood (Ed.), *Neurobehavioural sequelae of traumatic brain injury*. Hove, UK: Psychology Press.

Mattes, J. A. (1990). Comparative effectiveness of carbamazepine and propranolol for rage outburst. *Journal of Neuropsychiatry and Clinical Neuroscience, 2*, 159–164.

McLean, A. Jr., Dikmen, S. S., & Temkin, N. R. (1993). Psychosocial recovery after head injury. *Archives of Physical Medicine Rehabilitation, 74*, 1041–1046.

McMillan, T. M., Papadopoulas, H., Cornall, C., & Greenwood, R. J. (1990). Modification of severe behaviour problems following herpes simplex encephalitis. *Brain Injury, 4*, 399–406.

McMillan, T. M., & Oddy, M. (2001). Service provision for social disability and handicap after acquired brain injury. In R. Ll. Wood & T. M. McMillan (Eds.), *Neurobehavioural disability and social handicap following traumatic brain injury*. Hove, UK: Psychology Press.

Meichenbaum, D. (1986). Cognitive-behaviour modification. In F. H. Kanfer and A. P. Goldstein (Eds.), *Helping people change: A textbook of methods*. New York: Pergamon Press.

Miller, L. (1994). Traumatic brain injury and aggression. *Journal of Offender Rehabilitation, 2*, 91–103.

Miller, E., & Cruzat, A. (1981). A note on the effects of irrelevant information on task performance after mild and severe head injury. *British Journal of Social and Clinical Psychology, 20*, 69–70.

Monroe, R. R. (1989). Dyscontrol syndrome: Long-term follow up. *Comprehensive Psychiatry, 30*, 489–497.

Mooney, G. F., & Hass, L. J. (1993). Effect of methylphenidate on brain injury-related anger. *Archives of Physical Medicine and Rehabilitation, 74*, 153–160.

Nickels, J. L., Schneider, W. N., Dombovy, M. L., & Wong, T. M. (1994). Clinical use of amantadine in brain injury rehabilitation. *Brain Injury, 8*, 709–718.

Patterson, C. H. (1986). *Theories of counselling and psychotherapy* (4th ed.). New York: Harper and Row.

Powell, G. E. (1981). *Brain function therapy*. Aldershot, UK: Gower Press.

Prigatano, G. P. (1986). Psychotherapy after brain injury. In G. P. Prigatano, D. J. Fordyce, H. K. Zeiner, J. R. Roeche, M. Pepping, & B. C. Wood (Eds.), *Neuropsychological rehabilitation after brain injury*. Baltimore: Johns Hopkins University Press.

Prigatano, G. P. (1987). Psychiatric aspects of head injury: Problem areas and suggested guidelines for research. *BNI Quarterly, 3*, 2–9.

Prigatano, G. P. (1991). Disturbances of self awareness of deficit after traumatic brain injury. In G. P. Prigatano & D. L. Schacter (Eds.), *Awareness of deficit after brain injury: Clinical and theoretical issues*. New York: Oxford University Press.

Prigatano, G. P., Fordyce, D. J., Zeiner, H. K., Roueche, J. R., Pepping, M., & Wood, B. C. (1984). Neuropsychological rehabilitation after closed head injury in young adults. *Journal of Neurology, Neurosurgery and Psychiatry, 47*, 505–513.

Rao, V. R., & Lyketsos, M. D. (2000). Neuropsychiatric sequelae of traumatic brain injury. *Psychosomatics, 41*, 95–103.

Reeder, D. M. (1991). Cognitive therapy of anger management: Theoretical and practical considerations. *Archives of Psychiatric Nursing, 5*, 147–150.

Robinson, R. G., Kubos, K. L., Starr, L. B., Rao, K., & Price, T. R. (1983). Mood disorder in stroke patients: Relation to lesion location. *Comprehensive Psychiatry, 24*, 555–566.

Rohrbaugh, R. M., Siegal, A. P., & Giller, E. R. Jr. (1988). Irritability as a symptom of depression in the elderly. *Journal of the American Geriatric Society, 36*, 736–738.

Sazbon, L., & Groswasser, Z. (1991). Time-related sequelae of TBI in patients with prolonged post-comatose unawareness (PC-U) state. *Brain Injury, 5,* 3–8.

Scott, J. (1997). Advances in cognitive therapy. *Current Opinion in Psychiatry, 10,* 256–260.

Slagle, D. A. (1990). Psychiatric disorders following closed head injury: An overview of biopsychosocial factors in their etiology and management. *International Journal of Psychiatric Medicine, 20,* 1–35.

Starkstein, S. E., & Robinson, R. G. (1991). The role of the human lobes in affective disorder following stroke. In H. S. Levin, H. M. Eisenberg, & A. L. Benton (Eds.), *Frontal lobe function and dysfunction.* Oxford: Oxford University Press.

Stein, G. (1992). Drug treatment of the personality disorders. *British Journal of Psychiatry, 161,* 167–184.

Sukhodolsky, D. G., Solomon, R. M., & Perine, J. (2000). Cognitive-behavioral, anger-control intervention for elementary school children: A treatment outcome study. *Journal of Child and Adolescent Group Therapy, 10,* 159–170.

Van der Naalt, J., van Zomeren, A. H., Sluiter, W. J., & Minderhoud, J. M. (1999). One year outcome in mild to moderate head injury: The predictive value of acute injury characteristics related to complaints and return to work. *Journal of Neurology, Neurosurgery and Psychiatry, 66,* 207–213.

Watson, C., Rutterford, N., Shortland, D., Williamson, N., & Alderman, N. (2001). Reduction of chronic aggressive behaviour ten years after brain injury. *Brain Injury, 15,* 1003–1015.

Weddel, R., Oddy, M., & Jenkins, D. (1980). Social adjustment after rehabilitation: A two year follow-up of patients with severe head injury. *Psychological Medicine, 10,* 257–263.

Williams, W. H., & Jones, R. S. P. (1997). Teaching cognitive self-regulation of independence and emotion control skills. In B. Stenfert-Kroese, D. Dagnan, & K. Loumidis (Eds.), *Cognitive behaviour therapy for people with learning disabilities.* London: Routledge.

Wilson, B. (1989). Injury to the central nervous system. In S. Pearce & J. Wardle (Eds.), *The practice of behavioural medicine.* Oxford: University Press.

Wing, J. K., Cooper, E., & Sartorius, N. (1974). *Measurement and classification of psychiatric symptoms.* Cambridge: Cambridge University Press.

Wood, R. Ll. (1987). *Brain injury rehabilitation: A neurobehavioural approach.* London: Croom Helm.

Wood, R. Ll. (1988). Management of behaviour disorders in a day treatment setting. *Journal of Head Trauma Rehabilitation, 3,* 53–62.

Wood, R. Ll. (1990). Conditioning procedures in brain injury rehabilitation. In R. Ll. Wood (Ed.), *Neurobehavioural sequelae of traumatic brain injury.* Hove, UK: Psychology Press.

Wood, R. Ll., & Eames, P. (1981). Application of behaviour modification in the rehabilitation of traumatically brain injured patients. In G. Davey (Ed.), *Applications of conditioning theory.* London: Methuen.

Wood, R. Ll., & Worthington, A. D. (2001a). Neurobehavioural rehabilitation: a conceptual paradigm. In R. Ll.Wood & T. McMillan (Eds.), *Neurobehavioural disability and social handicap following traumatic brain injury.* Hove, UK: Psychology Press.

Wood, R. Ll., & Worthington, A. D. (2001b). Neurobehavioural rehabilitation in practice. In R. Ll. Wood & T. McMillan (Eds.), *Neurobehavioural disability and social handicap following traumatic brain injury.* Hove, UK: Psychology Press.

Yudofsky, S. C., Silver, J. M., Jackson, W., Endicott, J., & Williams, D. W. (1986). The Overt Aggression Scale for the objective rating of verbal and physical aggression. *American Journal of Psychiatry, 143,* 35–39.

NEUROPSYCHOLOGICAL REHABILITATION, 2003, *13* (1/2), 241–258

Episodic disorders of behaviour and affect after acquired brain injury

Peter Eames

*Beechwood House Brain Injury Rehabilitation Unit,
Pontypool, Wales*

Rodger Ll. Wood

University of Wales, Swansea, Wales

Psychological disorders that follow traumatic brain injury are possibly more complex and diverse than those associated with other forms of "brain damage". These may include organic aggressive, or organic affective syndromes that are episodic in nature and therefore require a more specific diagnosis, a different classification, and a different approach to treatment. Consequently, it is necessary for clinicians to learn to distinguish between "primary" psychiatric illnesses and those disorders of behavioural control and mood that stem specifically from brain injury. There is relatively little in the clinical literature that explains the relationship between variable states of behaviour, mood or temperament, and clinical disorders that may have long-term implications for patient management. This concept paper therefore addresses abnormalities of mood and behaviour that are episodic in character and are not recognisably included in the DSM and ICD classifications of psychological or psychiatric disorders.

INTRODUCTION

Among the many adverse consequences of acquired brain injury there is a group of disorders characterised by intermittent states of altered affect or behaviour. (The term "affect" is used here to indicate subjective emotional states; the term "mood" is avoided, because it tends to be used interchangeably with *either* emotional changes *or* episodes of changed behaviour, most typically anger or rage, and because these two are helpfully distinguished in understanding the disorders.) These conditions are not widely recognised and

Correspondence should be addressed to Rodger Wood, Department of Psychology, University of Wales, Swansea, Singleon Park, Swansea, SA2 8PP.

http://www.tandf.co.uk/journals/pp/09602011.html   DOI:10.1080/09602010244000435

can be readily confused with more standard forms of affective disorders such as "depression" or anxiety on the basis of a single consultation, even by psychiatrists, unless their essentially episodic nature is elicited in taking the individual's history.

They can be considered to form a group of disorders, because they share a range of characteristics. These include first and foremost their "episodicity": They are unpredictable, of sudden onset and brief duration, and usually stand out against a background of generally normal affect and behaviour as being "out of character" for the person. They may or may not be provoked by some external trigger, but if they are, it is nearly always something trivial. There may be partial amnesia for the period of the episode. After the episode the individual feels remorseful if he or she has behaved in an inappropriate way, or deeply regretful if it has involved an affective change; often there are also somatic symptoms, such as headache or fatigue and drowsiness. Typically the person expresses complete inability to control the change.

What distinguishes the varieties within the group is the nature of the affective or behavioural change. However, it is not uncommon for episodes to consist of a combination of an emotional state with explosive outbursts; occasionally a more complex combination of features may be seen. Certain other features are seen in association with these disorders in a substantial proportion of individuals. Those that emerge most clearly from the main studies (see below) are a general tendency to impulsivity, the use of a car or other vehicle as a weapon, and, more rarely, anomalies of sexual behaviour of an aggressive but unpredictable kind. Finally, these disorders have in common a failure to respond to treatment approaches that would be appropriate for their more usual psychiatric counterparts.

The most common *disorder of behaviour* is known as the episodic dyscontrol syndrome (EDS). Descriptions date back to the 19th century; Kaplan (1899) used the term "explosive diathesis". After the Second World War, Hooper, McGregor, and Nathan (1945) called it "episodic rage". The name "EDS" was coined by Ervin's group (Bach-y-Rita, Lion, Climent, & Ervin, 1971), who, in a large study, delineated certain "core features", later confirmed by Elliott (1982) in a further sample. It presents as episodes of rage, which may be associated with severe physical aggression, destructiveness or simple verbalised anger.

The most frequent form of *affective disorder* involves sudden changes into a state of non-specific dysphoria: The feelings are described in terms of irritable unhappiness and restlessness, often with disturbed sleep and appetite. Occasionally clinical pictures of retarded depression or hypomania may be seen that are distinguished from the corresponding primary psychiatric disorders only by the temporal pattern of the episodes. Several other variants occur much more rarely, with anxiety or alterations of cognition or perceptual disturbances as their leading features.

As a group these conditions have been referred to as "temporolimbic disorders" (Eames, 1990; Monroe, 1986). This comes from Monroe's experimental investigations (1970), which pointed to an association with abnormalities of medial temporal lobe and limbic structure dysfunctions. These disorders were found by Elliott (1982) not only as consequences of acquired brain injury, but also in a context of developmental disorders, particularly specific learning disabilities (such as dyslexia and dyspraxia), appearing in Elliott's work as "minimal brain dysfunction" (a term no longer used). The forms of acquired brain injury most likely to be followed by temporolimbic disorders are traumatic or subarachnoid haemorrhage associated with cerebral damage. Occasionally, such disorders have been found in association with complex partial epilepsy, especially of temporal lobe origin, or with tumours of the temporal lobe. Monroe and Lion (1978) argued that explosive aggression associated with temporal lobe injury occurs during the ictus (seizure), usually followed by amnesia for the event. Wood (1987) described three such cases of ictal aggression. However, aggression as an intrinsic feature of temporal lobe epilepsy is generally considered to be a rare event and peripheral to the disorders that form the core of this paper.

An important characteristic of episodic disorders is that they always appear after a delay or latent period. This is never less than a month, and most commonly between 3 and 18 months, but may be as long as several years. (Possible explanations are considered later.) Unfortunately, they appear to be more common also in individuals with sociopathic disorders, and may co-occur in "pseudo-psychopathic" disorders associated with frontal injury (Blumer & Benson, 1975). In such cases, the contrast between the episodes and the person's usual behavioural style may be less obvious, but there is still a need to try to distinguish between abnormalities of behavioural *states* and of behavioural *traits*.

After acquired brain injury, such disorders impose considerable stress on relatives, as much because of their unpredictability as from actual violence that may accompany the episodes, but also because they represent a marked change in a previously familiar person. They have been identified as an important factor underlying the breakdown of relationships after head injury (Wood and Yurdakul, 1997).

CLINICAL PICTURES

Episodic dyscontrol syndrome

The core features are sudden, unpredictable outbursts of rage identified by others as "out of character" (the expression "Jekyll and Hyde" is frequently offered), with either a trivial or no identifiable trigger, coming to an equally sudden end after no more than a few minutes, and followed by remorse.

Amnesia for events at the height of the outburst is seen in about one third of episodes (not of subjects). The frequency of episodes is very variable: They may occur almost daily, or there may be weeks or even months of freedom in between. An unexpected feature is that outbursts may be directed only towards furniture or the person's own valued possessions. When the outburst is directed towards people, it is far more likely to involve the person's own family than strangers, but children (unlike spouses) are extremely unlikely to be the victims of physical aggression. (This suggests that although control is lost in respect of the outburst itself, there may be a degree of control over the direction of the aggression.) These features reported by Bach-y-Rita et al. (1971) and by Elliott (1982) and reiterated by Silver and Yudofsky (1994) are consistent with the present authors' experience.

Affective disorders

When the leading symptom is dysphoria, episodes are equally sudden in onset, but may last for anything from an hour or two to several days, although not more than a week. They usually resolve quickly, but not as suddenly as the onset; many simply disappear overnight. States that closely resemble depressive illness rarely last more than a few days; hypomanic pictures are usually shorter; in some individuals there may be rapid swings between these extremes during the course of the episode; in others, either form may be seen in different episodes. It is these latter states, especially the depressed form, that are most subject to misdiagnosis in outpatient settings. The patient's appearance and mental state are so persuasive that antidepressants or sedatives are likely to be prescribed. When the patient is seen again two or three weeks later, and found to be well, the erroneous diagnosis seems confirmed; it may be only when a subsequent appointment coincides with a further episode that the appearance of a treatment response is seen to have been illusory. Disorders of these kinds were described by Kraepelin (1921), who thought they were initially precipitated by social stressors, but later evolved into episodes that occurred spontaneously. They were also described in detail by Monroe (1970). When the disorder is characterised by attacks of anxiety, these are usually short, lasting only up to an hour (Brodsky & Zuniga, 1978; Harper and Roth, 1962).

Other forms

Episodes of frank confusion, that have to be distinguished from partial status epilepticus, have been described by Pond (1957) and by Bacon and Haslam (1982). They may last from hours to a few days. Less severe degrees of obfuscation may be encountered, amounting to no more than a feeling of mental incompetence, with deficits of attention and information processing, perhaps accompanied by mild headache or "pressure in the head"; these again tend to last from hours to a day.

A few individuals present with episodes in which the leading feature is suspiciousness or even frank paranoia, sometimes accompanied by auditory hallucinations. They may be compounded by behaviours driven by these abnormal experiences. (See Bacon and Haslam 1982; Monroe, 1982; Pond, 1957). Such attacks usually last from hours to a few days, although the only cases seen by one of the present authors (PE) have involved episodes lasting for exactly 24 hours and brought to an end by a period of sleep.

CLASSIFICATION

There seems to be no proper place for episodic *affective* disorders in the ICD or DSM classifications, although both of these do include "brief affective disorder", largely based on the work of the Zurich group (Angst & Hochstrasser, 1994). Both classifications employ criteria that require "at least one episode a month for one year". This excludes individuals with less regular frequencies, for example, with several episodes in a week, but periods of freedom of more than a month.

Nor is there a formal classification of *explosive* disorders in either system. The cardinal features of sudden onset of aggressive or destructive behaviour precipitated by trivial or no triggers and followed by remorse are reflected in the DSM-IV (American Psychiatric Association, 1994) category of intermittent explosive disorder (DSM-IV 312.34). This refers to discrete episodes of failure to resist aggressive impulses, which result in serious assault or destruction of property. Aggression is designated as being out of proportion to the precipitating event. However, one of the main exclusion criteria is head injury. Additional criteria exclude the diagnosis if there is evidence of impulsivity or sociopathy, both of which are likely to be evident after injury to the frontal systems of the brain. In ICD 10, explosive disorders receive even less consideration, appearing as "impulse control disorders not elsewhere classified". Temporolimbic syndromes therefore have yet to find a proper place in the major classifications of psychiatric disorders.

Silver and Yudovsky (1987) reported a number of cases of aggression associated with frontal lobe and limbic damage. Later, the same authors (1994) argued that the impulsive aggression seen after traumatic brain injury should be classified as a specific form of psychiatric disorder, "organic aggressive syndrome", rather than the over-inclusive DSM-IV category, organic personality disorder. The present authors agree with the "rather than", but are doubtful about the suggested replacement. This is because it is also important, especially in relation to treatment, to distinguish carefully between EDS and other causes of aggression after brain injury, for example, the angry reactions in the context of poor inhibitory control discussed by Wood (2000). Undoubtedly, these episodic disorders need their own niches in classifications, but the definitions and criteria must match the clinical realities more closely than they do at present.

INCIDENCE

Currently there are no published data that allow an estimate of the incidence of temporolimbic disorders. Experience from a large district general hospital with a catchment population of about 350,000 people may give some insight into the issue. All patients admitted to hospital because of a head injury were referred at discharge to a head injury follow-up clinic. Some failed to attend, but over a 12-year period 743 patients were seen; many were followed up for several years; others who were discharged from the clinic but later developed either epilepsy or disorders of behaviour or affect were referred back by their family doctors (or often by themselves). Table 1 shows the numbers and forms of the disorders that emerged: 44 (almost 6%) had symptoms consistent with temporolimbic disorders. The majority had typical EDS; a minority had affective symptoms without EDS. (None of the variant forms was seen in this series of patients.) Since there can be a long delay before the disorders emerge (see below), and since some seen elsewhere may be misdiagnosed and treated as standard depressive illnesses, these data are likely to represent an underestimate.

In both published series (Bach-y-Rita et al., 1971; Elliot, 1982) there is a male:female ratio of about 3-4:1; in the series in Table 1, where all cases followed head injury, the ratio was 5.2:1. Bach-y-Rita et al. studied 130 patients seen in an inner-city emergency department, whereas Elliott reported on 286 patients seen in private practice. Thus it is unlikely that socioeconomic status is an important determinant.

THE ORGANIC BASIS

Monroe (1977) believed that these disorders resulted from epileptic distur-bances in various temporolimbic structures that did not propagate to neocortical areas and therefore did not lead to overt seizures or necessarily to alterations of consciousness or awareness. The argument is reasonable, because it is well established (in animal models at least) that when seizures are

Table 1
Head injury clinic admissions

Disorder type	Number
Episodic dyscontrol syndrome	35
Episodic disorder of mood	3
Episodic dyscontrol + mood	6
Episodic anxiety/panic disorder	0
Total admissions	743
Total with Temporo-limbic syndrome	44

"kindled" in limbic structures, they spread outside that system (i.e., to neo-cortex) only if the electrical discharge is exceptional. Some neurologists have argued that the hypothesis is weak because episodes are commonly provoked by external events, but this is far from persuasive, since many forms of frank epilepsy are known to be intrinsically "reflex" in nature. There are, for example, the forms known as reading, orgasmic or musicogenic epilepsies, but the most common is simple photosensitive epilepsy. Clearly, if a specific brain mechanism has an underlying defect, it is most likely to be subject to abnormal electrical discharges (i.e., epileptogenic activity) when it is being activated by its customary stimuli. Some support for Monroe's hypothesis came from his own experiments and electroencephalographic studies (1970).

Further support may be seen in a study of the delay in time of onset of post-traumatic epilepsy (PTE) and temporolimbic syndromes (TLS) after traumatic brain injury. Figure 1 presents data from the DGH clinic referenced above and compares the delays in onset of PTE and TLS: As can be seen, they are remark-ably similar ($r = 0.898$, $p < .01$, 2-tailed). This correlation suggests the two conditions may well have similar causal mechanisms.

There is as yet no clear understanding of what the mechanism might be, either for PTE or TLS. One candidate is the phenomenon known as "kindling". If a locus of grey matter (i.e., neuronal cell assemblies) is given daily periods of high-frequency repetitive electrical stimulation, there is little or no behavioural effect at first, but little by little a focus is produced that then becomes autono-mous, producing intermittent spontaneous electrical discharges that cause overt seizures. If produced within limbic structures (as distinct from neocortex), such discharges rarely propagate to neocortical areas, but may produce changes in emotional experience (e.g., fear or anxiety, Adamec, 1978, 1990; Pinel, Treit, and Rovner, 1977) or theoretically in behaviour (typically of

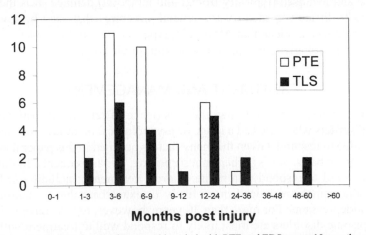

Months post injury

Figure 1. Admissions to a district general hospital with PTE and EDS over a 10-month period.

a "fight or flight" kind). At the moment the main difficulty with such a hypothesis is that there is no convincing evidence of kindling in man and some authorities do not believe it to be a phenomenon relevant to clinical epilepsy. It is also difficult on this basis to explain the very long latent periods often seen before epileptic or temporolimbic disorders emerge.

A more direct hypothesis relates to electrical disturbances that propagate in circuits that are known to be involved in the control of aggression, such as those within the limbic structures, principally the amygdala. These circuits may have their excitability raised, so that they are more likely to respond to legitimate provocative stimuli (Devinsky & Bear, 1984). An alternative possibility is the rather general proposition put forward by Penfield (1961) to explain what he called the "silent period of strange ripening" in relation to the delayed onset of PTE. This was that injury to the brain substance is repaired by scar tissue and, as in the skin and other organs, this gradually contracts over time. In this way, otherwise normal neurones surrounding the scar tissue are likely to be physically distorted. Since the electrical stability of neurones depends on the cell body membrane, across which the action potentials are ultimately developed, with increasing distortion the membrane may become unstable and therefore subject to spontaneous generation of discharges. If this occurs in a group (or "assembly") of neurones, it may then be capable of propagation sufficient to cause a behaviourally overt seizure.

It is obviously of interest to ask about the localisation of lesions that may generate the episodic disorders. In this paper, the authors are concerned principally with those disorders that occur in individuals who have suffered acquired brain injury. Unfortunately, the forms of injury that appear most likely to be followed by the later development of such disorders (i.e., head injury or subarachnoid haemorrhage) are characterised by widespread combinations of diffuse and localised (typically frontal and temporal) damage. It is therefore extremely difficult to identify the crucial structures that may be involved. Nevertheless it is clear that Monroe's experimental findings (1970, 1982, 1986) point strongly to medial temporal and limbic areas.

TREATMENT AND MANAGEMENT

The authors have frequently had the experience of referrals of patients with these disorders who have had a range of psychological therapies to which they have failed to respond. Given the many factors outlined in this paper that point to an organic basis, this is perhaps not surprising. It is as frequent a finding that they also fail to respond to a range of drug treatments, including sedatives (benzodiazepines are indeed more likely to exacerbate them), neuroleptics and antidepressants. For more than 30 years, however, reports have indicated that episodic disorders are most likely to respond well to treatment with antiepileptic agents (Bach-y-Rita 1971; Lewin and Sumners, 1992; Maletzky,

1973; Mattes, Rosenberg, & Mays, 1984; Monroe, 1989; Stein, 1992; Stone, McDaniel, Hughes, & Hermann, 1986). Just as with frank epilepsy, however, there are likely to be secondary problems of an emotional nature in reaction to the unsettling experience of unpredictable perturbations in the person's life and the feeling of vulnerability that results. These vary greatly depending largely on the stability and robustness of the individual's personality and on his or her interpersonal and social circumstances. They can be almost impossible to deal with unless the episodes are first controlled, but are then likely to need and benefit from psychological interventions that help to "re-orientate" the person to what is in effect a new way of life.

In the authors' experience, therefore, the approach most likely to be effective is first to institute trials of potentially appropriate drug treatments; only once control is achieved is it helpful to offer supportive psychological treatments. (This is the opposite of the recommendation published recently by Denmark and Gemeinhardt, 2002, that "all non-pharmacological alternatives should be considered first".)

Pharmacological methods

Before embarking on drug treatments, it is essential to make the diagnoses only if the core features are unequivocally present, because it is apparent that the appropriate treatments have little or no impact on other causes of "aggressiveness" (e.g., Wood, 2000) that may be encountered after acquired brain injury.

Relevant studies reported in the literature are sparse. There are none at all that deal with temporolimbic affective disorders. Of those that consider aggressive behaviour, very few specify EDS. Most are difficult to evaluate because they concern patients with "agitation" or "combativeness" in the *acute* stage of head injury, or refer to other populations, often behaviour-disordered children or adolescents, the elderly, or patients with severe learning disability. Most report either single case studies or small groups; few are controlled in any way. Several review articles (Corrigan, Yudofsky, & Silver, 1993; Fava, 1997; Mattes, 1986) conclude that benzodiazepines and neuroleptics are generally inappropriate medications, but lithium carbonate, beta-blocking agents (propranolol, but also metoprolol, which can be used safely in the presence of asthma) and anticonvulsants have shown promise in both efficacy and safety. There seems to be no doubt that lithium carbonate is effective in episodic disorders, but it is difficult to manage safely: Glenn et al. (1989) reported 10 patients of whom five showed a dramatic response, but three suffered potentially dangerous neurotoxic effects (a rather higher proportion than would be expected in patients treated with the drug for primary affective disorders). Mattes et al. (1984), reported a comparative study of propranolol and carbamazepine in 80 patients with outbursts of rage, of whom 51 were randomly assigned. They concluded that both provided benefit, but when there were also features of attention deficit disorder, the outcomes favoured propranolol.

However, most of the reports of successful treatment of episodic disorders have involved anticonvulsant (anti-epileptic) drugs. The earlier ones claimed that phenytoin (at that time the most commonly used anticonvulsant in North America) was helpful (Bach-y-Rita et al., 1971; Elliott, 1982; Maletzky, 1973; Monroe, 1970, 1982), although no data or details were given. The largest number have pointed to carbamazepine. Mattes et al. (1984), in their study of 80 subjects comparing this drug with propranolol, found that the former was favoured in cases of straightforward "intermittent explosive disorder". There are three impressive single-case studies (Lewin & Sumners, 1992; Morikawa et al., 2000; Stone, 1986). To date, the best designed study is by Azouvi et al. (2000), although it included patients with both acute-stage agitation and later episodic explosiveness (i.e., EDS): Of 10 patients, five had a very good response to carbamazepine, three had a moderate response, and two had no benefit.

In recent years there has been sporadic mention, mainly in review articles, of the use of derivatives of valproic acid, of lamotrigine or of gabapentin. There have been no reported studies of lamotrigine or gabapentin treatment of episodic disorders (Letterman & Markovitz, 1999), but they are reported, in the makers' data sheets (presumably on the basis of post-marketing surveillance data), occasionally to *provoke* explosive outbursts. One published study of valproic acid (Wroblewski, Joseph, Kupfer, & Kalliel, 1997) found that five patients with previously uncontrolled aggression or destructiveness responded dramatically, but there are no other studies that offer data.

On the basis of the above and from their own clinical experience, the authors recommend that carbamazepine be the first choice treatment of episodic disorders and that it be used in adequate dosage for a minimum period dictated by the length of time in which at least three episodes could be predicted, before concluding that it is unsuccessful. Clinical experience shows that most patients will need 400 mg morning and night. This is probably best reached in just two steps a week apart, starting with 200 mg morning and night: This will limit sedative adverse effects to two short periods and these will be well tolerated in the majority, provided they are warned and reassured in advance. Perhaps as many as a third will need (and will tolerate) 600 mg twice a day. Twice daily dosage is essential, even with "slow release" preparations, because otherwise the desired aim of a steady 24-hour level is not achieved. There is published evidence that generic versions of the drug are relatively unreliable in their bio-availability, so that it is wise to use only the original branded versions (Koch & Allen, 1987; Sachdeo & Belendiuk, 1987). Probably the best second choice, after epileptic agents, is propranolol, a beta-blocker (Elliott, 1977; Mattes et al., 1984).

There is no clear understanding of how anti-epileptic agents might have their effect in these conditions. Post and Uhde (1985), in a study on manic depressive illness, hypothesised that carbamazepine should stabilise dysregulated limbic neural activity because of its anti-kindling activity; unfortunately, it is significantly less effective at this than are derivatives of valproic acid (Bleck & Klawans, 1990), even though this is less effective in the treatment of episodic disorders. If Penfield's hypothesis is true, carbamazepine might be effective simply by increasing the electrical stability of neuronal cell membranes.

Psychological methods

Methods of behaviour management that are practised in specialist units can have a moderating impact on episodic aggression, but rarely if ever result in full control over the event (see Alderman, 2000; Wood, 1987). However, the majority of people with episodic disorders of mood and behaviour are not suitable for admission to specialist rehabilitation centres and require out-patient treatment. The methods of anger management proposed by Novaco (1975), used successfully to regulate aggressive reactions that have clear precipitants, often have little or no influence in cases of EDS. However, Fredriksen and Rainwater (1981) used a multiple approach for treating male psychiatric patients with intermittent explosive disorder that may have value in non-institutional settings. They began by conducting a behavioural analysis to identify such things as social skills deficits, cognitive attributions, expectations of outcome, and autonomic changes associated with the outburst. Patients were then trained in adaptive social skills involving alternative responses to situations that resulted in aggression. They employed instructional techniques, modelling, role playing, and relaxation methods. Only half of the 18 patients treated completed the programme but five of these achieved a clinically useful outcome.

Probably the most effective psychological intervention is cognitive–behaviour therapy, but only if the therapist has a full understanding of the biological and environmental factors that contribute to explosive behaviour (O'Neill, 1999). Motivation for treatment is often an issue, possibly related to problems of awareness and judgement that are implicit to dyscontrol syndromes. In some cases, individuals are simply unaware that they behave unreasonably, or have angry outbursts. In other cases, individuals will recognise that they can be inappropriately abrasive, even verbally aggressive, yet fail to register the impact this has on family members. In such cases, psychologists should on the one hand educate the family about the nature of episodic disorders, while on the other raise the injured person's awareness of somatic and emotional stimuli that often signal the incipient onset of a mood change. The patient will also need help to recognise the social and emotional impact of angry outbursts on family members. If individuals can come to recognise that their behaviour is unacceptable to others, they will have reached a stage where they can be helped to develop strategies that minimise the impact of the mood changes or outbursts (see Manchester & Wood, 2000).

Psychological interventions often involve simple strategies, such as telling family members that a mood change is expected and to ask for allowances to be made. This type of response operates on several levels. First, it facilitates awareness of an impending mood change. Second, it informs and educates others that some change is about to take place over which the individual has little or no control. The announcement acts as a form of verbal mediation that signals to the individual (as well as others) that some emotional or behavioural change is likely. This creates an opportunity for the individual to introduce some kind of strategy that may ameliorate the impact of the mood change.

CASE EXAMPLES

The following are real-life examples of isolated EDS, a temporolimbic affective disorder, and a more complex picture with a range of symptoms occurring together and leading to maladaptive behaviours during the episodes.

Case 1

A foreman electrician of 36 suffered a head injury in a road traffic accident, with a probable fracture of the base of the skull. He was unconscious for only 5 min, but had a post-traumatic amnesia (PTA) of three weeks. His prolonged but fluctuating confusional state was not clearly recognised by the orthopaedic team, so a computed tomography (CT) scan was not obtained. Within 3 months he made a full neurological and cognitive recovery and was able to return to work and perform satisfactorily. It can therefore reasonably be assumed that the prolonged PTA resulted from brain swelling and consequent mild brainstem compression in response to cortical contusions rather than a significant degree of diffuse axonal injury. This view was supported by marked fatiguability for the first 3 months. Four months after injury, once initial "shallow irritability" had resolved, he began to have sudden brief outbursts of verbal aggression and destructiveness, sufficiently dramatic to cause his 13-year-old daughter to avoid his presence. He was filled with remorse but the outbursts continued and gradually increased in frequency, from one a fortnight to almost daily, but the duration of each outburst remained the same. After a year he was referred back to a regional head injury clinic, where a diagnosis of EDS was made. He was prescribed carbamazepine, with a slowly increasing dose regime. After 3 weeks he felt unable to continue because of marked fatigue. The episodes continued and he was re-referred a year later. This time carbamazepine was introduced rapidly, during a 2-week holiday from work. Within that time he was tolerating it without adverse effects and the episodes disappeared. He was followed up over the next 3 years: After 2 years the drug was slowly withdrawn and by discharge he had continued free of episodes for 10 months without treatment.

Case 2

A girl aged 8 years was hit by a bus and suffered an isolated head injury, without initial loss of consciousness, but with a depressed parietal and basal fracture, and the rapid development of gross global brain swelling seen on CT scan. She was then unconscious for 2 days, confused for several days, and had subsequent PTA of just over a week. On the fifth day she developed a progressive left hemiparesis, which cleared within a week: This indicated a right frontal contusion. From the start she showed behavioural signs of significant frontal and temporal lobe injury, with deficits of attention and memory, as well as marked problems with literacy and numeracy, as well as disorganised, irritable and intemperate behaviour. Over the next 2 years these features improved, but even 9 years later she had a degree of social disinhibition that was slightly embarrassing to her family and her partner. From the first year, however, she started to have discrete outbursts of temper, often with physical aggression towards her family. By the time she was 13 these had diminished greatly, but had been replaced by "fits" of crying and self-deprecation every week or two, without obvious precipitants, in between which she was often brittle in manner. Within two more years, however, a clear pattern was established, with episodes of irritability and restlessness, with no discernible triggers and very sudden onset. They occurred at least once a fortnight and lasted between a day and a week, usually resolving over night. In these episodes she wept inconsolably, felt suicidal, talked constantly about death and about hating herself and everybody else, lost her appetite, but slept excessively. By this time she was working as a care assistant with elderly people, but the episodes put this employment at risk. She was living with a long-standing and supportive boyfriend, but her episodes had led to their splitting up on four occasions with diminishing intervals between. Happily she had an excellent response to carbamazepine, such that her episodes disappeared, although they recurred for a while when she stopped medication against advice, only to be controlled once more when it was re-instituted.

Case 3

Figure 2 illustrates the case of a young man who suffered a closed head injury at the age of 16. He was briefly unconscious but a PTA of several days was recorded and a CT scan showed a right-sided frontal contusion. He was referred to a rehabilitation unit 3 years after injury because of unpredictable behaviour that included episodes of heavy drinking. Most of the time the young man was a moderate drinker. His manner was generally amiable and placid. He lacked

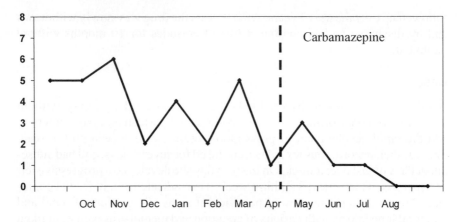

Figure 2.   Frequency of alcohol-related aggression before and after the introduction of carbamazepine.

drive and the ability to sustain goal-directed behaviour, but responded well to prompts and direction from staff on a post-acute rehabilitation unit. He could be moody and difficult on occasion, but these behaviours were never unmanageable. In contrast, there were episodes when his behaviour pattern changed. Initially, he tended to be unreasonable, suspicious and demanding. He found fault in staff and provoked arguments among other residents in the rehabilitation unit. At such times he usually displayed a rather grandiose and overbearing manner. He would then begin to drink heavily, which resulted in threatening and assaultive behaviour that, on more than one occasion, required police intervention.

There was no obvious social precipitant to these changes in his behaviour and he did not respond to a variety of psychological interventions. When the frequency of this behaviour pattern was plotted over time, a pattern emerged, with intervals of 12–15 weeks between episodes. This was interpreted as indicative of episodic dyscontrol. The anticonvulsant, carbamazepine was introduced. There followed a gradual reduction in these episodes. This more stable pattern of behaviour allowed a more consistent interaction with family, friends and staff, greater self-confidence, and a more positive attitude to his future.

RECOMMENDATIONS FOR FUTURE RESEARCH

Understanding episodic disorders of behaviour involves a complex interaction of maturational development, biological factors, learning mechanisms, and social forces that do not lend themselves easily to reductionist thinking. A multilevel, integrative research strategy is required to investigate these variables, in the context of different types of acquired brain injury.

The absence of a formal classification of episodic disorders means that the first step will be a large-scale prospective study to determine the incidence and prevalence of episodic disorders and their relationship (if any) to brain injury. This will allow a better definition of emotional states and behaviours associated with episodic disorders and distinguish between different syndromal clusters that may be linked to different types or patterns of brain damage/dysfunction. Neuroimaging studies could provide important information about relationships between cerebral pathology and function, that will allow correlations to be made with electrophysiological and neuropsychological measures. However, identifying biological processes will be a challenging task because of the episodic nature of the disorder and the problem of assessing cerebral activity during an episode, a time when the subject is least motivated or cooperative, and most agitated and volatile.

Until episodic disorders are properly classified in DSM or ICD format our understanding of the condition will remain patchy and effective treatment interventions will be slow to develop. The limited and sometimes conflicting information on antidepressant and anticonvulsant drugs makes clear the need for properly controlled studies on different pharmacological agents that regulate mood and behaviour. Such studies have taken place for agitated behaviour in dementia (see Tariot et al., 1998) and need to be conducted on a large scale in people who have agitated or aggressive episodes after head trauma or other acquired brain damage. These should not simply be placebo controlled studies but comparative studies, for example of the effectiveness of carbamazepine vs. valproate vs. selective serotonin reuptake inhibitors (SSRI) agents. Until a more systematic approach is brought to the identification and treatment of this disorder, many individuals and their families will experience serious and unnecessary difficulties in the wake of head trauma.

REFERENCES

Adamec, R. (1978). Normal and abnormal limbic system mechanisms of emotive biasing. In K. E. Livingston & O. Hornykiewcz (Eds.), *Limbic mechanisms* (pp. 405–455). New York: Plenum Press.

Adamec, R. E. (1990). Does kindling model anything clinically relevant? *Biological Psychiatry*, *27*, 249–279.

Alderman, N. (2000). Managing challenging behaviour. In R. Ll. Wood & T. M. McMillan (Eds.), *Neurobehavioural disability and social handicap*. Hove, UK: Psychology Press.

American Psychiatric Association (1994). *Diagnostic and statistical manual of mental disorder* (4th ed.). Washington, DC: Author.

Angst, J., & Hochstrasser, B. (1994). Recurrent brief depression: The Zurich Study. *Journal of Clinical Psychiatry*, *55*(4) (Suppl.), 3–9.

Azouvi, P., Jokic, C., Attal, N., Denys, P., Markabi, S., & Bussel, B. (2000). Carbamazepine in agitation and aggressive behaviour following severe closed-head injury: Results of an open trial. *Brain Injury*, *13*(10), 797–804.

Bach-y-Rita, G., Lion, J. R, Climent, C. E., & Ervin, F. R. (1971). Episodic dyscontrol: A study of 130 violent patients. *American Journal of Psychiatry, 127*, 1473–1478.

Bacon, C., & Haslam, M. (1982). Psychiatric presentation of psychomotor epilepsy. *British Journal of Clinical and Social Psychiatry, 2*, 16–17.

Bleck, T. P., Klawans, H. L. (1990). Convulsive disorders: Mechanisms of epilepsy and anticonvulsant action. *Clinical Neuropharmacology, 13*(2), 121–128.

Blumer, D., & Benson, D. F. (1975). Personality changes with frontal and temporal lobe lesions. In D. Blumer & D. F. Benson (Eds.), *Psychiatric aspects of neurological disease* (pp. 151–170). New York: Grune and Stratton.

Brodsky, L., & Zuniga, J. (1978). Refractory anxiety: A masked epileptiform disorder. *Paper presented to the Second World Congress of Biological Psychiatry*, Barcelona.

Corrigan, P. W., Yudofsky, S. C., & Silver, J. M. (1993). Pharmacological and behavioral treatments for aggressive psychiatric patients. *Hospital and Community Psychiatry, 44*(2), 125–133.

Denmark, J., & Gemeinhardt, M. (2002). Anger and its management for survivors of acquired brain injury. *Brain Injury, 16*(2), 91–108.

Devinsky, O., & Bear, D. (1984). Varieties of aggressive behaviour in temporal lobe epilepsy. *American Journal Psychiatry, 141*, 651–656

Eames, P. (1990). Organic bases of behaviour disorders after traumatic brain injury. In R. Ll. Wood (Ed.), *Neurobehavioural sequelae of traumatic brain injury*. Hove, UK: Psychology Press.

Elliott, F. A. (1977). Propranalol for the control of belligerent behaviour following acute brain injury. *Annals of Neurology, 1*, 489–491.

Elliott, F. A. (1982). Neurological findings in adult minimal brain dysfunction and the dyscontrol syndrome. *Journal of Nervous and Mental Disease, 170*, 680–687.

Fava, M. (1997). Psychopharmacologic treatment of pathologic aggression. *Psychiatric Clinics of North America, 20*(2), 427–451.

Frederiksen, L. W., & Rainwater, N. (1981). Explosive behaviour: A skill development approach to treatment. In R. B. Stuart (Ed.), *Violent behaviour: Social learning approaches to prediction, management and treatment* (pp. 265–288). New York: Brunner/Mazel.

Glenn, M. B., Wroblewski, B., Parziale, J., Levine, L., & Whyte, J. (1989). Lithium carbonate for aggressive behavior or affective instability in ten brain-injured patients. *American Journal of Physical Medicine and Rehabilitation, 68*(5), 221–226.

Harper, M., & Roth, M. (1962). Temporal lobe epilepsy and the phobic anxiety-depersonalisation syndrome. *Comprehensive Psychiatry, 3*, 129–151 & 215–226.

Hooper, R. S., McGregor, J. M., & Nathan, P. W. (1945). Explosive rage following head injury. *Proceeding of the Royal Society of Medicine, 2*, 458–471.

Kaplan, K. (1899). cited by Hooper, R. S, McGregor, J. M., & Nathan, P. W. (1945). Explosive rage following head injury. *Proceeding of the Royal Society of Medicine, 2*, 458–471.

Koch, G., & Allen, J. P. (1987). Untoward effects of generic carbamazepine therapy. *Archives of Neurology, 44*, 578–579.

Kraepelin, E. (1921). *Manic-depressive insanity and paranoia*. Translated by R. M. Barclay; Edited by G. M. Robertson. Edinburgh: E. S. Livingstone.

Letterman, L., & Markowitz, J. S. (1999). Gabapentin: A review of published experience in the treatment of bipolar disorder and other psychiatric conditions. *Pharmacotherapy, 19*(5), 565–572.

Lewin, J., & Sumners, D. (1992). Successful treatment of episodic dyscontrol with carbamazepine. *British Journal of Psychiatry, 161*, 261–262.

Maletzky, B. M. (1973). The episodic dyscontrol syndrome. *Diseases of the Nervous System, 34*(3), 178–185.

Manchester, D., & Wood, R. Ll. (2000). Applying cognitive therapy in neurobehavioural rehabilitation. In R. Ll. Wood & T. M. McMillan (Eds.), *Neurobehavioural disability and social handicap*. Hove, UK: Psychology Press.

Mattes, J. A. (1986). Psychopharmacology of temper outbursts: A review. *Journal of Nervous and Mental Disease, 174*, 464–470.

Mattes, J. A., Rosenberg, J., & Mays, D. (1984). Carbamazepine versus propranolol in patients with uncontrolled rage outbursts: A random assignment study. *Psychopharmacology Bulletin, 20*, 98–100.

Monroe, R. R. (1970). *Episodic behaviour disorders*. Cambridge, MA: Harvard University Press.

Monroe, R. R. (1982). Limbic ictus and atypical psychosis. *Journal of Nervous and Mental Diseases, 170*, 711–716.

Monroe, R. R. (1986). Episodic behaviour disorders and limbic ictus. In B. K. Doane & K. E. Livingstone (Eds.), *The limbic system: Functional organisation and clinical disorders* (pp. 251–266). New York: Raven Press.

Monroe, R. R. (1989). Dyscontrol syndrome: Long-term follow-up. *Comprehensive Psychiatry, 30*(6), 489–497.

Monroe, R. R., & Lion, J. R. (1978). Review of current research. In R. R. Monroe (Ed.), *Brain dysfunction in aggressive criminals* (pp. 105–120). Lexinton, MA: D. C. Heath.

Morikawa, M., Iida, J., Tokuyama, A., Tatsuda, H., Matsumoto, H., & Kishimoto, T. A. (2000). Successful treatment using low-dose carbamazepine for a patient of personality change after mild diffuse brain injury. *Nihon Shinkei Seishin Yakurigaku Zasshi (Japanese Journal of Psychopharmacology), 20*(4), 149–153.

Novaco, R. W. (1975). *Anger control: The development and evaluation of an experimental treatment*. Lexington, MA: D. C. Heath.

O'Neill, H. (1999). *Managing anger*. London: Whurr Publishers.

Penfield, W. (1961). Post-traumatic epilepsy. *Epilepsia, 2*, 109.

Pinel, J. P, Treit, D., & Rovner, L. I. (1977). Temporal lobe aggression in rats. *Science, 197*, 1088–1089.

Pond, D. A. (1957). Psychiatric aspects of epilepsy. *Journal of the Indian Medical Profession, 3*, 1441–1451.

Post, R. M., & Uhde, T. W. (1985). Are the psychotropic effects of carbamazepine in manic-depressive illness mediated through the limbic system? *Psychiatric Journal of the University of Ottawa: Revue de Psychiatrie de l'Universite d'Ottawa, 10*, (4), 205–219.

Sachdeo, R. C., & Belendiuk, G. (1987). Generic versus branded carbamazepine. *Lancet, I* (8547), 1432.

Silver, J. M., & Yudovsky, S. C. (1987). Aggressive behaviour in patients with neuropsychiatric disorders. *Psychiatric Annuls, 17*, 367–370

Silver, J. M., & Yudovsky, S. C. (1994). Aggressive disorders. In J. M. Silver & S. C. Yudofsky (Eds.), *Neuropsychiatry of traumatic brain injury* (pp. 313–353). Washington, DC: American Psychiatric Association.

Stein, G. (1992). Drug treatment of personality disorders. *British Journal of Psychiatry, 161*, 167–184.

Stone, J. L., McDaniel, K. D., Hughes, J. R., & Hermann, B. P. (1986). Episodic dyscontrol disorder and paroxysmal EEG abnormalities: Successful treatment with carbamazepine. *Biological Psychiatry, 21*, (2), 208–212.

Tariot, P. N, Erb, R., Podgorski, C. A., Cox, C., & Patel, S. (1998). The efficacy and tolerability of carbamazepine for agitation and aggression in dementia. *American Journal Psychiatry, 155*, (1), 54–61.

Wood, R. Ll. (1987). *Brain injury rehabilitation: A neurobehavioural approach*. London: Croom Helm.

Wood, R. Ll. (2000). Understanding neurobehavioural disability. In R. Ll. Wood & T. M. McMillan (Eds.), *Neurobehavioural disability and social handicap*. Hove, UK: Psychology Press.

Wood, R. Ll., & Yurdakul, L. K. (1997). Change in relationship status following traumatic brain injury. *Brain Injury, 11*, 491–502.

Wroblewski, B. A., Joseph, A. B., Kupfer, J., & Kalliel, K. (1997). Effectiveness of valproic acid on destructive and aggressive behaviours in patients with acquired brain injury. *Brain Injury*, *11*(1), 37–47.
Young, J. L., & Hillbrand, M. (1994). Carbamazepine lowers aggression: A review. *Bulletin of the American Academy of Psychiatry and the Law*, *22*(1), 53–61.

Intervention with families following brain injury: Evidence-based practice

Michael Oddy and Camilla Herbert

Brain Injury Rehabilitation Trust,
Burgess Hill, West Sussex, UK

The literature on brain injury and the family is examined to provide an evidence base for family intervention. In the absence of methodologically sound studies which evaluate the efficacy of family intervention, current practice should be based on the findings of studies that have investigated how families adapt and the difficulties they face in this process. The implications of this literature should be considered at all stages in the rehabilitation process and in all forms of contact with the family.

INTRODUCTION

There are frequent exhortations in the brain injury rehabilitation literature to include family members in the rehabilitation process and not to neglect their needs. There is a general acceptance that not only is the family a vital ingredient in the rehabilitation process but also that family members are themselves caught up in a particularly traumatic process (Brooks, 1991; Florian, Katz, & Lahav, 1989; Knight, Devereux, & Godfrey, 1998). Despite this recognition there are remarkably few studies evaluating the effectiveness of different types of family intervention. This review will attempt to describe the current evidence base for family intervention following brain injury. Family intervention will be broadly defined as any interaction between family members and rehabilitation professionals.

In most cases, much of the responsibility of caring for the brain injured person during their recovery falls on the family. This begins in the early acute phase of recovery when it is not uncommon for hospital staff to rely on family

Correspondence should be addressed to Michael Oddy, Brain Injury Rehabilitation Trust, 32 Market Place, Burgess Hill, West Sussex RH15 9NP.

http://www.tandf.co.uk/journals/pp/09602011.html   DOI:10.1080/09602010244000345

members to carry out a range of care tasks such as feeding, cognitive stimulation and even behavioural management. For many, particularly with injuries of moderate severity, there may be little or no formal rehabilitation phase. Discharge is from the acute hospital to home with only limited follow up and typically the family takes the primary role in caring for the injured person. Even where there is formal rehabilitation, the family is often asked (and wishes to be) continuously and fully involved. It is not surprising therefore that for many who suffer a brain injury, increasing social isolation occurs both for the individual and for the family itself (Kinsella, Ford, & Moran, 1989; Oddy, Coughlan, Tyerman, & Jenkins, 1985; Thomsen, 1984).

The relevance of family intervention derives from (1) the importance of the family in determining the recovery of the individual with a brain injury, and (2) the distress the family experiences as a consequence of the brain injury. These overlap and interact considerably as the family members' ability to cope emotionally and practically with the changes they experience are likely to have a direct impact on the brain injured person. There are no studies that explore the extent to which families can influence the overall outcome of recovery. There are studies of successful interventions involving family members (e.g., McKinlay & Hickox, 1987) and studies that have shown a correlation between family function and outcome (e.g., Douglas & Spellacy, 1996) but it is not possible to determine the direction of causation from these studies. Nor does research evidence demonstrate that families who make a better emotional adjustment are able to provide a more satisfactory environment for the injured person or even that separation is less likely. Nevertheless, promotion of the well-being of family members is a worthwhile end in itself and it is not unreasonable to hypothesise that there will be positive benefits for the injured family member.

Many studies suggest that families report a lack of information. It is equally clear that families may be given information but as a result of their emotional state they do not necessarily absorb it fully (Jacobs, 1991). There are few reports in the literature of families complaining that they were given too much information or that the information was alarming or unnecessarily depressing. Some families have been given a pessimistic opinion of the chances of survival of their relative in the acute stage. This makes them doubt guarded prognoses of further recovery. The doctors have been wrong once, why not again? Nevertheless it does appear that family members are able to filter out information that they are not ready to accept, and hear only what they can assimilate at that time. For this reason it is important to keep the family well-informed at each stage of the process and not assume that they will already understand the nature of the problems or of the interventions.

Information needs to be given in both written and verbal form. The latter can be tailored to the particular circumstances, and assessments can be made about what type and how much information the family requires. As discussed above the evidence to date suggests clinicians should err on the side of giving too much information rather than too little.

There are of course difficulties in giving specific information tailored to individual circumstances as the accuracy of prediction of outcome is far from precise. Families need to know this, although they may find the resultant lack of certainty confusing. Written information is available in the form of pamphlets from specific brain injury services and voluntary sector organisations such as Headway, and in the form of books such as Powell (1994), Gronwall, Wrightson, and Waddell (1990), and Stoler and Hill (1998).

The sense of the outside world, including extended family, not understanding the problems and difficulties is a common protestation from families (Hubert, 1995; Gosling & Oddy, 1999). A full understanding of their situation is of course impossible to achieve but it is important for the professional to be aware of the type of internal tensions that may exist within families. Perhaps the most commonly encountered tension is that between a spouse or partner and the brain injured person's parents. Commonly the latter live separately from the brain injured person and often do not fully appreciate the situation the spouse/partner is in. While a professional rehabilitation worker also cannot fully appreciate the position of the spouse they do at least have the benefit of two sources of knowledge. One is their knowledge and experience of the effects of brain injury and the other is their experience of having worked with many families who have experienced brain injury. This enables them to anticipate and appreciate problems that arise and can give them credibility in the eyes of close family members. The literature on the impact of brain injury on the family now contains considerable information on the predicament of different family members as well as the common difficulties families encounter (Brooks, 1991; Liss & Willer ,1990; Perlesz, Kinsella, & Crowe, 1999). Cognitive and "personality" changes appear to present greater difficulties to families than physical disabilities. This was suggested by early writers such as Panting and Merry (1972) and Thomsen (1974) and has been consistently substantiated by more systematic studies over the last 30 years (Brooks, 1991; Florian & Katz, 1991; Kreutzer, Gervasio, & Camplair, 1994; Oddy et al., 1985; Rosenbaum & Najenson, 1976).

Professionals also have the advantage of theoretical and conceptual models which provide a means of understanding otherwise baffling phenomena and enable predictions to be made about outcome and intervention. Current theory is stronger in terms of understanding the consequences of brain injury but relatively lacking in terms of understanding the family's response. A recent paper (Perlesz et al., 1999) has called for a more theoretically coherent framework by which to understand family adaptation after brain injury.

CONCEPTUAL MODELS

There are few, if any, fully articulated theories of family adaptation to brain injury. However, there are a number of conceptual frameworks and psychological theories that have some explanatory and predictive power. These are reviewed here and may provide a basis from which theory can be developed.

Denial

An early study of brain injury and the family by Romano (1972) took a psychodynamic approach and emphasised the role of denial. In an informal study of 13 families, Romano found that denial was a common phenomenon. She found that families tend to "fantasise" measurable improvement where none has occurred and to deny changes where these appeared obvious (e.g., "She's always been a messy eater" or "He's always had a bad temper"). Romano concluded that "personality death is an even greater loss than body death". Denial is undoubtedly a factor in the response of many families, probably more common in parents than spouses (Perlesz et al., 1999). It can act as a defence mechanism that enables families to filtrate their distress at a manageable rate. It can also be a long-term strategy that enables a positive attitude to be maintained indefinitely and despite evidence to the contrary (Thomsen, 1984). This will be discussed further in terms of coping theory.

Objective and subjective burden

More formal studies of the family were undertaken in the 1970s, notably by the Glasgow group (Brooks et al., 1986; McKinlay et al., 1981) who used a conceptual approach borrowed from studies of families of those discharged from long-term psychiatric hospitals to the community (Grad & Sainsbury, 1968). This approach describes families as suffering both objective and subjective burdens. Objective burden refers to the measurable severity of the person's disabilities and subjective burden refers to the relative's perception of the extent of their disabilities. In practice most studies that attempt to assess objective burden appear in fact to measure relatives' perceptions of their burden, rather than objective change and this distinction becomes blurred. Many authors are uncomfortable with a concept that implies that the injured person represents a burden on their family. A less value-laden approach is involved in the concepts of stress and distress, although the relationship between "burden", "stress", and "psychological distress" (such as anxiety and depression) is usually not clearly delineated.

Coping

More recently, many studies have employed psychological theories of coping such as the approach adopted by Lazarus and Folkman (1984). Coping theory tries to identify the nature of the differences between those who experience high or low stress in response to similar stressors. Thus it focuses on the personal resources of the family member rather than the injured person's limitations. It attempts to identify means by which families can respond to adverse circumstances in a way that minimises the negative impact. Perlesz et al. (1999) emphasise that not all families are found to be distressed following brain injury.

Lazarus and Folkman (1984) distinguish between problem-focused and emotion-focused coping. Problem-focused coping involves attempts by the individual to deal with stress by acting on the environment or the self. Emotion-focused coping involves a reappraisal of the stressful problem, entailing a change in the perceived meaning of the problem. This model provides a potentially useful framework for analysing the resources available to family members and for identifying who is most vulnerable to stress. It focuses attention on helping family members to find practical ways of problem solving as well as emphasising the role of attributions in the development of stress. This in turn provides a focus for dealing with the longer-term support needs of family members (Jacobs, 1991). There is a need to recognise that for most families the stress is not a single or short-term event but an ongoing set of circumstances. In studies of dementia in the elderly the concept of daily hassles has been used (Kinney & Stephens, 1989). While this has not been widely employed in studies of acquired non-progressive brain injury, it does emphasise the important distinction between stress following a single traumatic life event and continuing, unremitting forms of stress. For families of those who have suffered a brain injury it is not uncommon for both types of stress to be present.

Work with people experiencing chronic stress over which they have no control, such as those living with the after-effects of the disaster at Three Mile Island, suggests that under such conditions, problem-focused coping can be counter-productive and emotion-focused coping more likely to produce better outcomes (Collins, Baum, & Singer, 1983). This is an important factor to consider given the likelihood of a complex pattern of stressors within families following brain injury.

Cognitive adaptation

A variant of the "coping" approach is that of cognitive adaptation or positive coping. This refers to the process of thinking about a problem in such a way as to enhance (1) self-esteem, (2) a feeling of control, and (3) a sense of meaning (Taylor, 1983). It turns concepts such as "denial" or "rationalisation" on their heads and views recognition of the positive benefits that accrue from adverse circumstances as a positive adaptation to stress. Concepts such as "resilience" (McCubbin & McCubbin, 1991) and "salutogenesis" or discovering and learning how best to use one's own resources to meet challenges (Antonovsky, 1993) have been proposed to focus on the positive aspects of how families cope with adversity. For example "cognitive illusions", such as an overly favourable view of the self, an exaggerated sense of one's ability to control environmental events and a naive belief in the brightness of one's future, are seen as helpful and to be encouraged. Such concepts are related to the notion of "depressive realism" (Ackerman & De Rubeis, 1991). Depressive realism is the phenomenon whereby those suffering from depression have been found to make more realistic judgements about their performance or degree of control. Non-depressed people by contrast are shown to have a positive bias in terms of a positive view of themselves, an illusion of control and unrealistic optimism (Alloy & Abramson, 1979; Lewinsohn, Mischel, & Barton, 1980).

Families who appraise negative events in terms of challenge rather than threat, who make active attempts to alter stressful situations, and make constructive use of these illusions, are considered able to weather negative events with their self-esteem and well-being relatively intact. Minnes et al. (2000) found that both reframing and seeking spiritual support helped reduce stress. Koscuilek (1997) suggested that families adapt better if they are able to see the impact of brain injury as both manageable and meaningful. Other researchers have stressed the importance of finding meaning in adversity in family adaptation to learning disability (Turnbull & Turnbull, 1993) and mental illness (Stern et al., 1999). Qualitative work by Willer, Allen, Liss, and Zicht (1991) suggested that taking care not to attribute all family problems to brain injury, developing a realistic but optimistic outlook, maintaining enjoyable activities, and keeping the situation in perspective are successful strategies. Oddy (1995) has suggested that families vary in the extent to which they emphasise the continuities and discontinuities in the personality of the person with the brain injury. Those who perceive continuities more clearly are likely to cope better.

Bereavement and loss

Lezak (1986) presented a bereavement model of family adaptation after brain injury. The proposal is that families have to go through a similar process of accommodation to loss after a brain injury as after a death. Thus a series of stages have to be passed through before the family is able to reorganise itself (Perlesz & McLachlan, 1986). Lezak (1978) has emphasised the particular difficulties of this process when the person is still alive but their personality has changed. She emphasised the predicament of the spouse who is "living in a social limbo, unable to mourn decently, unable to separate or divorce without recrimination and guilt". The uncertainty of the recovery process with advances and setbacks leads to a disrupted grieving process that may last for years. Muir, Rosenthal, and Diehl (1990) have used the term "mobile mourning" to describe this disjointed process. Herbert (1998) explored the concept of unresolved grief with 34 relatives more than a year after brain injury. She found that for a subset of families, particularly those where the injuries were more severe, the identification of the loss and grieving process made sense to the relatives and potentially had a useful therapeutic role.

Family systems

The systems model emphasises the way in which the impact of brain injury reverberates through all members of the family (Minuchin et al., 1975). It draws attention to the notion of role strain and the difficulties inherent in the sudden changes that occur following a brain injury to a family member. Roles and "*sub-system*" boundaries are emphasised, together with related notions such as over-involvement, power struggles, and specific concepts such as "*the parental child*". This refers to a situation where one of the children, normally with the support of one parent, displaces the other parent and performs a pseudo-parental role within the family. This phenomenon is common following brain injury because of the loss of independence of the injured person. Systems theory uses a concept of circular as opposed to linear causality to explain family dynamics which has the effect of diffusing the issue of blame within families. Systems theory can also be helpful in explaining the way ramifications of the difficulties faced by one member may spread through the family in surprising and unexpected ways.

Concepts from systems family therapy such as cohesion and conflict have been applied in studies of brain injury. Frank et al., (1990) found that the increased passivity and dependency often reported following brain injury required families to be more cohesive to manage the greater dependency. Family therapy has been used explicitly to develop methods for resolving conflicts within the relationship patterns of the family system (Rosenthal & Muir, 1983). These authors described using homework assignments for the family to practise outside the sessions to foster generalisation of behaviour change.

INTERVENTION

Intervention with the family requires careful consideration at all stages in the rehabilitation process. In the early stages it involves keeping them informed of the progress of the injured person, what is likely to happen next, and some idea of prognosis. The provision of general information regarding brain injury is also important. Some counselling and emotional support may be required but is seldom available and its efficacy at this stage in recovery is untested. This is certainly the time of greatest anxiety (Oddy, Humphrey, & Uttley, 1978) but may not be a time when family members are most receptive to such assistance. The practical problems which relatives face (travelling to visit, simultaneous care of children, immediate financial pressures, fulfilling the injured person's role as well as their own) should not be underestimated (Gosling & Oddy, 1999).

Families need to be involved in decisions about the injured person's on-going care and rehabilitation. However, few will have any previous experience of brain injury and will require information to enable them to participate in this process.

The transition to a rehabilitation centre is an important stage for families. Many acute hospitals have extended visiting hours and relatives often become used to spending many hours at the bedside on a daily basis. This is less commonly the case in rehabilitation centres, partly because of the longer time-scales involved and the need to allow family members to resume some semblance of a normal life. An exception to this is described by Quine, Pierce, and Lyle (1988) who used relatives as voluntary helpers in an acute rehabilitation programme. However, family members can often feel excluded at this stage when a team of rehabilitation professionals takes over their usual function of caring for their relative. Gosling and Oddy (1999) cite a relative who likened the process to her husband being admitted to a religious sect. Doors were closed, she felt unwelcome and excluded, a strange and unfamiliar language was used and others now appeared "in control" of her husband's destiny. Careful consideration needs to be given to admission procedures to ensure relatives are kept well-informed, aims and objectives are discussed, information about the service is given, and questions are answered. Basic procedures such as receiving the person and their family on admission, proactively making regular contact, inviting close family to reviews, and adequately dealing with their concerns all need to be reliably in place. The brain injured person is much less likely to opt out of rehabilitation if his or her family is supportive of the rehabilitation centre's work.

More specific forms of intervention include educational programmes for families. These may take the form of individual counselling, the provision of written material, or group educational sessions aimed at family members. Kreutzer et al. (1994) suggested that such educational programmes should cover (1) the impact of subtle linguistic and cognitive deficits, (2) consistent and realistic information about behavioural difficulties and their likely impact on the family, and (3) ongoing training in behavioural management. Blosser and De Pompei (1995) have described a process whereby rehabilitation staff help families cope through a process they describe as mentoring.

Family support groups may provide either education and training or emotional support. Such groups may take place while the injured person is in a residential rehabilitation centre or following discharge home. Some such groups are "closed" in the sense that membership is determined at the outset while others are "open" to new members. They may be professionally led or self-help groups and run by other family members. In either case the leader must ensure that one or two members do not dominate, that criticism or negativity is avoided, and that the development of erroneous beliefs and minority views is prevented. In terms of experience it needs to be recognised that an experienced professional has second hand knowledge of a wide range of families in similar circumstances whereas a family member will have or will develop a deeper experience of brain injury but more limited to their own situation. Zarit, Anthony, and Boutselis (1987) found that peer-led groups are more effective than professionals in increasing informal support, whereas Toseland, Rossiter, and Labrecque (1989) found that professional-led groups are more effective than peers in increasing "well-being". Whitehouse and Carey (1991) found that parents continued to attend such a support group for longer than spouses and that families of the less severely brain injured attended for longer. However, there were more parents than spouses attending Whitehouse and Carey's group and this may have been the determining factor. In groups with a majority of spouses it is possible that they would be the more likely to continue. The finding that the families of the more severely brain injured attended for a shorter period may be due to the greater difficulty these relatives have in leaving their relative unattended. The timing of group meetings, their location and frequency needs careful consideration to avoid increasing the pressure on relatives. Whitehouse and Carey also found there was a preference for a semi-structured format to the group with guest speakers attending 25–50% of the time.

There are very few descriptions of the application of a formal family therapy approach following brain injury. There are no studies of the efficacy of this study only a small number of descriptive single case studies. Watzlawick and Coyne (1980) described a problem-focused family therapy approach to a patient with depression following stroke, encouraging his wife to avoid over-protecting him. Maitz and Sachs (1995) emphasised the importance of strengthening the parental sub-systems. This involved helping the non-injured partner to encourage the patient to resume parental responsibilities and to support their partner even if they disagree with the particular approach being taken. Maitz and Sachs (1995) argued that aggressive behaviour should be seen as resulting from a loss of position and power. Intervention needs to address the re-allocation of roles within the family. Solomon and Scherzer (1991) have emphasised the more directive nature of family therapy with this patient group. They offer guidelines for family therapists which include the use of logbooks, memory aids, visible reminders, and the role of routine and structure. Families have been encouraged to look at what is unacceptable behaviour and how they can tackle this.

Behavioural family therapy approaches have also been described. Muir et al. (1990) described "behavioural family training" as the establishment of specific operationalised goals and techniques for teaching family members to more effectively manage the problems presented by traumatic brain injury. The most thoroughly described model of behavioural family training is that of Jacobs (1991). He argued that by emphasising problem-solving techniques and outcomes, rather than processes, the participants take a stronger role in the development of selected interventions and can measure their accomplishments more concretely by the progress they make on specific issues. Jacobs (1989) suggested that the nature of treatment following brain injury may facilitate the development of learned helplessness to the extent that patients and families are repeatedly presented with problems rather than solutions, and "learn" that they have no control over major events that affect their lives. As a result they may become dependent, depressed, and passive. The family training model, with explicit targets and successes, seeks to overcome this sense of powerlessness. Jacobs argued that families can learn the critical skills that can be applied to future problems as they develop, rather than placing the responsibility and control of such processes with the therapist. Sohlberg, Glang, and Todis (1998) described three case studies that support this approach and indicated that successful intervention with caregivers did not need to go beyond recording the frequency of target behaviours. This in itself led to changes in caregiver behaviour which in turn resulted in reduced frequency of the challenging behaviour.

Many studies suggest there is also much to be gained by involving relatives in other aspects of rehabilitation and management, such as the improvement of physical function or increasing independence skills. Apart from the obvious gains to the patient and hence the decrease in dependency, relatives also benefit from having a clear role and feeling that they are contributing in a helpful and constructive fashion. The behavioural approach and other problem-solving approaches encourage relatives to see their efforts as experiments. This avoids disappointment if expectations are too high and goals are not attained (Zarit & Zarit, 1982). Carnevale (1996) describes a "mobile team approach" to helping families to manage challenging behaviour within the home. Of 35 families referred to the service over a 3-year period 11 completed the training pro-gramme and achieved an 82% improvement in target behaviour. However, as the authors acknowledge, this was not a well-controlled study and the positive results may reflect the fact that the service became involved at times of crisis. A more broadly based approach to helping families to provide home-based rehabilitation is described by Pace et al. (1999). In this service a team of profes-sionals provided both training for family members and direct therapy to the brain injured person. It was a condition however, that a family member would be present during the therapy session and would carry out therapists' recom-mendations for programmes and activities at other times. They report on 77 cases who achieved 77% of the rehabilitation goals by discharge. Follow-up data are encouraging in that achievements were generally maintained after

6 and 12 months but only 25 and 11 cases respectively were followed up at these intervals.

One of the less talked about aspects of recovery from brain injury is a difficulty in resuming sexual relationships. Sexual problems are common following brain injury and may require specific intervention (Oddy, 2001). Zasler and Horn (1990) emphasised the importance of a thorough assessment including sexual history, sexual physical examination, and clinical diagnostic testing as a basis for treatment. Price (1985) suggested that it is important for professionals to be aware of the possibility of sexual problems and to initiate discussion on this issue. She proposed that couple counselling is best left to later stages in rehabilitation as people are often extremely anxious following brain injury, particularly after mild or moderate injuries. There is a danger that to focus on the problem at this stage could well increase anxiety rather than reduce it. Setting appropriate goals is essential as it may be necessary to help a couple accept what cannot be changed. Price further suggested that clients should be discouraged as far as possible from adopting a dependent role as this is less sexually desirable. She recommended the use of appropriate strategies to help clients cope with body image and sexual identity problems and suggested that single clients will need more help with dating and general social skills than with sexual function per se. Self-control of inappropriate sexual behaviour should be encouraged by cognitive restructuring.

Elliot and Biever (1996) suggested that sex counselling or therapy is appropriate as long as the client has sufficient cognitive abilities to actively participate. They argued that behavioural sex therapy can help evaluate the current level of functioning for those with organic problems and then help the couple adjust to an altered level of function. Useful guides on sexual matters for people with brain injuries and their families have been provided by Griffiths and Lemburg (1993) and by Simpson (1999).

ASSESSMENT OF FAMILY FUNCTION

A review by Perlesz et al. (1999) concludes that the Family Assessment Device (FAD; Epstein, Baldwin, & Bishop, 1983) is the most commonly used measure of family functioning in brain injury studies. They suggest that the 12-item General Function (GF) subscale can be used as a valid and reliable screening instrument to distinguish between good and poor outcome in families following brain injury. They recommend its use both as a clinical screening instrument and as a research tool.

The Family Cohesion and Family Conflict scales of the Family Environment Scale (FES, Moos & Moos, 1981) have been found to be sensitive to changes in relationships within families seeking therapy after brain injury (Perlesz & McLachlan, 1986).

The Golombok and Rust Inventory of Marital State (GRIMS; Rust, Bennun, Crowe, & Golombok, 1988) has been used with couples following brain injury and found to be sensitive to change. The Golombok and Rust Inventory of Sexual Satisfaction (Rust & Golombok, 1986) is perhaps too intrusive for use with couples not explicitly seeking treatment for sexual dysfunction. However an eight-item version has been shown to be a reliable measure of sexual difficulties with a brain injured population (Gosling & Oddy, 1999).

There are no measures of family functioning specifically designed for families following brain injury in common use although a number have been designed for particular studies.

CONCLUSION

There is no direct evidence concerning the efficacy of intervention approaches with the families of those who have suffered a brain injury. However there is a body of evidence concerning the impact of brain injury on the family and remarkably consistent findings have been obtained in a wide range of studies over the last three decades. These data provide an evidential basis for planning such interventions which should be used in the absence of direct evidence from efficacy studies. Few case studies adopt an experimental approach and there is certainly a need for carefully conducted studies of family intervention utilizing both group and single case designs.

REFERENCES

Ackerman, R., & De Rubeis, R. J. (1991). Is depressive realism real? *Clinical Psychology Review*, *11*, 565–584.

Alloy, L. B., & Abramson, L. Y. (1979). Judgment of contingency in depressed and non-depressed students: Sadder but wiser? *Journal of Experimental Psychology: General*, *108*, 441–485.

Antonovsky, A. (1993). The implications of salutogenesis: An outsider's view. In A. P. Turnbull, J. M. Patterson, & S. Behret (Eds.), *Cognitive coping, families and disability* (pp. 111–122). Baltimore, MD: Paul H. Brookes.

Blosser, J., & De Pompei, R. (1995). Fostering effective family involvement through mentoring. *Journal of Head Trauma Rehabilitation*, *10*(2), 46–56.

Brooks, D. N. (1991). The head-injured family. *Journal of Clinical and Experimental Neuropsychology*, *13*, 155–188.

Brooks, N., Campsie, L., Symington, C., Beattie, A., & McKinlay, W. (1986). The five year outcome of severe blunt head injury: A relatives' view. *Journal of Neurology, Neurosurgery and Psychiatry*, *49*, 764–770.

Carnevale, G. J. (1996). Natural-setting behavior management for individuals with traumatic brain injury: Results of a three-year caregiver training program. *Journal of Head Trauma Rehabilitation*, *11*(1), 27–38.

Collins, D. L., Baum, A., & Singer, J. E. (1983). Coping with chronic stress at Three Mile Island. *Health Psychology*, *2*, 149–166

Douglas, J. M., & Spellacy, F. J. (1996). Indicators of long term family functioning following severe traumatic brain injury in adults. *Brain Injury, 10*(11), 819–839.

Elliott, M. L., & Biever, L. S. (1996). Head injury and sexual dysfunction. *Brain Injury, 10*(10), 703–717.

Epstein, N. B., Baldwin, L. M., & Bishop, D. S. (1983). The McMaster Family Assessment Device. *Journal of Marital and Family Therapy, 9*(2), 171–180.

Florian, V., & Katz, S. (1991). The other victims of traumatic brain injury: Consequences for family members. *Neuropsychology, 5*, 267–280.

Florian, V., Katz, S., & Lahav, V. (1989). Impact of traumatic brain damage on family dynamics and functioning: A review. *Brain Injury, 3*(3), 219–233.

Frank, R. G., Haut, A. E., Smick, M., Haut, M. W., & Chaney, J. M. (1990). Coping and family functions after closed head injury. *Brain Injury, 4*(3), 289–295.

Gosling, J., & Oddy, M. (1999). Rearranged marriages: Marital relationships after head injury. *Brain Injury, 13*(10), 785–796.

Grad, J., & Sainsbury, P. (1968). The effect that patients have on their families in a community and control psychiatric service. A two year follow-up. *British Journal of Psychiatry, 114*, 265–278.

Griffiths, E. R., & Lemberg, S. (1993). *Sexuality and the person with a traumatic brain injury: A guide for families*. Philadelphia: F. A. Davis.

Gronwall, G., Wrightson, P., & Waddell, P. (1990). *Head injury: The facts*. Oxford: Oxford University Press.

Herbert, C. M. (1998). The role of grief in family adaptation following traumatic brain injury. Psychology, unpublished doctoral thesis, University of Sheffield.

Hubert, J. (1995). *Life after head injury*. Aldershot, UK: Avebury.

Jacobs, H. (1989). Long-term family intervention. In D. W. Ellis & A.-L. Christensen (Eds.), *Long term family intervention from neuropsychological treatment after brain injury*. MS: Kluver.

Jacobs, H. (1991). Family and behavioural issues. In J. M. Williams & T. Kay (Eds.), *Head injury: A family matter*. Baltimore: Paul H. Brookes.

Kinney, J. M., & Stephens, M. A. P. (1989). Caregiving Hassles Scale: Assessing the daily hassles of caring for a family member with dementia. *Gerontologist, 29*(3), 328–332.

Kinsella, G., Ford, B., & Moran, C. (1989). Survival of social relationships following head injury. *International Disabilities Studies, 11*, 9–14.

Knight, R. G., Devereux, R. T., & Godfrey, H. P. D. (1998). Caring for a family member with a traumatic brain injury. *Brain Injury, 12*(6), 467–481.

Kosciulek, J. F. (1997). Relationship of family schema to family adaptation to brain injury. *Brain Injury, 11*(11), 821–830.

Kreutzer, J. S., Gervasio, A. H., & Camplair, P. S. (1994). Primary caregiver's psychological status and family functioning after traumatic brain injury. *Brain Injury, 8*(3), 197–210.

Lazarus, R. S., & Folkman, S. (1984). *Stress, appraisal and coping*. New York; Springer.

Lewinsohn, P. M., Mischel, W. C. W., & Barton, R. (1980). Social competence and depression: The role of illusory self-perceptions. *Journal of Social Behavior and Personality, 90*, 213–219.

Lezak, M. D. (1978). Living with the characterologically altered brain injured patient. *Journal of Clinical Psychiatry, 39*(7), 592–598.

Lezak, M. D. (1986). Psychological implications of traumatic brain damage for the patient's family. *Rehabilitation Psychology, 30*, 241–250.

Liss, M., & Willer, B. (1990). Traumatic brain injury and marital relationships: A literature review. *International Journal of Rehabilitation Research, 13*, 309–320.

Maitz, E. A., & Sachs P. R. (1995). Treating families of individuals with traumatic brain injury from a family systems perspective. *Journal of Head Trauma Rehabilitation, 10*(2), 1–11.

McCubbin, M. A., & McCubbin, H. I. (1991). Family stress theory and assessment: The resiliency model of family stress, adjustment and adaptation. In H. I. McCubbin & A. I. Thompson

(Eds.), *Families assessment inventories for research and practice*. Madison, WI: University of Wisconsin.

McKinlay, W. W., Brooks, D. N., Bond, M. R., Martinage, D. P., & Marshall, M. M. (1981). The short-term outcome of severe blunt head injury as reported by relatives of the injured persons. *Journal of Neurology, Neurosurgery, and Psychiatry, 44*, 527–533.

McKinlay, W. W., & Hickox, A. (1987). Family-based rehabilitation after traumatic brain injury. *Journal of Clinical and Experimental Neuropsychology, 9*(3), 276–276.

Minnes, P., Graffi, S., Nolte, M. L., Carlson, P., & Harrick, L. (2000). Coping and stress in Canadian family caregivers of persons with traumatic brain injuries. *Brain Injury, 14*(8), 737–748.

Minuchin, S., Baker, L., Rosman, B. L., Liebman, R., Milman, L., & Todd, T. C. (1975). A conceptual model of psychosomatic illness in children. *Archives of General Psychiatry, 32*(8), 1031–1038.

Moos, R. H., & Moos, B. S. (1981). *Family Environment Scale Manual*. Palo Alto, CA: Consulting Psychologists Press.

Muir, C. A., Rosenthal, M., & Diehl, L. N. (1990). Methods of family intervention. In M. Rosenthal, E. R. Griffith, & C. R. Bond (Eds.), *Rehabilitation of the adult and child with traumatic brain injury* (2nd ed.). Philadelphia: F. A. Davis.

Oddy, M. (1995). He's no longer the same person: How families adjust to personality change after head injury. In N. V. T. A. Chamberlain (Ed.), *Traumatic brain injury rehabilitation*. London: Chapman and Hall.

Oddy, M. (2001). Sexual relationships following brain injury. *Sexual and relationship therapy, 16*(3), 247–259.

Oddy, M., Coughlan, T., Tyerman, A., & Jenkins, D. (1985). Social adjustment after closed head injury: A further follow-up seven years after injury. *Journal of Neurology, Neurosurgery, and Psychiatry, 48*, 564–568.

Oddy, M., Humphrey, M., & Uttley, D. (1978). Stresses upon the relatives of head-injured patients. *British Journal of Psychiatry, 133*, 507–513.

Pace, G. M., Schlund, M. W., Hazard-Haupt, T., Christensen, J. R., Lashno, M., McIver, J., Peterson, K., & Morgan, K. A. (1999). Characteristics and outcomes of a home and community-based neurorehabilitation programme. *Brain Injury, 13*(7), 535–546.

Panting, A., & Merry, P. H. (1972). The long term rehabilitation of severe head injuries with particular reference to the need for social and medical support for the patient's family. *Rehabilitation, 38*, 33–37.

Perlesz, A., Kinsella, G., & Crowe, S. (1999). Impact of traumatic brain injury on the family: A critical review. *Rehabilitation Psychology, 44*(1), 6–35.

Perlesz, A., & McLachlan, D. I. (1986). *Grieving in abeyance: Head injury and family beliefs*. Paper presented at the Parkville Centre, Melbourne, Victoria, Australia.

Powell, T. (1994). *Head injury: A practical guide*. London: Speechmark Publishing Limited.

Price, J. R. (1985). Promoting sexual wellness in head injured patients. *Rehabilitation Nursing, 10*: 12–13.

Quine, S., Pierce, J. P., & Lyle, D. M. (1988). Relatives as lay-therapists for the severely head-injured. *Brain Injury, 2*(2), 139–149.

Romano, M. D. (1972). Family response to traumatic head injury. *Scandinavian Journal of Rehabilitation Medicine, 6*, 1–4.

Rosenthal, M., & Muir, C. A. (1983). Methods of family intervention. In M. Rosenthal, E. R. Griffiths, M. Bond, & J. Miller (Eds.), *Rehabilitation of the Head-Injured Adult* (pp. 407–419). Philadelphia: F. A. Davis.

Rosenbaum, M., & Najenson, T. (1976). Changes in life patterns and symptoms of low mood as reported by wives of severely brain-injured soldiers. *Journal of Consulting and Clinical Psychology, 44*(6), 881–888.

Rust, J., Bennun, I., Crowe, M., & Golombok, S. (1988). *The Golombok Rust Inventory of Marital State*. Windsor, UK: NFER.

Rust, J., & Golombok, S. (1986). *The Golombok Rust Inventory of Sexual Satisfaction*. Windsor, UK: NFER.

Simpson, G. (1999). *You and me: An education program about sex and sexuality after a traumatic brain injury*. Sydney, South Western Sydney Area Health Service.

Sohlberg, M. M., Glang, A., & Todis, B. (1998). Improvement during baseline: Three case studies encouraging collaborative research when giving caregiver training. *Brain Injury, 12*(4), 333–346.

Solomon, C. R., & Scherzer, B. P. (1991). Some guidelines for family therapists working with the traumatically brain injured and their families. *Brain Injury, 5*(3), 253 266.

Stern, S., Doolan, M., Staples, E., Szmukler, G., & Eisler, I. (1999). Disruption and reconstruction: Narrative insights into the experience of family members caring for a relative diagnosed with serious mental illness. *Family Process, 38*, 353–369.

Stoler, D., & Hill, B. A. (1998). *Coping with mild head traumatic brain injury*. New York: Avery.

Taylor, S. E. (1983). Adjustment to threatening events: A theory of cognitive adaptation. *American Psychologist, 38*, 1161–1173.

Thomsen, I. V. (1974). The patient with severe head injury and his family. *Scandinavian Journal of Rehabilitation Medicine, 6*, 180–183.

Thomsen, I. V. (1984). Late outcome of very severe blunt head trauma: A 10–15 year second follow-up. *Journal of Neurology, Neurosurgery and Psychiatry, 47*, 260–268.

Toseland, R. W., Rossiter, C. M., & Labrecque, M. S. (1989). The effectiveness of peer-led and professionally led groups to support family caregivers. *The Gerontologist, 29*(4), 465–471.

Turnbull, A. P., & Turnbull, H. R. (1993). Participatory research in cognitive coping: From concepts to research planning. In A. P. Turnbull, J. M. Patterson, & S. Behret (Eds.), *Cognitive coping, families and disability* (pp. 1–14). Baltimore, MD: Paul H. Brookes Publishing.

Watzlawick, P., & Coyne, J. C. (1980). Depression following stroke: Brief, problem-focused family treatment. *Family Process, 19*(March), 23–18.

Whitehouse, A. M., & Carey, J. L. (1991). Composition and concerns of a support group for families of individuals with brain injury. *Cognitive Rehabilitation* (*November/December*), 26–29.

Willer, B., Allen, K. M., Liss, M., & Zicht, M. S. (1991). Problems and coping strategies of individuals with traumatic brain injury and their spouses. *Archives of Physical Medicine & Rehabilitation, 72*, 460–464.

Zarit, S. H., Anthony, C. R., & Boutselis, M. (1987). Intervention with caregivers of dementia patients: Comparison of two approaches. *Psychology and Aging, 2*(3), 225–232.

Zarit, S. H., & Zarit, J. M. (1982). Families under stress: Interventions for caregivers of senile dementia patients. *Psychotherapy: Theory, Research and Practice, 19*(4), 461–470.

Zasler, N. D., & Horn, L. J. (1990). Rehabilitative management of sexual dysfunction. *Journal of Head Trauma Rehabilitation, 5*(2), 14–24.

Sexual changes associated with traumatic brain injury

Jennie Ponsford

Monash University and Monash-Epworth Rehabilitation Research Centre, Melbourne, Australia

Findings from numerous outcome studies have suggested that people with traumatic brain injuries (TBI) experience relationship difficulties and changes in sexuality. However, there have been few investigations of these problems. This paper reports the results of a study of sexuality following TBI, which aimed to identify changes in sexual behaviour, affect, self-esteem, and relationship quality, and their inter-relationships. Two hundred and eight participants with moderate-to-severe TBI (69% males) completed a questionnaire 1–5 years post-injury. Their responses were compared with those of 150 controls, matched for age, gender, and education. Of TBI participants 36–54% reported: (1) A decrease in the importance of sexuality, opportunities, and frequency of engaging in sexual activities; (2) reduced sex drive; (3) a decline in their ability to give their partner sexual satisfaction and to engage in sexual intercourse; and (4) decreased enjoyment of sexual activity and ability to stay aroused and to climax. The frequencies of such negative changes were significantly higher than those reported by controls and far outweighed the frequency of increases on these dimensions. A significant proportion of TBI participants also reported decreased self-confidence, sex appeal, higher levels of depression, and decreased communication levels and relationship quality with their sexual partner. Factors associated with sexual problems in the TBI group are explored and implications of all findings discussed.

INTRODUCTION

Sexuality in brain injury is a topic that has received relatively limited professional investigation relative to many other aspects of brain injury, despite the fact that sexual problems can cause significant distress. There are numerous

Correspondence should be addressed to Associate Professor Jennie Ponsford, Dept of Psychology, Bethesda Rehabilitation Centre, Epworth Hospital, 30 Erin Street, Richmond, Victoria, 3121, Australia. Fax: 61 3 94268742, Email: jennie.ponsford@med.monash.edu.au

This research was funded by a grant from the Transport Accident Commission of Victoria.

http://www.tandf.co.uk/journals/pp/09602011.html　　　DOI:10.1080/09602010244000363

definitions of sexuality. One that seems most appropriate in this context is that of Thorn-Gray and Kern (1983), who defined sex as "the verbal, visual, tactual and olfactory communication which expresses love and intimacy between two people" (p. 142).

Traumatic brain injuries occur predominantly in the 15–25 age group (Anderson & McLaurin, 1980; NHIF, 1984; Health Department of Victoria, 1991). The development of independence, a social network, sexuality, and formation of intimate relationships are major developmental tasks to be achieved during these years (Fryer, 1989). Findings from numerous outcome studies have shown that people with moderate to severe traumatic brain injuries (TBI) have significant difficulties in forming and maintaining relationships, due to changes in cognition, behaviour, and personality (Dikmen, Ross, Machamer, & Temkin; 1995; Oddy, Coughlan, Tyerman, & Jenkins, 1985; Ponsford, Olver, & Curran, 1995a; Tate et al., 1989). It has also become evident that there are changes in sexuality following TBI. Such changes potentially have a very significant impact upon the lives of these young people. However, sexual issues or problems tend not to be adequately investigated or addressed during the rehabilitation process. As Miller (1994, p. 19) has noted, "Professionals frequently ignore, avoid, or quite innocently overlook the sexual needs of their patients until they begin to exhibit "sexually inappropriate behaviour".

Human sexuality encompasses biological, physical, cultural, and psycho-social dimensions of personality and behaviour. TBI may disturb any or all of these dimensions. At a physical level, problems may include hypersexuality, or at the other end of the spectrum, reduced desire, ejaculatory dysfunction, anorgasmia, reduced sensation, or poor lubrication (Horn & Zasler, 1990). Although it is difficult to localise lesions, it is well known that TBI frequently causes damage to limbic structures, including the hippocampus, septal complex, amygdala, and hypothalamus, as well as the thalamus, cingulum, and frontal lobes—all of which have been shown to be involved, either directly, or via hormonal mechanisms, in the regulation of sexual responses (Horn & Zasler, 1990). Changes in motor control or sensation or pain may further inter-fere with the ability to engage in or take pleasure from sexual activity.

There are also secondary factors that may affect sexuality. Changes in body image, sexual identity and self-esteem, depression, and anxiety are well-documented consequences of TBI (Ducharme & Gill, 1990; Tyerman & Humphrey, 1984). Impaired cognitive function, including impaired behav-ioural control, communication, social judgement, and egocentricity can further affect capacity for interpersonal relationships (Ponsford, Sloan, & Snow, 1995b). Furthermore, significant others may experience feelings of depression, loneliness, anger and guilt in dealing with the cognitive, behavioural and physical changes in their spouse, with a consequent loss of affection and interest in sexual activity and general decline in relationship quality (Garden,

Bontke, & Hoffman, 1990). These changes have been comprehensively documented in numerous follow-up studies (Bond, 1976; Oddy, Humphrey, & Uttley, 1978; Ponsford et al., 1995a; Rosenbaum & Najenson, 1976; Weddell, Oddy, & Jenkins, 1980).

The person with TBI and his or her family depend upon rehabilitation professionals for assessment, guidance, education and support in dealing with sexual problems. Unfortunately, due to the multi-faceted nature of TBI and the reluctance of some staff members to deal with sexual problems, sexuality rehabilitation has made slow progress. There is a lack of consensus as to the specific impact TBI has on the sexuality of the patient and family. Some authors maintain that TBI results in disinhibition or hypersexuality (Miller, 1994), while others report that patients commonly suffer loss of libido or hyposexuality (Zasler & Horn, 1990; Garden et al., 1990).

Relatively few detailed studies of the frequency, nature and causes of sexual difficulties have been conducted. Moreover studies have tended to measure differing constructs, some evaluating the effect on the spouse, some on the patient, from either a physical or a psychosocial perspective. Of those studies focusing on TBI individuals themselves, Meyer (1971, cited by Sandel, Williams, Dellapietra, & Derogatis, 1996) surveyed 100 male survivors of TBI and found that 71% reported reduction of erection, and that erectile functioning was related to location and severity of injury. Kosteljanetz et al. (1981) studied a sample of 19 males with coma of up to 15-minute duration, but post-concussive symptoms lasting more than 6 months. A little over half reported decreased sex drive and/or erectile dysfunction. Kreutzer and Zasler (1989) studied a selected sample of 21 males, an average of 16.2 (SD = 14.1) months post-injury. Five were single and 16 married, and all reported sexual activity in the past 3 months. More than half (57%) reported a decrease in sex drive, a diminished ability to maintain an erection, and more than a third reported a decreased ability to achieve orgasm. Diminished frequency of sexual inter-course was reported by 62%. More than half reported decreased self-confidence and sex appeal and increased depression. On the other hand the quality of marital relationships was preserved, although 38% rated communi-cation as worse. All of these studies focused only on males and it is not clear how the samples were derived.

Sandel et al., (1996) investigated 52 out-patients with TBI, including 13 females, with a mean PTA duration of 54 days, an average of 3.7 years post-injury (range = 2 months–12 years). They found significant sexual dysfunc-tion, as measured on the Orgasm and Drive/Desire subscales of the Derogatis Interview of Sexual Function (DISF), relative to normative data, but not on other subscales. Time since injury was inversely related to reports of levels of sexual arousal.

The largest previous study conducted to date has been that of Kreuter et al. (1998). They studied 92 TBI individuals (65 men) 1–20 years post-injury, 53%

of whom had a stable partner. Forty percent reported a decreased ability to experience orgasm, 47% a decreased frequency of sexual intercourse, and 16% had low sexual interest. Reduced self-esteem, anxiety and depression were also identified in a significant proportion of participants. Level of disability was more strongly associated with sexual adjustment than was duration of post-traumatic amnesia.

All but the last two of these previous studies have focused only on males, ignoring the fact that a third of those sustaining TBI are female. Sample sizes have also been relatively small. However, above all, none of these studies has included a demographically matched control group, thereby making the assumption that all changes in sexual function reported were the result of the traumatic brain injury. Clearly, many people experience changes in their sexual function, desire, self-esteem, and relationships in the absence of a traumatic injury.

A study of sexuality following TBI has been conducted by the Monash–Epworth Rehabilitation Research Centre. The cross-sectional study, which has taken the perspective of the injured person, has aimed:

1. To identify changes in sexual function/behaviour following TBI, relative to a demographically matched control group.
2. To examine changes in affect, self-esteem, and relationship quality, relative to a demographically matched control group.
3. To examine the interrelationships between these and other factors.
4. To document participants' perceptions of the factors contributing to these changes.

METHOD

Participants

Participants with moderate to very severe TBI were recruited from the Bethesda Head Injury Rehabilitation Programme of Epworth Hospital. All patients treated in this programme are routinely invited to attend a follow-up clinic at 1, 2, 3, and 5 years post-injury. At the time of their attendance, they were asked if they were willing to participate in the project. It is therefore important to note that participants did not present because they were experiencing any particular difficulty. On average, 65% of those invited to the clinic attend at any time.

To date, a total of 208 individuals with moderate to severe TBI have completed the sexuality questionnaire, 143 (69%) of whom were males. They had an average age of 33.6 years (SD = 15.4, range = 14–79); 42% were aged 14–25 years, 22% 26–35, 15% 36–45, 8% 46–55, 12% 56–65 and only 2% > 65 years; 56% had never married. The mean PTA duration of participants was 29.3 days (SD = 31.4, range = 1–180 days); 23% had a PTA < 7 days, 43%

7–28 days and 34% > 28 days. There were no significant differences between those who participated in the study and those who did not in terms of gender, marital status or PTA duration. Those participating were slightly older, mean age = 33.6 years, SD = 15.4 vs. mean age for non-participants = 31.2, SD = 15.6; $z(1579) = -2.5, p < .01$. In the group participating there were somewhat fewer aged < 25 (42% vs. 51%) and somewhat more participants aged 56–65 years (12% vs. 5%, χ^2 (5) = 19.2, $p < .002$. Twenty-seven percent of participants were seen at one year post-injury, 45% at two or three years, and 28% at five years. Sixty-nine percent were taking no medication, 9% were taking medication for depression, 5% for epilepsy, 4% for headache, 5% for muscular pain, and 8% for other purposes.

The responses of this group were compared with those of a group of 150 controls, of similar age, gender and educational background, recruited from the general community. They had no history of previous head injury, neurological or psychiatric disturbance. The control group comprised 97 males (65%), with a mean age of 33.4 years (SD = 14.9, range = 15–76), and an average of 11.9 years of education (SD = 2.3, range = 7–19 years). Forty-eight percent had never married. There were no significant differences between the two groups in terms of age, gender, years of education, or marital status.

Measures and procedures

Hospital ethics approval was obtained before starting the study. At the time of attendance at the follow-up clinic, TBI patients were asked if they would be willing to participate in the project. A full, written explanation of the study was given to them. They were warned that some questions asked would be quite explicit, and it was made clear they were under no obligation to complete the questionnaires. Those who agreed to participate in the study signed a consent form.

TBI participants completed the Sexuality Questionaire. This questionnaire was adapted from those used by Kreuter et al. (1998) and Kreutzer and Zasler (1989), using language appropriate to both males and females. It covered perceived changes in the importance of sexuality, opportunities to engage in sex, sex drive, frequency of sexual activity, ability to give one's partner sexual satisfaction, ability to engage in sexual activity, enjoyment of sexual activity, ability to become aroused and to climax, self-confidence, sex appeal, level of depression, level of preoccupation with problems, and quality of communication and relationship with sexual partner/s. Changes were documented on a five-point scale: 1 = greatly decreased, 2 = decreased, 3 = same, 4 = increased, 5 = greatly increased. The scale also required the person to document reasons for the changes, as they saw them, choosing one or more from numerous alternatives.

The Hospital Anxiety and Depression Scale (HADS; Snaith & Zigmund, 1994) was also administered as an objective measure of anxiety and depression. Ponsford et al. (1999) found these scales to be sensitive to anxiety and depression following TBI. A score greater than 8 is said to be indicative of clinically significant anxiety and/or depression.

Controls also completed the Sexuality Questionnaire and the Hospital Anxiety and Depression Scales. On the Sexuality Questionnaire they were asked to compare their current state on each of the dimensions with how they had been one year previously.

Data analysis

Where the data were not normally distributed, non-parametric univariate analysis (Mann-Whitney U) was used for univariate comparisons. T tests were used for all other comparisons. Chi-square analysis was used for analyses involving categorical variables. Pearson's correlation coefficient was used to examine the relationship between sexuality scores and other variables. An alpha level of .05 was used.

RESULTS

Seventy-eight percent of TBI individuals said they were in a sexual relationship prior to their injury, versus 73% of controls, and 50% said they were in a relationship now, versus 60% of controls. This difference was not statistically significant. Seventy-nine percent said they had opportunities to engage in sexual activities with themselves or others, versus 80% of controls.

Overall, there was a far greater tendency for TBI individuals to report a decrease in the frequency and quality of their sexual experiences, relative to controls. TBI participants obtained significantly lower scores on the sexuality scale, indicating an overall decrease in quality on most variables, whereas most controls indicated no change, TBI mean = 24.3, SD = 10.3, control mean = 29.9, SD = 7.7, $t(270) = -5.2, p < .0001$. Thirty-seven percent of TBI individuals scored more than one standard deviation below the control mean, versus 14% of controls. Internal consistency of the sexuality scale, determined by Cronbach's alpha, was .92.

Pie graphs depicting the proportion of each group who reported an increase, decrease or no change for each of the domains are set out in Figure 1. Thirty-six percent of TBI individuals indicated that the importance of sexuality had decreased since their injury (vs. 15% of controls), and 39% said they had fewer opportunities to engage in sexual activities. Forty-one percent said their sex drive had decreased, and 54% said the frequency of engaging in sexual activities had decreased. Thirty-nine percent said their ability to give their partner sexual satisfaction had decreased. Thirty-eight percent reported a decreased

TBI   Control

Greatly Decreased
Decreased
Same
Increased
Greatly Increased

Importance
p<.0001

Opportunity
p<.002

Drive
p<.0001

Frequency
p<.01

Satisfaction
p<.0001

Engage
p<.0001

Enjoy
p<.0001

Arouse
p<.0001

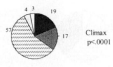

Climax
p<.0001

Figure 1. Sexual behaviour.

281

ability to engage in sexual intercourse, and 38% reported less enjoyment of sexual activity. Forty percent reported a decreased ability to stay aroused, and 36% a decreased ability to climax. The frequency of such reported decreases was significantly higher than those reported by the controls ($p < .01$ in all cases), as is depicted in Figure 1. A small percentage of TBI participants, generally 10% or less, indicated an increase on each of these dimensions, but that proportion was generally no different from the proportion of increases reported by the control group.

Results obtained for questions relating to affect and self-esteem are set out in Figure 2. These questions revealed that 52% of TBI individuals had decreased self-confidence since the injury, 47% felt their sex appeal had decreased, 42% reported higher levels of depression, and 45% reported an increased preoccupation with problems. These figures are all significantly higher than those seen in the control groups.

From Figure 3 it can be seen that 29% of TBI participants reported a decreased ability to communicate verbally with their partner, and 36% a decrease in the quality of their relationship with their sexual partner compared

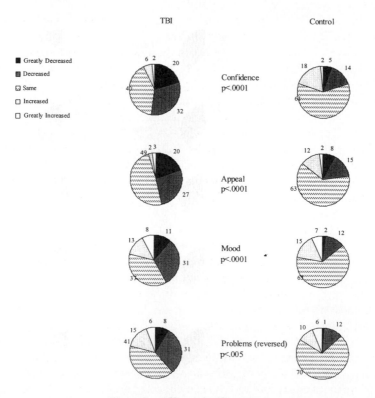

Figure 2.   Affect and self-esteem.

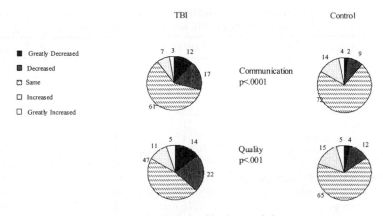

Figure 3. Relationship characteristics

with pre-injury. Again, these proportions were significantly higher than in controls, whereas reports of increases on these dimensions were reported to a similar or lesser degree than in controls.

When asked about the reasons for changes in their sexual behaviour/ enjoyment, 47% indicated fatigue was a contributing factor. Although 24% of controls also felt this to be the case, the proportion of TBI participants reporting this to be a problem was significantly higher. Decreased mobility was a factor for 31% of TBI individuals and only 2% of controls. Pain and loss or decrease in sensitivity were contributing factors in 22 and 19% of TBI cases respectively, and again very few controls. Low self-confidence and difficulties communicating were identified as contributing factors in 31% and 21% of cases. Feeling unattractive (23% vs. 12%), arousal/sex drive problems (17% vs. 10%), and having limited access to intimate social contact (19% vs. 10%) were also factors. These problems were also reported by controls, albeit to a lesser extent. Behaviour problems were also identified by 15% of TBI individuals and only 2% of controls (Table 1).

Table 2 sets out the correlations between scores on the sexuality scale and injury severity as measured by PTA duration, gender, age and time post-injury. There were no significant correlations between scores on the sexuality scale and PTA duration or gender. Time since injury did not appear to have a significant influence on scores. There was a very modest, but statistically significant correlation between sexuality scores and age, those aged < 25 being least likely to report decreases on any of the dimensions of sexuality. There was a progressive decline in scores, reflecting a decrease in the quality and frequency of sexual experiences with increasing age, the lowest scores being recorded for those aged 46–55 years, with a rise again for the small number of participants over 55 years of age (Figure 4). As can be seen from Figure 4, this pattern was not evident to the same degree in controls.

TABLE 1
Reasons for change in TBI and control individuals

Reasons for change	TBI %	Control %	χ^2	p value
Tiredness/fatigue	47	24	18.7	.0001
Decreased mobility	31	2	47.8	.0001
Low confidence	31	13	15.7	.0001
Feeling unattractive	23	12	6.4	.01
Pain	22	7	15.4	.0001
Difficulties in communicating	21	4	19.9	.0001
Loss or decrease in sensitivity	19	2	22.7	.0001
Decline in relationship	19	9	7.2	.01
Limited access to intimate social contact	19	10	6.1	.013
Arousal/sex drive problems	17	10	3.6	.06
Behaviour problems	15	2	16.6	.0001

TABLE 2
Relationship between total sexuality scores and age,
PTA, gender, and time post-injury

	Total sexuality score	
Variables	r	p value
PTA	+.079	.41
Age	−.266	.002
Gender	−.122	.24
Time post-injury	−.025	.69

PTA = post-traumatic amnesia.

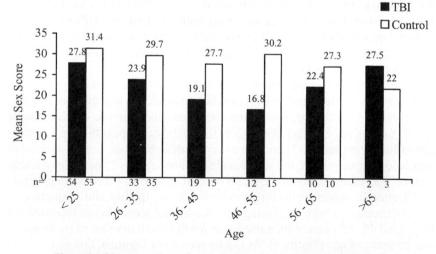

Figure 4.   Mean sexuality scale score by age group for TBI vs. control groups.

284

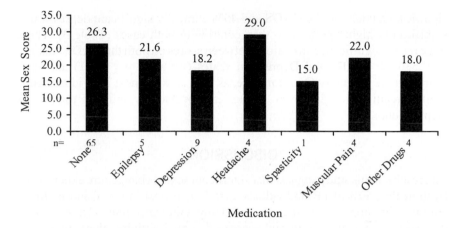

Figure 5.   Sexuality scale scores according to medication.

There was a significant, but very modest association between use of medication and sexual change reported ($r = -.28$, $p < .05$). There was a tendency for those taking medication to obtain lower scores and report more negative changes, the difference being statistically significant, mean sexuality score for no medication group = 26.3, SD = 8.6, vs. medication group mean score = 20.7, SD = 9.3, $t(90) = 2.79$, $p < .006$. An examination of sexuality scores in relation to medication being taken, as shown in Figure 5, revealed that those taking antidepressant medication obtained consistently lower scores. Those taking antispasticity medication also recorded low scores, but there were very few of these participants, and this may have been due to the extent of their physical disability.

Mean scores obtained by TBI participants and controls on the HADS are set out in Table 3. TBI participants exhibited significantly higher levels of anxiety and depression than controls. Of those with TBI, 56% exhibited clinically

TABLE 3
Results obtained by TBI participants and controls
on the Hospital Anxiety and Depression Scales (HADS)

| HADS | TBI | | | Control | | | | | |
	Mean	SD	Range	Mean	SD	Range	t	p value	χ^2
Anxiety	84	4.6	0–19	5.9	4.1	0–15	4.0	.0001	
Depression	6.9	4.9	0–21	3.2	3.2	0–14	7.1	.0001	
% Clinically significant									
Anxiety	56			29				.0001	15.8
Depression	45			9				.0001	31.4

significant anxiety on the HADS and 45% clinically significant depression, a significantly higher proportion than controls in both cases (Table 3). There were highly significant correlations between scores on both the HADS Anxiety ($r = .536$, $p < .0001$) and Depression scales ($r = .623$, $p < .0001$) and total scores on the Sexuality Questionnaire, as well as with most individual items, with correlations ranging from $-.26$ to $-.56$ for Anxiety and $-.35$ to $-.60$ for Depression.

DISCUSSION

The results of this study suggest that significant sexual changes are experienced by more than 50% of TBI individuals up to 5 years post-injury. Contrary to the common assumption on the part of many clinicians that TBI results in decreased sexual inhibition and increased sexual activity, there was a far greater tendency for TBI individuals to report a decrease in the frequency and quality of their sexual experiences. Only a small group of less than 15% reported increases on any of the dimensions of sexual performance, self-confidence, and sex-appeal. While acknowledging that there certainly is a sub-group of very severely injured individuals for whom this does occur, in the present study these proportions were generally equal to or less than those changes reported by controls relative to a year ago. Twenty-one percent of the TBI group reported improved mood and less preoccupation with problems, a similar proportion to that of the control group.

These findings are consistent with those of previous studies by Meyer (1971), Kosteljanetz et al. (1981), Kreutzer & Zasler (1989), Sandel et al. (1996), and Kreuter et al. (1998), all of which document decreases in both sexual function and desire following TBI, as well as a decline in affect and self-esteem. The use of a large and demographically similar control group in the present study considerably strengthens this finding, indicating that the changes do appear to be attributable to the injury in some way.

Participants attributed these changes to a variety of factors of both a physical and a psychological nature. Fatigue was clearly the most significant contributing factor for both TBI participants and controls, but it was reported with twice the frequency in the TBI group. The impact of fatigue on many aspects of the injured person's lifestyle appears to be immense. Other physical factors such as decreased mobility, pain, and loss or decrease in sensitivity were significant contributors for up to one third of TBI participants. These physical factors may potentially be investigated further with a view to their alleviation.

Reduced self-confidence, worsening mood, greater preoccupation with problems, and difficulties communicating were present for almost half of the TBI sample studied. About a third of the group attributed the decline in the quality of their sexual experiences to these factors. There were also significant associations between the presence of anxiety and depression, as measured objectively on the HADS, and scores on most items from the sexuality questionnaire. Those taking antidepressants were more likely to report a decline in their sexuality, although it was not clear whether this was due to the presence of depression or the medication itself. Otherwise, medication did not appear to have a significant impact on sexuality.

There was no significant association between sexuality scores and injury severity, as measured by PTA duration, gender or time post-injury. There was a significant age effect, those aged 46–55 reporting the greatest decreases in quality and frequency of their sexual experiences, a decline that was not evident in the control group.

It would appear, therefore, that sexual changes are attributable to numerous causes of a physical and psychological nature, which interact in a complex fashion, and are always going to be very difficult to disentangle, perhaps reflecting the diffuse and variable nature of traumatic brain injuries themselves. In this respect, this study has raised as many questions as it has answered. Indeed without objective measures of sexual functioning, it may never be possible to answer many of these questions. Although these TBI participants were acknowledging many sexual changes, there is also a need to study the perspectives of their sexual partners, who may have a different viewpoint. A separate study of this nature is currently under way.

What seems to be most important, given the frequency of these changes, is that assessing and addressing sexual issues becomes a routine part of the assessment and rehabilitation process. These are not easy issues for clients to raise. All rehabilitation staff need not only to be aware of the importance of sexuality, but also to be willing to talk with their clients about it. It is also essential that they have ready access to a designated health professional, ideally but not necessarily within the team, who has specialist therapeutic skills to address these complex issues, as well as an understanding of the impact of the injured person's cognitive impairments. Creating an atmosphere of openness and a protocol for addressing sexual issues is an important part of rehabilitation programme development. As Blackerby (1990) and Simpson (2001) have pointed out, this process should include the development of a philosophical consensus regarding approaches to sexuality in this context, clear guidelines for assessment and treatment of sexual concerns and who will undertake these, in both the short and the long-term, and provision of information resources and education for staff, clients and their partners or families. The "*You and Me*" programme, developed by Simpson (1999) represents one very good example of such a resource.

All potential causes of sexual difficulties need to be investigated and addressed, beginning with a full physical work-up along the lines of the GRASP (General Rehabilitation Assessment Sexuality Profile) developed by Zasler and Horn (1990). In some ways these physical aspects are more readily addressed, especially during the rehabilitation phase. Issues of self-esteem,

depression, communication and the quality of relationships are equally important at this stage, but tend to become more significant later on, after the injured
person has been discharged from rehabilitation. Active steps should be taken to
keep the lines of communication open to deal with these issues over a longer
time-frame—to encourage these young and not-so young people to seek help as
problems arise.

There is no doubt that a proportion of those injured at a young age lack the
social skills and self-confidence to initiate contact with and form relationships
with the opposite sex. The development and evaluation of methods of assessing
and re-training these skills is one of the greatest challenges to be faced in
improving many aspects of psychosocial outcome following TBI. However, it
is those in middle age who appear to be most affected, perhaps because they
already had established sexual relationships prior to injury, or because they are
more willing to admit to changes, or perhaps they are more susceptible to the
impact of fatigue. Potential causes for this do warrant more detailed investigation. The present study will continue longitudinally. This will provide the
opportunity to examine changes in aspects of sexuality in the same individual
over time. Of particular interest would be how and whether satisfaction with
and frequency of sexual behaviour change in response to the changing demands
of work and childrearing, and how this relates to those changes seen in the
general population. If nothing else, it is to be hoped that this study will
encourage clinicians to ask their clients how things are going sexually—this is
the most important first step.

REFERENCES

Anderson, D. W., & McLaurin, R. L. (Eds.) (1980). Report on the national head and spinal cord
    injury survey. *Journal of Neurosurgery, 53* (Supplement).
Blackerby, W. F. (1990). A treatment model for sexuality disturbance following brain injury.
    Journal of Head Trauma Rehabilitation, 5, 73–82.
Bond, M. (1976). Assessment of the psychosocial outcome of severe head injury. *Acta
    Neurochirurgica, 34,* 57–70.
Dikmen, S., Ross, B. L., Machamer, J. E., & Temkin, N. R. (1995). One year psychosocial outcome in
    head injury. *Journal of the International Neuropsychological Society, 1,* 67–77.
Ducharme, S., & Gill, K. M. (1990). Sexual values, training and professional roles. *Journal of Head
    Trauma Rehabilitation, 5*(2), 38–45.
Fryer, J. (1989). Adolescent community integration. In P. Bach-y-Rita (Ed.), *Traumatic brain
    injury* (pp. 255–286). New York: Demos Publications.
Garden, F. H., Bontke, C. F., & Hoffmann, M. (1990). Sexual functioning and marital adjustment after
    traumatic brain injury. *Journal of Head Trauma Rehabilitation, 5*(2), 52–59.
Health Department of Victoria, Community Services Victoria and Transport Accident Commission
    (1991). *Report of Head Injury Impact Study.* Melbourne: Health Department of Victoria.
Horn, L. J., & Zasler, N. D. (1990). Neuroanatomy and neurophysiology of sexual function. *Journal of
    Head Trauma Rehabilitation, 5(2),* 1–13.

Kosteljanetz, M., Jensen, T. S., Norgard, B., Lunde, I., Jensen, P. B., & Johnson, S. G. (1981). Sexual and hypothalamic dysfunction in the postconcussional syndrome. *Acta Neurologica Scandinavica, 63*, 169–180.

Kreuter, M., Dahllof, A.-G., Gudjonsson, G., Sullivan, M., & Siosteen, A. (1998). Sexual adjustment and its predictors after traumatic brain injury. *Brain Injury, 12*, 349–368.

Kreutzer, J. S., & Zasler, N. D. (1989). Psychosexual consequences of traumatic brain injury: Methodology and preliminary findings. *Brain Injury, 3*, 177–186.

Meyer, J. (1971). Sexual disturbances after cerebral injuries. *Journal of Neurovisceral Relations* (Suppl. X), 519–523.

Miller, L. (1994). Sex and the brain-injured patient: Regaining love, pleasure and intimacy. *Journal of Cognitive Rehabilitation, May/June*, 12–20.

NHIF (1984). *The silent epidemic*. Framingham, MS: National Head Injury Foundation.

Olver, J. H., Ponsford, J. L, & Curran, C. A. (1996). Outcome following traumatic brain injury: A comparison between 2 and 5 years after injury. *Brain Injury, 10*(11), 841–848.

Oddy, M., Coughlan, T., Tyerman, A., & Jenkins, D. (1985). Social adjustment after closed head injury: A further follow-up seven years after injury. *Journal of Neurology, Neurosurgery, and Psychiatry, 48*, 564–568.

Oddy, M., Humphrey, M., & Uttley, D. (1978). Subjective impairment and social recovery after closed head injury. *Journal of Neurology, Neurosurgery, and Psychiatry, 41*, 611–616.

Ponsford, J. L., Olver, J. H., & Curran, C. (1995a). A profile of outcome two years following traumatic brain injury. *Brain Injury, 9*, 1–10.

Ponsford, J., Olver, J., Nelms, R., Curran, C., & Ponsford, M. (1999). Outcome measurement in an inpatient and outpatient traumatic brain injury rehabilitation programme. *Neuropsychological Rehabilitation, 9*(3/4), 517–534.

Ponsford, J., Sloan, S., & Snow, P. (1995b). *Traumatic brain injury: Rehabilitation for everyday adaptive living*. Hove, UK: Lawrence Erlbaum Associates.

Rosenbaum, M., & Najenson, T. (1976). Changes in life patterns and symptoms of low mood as reported by wives of severely brain-injured soldiers. *Journal of Consulting and Clinical Psychology, 44*, 881–888.

Sandel, M. E., Williams, K. S., Dellapietra, L., & Derogatis, L. R. (1996). Sexual functioning following traumatic brain injury. *Brain Injury, 10*(10), 719–728.

Simpson, G. K. (1999). *You and me. An education program about sex and sexuality after traumatic brain injury*. Sydney: Brain Injury Rehabilitation Unit.

Simpson, G. K. (2001). Addressing the sexual concerns of persons with traumatic brain injury in rehabilitation settings: A framework for action. *Brain Impairment, 2*(2), 97–108.

Snaith, R. P., & Zigmond, A. S. (1994). *Hospital Anxiety and Depression Scale*. Windsor, UK: NFER-Nelson.

Tate, R. L., Lulham, J. M., Broe, G. A., Strettles, B., & Pfaff, A. (1989). Psychosocial outcome for the survivors of severe blunt head injury: The results from a consecutive series of 100 patients. *Journal of Neurology, Neurosurgery, and Psychiatry, 52*, 117–126.

Thorn-Gray, B., & Kern, L. (1983). Sexual dysfunction associated with physical disability: A treatment guide for the rehabilitation practitioner. *Rehabilitation Literature, 44*, 138–144.

Tyerman, A., & Humphrey, M. (1984). Changes in self-concept following severe head injury. *International Journal of Rehabilitation Research, 7*, 11–23.

Weddell, R., Oddy, M., & Jenkins, D. (1980). Social adjustment after rehabilitation: a 2-year follow-up of patients with severe head injury. *Psychological Medicine, 10*, 257–263.

Zasler, N. D., & Horn, L. J. (1990). Rehabilitative management of sexual dysfunction. *Journal of Head Trauma Rehabilitation, 5*(2), 14–25.

NEUROPSYCHOLOGICAL REHABILITATION, 2003, *13* (1/2), 291–306

Psychological adjustment, social enablement and community integration following acquired brain injury

Philip J. Yates

Mardon Neuro-Rehabilitation Centre, Exeter, UK
and University of Exeter, UK

Understanding and facilitating the process of psychological adjustment to acquired disability arising from brain injury continues to pose a considerable challenge to rehabilitation professionals. This paper reviews the literature on psychological adjustment to acquired disability and chronic health conditions as they may be applied to acquired brain injury. It is proposed that services are developed that address the psychosocial issues faced by survivors of brain injury. Case illustrations are provided that demonstrate a process of adjustment and integration towards participation in meaningful roles within the community.

There has been an extensive and growing interest over several decades in the psychosocial issues and processes related to adaptation or adjustment to acquired disability and chronic illness (Dunn, 2000). Attempts have been made to understand these from a variety of theoretical perspectives. This has resulted in theories, models and approaches being applied to psychosocial treatments and interventions to assist the individual or family in managing the change process following a sudden alteration in health status. More recently these perspectives have been applied in the field of brain injury rehabilitation, reflecting its increasing status as a major health issue internationally. This paper argues that community rehabilitation programmes utilising a bio-psycho-social model have a significant potential for improving psychosocial functioning and social role outcomes for brain injury survivors.

Community-based approaches to brain injury rehabilitation incorporate interventions that equate with the three dimensions inherent within the World Health Organisation *International Classification of Functioning* (WHO ICF,

Correspondence should be addressed to Philip Yates, Mardon Neuro-Rehabilitation Centre, Wonford Road, Exeter, Devon, EX2 4UD, UK.

© 2003 Psychology Press Ltd
http://www.tandf.co.uk/journals/pp/09602011.html   DOI:10.1080/09602010244000408

2001) (impairment—functional ability—participation potential). Neurological impairments can be realised in damage to brain structures that directly affect the ability of the individual to function independently within a social context. Recently these aspects have begun to emerge in the literature. For instance, Wilson (2002) has argued for the need to negotiate cognitive rehabilitation goals that address the various needs related to impairments, levels of activity, and participation. The importance of addressing the interaction of cognitive impairment with emotional dysfunction and the consequences for social functioning is addressed by Williams, Evans, and Fleminger (this issue) and Williams (2002). With regard to process and outcomes the concept of *empowerment* has emerged as a critical concept in the fields of mental health and disability (Fenton & Hughes, 1989). There are three common elements to definitions of empowerment: (1) perceived and actual power, including having choice and control; (2) a process involving "self in community", or community integration; and (3) access to valued resources such as material comforts and education (Nelson, Lord, & Ochoka, 2001). Neath and Shriner (1998) take a similar view of empowerment and stress the need to embed any understanding of the concept within a social context. Hence they convey three forms of power. The medical model of rehabilitation and disability has influenced an individualised notion of empowering people utilising counselling, psychological therapy, and psychiatry. This is referred to as *personal power* or the power of the individual to influence his or her environment. This is the most frequently addressed form in empowerment studies. A second from of power is *power over*, or hierarchical or authoritarian social power (for instance, the power of the medical profession or the state). The third form is *power with*, a form of social power where people come together as equals. This is prevalent in friendships, political groups, and self-help groups. Neath and Shriner relate these forms of power to people with disabilities within the workplace. However, they can also be applied to the functioning of the individual within the general community, and are located within the *participation* dimension of the proposed WHO ICF system (2001). The notion of empowerment as a key psychological construct that incorporates self-efficacy, participation and collaboration, sense of control, meeting personal needs, understanding the environment, personal action, and access to resources is articulated by Dempsey and Foreman (1997). This paper addresses the extent to which these concepts might be utilised alongside other process and outcome variables of adjustment within the WHO ICF and community rehabilitation frameworks.

INDIVIDUAL ADJUSTMENT AND ADAPTATION

In the literature the terms "adaptation", "adjustment", "acceptance", and "coping" are often used synonymously. The idea of "acceptance" or coming to terms with acquired disability can be traced back at least 70 years (Vasch,

1981). Wright (1960) addressed the concept of adjustment to disability in terms of it reflecting the interaction between a person's value system, level of emotional maturity and acceptance of self, and mental health status. Other constructs utilised in formulating her theory of adjustment to disability include the role of pre- and postmorbid self-concept, psychodynamic character defences disrupted by disability, a mourning type reaction to loss, group identification influencing the liking of others, and other social processes involved in the labelling of disabled people. This multi-factorial perspective includes a range of psychological, social psychological and social aspects that have contemporary relevance for the brain injury literature.

The theoretical interest in emotional reactions to disability was influenced further by the work of Kubler-Ross (1969) on death and dying. This led to acquired disability being viewed as a form loss for which a grieving response process occurred (Lindemann, 1981; Parkes, 1975). Horowitz (1982) conceived of a series of normal and pathological stress responses to illness, injury or loss. The normal phasic response includes outcry, denial, intrusion, working through, and completion or going on with life. The pathological responses include being overwhelmed, panic or exhaustion, extreme avoidance, flooded states, psychosomatic responses, and character distortions. These models are often referred to as *stage models* or *mental health models.* The empirical basis for such models has been questioned by Oliver (1981).

The concept of adjustment to chronic illness was reformulated by Moos and Tsu (1977) and Moos and Schaefer (1984) as the acquistion and use of different types of coping skills. This implied a more active role for the individual as opposed to the passive emotional response processes implied in stage models of adjustment. A coping process model in relation to brain injury and quality of life outcomes received attention from Moore and Stambrook (1995). Here the role of cognitive moderators such as attributional style, locus of control, and coping style are seen as influential in shaping the individual's cognitive belief system. This model also explicitly acknowledges the interaction between cognitive deficits and cognitive beliefs, and individual and family life-cycle factors. Other moderating factors extraneous to the individual are noted to affect the adjustment process, such as education, social network, cultural, financial and vocational factors, stigma, barriers, and resources. However, these are regarded as "beyond the control of the rehabilitation team" (p. 110). This model is important in delineating the coping process following brain injury and in determining the role of cognitive beliefs in influencing psychosocial outcomes. It does not explicitly address the context within which coping occurs and how social factors can be influenced to affect outcome.

Central to the coping models are cognitive components that are seen to influence the individual's behaviour in response to the illness, and determine the extent to which the individual adapts or maladapts. This basic tenet is manifest in *social cognition models* developed within the field of health psychology. For instance, Nerenz and Leventhal (1983) proposed a self-regulation theory of chronic illness. They argue that patients' mental representation of their illness, their coping style, and appraisal of their coping change according to the situation. The illness representations relates to the self-system in three ways: (1) it can be total (the self is the disease); (2) it is encapsulated (it is part of the self); or (3) the self faces constant outbursts of illness threat (acute symptoms). These three aspects interact with environmental factors to influence the mental representation of the illness. The model is dynamic as the appraisal components allow for a feedback loop to promote self-regulation and an alteration or maintenance of coping style. Other social cognition perspectives include the health belief model, risk perception theory, self-efficacy theory, the theory of planned behaviour, and the theory of reasoned action. These are reviewed in Baum et al. (1997). These perspectives have been developed in an attempt to further the understanding of individual differences in response to acute and chronic illness and acquired disabilities. Their relevance to the field of neurological rehabilitation has been recently explored by Curran, Ponsford, and Crowe (2000); Earll, Johnston, & Mitchell (1993); Herrmann, Curio, and Petz (2000); Johnston (1996); Martelli, Zasler, & MacMillan (1998); and Moore and Stambrook (1995).

SOCIAL THEORIES AND ADJUSTMENT

In contrast to these psychosocial perspectives there has been a developing critique of such formulations from exponents of sociocultural theory contributing to a *social model of disability* (Low, 1993; Oliver, 1990). This perspective is rarely referred to in the psychological literature but is associated with the views of people with disabilities and user-led organisations. Oliver (1989) has suggested that definitions of disability are relative rather than absolute. Thus the concept of disability can be viewed as a social construction. In this perspective the role of ideology is seen as important in shaping individual and social meanings of particular physical and mental impairments, public policy definitions, and ultimately the creation of social and psychological dependency. This contrasts with the purported *medical model of disability* where disability is equated with illness, with specialist health interventions provided in dedicated settings.

Chinnery (1990) describes the personal experience of a "process of being disabled" in both traditional rehabilitation and social contexts, with direct consequences for his well-being. Here it is argued that able-bodist attitudes, policies, practices and procedures dominate health, social and educational services to an unacceptable extent. In relating his own experience of acquired neurological disability he describes the reaction to the onset of disability as one of feeling "inferior" as he falls victim to his own premorbid value system and associated able-bodied prejudices. This provokes emotional reactions of anger and sadness, loss of confidence, and anxiety as being enhanced by social factors including environmental barriers and the emotional reactions of others. Such reactions include professionals feeling over-responsible for the disabled person, fulfilling a need to care and be kind, and denying the anger felt by the person with a disability: ". . . for the great majority of the victims of the process of being disabled, depression, anxiety, boredom, loneliness, anomie, alienation and a whole range of other self-destructive feelings characterise existence. Dependence, unemployment, isolation, segregation, relative poverty, ignominy and a whole range of other socially unacceptable states are the cause of these feelings . . ." (Chinnery, 1990, p. 48).

According to individual accounts many of the psychological states that disabled people may suffer from may be the product of being discriminated against and being made to feel inadequate, disillusioned, and unable to do anything about it (Marinelli & del Orto, 1984). Some psychologists might attribute such reactions to a process of "learnt helplessness" (Seligman, 1975), whereas Morris (1991) has characterised them as symptomatic of "internalised oppression".

ADJUSTMENT AND DISABLEMENT

A distinction between pathology, individual function and social context is made in the *International Classification of Impairments, Disabilities and Handicaps* (ICIDH) proposed by the World Health Organisation (WHO, 1980). Here disease or disorder gives rise to "*impairment*" which is a disturbance at the level of body organ. The consequences of impairment are realised at the level of the person in terms of functional performance. This is referred to as "*disability*". Impairment or disability can result in "*handicap*"—the social disadvantage that occurs in respect of individual's interaction with and adaptation to their surroundings. The key social roles affected that are regarded as the most disadvantageous are orientation, physical independence, mobility, occupation, social integration, and economic self-sufficiency.

Johnston (1996) criticised the WHO model for assuming that disability is the direct result of impairment. She cited research that did not support disease/impairment patterns of disability, nor different patterns of disability for different impairments. This research was used to suggest that disability is a behaviour and is shaped by environmental circumstance, coping and mental representations. Using the self-regulation theory, and in particular the theory of planned behaviour, she showed how mental representations and behavioural intention, or coping behaviour, may mediate between impairment and observed disability in a neurological rehabilitation setting.

This approach to conceptualising a psychological contribution to the WHO model provoked a critical debate on several grounds. Johnston's formulation was regarded by some as being located within an *individual model of disability*, therefore placing responsibility for disability upon the individual and implying a "victim blaming" perspective (Marks & Ungar, 1996). The social cognition formulation was viewed as removed from the social and relational environment in which the individual is ultimately required to function. Furthermore, Johnston's work has been described as "able-bodyist" in that it presumes that disabled people's lifestyles are deviant from able-bodied lifestyles. For example, "those who cannot get out of bed (an able-bodied aid to sleeping) have a worse level of disability. . ." (Finklestein, 1996, p. 342). However, Dodds (1996) argues that both the psychological (cognitive, behavioural, and emotional aspects), and those related to the concerns of disability studies (the social, environmental, cultural, and political aspects) need to be accounted for in an integrated form when considering the process of adjustment.

The concept of "normality" inherent in the WHO classification model has been the subject of increasing criticism. In reviewing reactions to the ICIDH, Pfeiffer (1998) notes that the language and paradigm of this system have been felt to be patronising and devaluing to disabled people. The reactions of the disability community in the United States led to the system not being adopted by the Center for Disease Control and Prevention and the US Public Health Service. The mounting criticisms have led to a revised system, the ICIDH-2, being proposed and this is presently awaiting final ratification. Currently it is referred to as the *International Classification of Functioning, Disability and Health* (ICF) (World Health Organisation, 2001). This incorporates new terms: *health condition* (disorder and disease) leading to either *impairment* (as previously defined under ICIDH-1), *activity* (the nature and extent of functioning at the level of the person), and *participation* (the nature and extent of a person's involvement in life situations).

In spite of the existence of the ICIDH, and its more recent revision, there have been very few attempts to relate the model to brain injury to measure outcome and analyse the critical components of disablement. Martelli, Zasler, and MacMillan (1998) have argued that the importance of understanding the variables mediating the relationship between impairments, disability and handicap cannot be underestimated when considering the potential for assessment and treatment interventions in relation to acquired brain injury. This approach has been particularly utilised in the quality of life (QOL) research. In a study of 758 brain injury survivors, Heinemann and Whiteneck (1996) demonstrated that enhanced life satisfaction is contingent upon a reduction in handicap and remediation of disability. Steadman-Pare et al. (2001) studied 275 individuals 8 to 24 years post moderate to severe brain injury and found that perceived mental health, self-rated health, gender, participation in work and leisure, and the availability of social and emotional support were significantly associated with QOL. Perceived mental health was the strongest predictor of perceived QOL after brain injury. Brown and Vandergoot (1998) examined QOL ratings as a function of brain injury severity. Those with mild severity had lower QOL ratings when compared with those with more severe brain injury. Also brain injury survivors had a greater range of unmet needs when compared to spinal injuries and non-disabled groups. The areas most affected were work, socialising, close friends, significant other, parenting, learning, and expressing self.

These QOL studies all concluded that there is a distinct lack of appropriate support available to address the long-term needs of this population. The results suggest that it may take years for individuals to re-engage in meaningful and functional life roles. These studies also demonstrate the potential for using QOL variables as rehabilitation outcome measures. The studies did not include measures related to the social environment including environmental barriers, social policies and attitudes influencing integration, and ongoing service contact. Two of the studies did not include measures of social support. These aspects are commonly neglected in the brain injury research to date, but remain critical factors that may affect the psychosocial adjustment process.

COMMUNITY INTEGRATION AND ENABLEMENT

An implication of the quality of life studies is that variables related to the handicap/social participation construct within the ICIDH/ICF WHO models can be critically important outcome measures from both client/service user and rehabilitation professional perspectives. The social model of disability promotes social inclusion for people with disabilities. This includes community integration and participation in valued social roles. There is now a growing recognition in the field of brain injury rehabilitation that a community-based approach is necessary for securing some of the positive outcomes that the research is now identifying (Morton & Wehman, 1995; Oddy & McMillan, 2001; Rowlands, 2002; Tyerman, 1997; Wall, Rosenthal, & Niemczura, 1998).

McColl et al. (1998) combined findings from both quantitative and qualitative studies to define community integration as "having something to do; somewhere to live; and someone to love". The key domains are therefore characterised as independent living, occupation, and social support. However, the process of reintegrating into the community following a traumatic brain injury has been described as a significantly stressful event requiring considerable adjustment (Karlovits and McColl, 1999) causing disruption in finances, employment, and personal relationships among others. Karlovitz and McColl studied 11 mostly male adults with severe brain injury on reintegration into the community. The participants identified nine stressors associated with reintegration: orientation, transportation, living situation, loss of independence, relationships, loneliness, routine, problems with studying, and work. With regard to coping, problem-focused strategies were most frequently used including avoiding, doing things differently, getting involved, and reaching out.

CASE ILLUSTRATION 1

RA is a 28-year-old female who sustained a severe traumatic brain injury at the age of 12 years. She continues to live with her parents. Her behaviour was described on referral to clinical psychology as withdrawn and she was socially isolated and she remained seizure prone despite high levels of anticonvulsant medication. Extensive investigations over several years supported the view that the seizures were non-clinical yet she remained on the medication. Her parents were in conflict over her management approach, her father favouring a more structured push towards independence, and her mother being more protective in respect of her social involvement. Neither parent was amenable to counselling about these issues. They did, however agree to meet with the team at two monthly intervals to discuss progress. The team comprised a clinical psychologist, occupational therapist, a community enabler and her manager, and a care manager, together with RA and her parents. A community enabler with substantial experience of working with brain injury survivors was allocated for 12 hours per week initially to meet with RA and slowly facilitate her social confidence ultimately away from the home. Over 9 months MT reached the position where she had explored supported employment options, developed regular leisure interests, including swimming, and independent shopping and had begun to state that she would like to think about leaving home and perhaps having her own flat. She wanted to make the decision as to when her reviews would be held and who should be present. Her depressive mood state was replaced with an increasingly more assertive and self-determined outlook. Her medication was reduced. During this initial period the enabler was supported by an occupational therapist and psychologist monthly in order to help her address cognitive, emotional, and behavioural issues within the functional social context. However, her mother became increasingly resistant to her ongoing enabling contact and it was thought she influenced RA's perspective on it. The package broke down after 18 months and the family, including RA, refused further contact.

This case demonstrates the challenge of community integration and the need to work with both individuals and families simultaneously to maximise outcomes and ensure sustained consistent intervention and support. There is considerable evidence that neither individuals who have acquired a brain injury nor their primary caregivers cope effectively with community integration without considerable support (Finset, Dyrnes, Krogstad, & Berstad, 1995; Rosenthal & Ricker, 2000). RA was experiencing considerable social isolation with consequent loss of self-esteem. In terms of McColl et al.'s (1998) formulation she had no personal relationships outside of the home (no one to love), she had no purpose (nothing to do), and felt she no longer needed to live with her parents (thus needing somewhere to live). The integration process was very difficult for her to sustain and had twice broken down over 15 years with significant psychosocial consequences. The QOL studies cited earlier support the issue in this case that she required considerable independent support over a long period (several years) to achieve her social and occupational independence, but she then would have required support to maintain her gains once they had been achieved or perhaps to develop them further.

Relatively few community-based approaches to brain injury rehabilitation have been outlined to date outside of residential or in-patient programmes for brain injured individuals. McMillan and Oddy (2001) note that community-based outreach services will have to be inherently flexible and based on local needs and geographical aspects. This point is acknowledged by Willer and Corrigan (1994) who describe a "Whatever it takes" (WIT) model for community-based services. This model focuses on empowering the individual through maximising self-determination. Ten core principles are described which include: recognising the need for organising services around the individual; teaching skills in the environment in which they are to be applied; manipulating the environment to assist with community integration; focusing upon life roles; facilitating enduring natural support mechanisms; working to prevent the individual from becoming "fragmentised" by service systems; promoting informed choice, respect and rights for the individual; and for services to recognise the long-term or lifelong needs of individuals with brain injury. Similarly, McCluskey (2000) has noted the important and unexpected roles that paid attendant carers hold in assisting people with brain injury in the community. These included the roles of attendant (practical help with daily tasks and routines), protector (both encouraging risk to promote learning and confidence, and minimising risk to prevent harm or abuse), friend (confidant, someone in whom the individual can trust, social contact), coach (facilitating skill development), and negotiator (mediator, advocate, and assisting in the regulation of appropriate behaviour). The training implications of such roles are considerable. However, the potential for trained individuals to enable people to reintegrate into the community is promising. The general role crosses the traditional divide between service agencies and different professional groups, allowing for a more co-ordinated approach to people with brain injuries.

CASE ILLUSTRATION 2

AB is a 40-year-old male, married with two children aged 15 and 13 years. He was diagnosed with a left frontal arterio-venous malformation, frontal lobe syndrome, and secondary epilepsy. He displayed personality change (aggression, tearfulness, and childlike behaviour) short-term memory problems, poor fluency, impaired sequencing, daytime fatigue, slurred speech and poor balance. On assessment his IQ was in the borderline range. He was found to be short-tempered, had a reduced stress tolerance, suffered from insomnia, had money management problems and his fits deteriorated over time. He had become depressed and was expressing increasing suicidal ideation. The marital relationship was mutually supportive but deteriorating significantly.

This resulted in neurology, psychiatry, clinical psychology, occupational therapy (OT) care manager and community enabling input being provided by consistent personnel over a 2-year period and reviewed every 3 to 6 months. His medication was reviewed. The clinical psychologist developed three roles: (1) fortnightly counselling sessions with a couples counselling session every two to three months—this role involved written summaries for AB and helped him to make sense of his frustrations; (2) to provide supervision on the under-standing and management of cognitive and behavioural aspects of his presentation for the enabler including anger management, attentional skills, memory strategies, confidence-building, and emotional regulation; and (3) continued case planning with the OT care manager, identifying stressors and planning preventative or risk-minimisation strategies. The OT care manager purchased a community enabler for 3 days a week to assist AB with purposeful activity throughout the week. This included attending weight reduction programmes, developing DIY skills and applying them at home, organising money and financial management, facilitating socialising, developing computer skills, and respite. Respite was built in for one week four times a year. AB chose to go away fishing with his enabler on these occasions and felt that it was only during these breaks that he truly relaxed. The enabler also functioned as a chosen advocate for AB at professional meetings and reviews. These activities and supports were pre-planned and built into his weekly and yearly calendars to provide structure and expectation to his daily routines. The outcomes were viewed by AB as very satisfactory. He continued to develop his interests and his stability was maintained with an 80% reduction in seizures and an improved mood state with no further depression and increased social activity.

AB's case highlights the frequency, intensity and structured nature of input required in the community setting for individuals whose neuropsychological status has widespread social consequences. One of the important features of this case was the need for the psychologist and enabler to work closely together. The roles identified by McCluskey (2000) were adopted by the community enabler who required support, training and supervision to carry them out consistently and appropriately. The principles of the WIT model (Willer & Corrigan, 1994) are appropriate in this case where creative approaches by a team organised around individual choice and need, crossing service bound-aries, over the long-term, in a collaborative relationship with the client could make a difference.

ENABLEMENT AND WORK

Perhaps the area that has received the most attention in the literature with regard to supporting the individual in the community post-traumatic brain injury is that of vocational rehabilitation. The outcomes related to enabling people with severe brain injury to develop work roles and thereby influence improved QOL self-ratings up to nine years post-injury are documented by O'Neill et al. (1998). Skord and Miranti (1994) point out that the literature supports an integrated approach towards job placement and supported employment for individuals with brain injuries and premorbid disadvantages. These involve addressing the individual's cognitive, psychosocial and physical functioning in the community within which they work. The primary methods involve advocacy and the development of occupational skills: Finding the participant a job; doing the job with them; doing things for employers and co-workers essential to job retention addressing other aspects that also affect job retention, e.g., transport, money management, and housing. Other roles may involve collecting information in order to enable the individual to make informed choices. Skord and Miranti stress that in their experience training all intra-disciplinary staff in basic advocacy and support services, including job placement, increases service effectiveness. They also argue for training in basic counselling skills, cognitive rehabilitation techniques and psychotherapeutic techniques for these staff. The range of treatment-training topics and themes that are included in these programmes are not fundamentally different from those carried out in in-patient brain injury rehabilitation units. The difference is that gains are maximised by learning and experience in the applied (work) environment. The encouraging outcomes from employment rehabilitation programmes that utilise a supportive or place-train model are reviewed by Wehman, West, and Fry (1989).

ENABLING TECHNOLOGIES

The ability of individuals post-injury to control their environment has received substantial attention in the field of medical rehabilitation. The use of environmental control systems (ECSs) that assist an individual to communicate, raise an alarm, operate intercom systems or light switches, home entertainment systems, heating appliances, page turn, open curtains, etc., has proliferated over the past 40 years. These have been reviewed by Carter (1997) and evaluated on a general population of people with disabilities by Harmer and Bakheit (1999). Harmer and Bakheit noted that the perceived benefits reported by users of ECSs were increased independence, increased feelings of self-worth and happiness, an increased feeling of control over the environment, and improved emotional state of informal carers. The role of ECSs in assisting people who have sustained more severe brain injuries such as those who may be "locked in" is compelling. However, their effectiveness has not received much attention in the literature. The potential for ECSs has been challenged on several grounds including the potential to reduce opportunities for social contact (Campbell, 1994), increase social isolation (Johnson & Moxon, 1998), and for focusing too much on individual deficit to the exclusion of the work environment where social barriers such as attitudes, the physical environment and technical barriers should receive much more attention (Roulstone, 1998). The field of cognitive rehabilitation utilises technological devices such as pagers, alarms, personal organisers, palm top computers, etc., to enable greater cognitive independence. For a review of these initiatives and their effectiveness for brain injury survivors see Wilson, Emslie, Quirk, and Evans (2001), and Evans, Wilson, Needham, and Brentnall (in press).

THE ENABLING ENVIRONMENT

The fields of rehabilitation psychology, social psychology and community psychology share the premise that both personal and situational factors have profound effects upon behaviour. Dunn (2000) notes that these disciplines owe much to the work of Lewin (1935) who expressed the idea that behaviour is a function of both person and the environment/situation in terms of the equation $B = f(P,E)$. Dunn notes that environmental constraints, for example a building's architecture, are more influential as behavioural constraints than are most disabilities. Therefore when considering enabling within a community context the issues noted by Moore and Stambrook (1995) as being "beyond the control of the rehabilitation team" may become crucial variables for manipulation if integration, adjustment and coping are to be properly facilitated. These may include education, social networks, cultural (or sub-cultural) issues, financial aspects, occupation, stigma, the physical environment, resources, and legal barriers. Underlying the difficulties people with disabilities face in these areas is the issue of attitudes of others in the community and how those shape and reinforce barriers or the opportunities that exist for integration. Dunn makes the point that research on attitudes and attitude change has generally targeted issues of acceptance and prejudice reduction, but has ignored ways to promote co-operation, interdependence, and mutual respect. Similar and more far-reaching processes are also noted by Campbell and Oliver (1996) when considering the criteria for evaluating the success of the social movement of disabled people. They argue that social change towards social inclusion should be measured in terms of: new political or economic changes; specific legislation; changes in public opinion and behaviour; the creation of new organisations or institutions; empowerment, consciousness raising, and education; internationalism; and human rights, civil rights, and citizenship. Psychologists have not as yet embraced the challenge posed in relation to change in many of these areas even if they can be accounted for in theoretical terms. However, if community-based rehabilitation is a future direction for brain injury services then these issues will impinge more so upon the individual survivor, as well as the team, and influence both process and outcome.

The literature reviewed in this paper has demonstrated the relatively recent consideration given by psychologists to social context in brain injury rehabilitation, and the potential for significant psychosocial gains to be made by focusing on applied context and the manipulation of environmental variables. The psychological literature has considered adjustment in terms of cognitive and emotional processes often to the exclusion of social context. In this sense the models have been too intrinsic. No study has related coping style to a particular context. Research in this area could form a very fruitful line of enquiry with implications for the reformulation of goal setting in rehabilitation. The emergence of qualitative methodologies and their relevance to health psychology (see Chamberlain, Stephens, & Lyons, 1997; Rowlands, 2002) holds promise for furthering our understanding of the "social meanings" related to the experience of brain injury, and can assist with the development of interventions. These methodologies are argued to be critical in assisting psychology to address the integration of the social, psychological and biological (Spicer & Chamberlain, 1996) and the constructs proposed by the World Health Organisation ICF model. Very recent work utilising quantitative and qualitative methodologies has occurred to develop coping theory, social theory, quality of life formulations, and community enabling interventions. These perspectives are able to contribute to an integrated community perspective on brain injury rehabilitation. The challenge for rehabilitation professionals in the field of brain injury is to now apply the substantial knowledge on psychological aspects of impairment and functioning following acquired brain injury to the environment in which the individual chooses to live and participate. The proposed WHO ICF (2001) classification system offers a useful bio-psycho-social framework to facilitate goal setting, outcome measurement, and service planning. The concept of "empowerment", particularly the elements of "personal power" and "power with" (Neath & Shriner, 1998) could be helpful in shaping community enabling interventions as part of a sustained long-term rehabilitation approach that recognises the flexibility and roles advocated by McCluskey (2000) and Willer and Corrigan (1994). The potential net gains of such an approach are compelling and may include a range of outcomes such as a reduction in mood disorders, increased social support networks, improved social relationships, physical and psychologically accessible environments, and meaningful vocation. There is currently an increasing trend towards the development of community-based brain injury services but the literature has yet to reflect this.

REFERENCES

Baum, A., Newman, S., Weinman, J., West, R., & McManus, C. (Eds.) (1997). *Cambridge handbook of psychology, health and medicine*. Cambridge University Press.

Brown, M., & Vandergoot, D. (1998). Quality of life for *individuals* with traumatic brain injury: comparison with others living in the community. *Journal of Head Trauma Rehabilitation*, *13(4)*, 1–23.

Campbell, J. (1994). Equipped for independence or self-determination? *British Journal of Occupational Therapy*, *3*, 89–90.

Campbell, J., & Oliver, M. (1996). *Disability politics*. London & New York: Routledge.

Carter, J. (1997). Environmental control systems for people with severe disabilities. *British Journal of Therapy and Rehabilitation*, *4*(12), 646–653.

Chamberlain, K., Stephens, C., & Lyons, A. C. (1997). Encompassing experience: meanings and methods in health psychology. *Psychology and Health*, *12*, 691–709.

Chinnery, B. (1990). The process of being disabled. *Practice*, *4*(1), 43–48.

Curran, C. A., Ponsford, J. L., & Crowe, S. (2000). Coping strategies and emotional outcome following traumatic brain injury: A comparison with orthopedic paients. *Journal of Head Trauma Rehabilitation*, *15*(6), 1256–1274.

Dempsey, I., & Foreman, P. (1997). Towards a clarification of empowerment as an outcome of disability service provision. *International Journal of Disability, Development and Education*, *44(4)*, 287–303.

Dodds, A. (1996). Letters. *The Psychologist, November*, 391.

Dunn, D. S. (2000). Social psychological issues in disability. In R. G. Frank & T. R. Elliott (Eds.), *Handbook of rehabilitation psychology*. Washington, DC: American Psychological Association.

Earll, L., Johnston, M., & Mitchell, E. (1993). Coping with motor neurone disease: an analysis using self-regulation theory. *Palliative Medicine*, *7*, 21–30.

Evans, J. J., Wilson, B. A., Needham, P., & Brentnall, S. (in press). Who makes good use of memory aids: Results of a survey of 100 people with acquired brain injury. *Journal of the International Neuropsychological Society*.

Fenton, M., & Hughes, P. (1989). *Passivity to empowerment*. London: Royal Association for Disability and Rehabilitation.

Finklestein, V. (1996). Letters. *The Psychologist, August*, 342.

Finset, A., Dyrnes, S., Krogstad, J. M., & Berstad, J. (1995). Self-reported social networks and interpersonal support 2 years after severe traumatic brain injury. *Brain Injury*, *9*(2), 141–150.

Harmer, J., & Bakheit, A. M. O. (1999). The benefits of environmental control systems as perceived by disabled users and their carers. *British Journal of Occupational Therapy*, *62*(9), 394–398.

Heinemann, A. W., & Whiteneck, G. G. (1996). Relationships among impairment, disability, handicap, and life satisfaction in persons with traumatic brain injury. *Journal of Head Trauma Rehabilitation*, *10*(4), 54–63.

Herrmann, M., Curio, N., & Petz, T. (2000). Coping with illness after brain diseases—a comparison between patients with malignant brain tumours, stroke, Parkinson's disease and traumatic brain injury. *Disability and Rehabilitation*, *22*(12), 539–546.

Horowitz, M. J. (1982). Stress response syndromes and their treatment. In L. Goldberger & S. Breznitz (Eds.), *Handbook of stress: Theoretical and clinical aspects*. New York: Free Press.

Johnson, L., & Moxon, E. (1998) In whose service? Technology, care and disabled people: The case for a disability politics perspective. *Disability and Society*, *13*(2), 241–258.

Johnston, M. (1996). Models of disability. *The Psychologist, May*, 205–210.

Karlovits, T., & McColl, M. A. (1999). Coping with community integration after severe brain injury a description of stresses and coping strategies. *Brain Injury*, *13*(11), 845–862.

Kubler-Ross, E. (1969). *On death and dying*. New York: Macmillan.

Lewin, K. A. (1935). *A dynamic theory of personality*. New York: McGraw-Hill.

Lindemann, J. E. (1981). *Psychological and behavioural aspects of physical disability*. New York: Plenum Press.

Low, C. (1993). The social model of disability. *Rehabilitation Network*, Winter, 5–7.

Marinelli, E., & del Orto, A. (1984). *The psychological and social impact of physical disability*. New York: Springer.

Marks, D., & Ungar, S. (1996). Putting disability into context. *The Psychologist*, July, 295.

Martelli, M. F., Zasler, N. D., & MacMillan, P. (1998). Mediating the relationship between injury, impairment and disability: A vulnerability, stress and coping model of adaptation following brain injury. *NeuroRehabilitation, 11*, 51–66.

McCluskey, A. (2000). Paid attendant carers hold important and unexpected roles which contribute to the lives of people with brain injury. *Brain Injury, 14*(11), 943–958.

McColl, M. A., Carlson, P., Johnston, J., Minnes, P., Shue, K., Davies, D., & Karlovitz, T. (1998). The definition of community integration: perspectives of people with brain injuries. *Brain Injury, 12*(1), 15–30.

McMillan, T. M., & Oddy, M. (2001). Service provision for social disability and handicap after acquired brain injury. In R. Ll. Wood & T. M. McMillan (Eds.), *Neurobehavioural disability and social handicap following traumatic brain injury*. Hove, UK: Psychology Press.

Moore, A. D., & Stambrook, M. (1995). Cognitive moderators of outcome following traumatic brain injury: A conceptual model and implications for rehabilitation. *Brain Injury, 9*(2), 109–130.

Moos, R. H., & Tsu, V. D. (1977). The crisis of physical illness: An overview. In R. H. Moos (Ed.), *Coping with physical illness*. New York: Plenum Press.

Moos, R. H., & Schaefer, J. A. (1984). The crisis of physical illness: An overview. In R. H. Moos (Ed.), *Coping with physical illness* (2nd ed.). New York: Plenum Press.

Morris, J. (1991). *Pride against prejudice*. London: Women's Press

Morton, M. V., & Wehman, P. (1995). Psychosocial and emotional sequelae of individuals with traumatic brain injury. *Brain Injury, 9*, 81–92.

Neath, J., & Shriner, K. (1998). Power to people with disabilities: Empowerment issues in employment programming. *Disability & Society, 13*(2), 217–228.

Nelson, G., Lord, J., & Ochocka, J. (2001). Empowerment and mental health in community: Narratives of psychiatric consumer/survivors. *Journal of Community and Applied Social Psychology, 11*, 125–142.

Nerenz, D. R., & Leventhal, H. (1983). Self-regulation theory in chronic illness. In J. G. Burnish & L. A. Bradley (Eds.), *Coping with chronic diseases*. New York: Academic Press.

Oddy, M., & McMillan, T. M. (2001). Future directions: Brain injury services in 2010. In R. L. I. Wood & T. M. McMillan (Eds.), *Neurobehavioural disability and social handicap following traumatic brain injury*. Hove, UK: Psychology Press.

Oliver, M. (1981). Disability, adjustment and family life—some theoretical considerations. In A. Brechin, P. Liddiard, & J. Swain (Eds.), *Handicap in a social world*. Milton Keynes, UK: Open University Press.

Oliver, M. (1989). Disability and dependency: a creation of industrial societies. In L. Barton (Ed.), *Disability and dependency*. London: Falmer Press.

Oliver, M. (1990). *The politics of disablement*. Basingstoke, UK: Macmillan.

O'Neill, J., Hibbard, M. R., Brown, M., Jaffe M., Sliwinski, M., Vandergoot, D., & Weiss, M. J. (1998). The effect of employment on quality of life and community integration after traumatic brain injury. *Journal of Head Trauma Rehabilitation, 13*(4), 68–79.

Parkes, C. M. (1975). Psychosocial transitions: Comparison between reactions to loss of a limb and loss of a spouse. *British Journal of Psychiatry, 127*, 204–210.

Pfeiffer, D. (1998). The ICIDH and the need for revision. *Disability & Society, 13*(4), 503–524.

Rosenthal, M., & Ricker, J. (2000). Traumatic brain injury. In R. G. Frank & T. R. Elliott (Eds.), *Handbook of rehabilitation psychology*. Washington, DC: American Psychological Association.

Roulstone, A. (1998). Disability and new technology: A barriers approach. In A. Roulstone (Ed.), *Enabling technology: Disabled people, work and new technology*. Buckingham, UK: Open University Press.

Rowlands, A. (2002). Circles of support building social networks. *British Journal of Therapy and Rehabilitation, 9*(2), 56–65.

Seligman, M. E. P. (1975). *Helplessness: On depression, development and death*. San Francisco: Freeman.

Skord, K. G., & Miranti, S. V. (1994). Towards a more integrated approach to job placement and retention for persons with traumatic brain injury and premorbid disadvantages. *Brain Injury, 8*(4), 383–393.

Spicer, J., & Chamberlain, K. (1996). Developing psychosocial theory in health psychology: Problems and prospects. *Journal of Health Psychology, 1*, 161–171.

Steadman-Pare, D., Clantonio, A., Ratcliff, G., Chase, S., & Vernich, L. (2001). Factors associated with quality of life many years after traumatic brain injury. *Journal of Head Trauma Rehabilitation, 16*(4), 330–342.

Tyerman, A. (1997). Head injury: Community rehabilitation. In C. J. Goodwill, M. A. Chamberlain, & C. Evans (Eds.), *Rehabilitation of the physically disabled adult* (2nd ed.). Cheltenham, UK: Stanley Thornes.

Vash, C. L. (1981). *The psychology of disability*. New York: Springer.

Wall, J. R., Rosenthal, M., & Niemczura, G. (1998). Community-based training after acquired brain injury: Preliminary findings. *Brain Injury, 12*(3), 215–225.

Wehman, P., West, M., & Fry, R. (1989). Effect of supported employment on the vocational outcomes of persons with traumatic brain injury. *Journal of Applied Behaviour Analysis, 2*, 395–405.

Willer, B., & Corrigan, J. D. (1994). Whatever it takes: A model for community-based services. *Brain Injury, 8*(7), 647–660.

Williams, W. H. (2002). Rehabilitation of emotional disorders following acquired brain injury. In B. A. Wilson (Ed.), *Neuropsychological Rehabilitation: Theory and Practice*. New York: Swets.

Wilson, B. (2002). Towards a comprehensive model of cognitive rehabilitation. *Neuropsychological Rehabilitation, 12*, 97–110.

Wilson, B. A., Emslie, H. C., Quirk, K., & Evans, J. J. (2001). Reducing everyday memory and planning problems by means of a paging system: A randomised control crossover study. *Journal of Neurology, Neurosurgery and psychiatry, 70*, 477–482.

World Health Organisation (1980). *International classification of impairments, diseases and handicaps: A manual of classification relating to the consequences of disease*. Geneva, Switzerland: World health Organisation.

World Health Organisation (2001). *International classification of functioning, disability and health – ICF*. Geneva, Switzerland: World health Organisation.

Wright, B.A. (1960). *Physical disability—a psychological approach*. New York & Evanston: Harper & Row.

Rehabilitation of the emotional problems
of brain disorders in developing countries

Tedd Judd

Diplomate in Clinical Neuropsychology, Bellingham, WA, USA

Emotional and behavioural problems of people with brain disorders are major undertreated problems in developing countries. These can be addressed by training lay volunteers in community-based rehabilitation. Training and programme implementation must be highly sensitive to local conditions. Basic concepts that can be trained in such conditions include case finding, triage, evaluation skills, emotional rehabilitation, restoration and compensation strategies, the continuum of responsibility, the zone of recovery, scaffolding, adjusting the person–environment fit, awareness of deficits, setting goals, communicating with others about the disability, disability rights, support groups, and circles of support.

INTRODUCTION

David, a healthcare worker, was visiting a rural Mexican mountain village when a father invited him home to meet his 13-year-old son, Pepe, who had never walked because he had had polio as a baby. David asked if they had tried crutches. The father replied that they could not afford to travel to the city to get some. David looked around, borrowed a machete, and cut branches to make crude crutches. The father protested they would not work, and, sure enough, when Pepe tried them, they broke under his weight. The father then took the machete and cut a more appropriate species of wood. Following David's example, he skillfully fashioned functional crutches. Within half a day Pepe was proudly walking for the first time in his life (Werner, 1990).

This episode illustrates a collaboration between a professional with specialised knowledge and a peasant with the knowledge and the skills to adapt that

Correspondence should be sent to Tedd Judd, Diplomate in Clinical Neuropsychology, 851 Coho Way, Ste. 301, Bellingham, WA 98225, USA. Tel: 001-360-734-7310, Fax: 001-360-647-8336, Email: tjudd@attbi.com

http://www.tandf.co.uk/journals/pp/09602011.html   DOI:10.1080/09602010244000309

knowledge to local conditions. The intervention would have been unsuccessful without the knowledge from both parties.

It is not usual to begin an article in an academic journal with storytelling. I have chosen to do so in order to illustrate the break from clinical convention that is often needed to be successful in applying clinical knowledge in settings in the developing world. This article can only present the clinical side of the knowledge needed for success. In a sense, this article will be only one hand clapping. I present here some promising approaches to interventions in the developing world for emotional problems resulting from brain lesions. The other hand clapping will be the knowledge of local resources and culture that comes from the individuals, families, and communities affected by those brain lesions.

The need

About 7% of the world's population is disabled (Mitchell, 1999b). Only about 1–2% (Johnston & Tjandrakusuma, 1982; World Health Organisation, 1981) or perhaps as much as 3% (Mitchell, 1999b) of people with chronic disabilities worldwide receive rehabilitation in their lifetimes. Within the population of disabled, the number of individuals affected by brain disorders is large. For example, Ardila and Rosselli (1992) have estimated that 3–5% of the population of Colombia is affected by some type of brain disorder, amounting to some 1 million people. Even in many developed countries, many people with brain disorders do not receive the services that have been developed. For example, only about 10% of individuals with traumatic brain injury (TBI) in the US receive adequate diagnosis and rehabilitation (Kreutzer, Gordon, & Wehman, 1989). Brain disorders may be more prevalent in developing countries than developed countries because of the prevalence of infectious diseases affecting the brain. Moreover, 90% of disability caused by motor vehicle accidents is in developing countries (Nantulya & Reich, 2002).

In developed countries, the emotional and behavioural changes resulting from brain disorders have been found to be more important than the physical and cognitive changes as significant barriers to effective functioning in family, work, school, and other settings (Morton & Wehman, 1995). Whether or not this is the case in developing countries remains to be seen. Differences in attitudes, the availability of rehabilitation, and community accessibility might rearrange the ordering of these factors.

In developed countries, the needs of family carers for adults with traumatic brain injuries are predominantly for information and emotional support (Sinnakaruppan & Williams, 2001). Whether or not these are the same priorities for carers in developed countries also remains to be seen. It seems likely, however, that these are among their needs.

Given the size of the population affected and the limited resources available, it is not realistic to expect that adequate direct interventions for emotional problems of brain disorders can be carried out primarily by neuropsychologists, by mental health or rehabilitation professionals, or even by professionals of any type. Interventions will need to be carried out by family members, co-workers, classmates, teachers, employers, community volunteers, and others (referred to as "intervenors" below). The available data suggest that the primary functions of such intervenors for people with brain injuries will be in providing education and support to them and their families with respect to emotional and behavioural problems.

Community-based rehabilitation

One prominent model that has been developed for general disability rehabilitation, particularly with the developing world in mind, is community-based rehabilitation (CBR). The World Health Organisation began supporting the model of CBR in 1978 (Mitchell, 1999a), and developed a manual for community workers over the following decade (Helander, Mendis, Nelson, & Goerdt, 1989, see also Werner, 1990). This model involves a three-tiered system. In the first tier, lay members of the community (local supervisors, LS), usually volunteers, are trained in basic rehabilitation techniques for common disabilities. They provide direct rehabilitation services to people with disabilities in their homes, in community centres, in schools, in community clinics, and in workplaces. The preparation of the LS varies from programme to programme and depends upon local conditions. In some programmes they may have little or no formal education, but they are typically literate, able to read the CBR manual, and may be high school or even college graduates. They are typically middle-aged women. They also train designated family members (family trainers) and others to continue with the training for their particular family member. They work in co-ordination with community institutions around issues such as transportation, childcare, social services, health services, disabled rights, community education, and other issues needing attention with respect to the needs of the person with disabilities. They also refer difficult cases to specialised rehabilitation services.

The second tier consists of district rehabilitation professionals who train and supervise the local supervisors. Their professions may vary, but they are typically healthcare professionals in the field of rehabilitation such as physical therapists, nurses, or physicians. The third tier is national co-ordination, ideally by the Ministry of Health (Mitchell, 1999a), but in some instances this could be by a nongovernmental organisation (NGO).

In a typical intervention, the LS gets her children off to school and puts on her tee-shirt (supplied by the programme) identifying her as an LS. She walks the few blocks to the house of a boy with a traumatic brain injury for her weekly visit, carrying her CBR manual and her notebook. She talks with the boy's older sister, who is the identified family trainer, about his progress during the week.

She watches the sister assist her brother as he walks with a walker, and she recommends that they advance to trying stairs, coaching them through their first attempts. She takes notes on problems and progress. On her way home she stops by the local school and arranges to visit the following week with the boy and his sister to arrange a return to class. Her niece is in the same class, and she will ask her to help. That same week she has her consultation group meeting with other LSs and a physical therapist at the local clinic. The group shares some of their experiences with the reactions of other children when a disabled child comes to class. The physical therapist recommends a referral for an orthotic and makes the appointment. Since she has never been to the orthotics clinic, another LS volunteers to go with her, the boy, and the sister on the bus.

In spite of initial enthusiasm, implementation of CBR remains very patchy. In accordance with the original model, implementation takes many different forms, adapting to local conditions in places such as Botswana (Nordholm & Lundgren-Lindquist, 1999), Laos (Inthirat & Thonglith, 1999), China (Zhuo & Kun, 1999), and the Philippines (Valdez & Mitchell, 1999). While formal evaluations of CBR are scarce, field reports are quite promising (Mitchell, 1999b).

CBR is one major context in which emotional and behavioural neuro-rehabilitation can take place. Other possibilities exist within medical, mental health, educational, social welfare, employment, and penal institutions and through religious and civic groups and NGOs. The major role of neuro-rehabilitation experts in such settings is training paraprofessionals and lay people with little or no background in mental health and rehabilitation, and often with little or no formal education. In these settings, the main job of neurorehabilitation experts is not to intervene or to provide therapy. It is to train others to intervene. In larger projects the neurorehabilitation experts' role might even be to train the trainers of intervenors. Since the intervenors in most of these settings have much broader mandates and goals, neurorehabilitation for emotions will be only a small part of their work, and interventions are likely to bear little resemblance to conventional psychotherapy.

THE FRAMEWORK OF TRAINING

Institutions

Training for intervention will most often take place within the context of an institution or system for intervention. Training must be reasonably congruent with the goals and motivations of the institution and the individuals within it to be effective. Understanding those goals and motivations is a critical part of the "other hand clapping", and is beyond the scope of this article. At the same time, some of those goals, motivations, and values may not be congruent with the implicit goals of neurorehabilitation or of the trainer. For example, the goals of the neurorehabilitation experts may be to help people with brain disorders to have greater understanding of and control over their own emotions and behaviour so that they can be empowered to be active, safe citizens and self-advocates. Some schools or penal institutions may be structured to produce docile labourers, or to isolate people and control and punish behaviour. Some orphanages and sheltered workshops may be structured to maintain dependence and servility whereas neurorehabilitation experts might advocate independence and dignity. Neurorehabilitation may be impossible in such situations, or it may require compromise or efforts directed at institutional change.

Physically, the interventions and even the training may well take place outside of traditional clinical settings of hospitals and clinics. It may take place in homes, community centres, churches, schools, gaols, workplaces, or even outdoors.

Attitudes

The mindset of neurorehabilitation includes certain attitudes and perspectives regarding neurodisabilities that may not be shared initially by the trainees. These differing attitudes and perspectives may not be initially evident or articulated. Examples of these contrasts are presented in Table 1. Some of these contrasts can be finessed or accepted in intervening. One example would be a family that is willing to carry out a neurorehabilitation programme while continuing to pray for a miracle. For some contrasts, it is critical that the neurorehabilitation experts examine their own attitudes and consider adjustments and compromises. For example, neurorehabilitation experts will need to show respect for local culture, authority, and ways of thinking in order to gain acceptance and to be effective in that context (like the volunteer, David, in the opening story). For some contrasts, the neurorehabilitation experts will need to work towards changing others' attitudes, values, and beliefs, particularly concerning respect for people with disabilities and the role of rehabilitation. This work may at times be through explicit advocacy, but more often it will be conveyed implicitly through example.

Methods of instruction

Instructing intervenors involves imparting information to them, training them in intervention skills, and facilitating a shift in their attitudes. Traditional classroom instruction is likely to play only a minor role, particularly if the learners have little background in that type of setting. Information may be imparted, instead, through storytelling (formally known as case histories), demonstration, Socratic dialogue, metaphor, answering questions, and visual aids. Locally produced videos have been demonstrated to be an effective CBR instructional tool in Africa (Holloway, Lee, & McConkey, 1999).

TABLE 1
Contrasting values, beliefs, and attitudes in the neurorehabilitation context

Domain	Neurorehabilitation values, beliefs, attitudes	Contrasting values, beliefs, attitudes
Proximate causes of disability	Infections, accidents, assaults, toxicities, vascular disorders, tumours, etc.	Witchcraft, spirit possession
Distal causes of disability	Hypertension, diabetes, lack of sanitation, unsafe conditions, lack of medical care	Skewed political priorities, economic injustice, divine intervention or punishment, moral retribution, ancestral misdeeds
The person with a disability	A whole individual worthy of respect, dignity, and self-determination to the extent possible	Less than a full person, in need of protection, not fully capable of decisions or self-determination, childlike
Causes of unusual emotions and behaviour in the person with a neurodisability	A combination of direct organic change in the mechanisms of emotion, reactions to illness, and pre-illness personality	Spirit possession, attributing all to pre-illness personality, or not acknowledging that the behaviour is unusual
Possibility of change	Change occurs gradually	Change may occur suddenly and miraculously through divine or magical intervention in response to the appropriate appeals, change may not be possible
Role of rehabilitation	Change occurs through the professionally guided hard work of the person with the disability	Rehabilitation is a treatment actively performed by the professional on the passive recipient
Goals of rehabilitation	Personal independence	Restore function in an interdependent context
Knowledge	Science is the highest standard, professionals are the authorities	Religion or tradition may be the highest standard, elders or other leaders may be the highest authorities

Training skills most usually requires demonstration, imitation, and practice under supervision. Since neurorehabilitation experts may be training trainers, the "see one, do one, teach one" principle of medical training may be usefully adapted to this context.

Shifts in attitude tend to occur over time, through repeated example, and within a social context. An important component of training is periodic discussions among CBR workers with access to neurorehabilitation experts. One particularly valuable training resource is Werner and Bower's (1982) *Helping health workers learn*.

Case finding

Existing institutions and systems will have case-finding mechanisms in place. Emotional and behavioural disorders may not be recognised as reasons for case identification, however. Often these problems are not viewed as a consequence of the brain disorder or as an appropriate target for rehabilitation. If no physical rehabilitation or medical needs arc identified, potential cases may get passed over, or shunted into systems where their problems are not recognised as being due to brain disorder. It may be necessary to educate referral sources about what to look for. Specific questions might be incorporated into structured interviews (for example, "What happens when s/he gets angry?" "How does s/he get along with friends?"). There may be outreach to the systems where such people may get shunted. The specific content of the education of referral sources will depend on the priorities of the interventions planned, and may be selected from ideas presented below.

Case selection

Case selection must take into account both need and likely benefit. In my experiences in introducing neuropsychological rehabilitation concepts in developing countries, it is not unusual to encounter a "test the expert" session. I still vividly recall after 15 years the futility of attempting to do a grand rounds presentation with a 300 lb young man with a severe traumatic brain injury. They brought him from the back ward of a national psychiatric hospital, and he never stopped running during the entire (mercifully brief) event.

Since resources are limited, it is virtually always necessary to exercise a certain amount of neurorehabilitation triage   focusing efforts on those most usually moderately disrupted individuals where intervention is likely to be effective and likely to make a substantial functional difference. The intensive and expensive interventions that are sometimes expended on severely injured individuals (such as my grand rounds case) in the developed world may not be practical in developing countries. Similarly, extensive interventions producing modest functional gains for those with mild traumatic brain injuries may not be a high priority. Priorities in case selection, therefore, must be collaboratively adjusted to local conditions and values.

Evaluation

For those neuropsychologists who are greatly enamoured of their tests and evaluation abilities, the prospect of formal, normative-based, culturally appropriate cognitive neuropsychological evaluation in the context of a CBR or similar programme may seem daunting, to say the least. Fortunately, such an effort is not necessary in many circumstances for at least two reasons. First, because of the triage principle just discussed, the main focus of such efforts will be towards individuals whose deficits are sufficiently obvious that formal testing may not be needed to demonstrate them. Although formal testing could contribute to understanding the details of those deficits, interventions may proceed reasonably well with alternative evaluation techniques. Second, formal testing is less important to the evaluation of the organic emotional changes at issue here than it is for the evaluation of cognition. Furthermore, even in developed countries we are still just learning to use the first generation of formal neuropsychological tests and scales for the evaluation of organic emotional changes (Judd & Fordyce, 1996).

Space does not allow for a full elaboration on how to train CBR workers in evaluation of emotional changes due to brain disorders. The following principles, however, can give the reader an impression of such a programme:

1. Evaluation of emotions and behaviour should be a routine part of any neurorehabilitation evaluation.
2. CBR workers should be given a framework for understanding the major organic emotional changes so that they know what to look for.
3. CBR workers should routinely take information from family members or other informants in addition to the person with the brain disorder.
4. CBR workers should be trained to follow up on any complaints about emotional or behavioural problems with inquiries about examples, situations in which the problem occurs, practical consequences, and so on.
5. CBR workers should be trained to inquire about whether or not and to what extent the problem in question was present prior to the brain disorder.
6. CBR workers should be trained to observe and make note of unusual behaviours that may indicate a problem.
7. CBR workers should have the on-going opportunity to review their work with peers and supervisors.
8. CBR workers should be trained and encouraged to recognise when they are uncertain about what they are dealing with and to seek consultation with their supervisors.

CONTENT OF TRAINING

The fields of physical and cognitive neurorehabilitation are fairly well developed and researched. Specialised models of neurorehabilitation for emotional and behavioural problems are less well developed (Judd, 1999), and less fully researched (this issue). There is even less development of these models and research with respect to applications in the developing world. In lieu of such research, the remainder of this article will present those basic concepts in the neurorehabilitation of emotion, derived from empirical research, that I have found in my clinical and teaching experience to be teachable, understandable, and useful in developing countries. Most of my experience is in Latin America, and so significant modifications may be needed for other settings. I propose the use of these concepts as a starting point in developing components for the neurorehabilitation of emotion within CBR programmes and similar undertakings. These, and related concepts, are elaborated in Judd (1999) and Judd and DeBoard (in press).

Emotional rehabilitation

The emotions and personality of a person with a brain disorder can be thought of as having three components or sources:

1. The person's personality prior to brain disorder.
2. Emotional reactions to the experience of illness, injury, disability, and the consequences of disability.
3. Organic changes in emotional functioning resulting from damage to the brain.

Many people tend to attribute all but the most obvious of organic changes to the first two components, and to deal with the person accordingly. Getting lay people to understand when a change is a direct consequence of damage to the brain's emotional mechanisms is a critical step in helping them to orient towards appropriate interventions. This understanding can often defuse blame placing and inappropriate punishment and restrictions. Mechanical metaphors are often helpful here—cars with faulty brakes (disinhibition of behaviour or emotions) or dead batteries (impaired initiation), sieves with holes ripped in them (disinhibition), broken telephone lines (impaired emotional expression), and so on.

Once emotional problems are seen as organic, they can then be seen as candidates for rehabilitation. Here an analogy with physical (and sometimes cognitive) rehabilitation is useful. Just as someone may need to relearn through practice how to control their leg, they may need to relearn through practice how to control their anger, their crying, or their anxiety. Just as they may need a cane to help them walk, they may need a cue card to help them get through a difficult meeting. Just as they may need to avoid the middle of the market so they do not get jostled and knocked down, they may need to avoid the middle of the crowd at a soccer game so they do not get over-aroused.

This article focuses only on the rehabilitation of organic changes in emotional functioning. A complete rehabilitation programme would also address emotional reactions to disability and its consequences and differentiating them from organic changes.

Restoration and compensation strategies

Rehabilitation strategies can be broadly divided into restoration (relearning) strategies and compensation strategies. Restoration strategies are those aimed at retraining lost or damaged abilities. They are typically time-consuming and costly and require considerable motivation and effort, but when successful they are typically more satisfying and normalising, and less stigmatising. Traditional examples include retraining in walking, talking, writing, money management, and work skills. Emotional rehabilitation restoration strategies include retraining of self-control of anger, emotional modulation of tone of voice, and social skills.

Compensation strategies involve deploying aids or alternative approaches that allow the person to accomplish a functional activity in spite of a disability. These are typically less time-consuming and require less effort, but they do require training in the use of compensation, and maintenance of the compensation. Cost varies depending upon the aid used. Emotional rehabilitation compensation strategies include identifying and avoiding specific situations that provoke unacceptable emotional reactions, using other people to cue behaviours, using cueing devices (described below), and expressing emotions in words when they cannot be expressed in tone of voice. The physical rehabilitation analogy is also useful in educating about emotional compensations ("brain canes").

Compensations are sometimes a temporary tool leading to restoration. For example, someone relearning how to walk may progress from a walker to a cane to no aid. Someone relearning anger control may go from cued time outs to self-cued time outs with a cue card to self-calming in context.

Learning to distinguish between restoration and compensation strategies can be done through analogy with physical rehabilitation. The distinction is an aid in goal-setting and in choosing realistic approaches. It can also help to direct creative energy to finding new solutions and new hope. For example, if a restoration approach fails or appears impossible, one can fall back on a compensation approach. Many young people with mobility limitations struggle for years, walking only short distances painfully slowly with crutches until they discover that a wheelchair can be liberating and allow them to go many more places much more easily. Similarly, a family might wait or nag or hint for years in hopes of getting someone with impaired initiation to be more spontaneous before they accept or discover that the person will happily participate if they are told what to do.

Gradual progress

The continuum of responsibility.   People who are unconscious or disoriented and confused are not responsible for their behaviour, but caregivers are. If and when they have fully recovered, they are fully responsible for their behaviour. The process of recovery includes caregivers gradually turning over to these people responsibility for their own behaviour along a continuum of responsibility (Sbordone, 1991). CBR workers who understand this can help participants understand their roles and reduce conflict, overprotection, and underprotection.

Intervention techniques vary according to the ability of the person with the brain disorder to participate. For example, behaviour management (such as manipulating the level of stimulation) may be applied in early stages of recovery from a severe TBI. As successful techniques are discovered, they are explained to the person as they are used. As the person recovers, he or she is given specific roles in implementing the techniques. Cues from caregivers for using these techniques are gradually faded in favour of external compensations such as written instructions, avoiding certain situations, asking for help, and so on. Finally, the therapist helps the person make the transition from external to internal techniques such as self-talk (Cicerone & Giacino, 1992; Meichenbaum, 1993).

The zone of recovery. If a given activity is too easy, the person recovering from a brain injury may become bored by it and even resentful of being given a child's task or too little responsibility (Table 2). If it can be done independently and easily, then it may not contribute much to recovery. Someone who is only allowed to do this kind of activity is being overprotected. On the other hand, if an activity is too difficult, the person may get frustrated and angry, and eventually discouraged and depressed. An activity that is most appropriate for facilitating recovery is one that is a manageable challenge, and that the person can do with some help (physical help, directions, reminders, or other cognitive strategies).

TABLE 2
Zone of recovery

Zone of recovery		
Too easy	*Just right*	*Too hard*
Can do the task easily, independently	Can do the task with some help	Can't do the task without much help
Bored, overprotected	Challenged	Frustrated, angry, discouraged
Do it for them	Show, guide, cue	Trial-and-error
Tell, but don't involve	Person and helper are active	Guessing
Person is passive		Helper is passive

Adapted by Cicerone and Tupper, 1990 from the zone of proximal development (ZPD) Vygotsky 1978.

Navigating the zone of recovery is, in some respects, an art. Some people are very good at it; others are not. Parents and teachers have often developed this skill. The CBR worker can help other people to develop this skill, to recognise how to break down a task into components, to find which components to attempt, and to know how and when help is needed. The concept of the zone of recovery can be used to help select social and emotional challenges that are appropriate and can facilitate emotional recovery. A classic psychotherapy example of this type of work applicable in neurorehabilitation of emotions is the construction of a hierarchy in the systematic desensitisation of phobia.

Scaffolding.   Scaffolding (Vygotsky, 1978) refers to the support, compensations, cues, help, and encouragement that people with brain disorders need in order to accomplish an activity. The CBR worker can help family members to determine how much scaffolding is needed for given goal activities. As people get better at doing these things, the scaffolding is gradually removed to allow them to gain greater mastery over the activity. Although Vygotsky articulated this concept in the field of cognitive development as an educational tool, it can be applied to emotional rehabilitation. For example, suppose a 10-year-old boy would like to return to school after a TBI, but his behaviour is to disinhibited for the classroom, with emotional outbursts, calling out, and teasing. Possible forms of scaffolding might include erecting a partition or having him sit outside so that he can see the teacher but not the class, having a parent or older sibling accompany him and sit next to him, and giving him permission to go to a quiet space to calm down when he needs to and cueing him to go there. The gradual dismantling of the scaffolding might include gradually decreasing the size of the partition or moving him closer to the class, moving the person monitoring him further away from him, finding another student who could take over the monitoring and cueing, training him to self-cue when he needs to go to the quiet place, and training him in self-calming.

Overprotection vs. interdependence and adjusting the person–environment fit.   Personal independence is such a dominant value in most developed countries that it has been enshrined as the metric of rehabilitation success in the widely used Functional Independence Measure (Granger, 1998). There are societies, however, in which interdependence (Condeluci, 1995) takes greater priority, especially within the family. In such families, it may be more important that everyone has a role and is valued than that everyone is autonomous. From a rehabilitation perspective, sometimes this interdependence can result in what appears to the Western professional to be overprotection of the person with the disability. The CBR worker may need to approach such situations by mobilising hope regarding what might be possible with rehabilitation, but also by proceeding gradually in small steps along the continuum of responsibility. This may allow family systems to adjust. By working with family members as the providers or facilitators of rehabilitation, the CBR worker brings them along in changing the balance of the family interdependence.

The dominant (although changing) rehabilitation model worldwide has been that of the repair shop, in which the damaged person is brought into the hospital to be fixed before being returned to service. With an emerging movement for the rights of people with disabilities, societies are shifting to recognise the need to accommodate all of their citizens in architecture, transportation, housing, education, employment, and other domains. The repair shop model is being replaced with a model that involves adjusting the fit between the person and the environment. CBR workers can be trained to consider both the direct rehabilitation of the person with the brain disorder and the changes in that person's environment (physical and social) that might make for a better fit.

Awareness of deficits

People with TBIs are often impaired in their ability to evaluate their own abilities (Prigatano, this issue). It is very important for CBR workers and families to recognise if people with TBI think they are more capable than they are (anosognosia) or if they think they are less capable than they are (catastrophising), and to understand that as an organic change.

Setting goals

Setting functional goals is a well-established practice in many rehabilitation settings. Such goal setting also serves a purpose for emotional rehabilitation. It gives direction and purpose to the interventions, as in the scaffolding example above. Goal setting makes it much more possible to focus attention on emotional rehabilitation because it then becomes necessary to identify what is keeping the person from reaching the goal. Goal setting also allows for the measurement of progress and to inform decisions as to whether to continue with an effort, revise the approach, or give up.

Emotional reaction versus emotional communication

For those working with people with TBIs it is important to understand that emotional reactivity can be organically altered (Judd, 1999). Reactivity can increase for one or more emotions, so that the person may over-react to certain situations. Finding ways to cope with these changes can come from recognising and labelling it as an organic change, setting functional goals, putting compensating scaffolding in place, and working gradually towards self-control, as will be illustrated below for impulsive anger. Emotional reactivity can also decrease. This may be less problematic initially, but potential interventions are also less clear. Cueing and structured involvement in emotional experiences may be some help.

For those working with people with strokes it is important to understand that emotional communication can be organically altered (Judd, 1999). One's facial expressions, tone of voice, body language, and even emotional words may not accurately reflect one's feelings. An expressionless face or flat tone of voice may belie an active internal emotional life. This can be relatively easily tested and demonstrated to families by asking the person to demonstrate various emotions (Ross, 1993). It is also relatively easily compensated for by having the person say their feelings in words.

At the opposite extreme, reflex crying and laughing and automatic cursing may communicate feelings that are not felt. Reflex crying and laughing can be compensated for by educating the person and the family about the phenomenon. Restoration is often possible through simple self-control techniques (Judd, 1999).

Organic changes in emotional reactivity and communication are somewhat difficult to describe convincingly in words. They are relatively easily learned through direct experience with people so affected. Education about these phenomena should be conducted through direct experience or video whenever possible.

Impulsive anger

Impulsive anger is arguably the most important organic emotional change resulting from TBI. It is a frequent problem and it causes considerable disability, disruption, and distress in those who have it and in their communities.

Organic impulsive anger typically has its onset after a TBI. It is an overreaction to sometimes trivial events that is out of character and often distressing to the person. It typically does not serve any purpose for the person. It usually comes on and goes away rapidly.

The following is an abbreviated protocol for working with a person with impulsive anger that can be implemented with relatively little training:

1. Identify and characterise the problem.
2. Determine violence risk level. If it is significant take appropriate action (remove weapons, make a safety plan, refer as needed).
3. Determine anger risks and triggers. Reduce exposure to these as necessary and possible.
4. Determine anger warning signs.
5. Determine what is helpful for calming the person down.
6. Establish an agreed time out and calm down plan for anger episodes. Include agreement about who needs to be responsible for cueing the time out.

7. Record the plan in some form (cue card, drawings) and put it where it is needed.
8. Practise the plan (simulation).
9. Monitor and adjust the use of the plan.
10. Move towards self-cueing and self-calming in place, as possible.
11. Reduce the scaffolding as possible.
12. If there is sufficient success in self-control, make a gradual and planned return to exposure to anger risks and triggers.

Initiation

Difficulty initiating activity is a common problem in brain disorders. It can be taken for depression or lack of motivation. Properly identifying it eliminates many problems of misattribution. The most useful interventions are structure, schedules, and cueing. If the person affected is someone of authority such as a parent, elder, or supervisor, some work may be required in getting others to feel comfortable telling them what to do.

Cueing devices

Direct cues from other people are a very important part of early stages of intervention for organic emotional and behavioural problems. Moving from those stages towards more self-control often entails moving from human cues to cueing devices. These can range from sophisticated personal digital devices to alarms, calendars, and simple cue cards with a few words written on them, such as an anger time out sequence. For those who cannot read, pictures can be used, or other symbols such as rosary beads. I had a client who wore a Buddha around his neck, and during each time out he would talk to Buddha. Similar individualised adaptations can be sought when compensations are needed to help someone remember to follow a behaviour plan.

Communicating to others

What to tell others in the community about one's disability or the disability of one's family member is a critical part of how that person is received and how the person–environment fit becomes structured (Judd, 1999). This is a legitimate focus of intervention by CBR workers and others. It may be best approached after a few months of rehabilitation work when understanding has improved and attitudes have shifted somewhat. It can be an ongoing focus of discussion in the rehabilitation process, in the CBR worker consultations, and in support groups. The most effective ways of telling the story will vary widely depending upon the values of the community and the purpose of the communication. For example, in some settings the CBR worker may talk with family and community members individually. In other settings the affected individual may practise what to say to others.

Empathy and rights

Listening well and developing accurate empathy should be an important and explicit part of CBR worker training. When CBR workers come to understand the desires, dreams, and perspectives of people with disabilities and their families they will be better able to assist them. This can also become the foundation of advocating for their rights.

Support groups

If a critical mass of affected people exists and if the culture allows it, the formation of support groups around types of disabilities can play a major role in emotional rehabilitation (Mann & Ditmar, 1992; Miller, 1992, 1993). Support groups consist of a number of individuals affected by a particular disability, and sometimes their family members. Support groups also become a focal point for exchanging information and skills, for advocacy, for changing community attitudes, and for collective action on such issues as civil rights, access to services, and accessibility. Support groups are distinct from therapy groups in that they are run by and for their members rather than by professionals. Professionals may facilitate their formation, but do not participate unless invited. When support groups are functioning well and independently they may even have creative tension or conflict with professionals and rehabilitation workers that allows them to get their needs better met.

Circles of support

Circles of support are groups of natural supporters within the community who come together periodically to help a particular person with a disability known to them, to realise their dreams (Willer, Allen, Anthony, & Cowlan, 1993). The immediacy of these groups, their attachment to the focus person, and their connections to the community allow them to accomplish many things that professionals cannot. CBR workers are in an especially favourable position for facilitating the development of circles of support for individual disabled people.

In the context of CBR this might work as follows: The CBR worker discusses with the focus person who to invite into the circle (specific family members, friends, acquaintances, community members, teachers, clergy, etc.). The CBR worker invites each of those people personally, explaining the purpose of the group. The CBR worker co-ordinates the first meeting. The participants introduce themselves, and the focus person describes his/her dreams and desires for the future. The participants then undertake problem solving to help realise those dreams. This may involve practical help, community connections, raising money, or consulting professionals. They meet as often as necessary. If those dreams involve behavioural or emotional goals, or if the circle sees a need to work on such goals to achieve the dreams, then the CBR worker or rehabilitation professionals, if needed, can educate and train those members of the circle who will assist with those goals.

For example, suppose a young man with a TBI with social disinhibition and poor quality control would like to date and marry. His circle may recognise that his behaviour is responsible for his poor success at dating. The circle would be likely to figure out on its own that he needs help with his appearance and there would likely be members who could help him to get appropriate clothes and instruct him in grooming. But they might be more at a loss as to how to help with his disinhibition. The CBR worker, following principles of the zone of rehabilitation and scaffolding, might, at the circle's request, help them to construct a progressive sequence of social events leading to dating, and identifying individuals who could coach him through those events.

CONCLUSIONS

Experienced neurorehabilitation experts are typically in awe of the number, complexity, and combinatinos of specific problems that can arise from brain disorders. In spite of this, themes and patterns are common. We cannot solve all of the problems all of the time. But a small number of simple concepts applied within a basic framework have the potential to alleviate considerable distress and disability. That potential can only be realised, however, in collaboration with the individuals, families, and communities affected by brain disorders.

REFERENCES

Ardila, A., & Rosselli, M. (1992). *Neuropsicología Clínica* [Clinical Neuropsychology]. Medellín: Prensa Creativa.

Cicerone, K. D., & Giacino, J. T. (1992). Remediation of executive function deficits after traumatic brain injury. *NeuroRehabilitation, 2,* 12–22.

Cicerone, K. D., & Tupper, D. E. (1990). Neuropsychological rehabilitation: Treatment of errors in everyday functioning. In D. E. Tupper & K. D. Cicerone (Eds.), *The neuropsychology of everyday life: Issues in development and rehabilitation.* Boston, MA: Kluwer Academic.

Condeluci, A. (1995). *Interdependence: The route to community.* Boca Raton, FL: CRC.

Granger, C. V. (1998). The emerging science of functional assessment: Our tool for outcomes analysis. *Archives of Physical Medicine and Rehabilitation, 79,* 235–240.

Helander, E., Mendis, P., Nelson, G., & Goerdt, A. (1989). *Training in the community for people with disabilities.* Geneva: World Health Organisation.

Holloway, S., Lee, L., & McConkey, R. (1999). Meeting the training needs of community-based service personnel in Africa through video-based training courses. *Disability and Rehabilitation, 21,* 448–454.

Inthirat, T. R. S., & Thonglith, S. (1999). Community-based rehabilitation in the Lao People's Democratic Republic. *Disability and Rehabilitation*, *21*, 469–473.

Johnston, M., & Tjandrakusuma, H. (1982). Reaching the disabled. *World Health Forum*, *3*, 307–310.

Judd, T. (1999). *Neuropsychotherapy and community integration: Brain illness, emotions, and behavior*. New York: Kluwer Academic/Plenum Publishers.

Judd, T., & DeBoard, R. (in press). Natural recovery: An ecological approach to neuropsychological recuperation. In B. Uzzell (Ed.), *International handbook of cross-cultural neuropsychology*. New York: Kluwer Academic/Plenum Publishers.

Judd, T., & Fordyce, D. (1996). Personality tests. In R. J. Sbordone & C. J. Lond, (Eds.), *Ecological validity of neuropsychological testing* (pp. 315–356). Delray Beach, FL: GR Press/St. Lucie Press.

Kreutzer, J. S., Gordon, W. A., & Wehman, P. (1989). Cognitive remediation following traumatic brain injury. *Rehabilitation Psychology*, *34*, 117–130.

Mann, W. C., & Dittmar, S. S. (1992). Consumer advocacy and professional education: Traumatic brain injury. *Journal of Cognitive Rehabilitation*, *10*(6), 8–11.

Meichenbaum, D. (1993). The "potential" contributions of cognitive behavior modification to the rehabilitation of individuals with traumatic brain injury. *Seminars in Speech and Language*, *14*, 18–31.

Miller, L. (1992). When the best help is self-help, or, everything you always wanted to know about brain injury support groups. *Journal of Cognitive Rehabilitation*, *10*(6), 14–17.

Miller, L. (1993). *Psychotherapy of the brain-injured patient: Reclaiming the shattered self*. New York: Norton.

Mitchell, R. (1999a). Community-based rehabilitation: The generalized model. *Disability and Rehabilitation*, *21*, 522–528.

Mitchell, R. (1999b). The research base of community-based rehabilitation. *Disability and Rehabilitation*, *21*, 459–468.

Morton, M. V., & Wehman, P. (1995). Psychosocial and emotional sequelae of individuals with traumatic brain injury: A literature review and recommendations. *Brain Injury*, *9*, 81–92.

Nantulya, V. M., & Reich, M. R. (2002). The neglected epidemic: Road traffic injuries in developing countries. *British Medical Journal*, *324*, 1139–1141.

Nordholm, L. A., & Lundgren-Lindquist, B. (1999). Community-based rehabilitation in Moshupa village, Botswana. *Disability and Rehabilitation*, *21*, 515–521.

Ross, E. D. (1993). Nonverbal aspects of language. *Behavioral Neurology*, *11*, 9–23.

Sbordone, R. J. (1991). Psychotherapeutic treatment of the client with traumatic brain injury: A conceptual model. In J. S. Kreutzer & P. H. Wehman (Eds.), *Cognitive rehabilitation for persons with traumatic brain injury: A functional approach*. Baltimore: P. H. Brookes.

Sinnakaruppan, I., & Williams, D. M. (2001). Family carers and the adult head injured: A critical review of carers' needs. *Brain Injury*, *15*, 653–672.

Valdez, L. S., & Mitchell, R. A. (1999). Community-based rehabilitation: A development program in Negros Occidental. *Disability and Rehabilitation*, *21*, 495–500.

Vygotsky, L. S. (1978). *Mind in society: The development of higher psychological processes*. Cambridge, MA: Harvard University Press.

Werner, D. (1990). *Disabled village children*. Palo Alto, CA: Hesperian Foundation.

Werner, D., & Bower, B. (1982). *Helping health workers learn*. Palo Alto, CA: Hesperian Foundation.

Willer, B. S., Allen, K., Anthony, J., & Cowlan, G. (1993). *Circles of support for individuals with acquired brain injury*. Buffalo, NY: Rehabilitation Research and Training Center on Community Integration of Persons with Traumatic Brain Injury.

World Health Organisation. (1981). *Disability prevention and rehabilitation: Report of the WHO expert committee on disability prevention and rehabilitation*. Geneva, Switzerland: World Health Organisation.

World Health Organisation. (1982). *Community based rehabilitation*. (Report of a WHO inter-regional consultation, Columbo, Sri Lanka, 28 June–3 July.) Geneva, Switzerland: World Health Organisation.

Zhuo, D., & Kun, N. D. (1999). Community based rehabilitation in the People's Republic of China. *Disability and Rehabilitation, 21*, 490–494.

Subject Index